The Other South

The Other South

Southern Dissenters in the Nineteenth Century

CARL N. DEGLER

1817

HARPER & ROW, PUBLISHERS

New York, Evanston, San Francisco, London

FIRST EDITION

Designed by Patricia Dunbar

Library of Congress Cataloging in Publication Data

Degler, Carl N.
  The Other South: Southern Dissenters in the Nineteenth Century
  Bibliography: p. 372
  1. Confederate States of America—Politics and government. 2. Slavery in the United States—Anti-slavery movements. 3. Southern States—Politics and government—1865–1950. I. Title.
E487.D327   320.9'75'04   73–4076
ISBN 0–06–011022–8

To the memory of Lyndon B. Johnson,
the most effective and courageous President
from The Other South

Contents

I

Some Conclusions by Way of Introduction

This book is about losers. In fact, its subtitle might well be E. H. Carr's phrase "the truths of the defeated." It is about white Southerners during the nineteenth century who stood out against the prevailing views and values of their region while remaining there. The chief characters are those Southerners who opposed slavery, supported the Union, became Republicans during Reconstruction, rejected the Democratic party in the 1880's, and joined the People's party in the 1890's. All of these dissenters lost their immediate fight; yet in time each fight was ultimately won. Slavery was ended, the Union was restored, and today the South has a two-party system that includes blacks as well as whites.

The story that is told here, however, is not a success story. Since the book ends with 1900, there are few successes, and even those that did occur often came too late to comfort those who once had sought them. Hence the book is indeed about those Southerners who were defeated. The story of them and their dissent offers a different view of the South from that usually associated with the region. Yet it is one that is necessary to know if we would comprehend the region or the nation of which it is a part.

It should also be said that in dwelling upon the "Other South," I do not intend to imply that with a little luck, or perhaps with a shift in a few ballots, the Other South might have become the Majority South. What the South is and how it got that way are

1

more complicated than that. In fact, if I were asked whether the South's history might have been different from what it was, I believe my answer would be no. And I say that not because I deny the theoretical existence of crucial turning points in history. Certainly there are moments in history when a different decision or a different leader would have caused history to move in a new direction. But in the history within these covers, there do not seem to be any such pivotal moments.

The defeated depicted here were soundly beaten. Indeed, one rather inescapable conclusion from the story of the efforts to build a biracial party in the South after the Civil War is that defeat came not once, but three times. That can hardly serve as an example of "what might have been." Or take another example. Whether secession could have been prevented by a more united front of Unionists in the South in 1860–61 is somewhat less clear. But if one recognizes the social and moral anomaly that slavery had become by the middle of the nineteenth century, it seems evident that Northern hostility toward the institution would not have died down. At the same time, the long history of Southern emphasis on constitutional protections for slavery, including secession, suggests that Southerners were very likely to have persisted in seeking to leave the Union in an effort to protect slavery from Northern attacks. In short, it does not seem that secession could have been postponed indefinitely, even if it had been postponed in 1860–61. It is true, as David Potter has argued, that once a crisis is passed no one can be certain what course subsequent events will take. But since all historical explanation is a balancing of probabilities, we can only say that the probabilities in 1861 pointed to another crisis later rather than to a final resolution of the issue of slavery without secession and without war. After all, a crisis over the Union was compromised away once before—in 1850—only to return in 1860.

No, the purpose of this examination of the Other South is not to suggest that there were narrow escapes or near-misses, that things might have been different. Rather it is to illustrate concretely something that is often forgotten in thinking about the American South. It is that the South is not and never has been a monolith. Always there have been diversities and divergences within its history and among its people, not only between the races, but among the whites as well.

Nor have the divisions among the whites been only those of class. Eugene Genovese has been the most consistent advocate of the view that the antebellum South was dominated by a self-conscious planter class. In his brilliant and influential book *The Political Economy of Slavery* he has argued that secession was the natural consequence of the efforts of a self-conscious slaveholding elite to save its civilization, which was not only based upon slavery but was also shaped by it.

Genovese's class interpretation of antebellum Southern history has much to be said for it; certainly it has caused many historians to rethink and re-examine traditional ways of looking at the Southern past. The story told in this book, however, does not lend much support to Genovese's conception of a self-conscious planter class seeking to protect its civilization against an outside threat. For as we will see, the pattern of support for and opposition to that civilization within the South did not follow neat class lines. There simply were too many slaveholders and planters who opposed slavery and worked for the perpetuation of the Union to allow Genovese's formulation to be persuasive. This is not the place to examine in full the implications or imperfections of Genovese's conception of the Old South, but certainly one of those imperfections is his failure to deal with the divisions within the so-called ruling class over secession and even over slavery itself.

But if my intention is to point to the diversities within the South, I do not intend to deny that there is a South—a region that is different from the rest of the nation. There is indeed an overall unity that embraces the diversity. Some years ago Howard Zinn in his book *The Southern Mystique* argued that the South was not truly distinctive at all. He did this by examining the various traits of Southern culture that have been singled out to show how the South differs from the rest of the United States. Yet each of those traits, Zinn concluded, was merely a concentrated or more heightened manifestation of practices or values that all Americans shared, though perhaps in weaker degree. There is truth in Zinn's contention if only because the South has never had a monopoly on racism, or violence, or even on the one-party system. But as Friedrich Engels taught us long ago, differences of degree, if great enough, become differences of kind. Three conspicuous examples —which Zinn does not mention, incidentally—are the South's relative lack of urbanization, industrialization, and immigration from Europe and Asia. Moreover, as this book seeks to show, even its dissenters were distinctive. Southern antislavery arguments took a different form and emphasis from those heard in the North, however much the arguments may have overlapped. Southern Unionists, too, differed from their Northern counterparts, as did Southern Republicans and Southern Populists.

To talk of the ways in which the South is distinctive tempts us to grapple with the tangled but fascinating puzzle of the nature of Southern identity. But that temptation will be resisted here. Let it simply be said that even those commentators who would homogenize the South and the rest of the United States must recognize one experience, at least, that is uniquely Southern. As C. Vann Woodward pointed out in *The Burden of Southern History,* of all Americans, only white Southerners have been defeated in a war and occupied by the enemy. This unique experience has indeed given Southerners a double history. They have been both Americans *and* Southerners. New Englanders or Midwesterners have never experienced an incongruence between their local and their national loyalties. Indeed, as one Southern historian once remarked, only half-humorously, the history of the United States *is* the history of New England. The double history of Southerners has a particular significance for a study of Southern dissenters, for they experienced the tug of contrary pulls even more compellingly than traditional Southerners. They experienced it not only during the Civil War, but throughout the nineteenth century, for by definition they were at odds with their fellow Southerners.

At no time was the double history of the South more acute than during the secession crisis. Most Southerners were never torn by the wrong of slavery, but every Southerner had to confront at the time of secession the conflict in loyalties to region and to nation. Nothing points up the double history of Southerners more than an examination of the conflict going on inside those men and women of the South who called themselves Unionists. For Unionism could not be an abstraction for Southerners as it often was for Northerners. In the South, by 1861, its definition was intimate, concrete, and intensely personal. Consequently, I have devoted a full chapter to trying to do justice to the variety of choices involved, and to the personal courage and anguish that often accompanied that double history at its most poignant moment—during the crisis of secession. This may not be a book about "what might have been," but it is an attempt to show what it was like to face a choice between nation and region as well as between individuals and the majority.

If Southerners have had a double history, the dissenters in this book might be said to have had a triple history. The values many of these men and women espoused were close to those held by Americans in general, but from the viewpoint of the non-South even the dissenters were Southerners. To Northerners, for example, Hinton Helper was always a Southerner, even if he did oppose slavery; Southern Republicans in the eyes of Northerners were first Southerners and only secondarily Republicans. All of which is but another way of saying that the South is a distinctive region, which made those who dissented from it at once a part of it and yet outside it. As dissenters who remained within the South, these men and women suffered the consequences of defeat in Civil War along with other Southerners, but at the same time they also experienced their own defeats at the hands of the Majority South. It is time, I believe, that their place and history in the life of the South received recognition, too. They are not only a part of the region, but their dissent tells us something important about the South as a whole.

Traditionally, the history of the South, even more than the history of the nation, is divided by the Civil War. In view of the fact that the South was the battlefield, the choice of that war as a dividing line is understandable. Moreover, out of that war came not only devastation, but also the destruction of slavery and the society that rested on it. The Civil War, however, is only one of the discontinuities or breaks in the history of the South that some historians have called attention to. C. Vann Woodward, for example, has seen Reconstruction and the Populist era as other discontinuities in the history of the region. This book, however, does not emphasize the discontinuities in the Southern past. Rather it offers testimony to the continuity among dissenters, even across the chasm of civil war and emancipation. New bases of conflict and contention within the South were certainly added as time went on; nevertheless the issues and conflicts of the antebellum years continued to move men and parties in the years after Appomattox.

Undoubtedly the most convincing continuity in the South's history, as well as one of the principal reasons for seeing the South as distinctive, is that throughout the nineteenth century the vast majority of American Negroes lived there. When I began work on this book, I saw myself as writing only about whites. For "the South" has always meant the white South, and a Southerner has been a white person only. And it is true that there are few individual black people in these pages; yet blacks are never absent. A half-century ago the great Southern historian Ulrich B. Phillips discerned what he called "the central theme of Southern history." It was that the South "shall be and remain a white man's country." Phillips never wrote about those white people who dissented from their region; his primary concern always was with those people, both black and white, who made up the mainstream of Southern history. Still, in an important sense, this book is an illustration of his central theme. Behind all these dissenters, as behind all of the white South's great concerns during the nineteenth century, has stood the black eminence. Negroes have never been passive in the South, not even under slavery, but it has not been their resistance or even their violence that has made them the central concern of all Southerners—traditionalists and dissenters alike. It was simply their presence that mattered. So, strange as it may seem, although there are few individual Negroes in this book, it is about black Southerners, too.

In writing this book I discovered further that one cannot write about the South, or even think about the region, without recognizing that the South's history is truly the result of the interaction of black and white down through the centuries. It is this interaction, more than anything else, that sets the South apart from the rest of the United States. No other section of the country ever came close to duplicating that experience, that intimate mingling of European and African, of master and slave. For as W. J. Cash has written, "Negro entered into white man as profoundly as white man entered into Negro—subtly influencing every gesture, every word, every emotion, and idea, every attitude." The fact is that everything in the outward culture of Southerners, too, from the vocabulary and accent of their speech, through the foods and cooking, to the politics and the economy, has been shaped by the historic love-hate relationship between black and white on the Southern earth under the hot Southern sun. One might well rephrase the central theme of Southern history to be the effort of white Southerners to escape or to prevent that interaction, for they knew that it set them apart from other Americans.

To say that the central theme of Southern history is that the region shall remain a white man's country is to place racial consciousness ahead of class consciousness. And in a sense this book is a study in the way class has been subordinated to race in the life of nineteenth-century Southerners. Again and again certain Southerners sought to unite black and white in the name of common class interests only to have the effort shattered by an appeal to color. This book, to be sure, offers evidence that there were many white Southerners who ignored race in the name of class solidarity, but it also makes clear that most white Southerners could not follow that example. To them race was always more fundamental than class.

One political consequence of the presence of blacks has been the Solid South. A good part of this book is taken up with describing efforts to break up that solid front. Yet only sporadically and intermittently was that goal achieved in the nineteenth century. For almost half a century after the end of Reconstruction in 1877 not a single Republican presidential candidate was able to carry a state of the former Confederacy. Warren Harding in 1920 was the first to do so. In the election of 1972 Republican Richard Nixon captured every state of the South for the first time in the history of his party. Not even Ulysses S. Grant in the midst of Reconstruction achieved as much.

Richard Nixon's accomplishment, however, was not a triumph of the Other South. For by 1972 the Republican party was not the same party it had been a hundred years before. In 1872 it was the champion and the vehicle of Negro suffrage and Negro rights. By 1972 that role was being played by the Democratic party, the result of a political somersault that began many years before under Presidents Truman, Kennedy, and Johnson—two of whom, incidentally, were Southerners. The purpose here is not to describe the way that reversal took place. Rather it is to observe that although great national parties may change, the Majority South remains the same. It is yet another example of the continuity of Southern history and the persistence of the central theme. The support that the white South today gives to the once-detested Republican party is but a measure of the fact that the Republican party is no longer the Negro's champion and that instead the South's traditional party, the Democratic party, has assumed that role. One can be quite confident that if the Republican party should repudiate President Nixon's "Southern Strategy" a good part of the white South would ignore both parties as it did in 1948 with the Dixiecrats and threatened to do in 1972 with George Wallace's American party.

By the last quarter of the twentieth century, however, the solidity of the Majority South is weakening. The central theme no longer attracts as many white Southerners as it once did. Today the Democratic party in large areas of the South is a genuine biracial party and literally hundreds of elected officials in the South are black; legal segregation is clearly on the way out. The South today, in short, is less of a monolith than ever.

This book does not treat the twentieth-century South; hence the dissenters of today find no place here. But even as one recognizes the continuing and deepening diversity within the region, it is well to recall how premature have been earlier assertions of the end of the South's distinctiveness. In 1957, for example, Harry Ashmore wrote a book he called *Epitaph for Dixie,* in which he emphasized the changes in the South since 1945, which were making it more like the rest of the nation. Yet in 1964 five states of the deep South deserted a Southern-born Democratic President because he had successfully fought for the passage of the most powerful and comprehensive civil rights act ever enacted in the United States. And the remainder of the white South was hardly much more enthusiastic about Lyndon Johnson. The South, in short, endures, despite its historical and continuing diversity. The central theme remains. For if diversity has always been a part of its history, its distinctiveness is just as much a part of that history. And that sense of difference, felt outside the South as well as within, promises to continue for years to come. Those circumstances, events, and common experiences that have set Southerners apart from other Americans in the past will not soon be cast off.

It is at once an assumption and a conclusion of this book that the burden of the past is felt even by those who, like the dissenters discussed here, consciously seek to throw off that burden. The South's burden of history and the efforts of some Southerners to transcend that past have long been sources of my own interest in the South. I am not a Southerner, neither by birth nor by adoption. My interest in the region derives rather from my conviction as a historian that the past limits options for change in the present. Nowhere else in American history is the truth of that conviction more clearly observed than in the history of the South. And nowhere in that history is it so obvious as in the story of those dissenters who sought to escape their Southern past.

Historians recognize that the ultimate paradox of history is that the only sure escape from the power of the past is by understanding it. Only by consciously knowing one's history can one begin to transcend it. And that, I suppose, is my ultimate reason for writing this book, or any book of history, for that matter. But in this particular case, by knowing those of an earlier time who struggled to escape their Southern past, those of us today who seek to change not only the South's inheritance but the nation's as well can gain spiritual support for our own efforts together with understanding of the past.

In the nineteenth century no institution or cultural trait more sharply set apart the South from the rest of the nation than slavery. At one time, to be sure, slavery had been established in every state of the original Union. But by the opening of the nineteenth century slavery had been ended or was on the way to abolition in all the states north of the Ohio River and Maryland. And as the century moved on, the continued existence of the institution in the Southern states became more and more of an anomaly. Yet the more slavery differentiated the South from the rest of America, the more Southerners felt called upon to defend it. In time, their identification with slavery became so close that many Southerners spoke of it as "our peculiar institution."

Despite this identification, there always were white Southerners who not only harbored doubts about slavery but also expressed hostility toward it. For those Southerners the past was not entirely controlling; they had transcended it, at least in part. Who were these Southern opponents of slavery and why did they object to so Southern an institution? What do their arguments reveal about them and the South? These questions the next two chapters seek to answer.

BOOK

I

SOUTHERNERS
AGAINST SLAVERY

2

Enemies of Slavery
in Behalf of Blacks

In the early morning hours of August 22, 1831, a black slave preacher in Southampton County, Virginia, gave a signal to a group of slaves to rise up in rebellion against their masters. Almost systematically Nat Turner's handful of followers went from one farmhouse to another, maiming or killing the occupants. The suddenness of the rebellion caught the whites completely unawares, for none of the blacks privy to the long-planned plot had breathed even a hint. In fact, many of the farmers of the region had left the county for the campgrounds of neighboring North Carolina for a little religious refreshment. As the rebels moved slowly in the general direction of the Dismal Swamp of North Carolina during the first day of the insurrection, they were virtually unopposed. As a result, the death toll of the whites was probably the highest ever recorded in a single slave uprising on the North American continent. By the time militia and troops arrived on the scene some sixty whites lay dead. Eventually three companies of federal troops as well as state militia and scores of armed citizens were deployed. Although no one will ever know how many blacks died in the white frenzy of fear and fury, dozens were killed outright before the troops intervened to temper the local whites' violent repression.

Although the outbreak was put down within a day, the excitement and fear persisted much longer, if only because Turner, the leader of the band, was not captured for two months. Moreover, the bloody black heads of the rebels fixed on poles along the roads, though intended as a warning to potential rebels, must also have reminded the whites of the terrible events of August 22 and 23. As late as November 21, the governor was receiving urgent requests from Virginia citizens for arms to protect themselves against possible slave insurrections.

DRIVEN BY FEAR

News of the uprising spread across the South, accompanied by the fear that the plot extended beyond Virginia's borders. The governor of South Carolina proposed to the governors of North Carolina and Virginia that they consult on joint action to forestall such events in the future. In New Bern, North Carolina, federal troops had to be brought in to calm the fears of the people that rebellion would spread to their slaves. As far away as Louisiana the governor called the legislature into session, fearful that some Virginia slaves in Louisiana would have brought ideas of insurrection with them. Some Northern newspapers reported the spread of rebellion, though in fact no other uprising occurred. Many years later, Daniel R. Goodloe, a North Carolina antislavery man, recalled the fear generated in Oxford, North Carolina: "I was then in my seventeenth year. I volunteered and had my first military service in marching over the town and neighborhood to suppress imaginary combinations of insurgent negroes."[1]

Goodloe's recollection was a good deal calmer than the reaction at the time, especially in Virginia. Throughout the state, but especially in the tidewater area, where the slave population was concentrated, white men anticipated violence and bloodshed, if not worse. One sympathetic Northerner then visiting in Virginia wrote that Virginians "lie down to sleep with fear. They hardly venture out on nights. A lady told me, that for weeks after the tragedy, she had quivered at every blast of wind, and every blow of the shutter. Bolts and bars were tried, but the horrid fear haunted the whole population day and night."[2]

1. "Autobiographical Sketch," in Goodloe Papers, Folder 3.
2. Quoted in Joseph Clarke Robert, *The Road from Monticello: A Study of the Virginia Slavery Debate of 1832* (Durham, N.C., 1941), pp. 7–8.

The Turner Rebellion broke out at a low point in the history of white Virginia. Like much of the upper South, which did not grow the miracle crop of cotton, Virginia depended upon tobacco and wheat; these crops did not bring the prices and profits associated with the Cotton Kingdom, then in its rise to dominance. Instead, Virginia agriculture languished in 1831, and men wondered whether the Old Dominion might not have passed its prime, economically as well as politically. The recent census of 1830 had offered documentation to support the fears. As late as 1810 Virginia had stood first in population among the states of the Union, but by 1820 it was in second place, and now in 1830 it was third. But this declension in national standing was more of a worry to those Virginians who competed on the national scene; for the average farmer or planter much more immediately worrisome was another fact revealed by the census. This was the rapid growth, east of the Blue Ridge Mountains, of the black population as compared with the white. At the first census in 1790 whites outnumbered blacks even east of the Blue Ridge, but by 1800 the proportion was reversed, if only slightly. By 1820 the difference was 65,000 in favor of blacks, and by 1830 blacks outnumbered whites by 81,000. In such a demographic context the Turner uprising could seem only ominous to the average white Virginian.

Between August and December, when the legislature was scheduled to meet, Virginians of all classes wrestled with the question of how to prevent another Southampton. Some people thought that it was necessary only to reduce the imbalance between white and black in the east by some scheme of deportation—either of free blacks or of slaves. A few white Virginians acted to translate the thought into reality. Before the end of the year some two hundred free Negroes of Southampton County were impelled by whippings and other means to accept the offer of the American Colonization Society to transport them to Liberia for permanent settlement. Governor John Floyd, on the other hand, who owned a dozen or more slaves himself, wrote in his diary in November: "Before I leave this Government I will have contrived to have a law passed gradually abolishing slavery in this state, or at all events to begin the work of prohibiting slavery on the west side of the Blue Ridge

Mountains."[3] Before the legislature met, he drew up a plan for the gradual elimination of slavery through purchase and the removal of the freed blacks. The legislature received a number of petitions from citizens asking for the end of slavery, some because of the fear of another insurrection, others taking the occasion to object to slavery in general. One such petition from Nelson County in the piedmont region was signed by 332 names. Newspapers also seriously canvassed the possibility of emancipation. "A few months have wrought a great change in public sentiment" concerning slavery, commented one Virginian early in December, 1831.[4]

In his message to the legislature in December, Governor Floyd did not recommend or even mention emancipation, though he devoted most of his remarks to the Southampton uprising. Behind the scenes, however, Floyd worked closely with those members of the House of Delegates who believed that an end to slavery was the proper answer to the threat aroused by Turner's rebellion. They were sufficiently numerous so that when an effort was made to prevent the question of emancipation from being discussed at all, it failed. The stage was now set for a historic and highly dramatic event. From January 16 to January 25, 1832, the Virginia House of Delegates debated, as no legislature in the South ever had or ever would again, the merits of Negro slavery.

Momentous as the occasion undoubtedly was, it needs to be recognized that at no time did the House have before it a resolution calling for the ending of slavery or even a plan of gradual emancipation. The debate was over whether a committee's report ought to recommend the ending of slavery or not. That technical limitation, however, did not prevent those who thought slavery wrong or inexpedient from voicing some of the harshest judgments on slavery ever to be heard in a public forum in North America. The speeches on both sides were carried in the Virginia newspapers and in others throughout the nation.

As the debate proceeded it soon became evident that the House of 134 members was divided three ways on the question. About sixty members—most, but not all, of whom came from the non-

3. Clement Eaton, *Freedom of Thought in the Old South* (Durham, N.C., 1940), p. 93.
4. Robert, *Road from Monticello*, p. 14.

slaveholding western part of the state—wanted some kind of legislative action looking toward the ending of slavery. Another sixty members agreed that slavery was an evil, but said that they could envision no practical way to end it. Not all the members of this group, incidentally, were slaveholders from the east. The third group, embracing only twelve members, favored emancipation, but they were not prepared to vote for legislation at that particular time. As a result, it can be said that this group, by voting with the second group, determined that slavery in Virginia would not be set on the road to extinction.

In view of the persistent stories—even from historians who should know better—that antislavery lost by only one vote in the Virginia legislature in 1832, it is worth noting that no vote was that close. The vote on the motion to have the legislature consider the possibility of legislation to end slavery was lost 73 to 58. The closest tally was on a motion to label slavery an evil but inexpedient to legislate upon at that time; that count was lost by seven votes (67 to 60). Furthermore, even if the House had voted to *consider* antislavery bills, what the outcome of that consideration would have been is not at all clear. And finally, even if the House of Delegates had voted to end slavery—in the most gradual manner and with compensation to owners—the whole package still had to pass the conservative Senate. In sum, the point in looking at the Virginia Debates on slavery in January, 1832, is not to suggest that history might have been different if only a few men had switched their votes, but to provide some insight into the thoughts of these Southerners who opposed slavery.

THE ROOTS OF SOUTHERN ANTISLAVERY

Although the Virginia Debates provide some of the most cogent and wide-ranging arguments against slavery in the history of the nineteenth-century South, the arguments did not spring forth without antecedents. The roots of Southern antislavery thought go back much further than 1832. There will be, however, no attempt here to survey the whole history of Southern antislavery thought and action. The purpose is to examine the nature of Southern antislavery ideas when slavery was at its height—roughly between 1820 and 1860. As an introduction to the subject, though, it is worth looking at some of the expressions of antislavery thought in previous years, for they suggest the antiquity of Southerners' reaction against slavery.

Probably there is no native Southerner whose objections to slavery are better known than Thomas Jefferson's. Actually, Jefferson's doubts and reservations about slavery—and they probably ought not to be called much more than that—were echoed by a number of his Virginia contemporaries like James Madison, Patrick Henry, and above all George Mason. Even George Washington freed his slaves at his death, an antislavery gesture that the Sage of Monticello failed to make. The Jeffersonian doubts about the desirability of slavery manifested themselves, too, when both Kentucky and Tennessee—those two early offspring of Virginia— came to draw up their constitutions. David Rice, for example, led a fight to prohibit slavery in Kentucky at the state's first constitutional convention in 1792. The fight, of course, was lost by a vote of 26 to 16. Four years later an effort to provide in the constitution of Tennessee for the gradual end to slavery in that state was also defeated, but there, as in Kentucky, it was evident that some Southerners recognized the evil of the institution. Occasionally, even in the deep South in those early years, doubts about slavery came to the surface. A judge in Chatham County, Georgia, in 1804 told a grand jury that the hour was getting late for ridding the state of the curse of slavery. Slavery, he emphasized, was the work of men, not of God. If it is kept, he asked, "What then are we eventually to expect!! What but blood, massacre, and devastation!" He urged the jury to consider his plan for gradual emancipation and religious instruction for those who were freed.[5]

Perhaps the most outspoken and sustained admissions by prominent Southerners of their doubts about slavery prior to 1832 were made in Congress during the debates over the admission of Missouri in 1820. Typical of Southern antislavery remarks at that time were those of Congressman Robert Reid of Georgia. "Believe me, sir, I am not the panegyrist of slavery. It is an unnatural state; a dark cloud which obscures half the lustre of our free institutions!"

5. Ruth Scarborough, *The Opposition to Slavery in Georgia Prior to 1860* (Nashville, 1933), pp. 243–44.

But his doubts about the institution, as Reid and most of his fellow antislavery Southerners in Congress soon made clear, did not mean he favored abolition or even gradual emancipation. Slavery, he said, "is a fixed evil, which we can only alleviate. Are we called upon to emancipate our slaves? I answer their welfare—the safety of our citizens, forbid it. Can we incorporate them with us and make them and us one people? The prejudices of the North," he correctly observed, "and of the South rise up in equal strength against such a measure."[6]

The ambivalent and ambiguous objection to slavery expressed by Reid, which might be called the Jeffersonian outlook, was not the only form that antislavery sentiment assumed in the South prior to 1832. Soon after the Missouri question was settled, Benjamin Lundy, a New Jersey-born abolitionist who had lived in Virginia and Missouri for years, moved to eastern Tennessee to continue the publication of his antislavery newspaper, *The Genius of Emancipation.* Eastern Tennessee already had a small antislavery movement when Lundy joined it; its criticisms of slavery were often much more severe than those expressed in Congress or by Thomas Jefferson. It is sometimes said that one of the sources of Southern hostility toward Northern abolitionists, especially after 1830, was their habit of impugning the morality of slaveholders in addition to attacking slavery. An acquaintance with Lundy's newspaper and with the Southerners who supported it makes evident that attacks on the morality of slaveholders were not confined to Northerners. In 1823, for example, while his newspaper was being published in Tennessee, Lundy wrote that many of the slaveholders "are ipso facto the most disgraceful whoremongers upon earth; they make a *business* of raising bastards and selling them for money;—they keep poor miserable degraded females for this identical purpose; they compel them to submit to their abominable and *avaricious* and brutal lusts; they oppose the work of emancipation *on this ground.*" Elihu Embree, who preceded Lundy as an antislavery publisher in Tennessee, was a native Southerner. Nevertheless he was no more reluctant than Lundy to attack the

6. *Annals of Congress,* 16th Cong., 1st Sess. (Washington, D.C., 1855), pp. 1025–26.

morality of slaveholders. In 1820, for example, Embree called slaveholders "monsters in human shape." About the same time another Tennessean referred to them as "bloodsuckers," while still another antislavery Southerner said they were "Miserable sons of avarice," "Infant Neros . . . these Caligulas of the North American Republic."[7]

Some early Southern antislavery thinkers put their views in book or pamphlet form. In 1824 Joseph Doddridge, an Episcopal minister in western Virginia, published a book condemning slavery and, more remarkable, condemning the racial defense of the institution. "We debase them to the condition of brutes," he wrote, referring to the black slaves, "and then use that debasement as an argument for perpetuating their slavery." Better known as an early antislavery writer in the South was Robert J. Breckinridge of Kentucky, who wrote letters opposing slavery to newspapers and in 1830 brought out *Hints on Slavery*. Because of these pronouncements he had to resign from the legislature, but he neither left the South nor desisted from his vocal opposition to slavery.

Breckinridge's assault on slavery was unambiguous. "Never was there a more fallacious idea," he wrote, "than that slavery contributed anything towards the permanent resources of a state. It is an ulcer eating its way into the very heart of the state." Gradual emancipation, he contended, would reduce the value of the remaining slaves and thereby give the "poor and laboring whites . . . just protection, aid, and encouragement for which they have been so long deprived, and *which our humanity has for so long lavished on the blacks*." If Breckinridge's primary concern was whites, he still thought that the moral life of blacks was a casualty under slavery, too. It broke up the slave family and encouraged promiscuous breeding, he pointed out. Furthermore, slavery denied the essential humanity of Negroes. "Men will not always remain slaves," he warned. "No kindness can soothe the spirit of a slave. No ignorance, however abject, can obliterate the indelible stamp of nature, whereby she decreed man free. No cruelty of bondage,

7. Merton L. Dillon, *Benjamin Lundy and the Struggle for Negro Freedom* (Urbana, Ill., 1966), pp. 53–54.

however rigorous, can suppress forever the deep yearnings after freedom."[8]

Expressions of antislavery views in the years before the Virginia Debates were not confined to isolated individuals. In 1825, for example, the Raleigh *Register* asked "Ought Slavery to Exist?" The newspaper's answer was clearly antislavery and suggested that its view was not unique in the South: "We presume but few would answer in the affirmative, and still fewer would be found to advocate the practice as being right in itself or to justify it except on the broad plea of necessity." Yet this was within the ambiguous and ambivalent Jeffersonian tradition. More consonant with the hard moral line against slavery that would later be associated with Northern abolitionists was *An Address to the People of North Carolina on the Evils of Slavery,* published in 1830 by the Manumission Society of North Carolina. In the pamphlet slavery was attacked as "radically evil" and "founded in injustice and cruelty." It corrupts not only those who are associated with it, but it "is contrary to the plain and simple maxims of the Christian Revelation, or religion of Christ." The pamphlet advanced a scheme for the gradual emancipation of slaves in the state.[9]

None of the manumission or antislavery societies in the South of the 1820's was large in membership; yet those in the North were even less impressive in size or in number. Benjamin Lundy, whose *Genius of Emancipation* was one of the earliest abolitionist newspapers in the United States, estimated in 1827 that there were 106 antislavery societies in the South as compared with 24 in the Northern states. He thought that the Southern membership of such societies reached 5,000, while the Northern was only 1,500. Inasmuch as many of these antislavery societies, at least in the South, were actually branches of the American Colonization Society, it is

8. Patricia P. Hickin, "Antislavery in Virginia, 1831–1861," unpublished Ph.D. dissertation, University of Virginia, 1968, pp. 526–27; Robert Jefferson Breckinridge, *Hints on Slavery* (n.p., n.d., title page refers to publication in *Kentucky Reporter* in 1830), pp. 20–26.

9. R. H. Taylor, "Humanizing the Slave Code of North Carolina," *North Carolina Historical Review*, II (1925), 330; *An Address to the People of North Carolina, on the Evils of Slavery* (Greensboro, N.C., 1830).

necessary at this point to stop to examine the colonization movement.

THE AMBIVALENCE OF COLONIZATION

The American Colonization Society was founded in Washington, D.C., in 1817 to provide a means for removing free Negroes from the United States. The society established the colony of Liberia on the west coast of Africa as a haven for former American slaves. In origin the society was not antislavery, since its stated purpose was to remove only free blacks who volunteered to move to Africa. In time, however, the work of the society came to include the removal of any blacks, whether born free or recently freed. Thus the society provided an answer for those slaveholders who wished to free their slaves, but who did not think it advisable for the freed blacks to remain in the United States. Understandably, during the 1820's, when the society flourished and excited the least controversy, the great majority of its local organizations were located in the slave states, where blacks were concentrated. In 1826, for example, forty-four of the fifty-seven such organizations were in the South.

Early in the 1830's the American Colonization Society in particular and the idea of colonization in general came under violent attack from William Lloyd Garrison, the Massachusetts abolitionist. From that onslaught, the society's reputation for being sympathetic toward Negroes never recovered. In essence Garrison argued that colonization was a ruse for preserving slavery rather than a scheme for ending it. The removal of free Negroes made slavery more palatable to whites who resented or feared a disproportionate number of blacks around them. Because some of the proponents of colonization were of this persuasion and also because the great majority of Negroes were native Americans and not Africans in anything but remote ancestry, historians have generally followed Garrison's argument. Within the context of the nineteenth-century South, however, the Garrisonian interpretation of colonization and its significance obscures more than it reveals. By lumping colonization with proslavery people, the Garrisonian view ignores the fact that colonization in the 1820's and 1830's attracted people who were opposed to slavery. They may not have opposed it with the same intensity or belief in Negro equality that animated Garrison, but they were not defenders of the institution either, as Garrison's simplified categories would lead one to believe.

One reason for making the distinction, too, is that in the minds of proslavery advocates, colonization and emancipation were allied. A particularly revealing example of this association and reaction occurred in the middle twenties. In January, 1824, the legislature of Ohio invited Congress and the legislatures of the other states to consider a plan for gradual emancipation of all the slaves in the country through colonization abroad of the free Negroes. The costs of the plan were to be borne by the federal government on the assumption that slavery was a national, not a sectional, problem. Within a matter of months, eight Northern states, including all of those in the newly settled Northwest, endorsed the idea. In February, 1825, Rufus King, senator from New York, introduced a bill in the Senate to create, from the sale of public lands, a fund to carry out the plan. The reaction of Georgia and South Carolina was instantaneous and hostile. As Charles Sydnor, a modern Southern historian of the period, has remarked, "The harshness of the Southern rejoinder to these proposals can hardly be explained." Nevertheless it makes evident that colonization in this context was seen as a severe threat to slavery even before a strong antislavery agitation was mounted in the North. Needless to say, nothing came of the King proposal once the vehement opposition of the lower South became known.

Even after Garrison denounced colonization as a ruse to protect rather than a way to end slavery, many Southerners still identified the idea with opposition to slavery. Thus, when in 1832 the legislature of Virginia refused to move toward emancipation, it turned to colonization. The Virginia House of Delegates voted 79 to 41 to provide funds to pay for the removal of free blacks who had been voluntarily manumitted and who also gave their consent to being deported. In that vote there was no clear division between antislavery and proslavery men, but in the Senate there was. There the bill was amended to prohibit the use of funds for transporting manumitted slaves, thereby confining the application of the bill to free Negroes only. With this change, which was obviously intended to remove the slightest antislavery aspect from the original measure, the bill was supported by fifteen of the nineteen senators from the eastern (slaveholding) counties and opposed by nine of the eleven from the western (nonslaveholding) counties. Having made their point, the defenders of slavery in the Senate then made a motion to postpone indefinitely the whole measure, which passed 18 to 14.

There were other signs after 1830 that colonization was interpreted by Southerners as signifying opposition to slavery. Patricia Hickin, for example, in her thorough and admirable study of antislavery in Virginia, points out that colonization as an idea was very unpopular in the tidewater and rural south side of the state, where the slaves were concentrated, but popular in the west, where the slaves were few. Robert Breckinridge of Kentucky, who spent most of his public life seeking to rid his state of slavery, emphasized the antislavery basis of colonization in a speech in 1831. Colonization assumed that slavery was an evil, morally and politically, he pointed out, and the Colonization Society for which he spoke "cherished the hope and the belief also, that the successful prosecution of its objects would offer powerful motives and exert a persuasive influence in favor of emancipation. And it is with this indirect effect of the society that the largest advantage is to result in America." Similarly, a few years later, in 1836, the Louisville *Journal* placed itself on record in favor of colonization as the only way to end slavery in the South. "Its object is not to pronounce the Negro free and equal to the white but to endeavor to make him so—not simply to break the chains from his limbs, but to place him in a position to deserve and enjoy freedom."[10]

The records of the Colonization Society also attest to the connection in many Southerners' minds between opposition to slavery and colonization. In those records are examples of large planters who willed their slaves to the society or in some instances turned over their whole estates to the society for the purposes of furthering colonization and freeing their own slaves. Historians in examining the files of the American Colonization Society have come to

10. Asa Earl Martin, *The Anti-Slavery Movement in Kentucky* (Louisville, 1918), pp. 53–56.

a similar conclusion. "In reading countless official reports, documents, and articles of various kinds," in the society's files, remarks Frederic Bancroft, "not one positively proslavery official word has been found. The general tenor of it all was at least mildly, often positively antislavery. And about four-sevenths of the real colonists before 1852 had been emancipated in view of emigrating to Africa."[11] Finally, as we shall see later, some of those Southern opponents of slavery who were indisputably concerned about the welfare of the Negro in slavery, like Samuel Janney and Mary Minor Blackford, did not find a conflict between their outlook and colonization since they supported colonization.

VARIETIES OF SOUTHERN ANTISLAVERY

If the meaning of colonization could be ambiguous in the South, the meaning of antislavery was even more so. This is perhaps the place to make clear the varieties of motives that lay behind that antislavery sentiment. Just as some men favored colonization merely to get rid of blacks in their midst, so some men opposed slavery because it brought blacks into their midst. William H. Roane, a member of the House of Delegates during the Virginia Debates of 1832, was certainly of this persuasion. Although he spoke against slavery, he made it clear he was not thinking about the welfare of the blacks. "I am not one of those who have ever revolted at the idea or practice of slavery, as many do. . . . I think slavery as much a correlative of liberty as cold is of heat. . . . Nor do I believe in that Fan-faronade about the natural equality of man. . . . I no more believe that the flat-nosed, wooly-headed black native of the deserts of *Africa,* is equal to the straight-haired white man of Europe, than I believe the stupid, scentless greyhound is equal to the noble, generous dog of *Newfoundland.*" As Roane made clear, his objection to slavery was that it brought blacks and whites into the same country. "I lay it down as a postulatum," he asserted, "that free white people, free blacks, and

11. Frederic Bancroft, "The Colonization of American Negroes, 1801–1865," in Jacob E. Cooke, ed., *Frederic Bancroft: Historian* (Norman, Okla., 1957), p. 190. The standard and most recent study on the colonization movement is P. J. Staudenraus, *The African Colonization Movement, 1816–1865* (New York, 1961).

slave blacks cannot and ought not to constitute one and the same society."

Still other antislavery Southerners sought to end slavery because they feared the violence of outraged black slaves. Certainly this was in the mind of many Virginians after Turner's uprising. As James McDowell, an antislavery man, phrased it during the Virginia Debates of 1832, "Was it the fear of Nat Turner and his deluded and drunken handful of followers which produced or could produce" this discussion? Was that why distant counties armed themselves? he asked. "No, sir, it was the suspicion eternally attached to the slave himself, the suspicion that a Nat Turner might be in every family, that the same bloody deed could be acted over at any time in any place, that the materials for it were spread through the land and always ready for a like explosion."[12]

Actually, the number of Southern antislavery men who rested their case against slavery on racism alone were few, so far as the evidence reveals. The irony is that hostility to blacks as a primary reason for opposing slavery was probably more widespread in the North than it was in the South. This is not to say that there were not Southerners who disliked or even hated Negroes. For Hinton Rowan Helper, as we shall see, certainly was as Negrophobic as anyone in the United States. Rather it is to say that the preponderance of Southern antislavery people did not have hatred of Negroes as their primary objection to slavery, as it was for a number of Northern antislavery men. Most of the Negrophobes among the antislavery Southerners actually opposed slavery for another, albeit related reason. They objected to slavery and wanted to have it ended in the South because they thought it was an economic and social system harmful to white men. To this large class we shall turn in some detail, in the next chapter.

A third class of Southern arguments against slavery was those that stemmed primarily or largely from a concern for the Negro. This argument is most often associated in modern minds with Northern abolitionists. Certainly the kind of moral horror over slavery that was developed and propagated by William Lloyd Garrison, Lydia Maria Child, or Wendell Phillips in the North

12. Robert, *Road from Monticello*, pp. 80–81, 103–4.

derived almost wholly from a concern for the black who was a slave. There is no need here to recapitulate the Garrisonian view that slavery was a sin which must be immediately ended. It is necessary, however, to point out that there were no Garrisons or Grimké sisters or Theodore Parkers in the South. True, a highly moral attack on slavery and slaveholders that came close at times to the position mounted by the extreme Northern abolitionists can be found among a few Southerners, particularly among Quakers. But to all intents and purposes in the antebellum South the strongly moral Garrisonian type of argument against slavery is virtually unrepresented. Indeed, it was almost a necessary ritual for a Southern antislavery advocate after 1831 to deny having any affinity with Garrison's ideas before he could expect to receive a hearing at all.

Furthermore, it is worth recalling that in the North, too, radical abolitionists were a mere handful, even among the opponents of slavery. The mass of antislavery people in the Republican party, for example, were opposed to slavery principally because of its impact upon white men, rather than because of its harm to blacks. Certainly this was the position of the party's national leaders like William Seward, Abraham Lincoln, or Horace Greeley. Alexis de Tocqueville was not confining the application of his remarks to the South when he wrote in 1835, "It is not for the good of Negroes but for that of the whites that measures are taken to abolish slavery in the United States."[13]

With that introduction let us now turn to an examination of the nature of the antislavery argument as it was set forth in the South between roughly 1830 and the outbreak of the war that ended Negro bondage. In the remainder of this chapter we shall look at the arguments that rested on a concern for the welfare of blacks; then in the next chapter we will scrutinize those attacks on slavery that arose from a primary concern for whites.

13. Alexis de Tocqueville, *Democracy in America,* ed. by Phillips Bradley (New York, 1948), I, 360. For a good summary and analysis of Northern Republican views of the Negro and the racism underlying their antislavery outlook see Eric Foner, *Free Soil, Free Labor, Free Men: The Ideology of the Republican Party Before the Civil War* (New York, 1970), ch. 8. For a general view of Northern anti-Negro practices during the antebellum years see Leon F. Litwack, *North of Slavery* (Chicago, 1961).

MADE IN THE IMAGE OF GOD

If there were no Theodore Welds or William Lloyd Garrisons in the South, there were people who saw slavery as wrong because of what it did to Negroes. In a sense, one of the earliest criticisms of slavery by a Southerner that stemmed from concern for blacks came from Thomas Jefferson, who in a private letter in 1786 referred to "our suffering brethren," the slaves. Several of the critics of slavery during the Virginia Debates echoed this Jeffersonian argument. Philip A. Bolling, from a county in the piedmont, asserted that no matter how one might defend slave labor one "could not justify the traffic in human beings. High-minded men ought to disdain to hold their fellow creatures as articles of traffic—disregarding all the ties of blood and affection—tearing asunder all those sympathies dear to men—dividing husbands and wives, parents and children, as they would cut asunder a piece of cotton cloth. They have hearts and feelings like other men. How many a broken heart—how many a Rachel mourns because her house is left unto her desolate. . . . This, sir, is a Christian community. They [*sic*] read in their Bibles 'do unto all men as you would have them do unto you'—and this golden rule and slavery are hard to reconcile." It is not known whether Bolling himself was a slaveholder, though he came from a slaveholding county. But Henry Berry identified himself as a substantial slaveholder who owned a plantation a hundred miles east of the Blue Ridge—that is, in the midst of the slaveholding region. "Pass as severe laws as you will to keep these unfortunate creatures in ignorance," he told his fellow legislators, "it is in vain, unless you can extinguish that spark of intellect which God has given them. . . . Sir, we have, as far as possible closed every avenue by which light might enter their minds; we have only to go one step further—to extinguish the capacity to see the light, and our work would be completed; they would then be reduced to the level of the beasts of the field, and we should be safe. . . ."[14]

As might be anticipated, Virginia's great Quaker opponent of

14. Robert, *Road from Monticello*, pp. 110, 99.

ducers and oppressors of the Africans, have descended, were exceedingly ignorant, superstitious and degraded." It was only the introduction of Christianity to the Anglo-Saxons and Germans that raised them to a civilized position. "Thus if this boasted and boasting Anglo-Saxon race, with an open Bible in their hands and with the ameliorating and humanizing influences of Christianity steadily bearing upon them all the time have been fifteen hundred years in arriving at their present low stage of progress, how dare we say that the Africans, who have been for long centuries shut out from this light of heaven and from these benign influences, and have been moreover debased and stupefied by that abominable traffic, the slave trade, are an inferior race?"

His argument closed with a defense of the natural rights of Negroes: "Even if they were as inferior as the advocates of slavery assert, they certainly have as good a right to the free use of whatever power the creator has given them as the weak minded among the whites or as those who have been more liberally endowed."[16]

Long before Caruthers wrote, the men in the Virginia Debates who questioned slavery had advanced the argument that neither natural law nor the superiority of one culture justified the enslavement of men of a less advanced society. George W. Summers, who came from the nonslaveholding west, was indirect in his questioning of slavery, but the issues he raised were those spelled out by Caruthers and Goodloe later. "I will not advert to the great principles of eternal justice, which demand at our hands the release of this people," he began. "I will not examine here, the authority upon which one part of the human family assumes the right to enslave the other—I will not open the great volume of nature's laws, to ascertain if it is written there that all men are alike in the sight of Him, who must regard with equal beneficence the creatures of his hands, without distinction of color or condition." More direct was Thomas Jefferson Randolph's questioning of the biblical defense of slavery. Randolph was Thomas Jefferson's nephew and a slaveholder himself. "The gentleman has appealed to the Christian religion in justification of slavery," he began, referring to a

16. Manuscript entitled "American Slavery and the Immediate Duty of Southern Slaveholders" in Eli Washington Caruthers Papers, Preface and pp. 13–28.

previous speaker. "I would ask him upon what of those pure doctrines does he rely; to which of those sublime precepts does he
avert to sustain his position? Is it that which teaches charity,
justice and good will to all, or is it that which teaches 'that ye do
unto others as ye would they should do unto you'?" Another antislavery speaker, Williams from Harrison County in the Valley,
carried the attack upon the biblical defense of slavery a step further
by observing that the failure to condemn slavery in the Bible was
not, as the defenders of slavery asserted, tantamount to the
acceptance of the institution. After all, Williams pointed out, "The
Savior did not come into the world to teach us politics of munici-
pal regulations; but to offer himself as a sacrifice for the transgres-
sions of men. He spoke . . . after the manner of men, and so did
Joshua, when he bade the sun to stand still. But the gentleman
very well knows that it was the earth and not the sun, whose
motion was arrested. From these facts, it is plain the Bible does
not afford either a system of astronomy or politics . . . suited
to the present time. . . ."[17]

As might be expected, moral arguments against slavery appealed particularly to clergymen who opposed the South's peculiar
institution. The great preponderance of Protestant ministers in the
antebellum South, to be sure, accepted the traditional biblical and
other defenses of slavery. But here and there some spoke out, like
Caruthers, or published works against the institution, like Samuel
Janney. And there were a few others. William Sparrow, an Episco-
palian minister at Alexandria, Virginia, was one; J. M. Pendleton,
a Baptist of Nashville, Tennessee, was another; and John McLean
of Texas, a Methodist, was still a third. Another Methodist
preacher, John Hersey, soon after the Virginia Debates, wrote a
book called *Appeal to Christians on the Subject of Slavery*, which
went into several editions. Proclaiming black men to be the
brothers of white men, he added, "Would it be esteemed honorable, or merciful, or affectionate in any human being to hold his
own brother in bondage for life, and make a slave of him?"
Although Hersey made evident that he was concerned for the
black men, he still did not favor emancipation without coloniza-

17. Robert, *Road from Monticello,* pp. 84–85, 97, 94.

tion. In his view, America was simply not a place in which a black person could achieve dignity and respect. Instead he called for the expenditure of a million dollars a year to colonize blacks in Africa.[18]

The Manumission Society of North Carolina in 1830 published a similar call for recognition of the contradiction between slavery and humanity. To argue that Negroes could be justifiably enslaved because they had been slaves in Africa, the pamphlet pointed out, was to place Western civilization on a level with African, though it was generally presumed by those who defended slavery to be higher. Besides, "Negroes are *human beings,* and are capable of loving, of being endeared to each other," while slavery violated those tender relations. Furthermore, the address went on, "liberty is the *unalienable birth-right* of every human being" and "God has made no difference in this respect between the *white* and *black.*" From a national or an individual point of view, there is no distinction between the races; the Negro is "entitled to the same measure of justice with the white man" and "neither his skin" nor any other physical attribute should be used as a "pretext of his oppression." The pamphlet closed with a plan for gradual emancipation and a recognition that the "debt we owe to the Negroes" cannot be discharged by freedom alone—the nation must educate and uplift the Negroes so "that they may be prepared both to enjoy and appreciate liberty."[19]

One of the most remarkable Southerners who opposed slavery on religious grounds was Mary Berkeley Minor Blackford of Fredericksburg, Virginia. The wife of a prominent publisher and supporter of the American Colonization Society, Mary Blackford made no secret of her opposition to slavery and the culture it shaped. Although her five sons were destined to serve in the Confederate army, she tried early to induce at least two of them to leave Virginia and the South to escape the effects of a slave society. Like some other colonizationists, she thought it was best for blacks to move to Africa if they would be truly free. In 1827 she freed her two house servants with the expectation that they would leave

18. Hickin, "Antislavery in Virginia," p. 374.
19. *An Address to the People* . . . , pp. 31–33, 39, 65–66.

for Africa, but they refused. Mary Blackford then hired them as
her servants. Her many entries over the years in a diary on the
enormities of slavery reveal that her primary objection to the
institution was her concern for blacks.

One incident in 1832 illustrates not only her concern for the
humanity of slaves but also her remarkably detached attitude
toward the recent Southampton uprising of Nat Turner, about
which most white Virginians were highly emotional. Across the
street from where she lived in Fredericksburg was the home of a
slave trader named Finnell. Confined in the basement of Finnell's
house was a young Negro who had recently been sold by his
master because the slave had been suspected of planning to run
away. When the boy's mother tried to see him to say goodbye
before he was transported to the South, the guard refused to let her
in. Mary Blackford learned of the refusal and offered to intercede.
Crossing the street, she confronted the guard, only to be refused as
adamantly as the mother was. "When I found all hope of prevailing with him was over," she wrote later, "I fixed my eyes steadily
upon the hard hearted being before me and asked him if he did not
fear the judgments of an offended God. I warned him that such
cruelty could not long go unpunished and reminded him of the
affair at Southampton which had just occurred. He seemed to quail
under my rebuke." Nevertheless, the mother was not allowed to
see her son until he was moved out to be sold down South. It was
after this incident that Mary Blackford commented wryly in her
diary: "How the practice of injustice hardens the feelings is perfectly wonderful; what is done under our own eyes would shock us
to the last degree were it not for this hardening process. I am
convinced that the time will come when we shall look back and
wonder how Christians could sanction slavery." How strange, she
commented, that even professors of religion—like the owner of the
slave who was being sent South—"think themselves justified when
a slave attempts to make his escape to a Free State from a most
natural and laudable desire of freedom to have him immediately
sold to a Negro buyer, seeming to consider he had committed a
great crime."[20]

20. L. Minor Blackford, *Mine Eyes Have Seen the Glory* (Cambridge,
Mass., 1954), pp. 39–40, 42.

Blackford's reference to the Southampton uprising in her encounter with the slave-pen guard is not the only evidence that she was much more detached about Turner's rebellion than most white Virginians. About a year after the insurrection she visited friends in Southampton County and while there talked with surviving members of the Whitehead family—most of whom had been killed in the early hours of the uprising. She questioned the Whiteheads about those slaves who had remained faithful to their masters "to show that justice had not been done them generally in the recital of the crimes committed by a comparatively small number." Her desire to understand the slave's position also explains her admiration for *Uncle Tom's Cabin*—another act of detachment from her society that required courage as well as concern for blacks.

Sometimes she could see the interest of the blacks clearer than they saw it themselves. Once when Fredericksburg celebrated Washington's birthday in its usual fashion with a parade, she wrote in her diary: "I always feel strongly affected when I see the mob of poor slaves that follow our troops of Volunteers who come marching in the streets on our great anniversaries. I think how little reason they have to rejoice in an independence that has left them in such abject slavery, and yet so profoundly ignorant as not to understand why they have no interest in the rejoicing." Even more ironic, she noted, was the fact that the companies had been formed since the Turner uprising. "It grieves my heart that my brave countrymen should be preparing for a servile and dishonorable warfare when the way is opened to gradually abolish slavery, the cause of so much wrong."[21]

Aside from freeing her slaves and contributing money to the Colonization Society, Blackford showed her interest in and concern for blacks by running a Sunday school for slaves. The law, of course, prescribed a fine or imprisonment for such behavior. "I have myself been twice threatened by the Grand Jury for teaching on Sunday a few colored children to read their Bibles," she admitted. "I know they cannot get any white witnesses to witness against me [presumably because no white person would agree to do so] and the colored people would not be received as witnesses

21. *Ibid.,* pp. 25–26, 43.

in the eyes of the law, even if they were willing." But she recognized that if she took on any more of the many children who applied for instruction "the threat so often given of breaking it up might be put into execution."[22] (During the 1850's Samuel Janney joined with a fellow Virginian, Moncure Conway, then a minister in Washington, D.C., in petitioning the legislature to repeal the prohibition against teaching slaves to read. Janney was still interested in a Quaker First Day school for black children, which he had started years before. The prohibition was not rescinded, nor did the legislature respond favorably to the request for a law prohibiting the separation of slave families.)

Mary Blackford lived through the Civil War and witnessed the end of slavery. A year after Appomattox she brought to a close her "Notes Illustrative of the Wrongs of Slavery," which she had been keeping for so many years. The entry for March, 1866, reads: "A new era has dawned since I last wrote in this book. Slavery has been abolished!!!" Three months later she described a procession of nearly one thousand black children who were attending the local schools. The occasion was the celebration of the first anniversary of schools for Negro children. "It was the most interesting public occasion I ever witnessed," she observed. "For when I thought that this was the anniversary of the day when the little ones were no longer shut out of the light of God's truth, that the fetters of ignorance were at last broken, and that they might not be forced from their parents and sold at public auction to the highest bidder my heart went up in adoring gratitude to the Great God, not only on their account, but that *we white people* were no longer permitted to go on in such wickedness, heaping up more and more the wrath of God upon our devoted heads."[23]

FREEDOM'S FOR ALL MEN

Concern for the blacks held in slavery was not confined to those who drew upon religious commitments. At the Virginia Debates

22. *Ibid.*, pp. 44–45.
23. *Ibid.*, pp. 249–50. Italics in original.

the most prominent attack on slavery stemmed from political rather than religious considerations, though in early nineteenth-century America political and religious values were never sharply separated. The assertion that black men were human beings and possessed of the same urge to liberty as other men was advanced especially against those who liked to emphasize the benign character of slavery in Virginia. When James C. Bruce of Halifax asserted that the Virginia slave was happy and contented and that his condition was preferable to that of the laboring classes in Europe, William Preston, of Montgomery County, which was west of the Blue Ridge, rose to his feet, protesting. "Mr. Speaker, this is impossible: happiness is incompatible with slavery. The love of liberty is the ruling passion of man; it has been implanted in his bosom by the voice of God, and he cannot be happy if deprived of it." Other speakers could hardly contain their contempt for those who would argue that slaves preferred slavery to freedom. "Perhaps one of the most remarkable arguments in the whole course of the debate," exclaimed George Williams, from west of the Blue Ridge, "was that by which the gentleman from Petersburg . . . endeavored to maintain that our slaves do not wish to be liberated —that servitude is sweet, and that the yoke and the fetter sit as lightly on their limbs as garlands of flowers and wreaths of palm." Only someone carried away by his own rhetoric, Williams pointed out, could paint such an unrealistic picture of slavery. "The poorest, tattered Negro who tills the planter's field, under his task master and labors to produce those fruits which he may never call his own, feels within him that spark which emanates from the deity— the innate longing for liberty—and hears in the inmost recesses of his soul, the secret whisperings of nature, that tell him he should be free. The love of freedom is a universal animal principle—it is concommitant with vitality. No human being was ever born without the wish for liberty implanted in his breast. God never made a slave—for slavery is the work of man alone."

In the minds of these men—and others like them—there could be no question that blacks were human beings and that slavery could not be justified by race any more than it could be supported by justice. For the very principles of the republic denied it. After denouncing slavery for what it did to white men, Samuel Moore, a delegate from a county west of the Blue Ridge, remarked: "I must now take a short view of slavery as it affects the slaves themselves. 'That all men are by nature free and equal' is a truth held sacred by every American and by every Republican throughout the world. And I presume it cannot be denied in this Hall, as a general principle, that it is an act of injustice, tyranny, and oppression, to hold any part of the human race in bondage against their consent." Although circumstances may require slavery, they cannot justify it. "The right to the enjoyment of liberty is one of those perfect, inherent and inalienable rights, which pertain to the whole human race, and of which they can never be divested, except by an act of gross injustice."[24]

Among public figures in the antebellum South who opposed slavery, there were few who permitted their concern for the slave to carry over to a concern for the free Negro. Indeed, it was common knowledge that many antislavery people, even in the North, were remarkably unconcerned with the fate or condition of free blacks. Yet William Gaston, judge of North Carolina, made no secret of his efforts to stand by the rights of free Negroes.

As a judge of the Supreme Court of North Carolina, Gaston was known for his landmark decision in the case of *State* v. *Will* (1834), in which it was held that a slave could resist a white man to save his own life. "The prisoner is a human being," Gaston wrote in that decision, "degraded indeed by slavery, but yet having organs, dimensions, senses, affections, and passions like our own." In 1832, six months after the Virginia Debates and less than a year after the Turner Rebellion in neighboring Virginia, he counseled students at the University of North Carolina at Chapel Hill to assume "the duty which has been too long neglected, but which cannot with impunity be neglected much longer." The duty, of course, was "the ultimate expiration of the worst evil that affects the Southern party of our Confederacy. Full well do you know to what I refer, for on this subject there is, with all of us, a morbid sensitiveness which gives warning even of an approach of it. Disguise the truth as we may, and throw the blame where we will,

24. Robert, *Road from Monticello*, pp. 83, 93–94, 63–64.

it is Slavery which, more than any other cause, keeps us back in the career of improvement."

In that address Gaston emphasized the way in which slavery harmed the economy of the whites, but in his defense of the rights of free Negroes in the constitutional convention of 1835 he showed that a concern for black men was also an important part of his objection to slavery. The convention sought to disfranchise free blacks, who up to then had been able to vote if they could meet the same property qualifications as white men. Gaston objected to disfranchisement, arguing that a black person who possessed the necessary property for voting ought to have that privilege and not have an additional stigma placed upon him because of his color. The convention did not heed Gaston, and blacks were disfranchised in North Carolina. Not surprisingly, when Gaston died, large numbers of Negroes from his district in New Bern attended his funeral. It was reported that his picture was placed in the home of every free Negro in town. The Negroes of New Bern met at his death and commented on his being a "friend and kind protector" as well as praising his treatment of his own slaves.[25]

Politically, it is worth noting, in view of his dissenting position on slavery and blacks, Gaston was no radical or even liberal. (Religiously, he was conservative, too, for he was a Roman Catholic.) He remained, as one of his biographers has remarked, "a Federalist until his death." Thomas Jefferson, for example, was viewed by Gaston as a "grand Machiavellian Humbugger," despite his well-known opposition to slavery.[26] Since Gaston lived long after the Federalist party itself was dead, the characterization of him as a Federalist sums up an attitude of mind as well as a political affiliation. We shall have occasion in the next chapter to

25. J. Herman Schauinger, *William Gaston, Carolinian* (Milwaukee, 1949), p. 166; William Gaston, *Address Delivered Before the Dialectic and Philanthropic Societies at Chapel Hill, N.C., June 20, 1832* (5th ed., Chapel Hill, 1858), pp. 23–24; Edward F. McSweeney, "Judge William Gaston of North Carolina," in Thomas F. Meehan, et al., eds., *Historical Records and Studies* (New York, 1926), pp. 180, 184.

26. R. W. D. Connor, "William Gaston: A Southern Federalist of the Old School and His Yankee Friends, 1778–1844" (Worcester, Mass., 1934), a reprint from the *Proceedings of the American Antiquarian Society,* Oct., 1933, pp. 47, 3–4.

return to this coincidence between antislavery sentiment and political and social conservatism.

Charles Fenton Mercer was an antislavery Virginian who was as prominent socially and politically as Gaston. Mercer, for example, served in Congress from 1817 to 1840 without interruption. Unlike Gaston, however, Mercer did not publicize his views, for his major work on government, in which his severe indictment of slavery is contained, was published anonymously and privately in 1845. Although the purpose of his book was a criticism of the United States government as it was then operating, Mercer made clear his concern for the Negro in his almost bitter denunciation of white society for its perpetuation of slavery. In describing the population of the United States he observed that three million "human souls are a blank in creation, are worse than dead—they are slaves. . . . They stand not only fixed and sunk, but lower and lower are they sinking in the scale of creation; no bright spot shows their features, though made in God's own image. All the light that shines illuminates them not; all the ameliorations of society reach not them; no rational enjoyments embrace them; no law is enacted for them; no vote, no voice, no cry of joy issues from their dark and deep dungeons!" Moreover, "they beget children for their master's use and behoof; marry only to promote a master's means; and what shows the lowness and meanness of their condition is that they are willing to propagate and take care of children to be abused as slaves."

Like Gaston, Mercer was one of those rare antislavery Southerners—or Northerners, for that matter—who carried his attack on slavery's degradation to a realistic appreciation of the effect of the institution on free Negroes. Like Tocqueville, Mercer recognized that color and slavery were intimately and inescapably associated; the degradation of the status contaminated the color. "The coloured man must be a slave, or the descendant of a slave; the brand of disgrace is upon him." As a result, free Negroes have few rights; they are "out of the pale of all right and protection." Even in the North, he correctly pointed out, the free Negro is "a vagabond on the face of the earth. . . ." The only thing worse than slavery, Mercer declared somewhat exaggeratedly, was "the state of a free coloured person, which is still more degrading and more deplorable," for the slave had at least his master to take an interest in him; the free black had no one.[27]

All of the antislavery Southerners we have looked at so far, particularly those who expressed a clear concern for the Negro, lived and worked in the upper South—that is, Tennessee, Kentucky, Virginia, or North Carolina. Indeed, as will be noticed in more detail in the next chapter, expressions of Southern antislavery sentiment are almost entirely confined to the upper South. Yet there is one example of concern for black people by a white Southerner from the deep South which deserves to be examined, even if it does not fit easily under the rubric of antislavery.

A STRANGE AND WONDERFUL MAN

John McDonogh of Louisiana was not an opponent of slavery in the obvious sense. He left no body of documents bespeaking his opposition to the institution; there are no fine speeches by him denouncing slavery or expressing faith in the potentialities of black people. Yet in his life and in his relations with his slaves John McDonogh properly falls into the category of white Southerners who sympathized with blacks who were slaves and, more than that, helped them to escape the burden of slavery.

McDonogh was not a native of Louisiana, for he was born in Baltimore, but he migrated to New Orleans permanently when he was twenty-five years old. Although he was remarkably successful as a merchant in New Orleans, he chose to live across the Mississippi River in seclusion on his plantation at McDonoghville. There he raised vegetables and other crops for the local New Orleans market and added to his wealth through land purchases and speculation. During the 1830's and 1840's, when he was at the height of his activity, he was reputed to be among the richest men in the United States, let alone the South. His great wealth attracted attention, as was to be expected, but perhaps more striking to those who knew him well was the industry and efficiency of his slaves. For many years McDonogh would not reveal the secret of

27. [Charles F. Mercer], *The Weakness and Inefficiency of the Government of the United States of North America* (London, 1863), pp. 335, 122–23. The original private edition was published in 1845.

his success in employing slaves on his lands and in his business. He used slaves to collect his rents, manage his urban properties, keep his accounts, run his agricultural enterprises, and care for his slaves. Between his wealth and his uncanny ability to manage slaves, McDonogh earned a reputation or notoriety in New Orleans for eccentricity at least, and miserliness and mystery at most. His reputation for miserliness stemmed primarily from his insistence upon prompt payment by his white tenants, and from his general refusal to grant concessions to his debtors. Although he was almost fanatically religious, that attitude did not preclude his relentlessly foreclosing a mortgage that was overdue. His strict and rigid ways in dealing with others did not endear him to white New Orleans. When he died, the few whites who came to the graveside stood stony-faced and unmoved.

The records do not offer any light on the matter, but one suspects that another reason why the whites of New Orleans did not like John McDonogh was because of his special relationship with his Negroes. It all grew out of "the plan," which McDonogh put into practice in 1825. Like many antislavery proposals, Mc-Donogh's stemmed from his religious convictions—he was a strict Scottish Presbyterian. He noticed that although his slaves had Sunday off they still had to work around their own houses and plots on the Sabbath because of the long hours they had worked during the week. Determined that his slaves would keep the Sabbath sacred by not working at all, he struck a bargain with them. If they would desist from any work on Sunday he would grant them Saturday afternoon off so that they could complete their own chores. (Many planters in the South, incidentally, generally granted Saturday afternoon to the slaves anyway, a fact that testified further to McDonogh's strictness.) As he later wrote, after he put his idea into effect he noticed a marked improvement in the working habits of his slaves. Then, in 1825, he conceived of the plan of letting the slaves work for wages on Saturday afternoon and two extra hours each day, if they worked for him. Since he paid the males 62½ cents per day in the summer and 50 cents in the winter it was easy to calculate how long it would take for a slave "to buy" more time and eventually his freedom. When a slave had worked enough to pay off a sixth of his price, then he was free for a whole day, and so on until he had worked off his full price. Although buying the first day would take a long time since the number of working hours on his own behalf were few, thereafter the purchase of free time became easier and easier. To buy his complete freedom a slave required fifteen years, McDonogh calculated. Once a slave was free he could then work to buy off his relatives.

After working out his plan, McDonogh presented it to a dozen or so leaders of his many slaves for their consideration. He gave them a week to think over the proposition, with the understanding that if they accepted, he would agree to a stated price for each of them ($600 for men, $450 for women, and proportionally less for children) and that he would set forth the plan in writing and also in his will in order to protect the slaves' interest in the event of his death prior to the complete implementation of the plan. He expressed the hope that they would all work together "so that the whole company shall go on the same day on board ship and sail for your fatherland." One of the requirements of the plan was that the freed blacks emigrate to Africa. "My object is your freedom and happiness in Liberia," he told them, "without loss or cost of a cent to myself from sending you away and conferring that boon, as the humble instrument of the Most High on you and on your children." He also insisted, on pain of sale, that they live "moral lives," free of crime while working for him.

Paternalistic and even harsh-sounding as the plan may have been, it was more generous in fact than in expression. By giving them free time he was making a concession to them which other slave owners did not make. Actually there was a pedagogical rationale behind McDonogh's tough, Presbyterian demand that the slave work off his entire cost. If a slave were merely granted his freedom after a term of years, McDonogh argued, the boon "would appear as a gift of his master who might, as the slave would fear, repent and retract his promise." Under his method, however, "the slave would have gained it—have purchased and paid his master for it. Hope would be kept alive in his bosom; he would have a goal in view, continually urging him on to faithfulness, fidelity, trust, industry, economy, and every virtue of good work."[28] Even though his statement is taken from a justification of his plan that McDonogh wrote for white, slaveholding readers, it is evident that he saw his plan as a way of inculcating into slaves who were to be free those attitudes and habits that would fit them for a world of work and competition.

Because McDonogh did not tell outsiders of his plan while it was in operation, he earned from some people an enviable reputation for having hard-working slaves, while other, more compassionate observers condemned him for working his slaves beyond the usual hours. (The fact was that his slaves worked two extra hours each day as a way of speeding up the achievement of their freedom.) At least one early-rising neighbor noticed that one of McDonogh's slaves got to work before he did. Why, said the neighbor once to McDonogh, your people don't walk to their work, "they run all day. I never saw such people as those, sir, I do not know what to make of them."[29] McDonogh merely smiled and said nothing.

When talking to his fellow white Southerners, John McDonogh emphasized his practicality and unemotional relationship with his blacks. When he told of his plan for the first time in 1842 in a New Orleans newspaper he justified it on the grounds that his slaves worked better than others and that the money they paid him for their freedom "will enable me to go to Virginia or Carolina and purchase a gang of people of nearly double the number of those I have sent away." Once he told his slaves, "I would never consent to give freedom to a single individual among you, to remain on the same soil as the white man." But from a letter he wrote in answer to a request for a bequest to a Negro college, it is clear that McDonogh's belief in colonization was not simply a dislike of blacks. "My own opinion is," he wrote, "and I have long entertained it, and every day's observation confirms it more strongly on my mind, that without separation of the races, extermination of one or the other must inevitably take place. The two races can never inhabit together in a state of equality in the same country.

28. Lane Carter Kendell, "John McDonogh—Slave-Owner," *Louisiana Historical Quarterly*, XVI (1932), 125, 129; William Talbot Childs, *John McDonogh: His Life and Work* (Baltimore, 1939), pp. 79, 84–85.
29. Kendell, "John McDonogh," pp. 130–31.

They may for a short time, even in the capacity of master and slave; as equals and brethren, never." Consequently, for the happiness of the blacks he insisted upon their removal to Africa and urged that Congress do something to make it possible on a broad scale.[30]

That his belief in colonization stemmed from concern about the future of the Negroes rather than from his hatred of them is shown by the relations he had with his slaves while they were working their way to freedom. All the disciplining of his slaves was carried out by a jury of five or six male slaves whose recommendations were reviewed by him; usually, he contended, he had to make the punishments more lenient. For more than twenty years, he boasted later, there had been no white overseer over his slaves. The whole plantation and business was run by blacks, who reported to him each night. McDonogh, in turn, was open and honest with them, showing the slaves his accounts of their time every six months and explaining where each stood. As he shrewdly advised other planters, his plan for emancipation could work only where the slaves trusted the master, "for no one is better acquainted with the character of his master than the slave himself." When McDonogh could not get the legislature to grant him an exception to the prohibition against education of blacks he sent, at his own expense, two of his slaves to Lafayette College in Easton, Pennsylvania, to be trained in the ministry and in medicine for work among the freed slaves in Liberia. Upon the completion of their education both were freed, but only one actually went to Liberia. For those left at home McDonogh provided rudiments of education and religious training. In his development at McDonoghville, McDonogh readily sold lots to free blacks, even as he used black slaves as rent collectors among the white tenants. He also delighted in dining with Andrew Durnford, a free Negro planter whose son Thomas was McDonogh's godchild. Thomas sometimes vacationed at McDonogh's house and at other times helped McDonogh in the management of his landholdings.

After the slaves were freed and in Liberia, McDonogh kept in affectionate touch with them, advising them and encouraging them. David McDonogh, one of the two blacks whom McDonogh sent to Lafayette College, wrote from Liberia in 1846: "When I was

30. Childs, *John McDonogh,* pp. 86, 68, 121.

young and foolish you took me from my father and mother into your own dwelling and brought me up as a son instead of a servant." Something of the relationship between the black boy, now grown, and the austere Presbyterian is revealed in his closing lines: "I should like very much dear father to see you once more before we leave this world. . . . But I will never consent to leave this Country . . . for this is the only place where a colored person can enjoy his liberty."[31] That last statement was undoubtedly a reflection of McDonogh's view, too.

When McDonogh died in 1850 at the age of seventy-one he was placed in a prearranged tomb located in the burying ground of his slaves, where he was to remain until his body was removed to Baltimore. At his funeral the eyes of the few whites who attended were dry, while the many blacks who came wept openly at the loss of their friend.

The study of John McDonogh can stand for much in an analysis of Southern antislavery thought. McDonogh freed his slaves, but over a long period of time and at their own expense, so to speak. Moreover, slavery was wrong in his eyes, but it was not so wrong that it called for an immediate remedy. Even as a religious person, McDonogh did not view slavery as a sin, and certainly he did not see those who held slaves as guilty of sinning thereby. Yet, withal, John McDonogh thought slavery wrong because of what it did to black people. His primary objection was not that slavery may have harmed whites, but that it denied freedom to people who happened to be black.

There were other Southern opponents of slavery, however, who thought that the harm slavery brought to white society was the most important reason for ending it. To them, the concern for black persons, which animated those Southerners we have been looking at up to now, was secondary. It is time, now, to turn to an examination of the arguments of those antislavery Southerners.

31. Arthur G. Nuhrah, "John McDonogh: Man of Many Facets," *Louisiana Historical Quarterly*, XXXIII (1950), 125–26.

3

Enemies of Slavery
in Behalf of Whites

Inasmuch as the antislavery movement in the North was rooted in a concern for the white man, it comes as no surprise to observe that the Southern antislavery argument was dominated by a similar justification. This aspect of the Southern antislavery movement was not only dominant, but complex and sophisticated as well.

Those Southerners who opposed slavery knew the institution well. Some of them were slaveholders themselves, just as many of those who opposed slavery because of what it did to Negroes were slaveholders. They could not help being aware of the many ways in which the institution adversely affected their lives and their futures. Thus during the debate over slavery in the Virginia legislature in January, 1832, Henry Berry, a slaveholder from the piedmont, expressed his surprise "to find that there are advocates here for slavery, with all its effects. . . . That slavery is a grinding curse upon this state I had supposed would have been admitted by all, and that the only question for debate here, would have been, the *possibility* of removing the evil." Charles Faulkner, on the same day, spelled out the evils as he saw them from the standpoint of the western part of the state, where slaves were few. "It banishes free white labor—it exterminates the mechanic—the artizan—the manufacturer. It deprives them of occupation. It deprives them of bread." But it was a slaveholder, Thomas Marshall, son of the Chief Justice of the United States, who spoke for most

Southern antislavery men when he exposed the primary source of
his opposition to slavery. "The ordinary condition of the slave is
not such as to make humanity weep for his lot," he began. "Compare his condition with that of the laborer in any part of Europe
and you will find him blessed with a measure of happiness, nearly,
if not altogether equal. . . . It is not for his sake, nor to melio-
rate his condition, that abolition is desirable. Wherefore, then,
object to slavery? Because it is ruinous to the whites. . . ." Then
was revealed the deep-seated fear: "The evil admits of no remedy.
It is increasing, and will continue to increase, until the whole
country will be inundated by one black wave, covering its whole
extent, with a few white faces here and there floating on the surface." More elaborately poetic, but no less damning, was the
indictment set forth by Samuel Garland of Amherst County,
located in the slaveholding piedmont. Thanks to slavery, he said,
Virginia, "in the May-day of life . . . wears upon her countenance the evidence of premature decay, and the yellow leaf of
autumn has followed too soon the budding blossoms of Spring."
He called slavery "this cancer which destroys at the fountain, the
streams of vigorous and healthful existence." Although Virginians
enjoy as much talent as other men and their territory harbors
resources as rich as any other, all have "been lost and paralyzed by
this national calamity. Like a pestilence it has swept over our land
withering and blighting whatever it breathed upon. . . ."[1]

THE UNDUE WEIGHT OF SLAVERY

Antislavery Southerners, however, were not content to speak in
general terms when they condemned slavery. Perhaps the most
widely used argument against slavery as an economic system
harmful to whites was a comparison of the South's progress with
that of the North. "Sir, if there be one, who concurs with that
gentleman in the harmless character of this institution," said
Charles Faulkner during the Virginia Debates, "let me request him
to extend his travels to the northern states of this union—and beg
him to contrast the happiness and contentment which prevails
throughout that country . . . with the division, discontent, indo-

1. Joseph Clarke Robert, *The Road from Monticello: A Study of the
Virginia Slavery Debate of 1832* (Durham, N.C., 1941), pp. 99, 77–78, 92.

lence, and poverty of the southern country."[2] The same argument was elaborated upon in several books and articles over the years by other antislavery Southerners, notably Daniel Reaves Goodloe. Goodloe, a native North Carolinian, was one of the most prolific and informed of the Southern antislavery writers. As a young printer in a newspaper office he had ready access to reports on the Virginia Debates contained in the newspapers his office exchanged with Virginia publishers. Later he wrote that it was in reading about "the debate that fixed me as an Emancipationist, from which I never swerved back." He began writing against slavery as early as 1841, but usually anonymously. Only later, when he left North Carolina to become an editor of the *National Era,* a moderate antislavery newspaper in Washington, D.C., did he acknowledge his antislavery publications. Always his aim was to move beyond moral objections to slavery, though as we have seen already, he was not without compassion for blacks. As he wrote in his first tract, "my present purpose will be to show, that the chief evils of slavery to the body politic result from principles more stubborn and powerful than its moral effects upon the people." His main work was also his first; its title set forth the kind of argument he developed: *Inquiry into the Causes Which Have Retarded the Accumulation of Wealth and Increase of Population in the Southern States: in Which the Question of Slavery is Considered in a Politico-Economical Point of View.*

In this pamphlet Goodloe introduced a systematic statistical comparison between New York and Virginia to show the allegedly harmful effects of slavery on population growth. Then he compared Pennsylvania with Virginia and Ohio with Kentucky to the same effect. Later, in 1849, he published a pamphlet against Ellwood Fisher, a proslavery advocate, in which the burden of the argument was once more the superiority of the Northern to the Southern states economically, again measured by statistics. When the Kansas question arose in the 1850's, Goodloe wrote a pamphlet entitled *Is It Expedient to Introduce Slavery into Kansas?*— to which question the answer was no surprise. Again the argument against slavery is a comparison between the economic achievements of comparable Northern and Southern states. Thus Illinois

2. *Ibid.,* p. 77.

and Missouri, as relatively new western states, are compared in amount of railroad trackage, with the slave state (Missouri) lagging behind the free state; New York and Virginia are compared on miles of canals; Massachusetts and South Carolina on amounts of commerce, always to the disadvantage of the slave state. A table of figures comparing Northern and Southern states, he pointed out, "demonstrates the great superiority of Freedom over Slavery, as regards the mechanic arts and manufacturing."

Such comparisons were popular among a number of Southern antislavery writers. Henry Ruffner, a slaveholder in western Virginia and president of Washington College (now Washington and Lee), in 1847 published his argument for gradual emancipation entitled *Address to the People of West Virginia*. Since Ruffner's admitted purpose was to show that abolition of slavery would be beneficial to white men—including slaveholders like himself—he made much of a comparison between the Northern and the Southern economies. "Nowhere, since time began," he asserted, "have the two systems of slave labor and free labor, been subjected to so fair and so decisive a trial of their effects on public prosperity, as in these United States. . . . No man of common sense, who has observed this result, can doubt for a moment that the system of free labor promotes the growth and prosperity of States, in a much higher degree than the system of slave labor." Knowing the South's commitment to agriculture, Ruffner made a special point to show that even in agriculture the free states of the Atlantic seaboard outproduced the Southern seaboard states in value of crops and in land values. "Even New Englanders on their poor soils and under their wintry sky," he taunted his fellow Southerners, "make nearly forty per cent more, to the hand, than the old Southerners [old, coastal Southern states] make in the 'sunny South' with the advantage of their valuable staples, cotton and tobacco."[3]

3. "Autobiographical Sketch," in D. R. Goodloe Papers, Folder 3; [Daniel Reaves Goodloe] *Inquiry into the Causes Which Have Retarded the Accumulation of Wealth and Increase of Population in the Southern States: in Which the Question of Slavery is Considered in a Political-Economical Point of View* (Washington, D.C., 1846), p. 8; Henry Ruffner, *Address to the People of West Virginia; Showing that Slavery is injurious to the public welfare and that it may be gradually abolished, without detriment to the rights and interests of slaveholders* (Lexington, Va., 1847; reprinted, Bridgewater, Va., 1933), pp. 11–12, 18–20.

The comparative argument was so convenient and demonstrable that it was used wherever the effects of slavery were discussed. Antislavery men of the North used it as frequently as Southerners. During the debates in Congress over the measures that became the Compromise of 1850, for example, a favorite argument for opposing the spread of slavery was just this comparison between the economic progress of the Northern and the slave states.

Undoubtedly the most widely disseminated example of the argument was Hinton Rowan Helper's *The Impending Crisis of the South,* which was first published in 1857 and then reprinted and widely circulated in 1859–60 as a Republican campaign document. Like Goodloe, Helper was a native North Carolinian; we shall have occasion to look more closely at him and his book a little later. Here it is necessary only to observe that in *The Impending Crisis,* Helper carried Goodloe's statistical argument to its ultimate expression. Drawing upon the census of 1850, which had been supervised by the Southern nationalist James D. B. De Bow, Helper filled page after page of his book with tables of statistics that showed the economic superiority of the nonslave states over the slave states. Not all of Helper's comparisons were scrupulously fair or even intended to be, but none of his errors or misinterpretations more annoyed the proslavery advocates than his calculation that the value of the North's hay crop was greater than that of the whole cotton crop of the South. For a region that called cotton King, to make lowly hay its superior was to do more than put up a straw man.

Inasmuch as Goodloe and Helper were antislavery North Carolinians as well as good friends, it is tempting to credit Goodloe with some direct influence on Helper's book. But by the 1850's the comparative argument was so commonplace among antislavery men, North as well as South, that Helper could have picked up the idea from many sources. In fact, as we have seen, at the Virginia Debates a primitive version of the idea was already being invoked, and Tocqueville used comparison in his *Democracy in America,* which appeared in its first American edition in 1838.

Goodloe is worth calling attention to for more than his comparison argument. Many of the antislavery Southerners who put the white man's interests first were colonizationists or deportationists;

Goodloe was not. It is true that he liked to assert, as we have seen, that his objections stemmed from economic reasons and from his ambitions for the prosperity and diversity of his native region. And from the standpoint of effectiveness in persuading white Southerners that was undoubtedly the best approach to take in attacking slavery. But as we have seen already, Goodloe was among those antislavery Southerners who also were concerned about the future of blacks. More than that, at no time, so far as the record shows, did Goodloe come out for removal of blacks once they had been emancipated. Unlike Lincoln, for example, who, when an end seemed in sight for slavery during the Civil War, sought to find ways to remove the Negroes, Goodloe never suggested the removal of the freed slaves. In his pamphlet *Emancipation and the War*, which appeared in 1861, he argued that freeing the slaves would not harm the South or the nation, even if the freed blacks did not leave the country. He pointed out that the experience of the British West Indies, where the slaves had been emancipated in 1833, showed that even when the blacks made up a preponderance of the population they did not threaten the whites. He boldly described the "danger of turning loose the four million of black slaves" upon the South as "imaginary."

After the war, when the blacks were in fact free, he continued to believe that Negroes could fit into the going society. As early as September, 1865, for example, he wrote in the Greensboro, North Carolina, *Patriot* to advocate the abolition of laws discriminating against Negroes, including those that prohibited blacks' testifying against white men. Moreover, he wrote later, "I insisted that the right of suffrage should be made to depend on education, intelligence, and character; not on the color of the skin."[4]

Years before the war began, Goodloe's antislavery convictions had brought him into the Republican party, which, as a refugee from the South, he continued to support throughout the war and after. But as one might expect, Goodloe was not a Radical Republican. Like President Lincoln, he supported emancipation with compensation, on the ground that it was fair, and because it would

4. Daniel R. Goodloe, *Emancipation and the War* (n.p., n.d., but from internal evidence, around Aug., 1861), pp. 11–12; Daniel R. Goodloe, *The Marshalship of North Carolina* . . . (n.p., n.d., but apparently 1869), p. 4.

help in the restoration of the Union. Not surprisingly, in view of their agreement, Lincoln appointed him to the commission charged with carrying out compensated emancipation in the District of Columbia during the Civil War. Unlike Lincoln's successor and Goodloe's fellow Southerner, President Andrew Johnson, Goodloe was realistic enough to recognize that the Fourteenth Amendment, which ten of the former Confederate States refused to ratify in 1866, "was certainly a very mild measure. . . . The people were very unwise," he wrote in 1868, "not to accept it. I endeavored to persuade them to do so and to accompany the acceptance with an extention of the right of suffrage to all colored men who could read and write." He also thought that Johnson's Reconstruction policy was defective in that "it failed to furnish a proper guaranty [*sic*] for the liberty of the blacks, and for the safety of those whites" who had supported the Union during the war. But Goodloe was never a supporter of unrestricted black suffrage; he thought the former slaves too gullible and prone to vote their color. Moreover, the Radical policy of disfranchising numbers of whites while enfranchising all male blacks seemed to the conservative Goodloe "to turn society upside down." His doubts about black enfranchisement and Radical policies in general were reflected in his allying himself with the conservative wing of the Republican party in North Carolina when he returned after the war.[5] We shall hear of him again during Reconstruction.

WORKERS WITHOUT INCENTIVE

Not all antislavery Southerners became Republicans, of course, but virtually all of them condemned slavery for its inefficiency as a labor system. Antislavery thought in the North also was suffused with the liberal idea that self-interest was the best guarantee of an efficient worker. Northerner Frederick Law Olmsted, who wrote perhaps the most famous book of travels in the antebellum South, made the observation over and over again that slaves could not compete with free men because they did not receive the fruits of their work. Like Olmsted, many antislavery Southerners believed

5. Daniel R. Goodloe, *Letter to Hon. Charles Sumner on the Situation of Affairs in North Carolina* (Raleigh, 1868), pp. 9–10.

slavery to be an outmoded system of labor. "Why, sir, is slave-labor more expensive and consequently less profitable than the labor of the white man?" asked Philip Bolling at the Virginia Debates. The answer, he went on, is that slaves "have no *immediate self-interest* to act upon them. . . . This great, this all-powerful motive of action is wanting to stimulate the slave to labor." It is noticeable that Bolling blames the inefficiency of slavery on the system and not on the race of the slaves—a distinction that Northerner Frederick Olmsted was not always careful to make.

The same argument, though dressed up in academic garb, was advanced by George Tucker in his book *The Laws of Wages, Profits & Rent Investigated,* published in 1837. Tucker, a professor at the University of Virginia, said in his preface that he had been offering the lectures contained in the book for the previous ten years to his classes. He plainly condemned slavery as less productive than free labor because fear cannot be as efficient and constant a motive as self-interest. Besides, he acknowledged, the self-interest of the slave is actually at variance with that of the slaveholder and the community. Moreover, slave labor is "not likely to be of that refined and ingenious character as it would be if it were to feel the stimulus of competition and the prospect of proportionate recrimination." In short, Tucker found slave labor unimaginative, not because the slaves were black, but because they were unfree. The very inefficiency of slave labor, Tucker told his classes, decreed its end as soon as the sugar- and cotton-growing states, which at the time provided the only reason for its continuance, were able to obtain sufficient labor from other sources.[6]

As Henry Ruffner pointed out in his pamphlet of 1847, there could be no question that slavery produced a profit. The issue was that Southerners were employing "a sort of labor that yields only half as much to the hand as" free labor. Farming carried on by slaves, he said over and over again, is at once "extensive and exhaustive." By misusing the soil, slave labor kills "the goose that lays the golden egg." But that is the disadvantage that slaveholders must always labor under; they "cannot do otherwise with laborers

6. Robert, *Road from Monticello,* pp. 108–9; George Tucker, *The Laws of Wages, Profits & Rent Investigated* (New York, 1964, reprinted from 1837 ed.), 46–47, 49.

who work by compulsion, for the benefit only of their masters; and whose sole interest in the matter is, to do as little and to consume as much as possible."[7]

The objection of antislavery Southerners to slave labor went further than its inefficiency and excessive cost to the individual slaveholder. Such labor, they insisted, was bad for the region as a whole because it kept the South economically backward or under-developed. "Even the common mechanical trades do not flourish in a slave State," Henry Ruffner complained. "Some mechanical operations must, indeed, be performed in every civilized country" except the South, he scornfully observed. It manages "to import from abroad every fabricated thing that can be carried in ships" but which free societies are accustomed to make for themselves. He then went on to develop an argument that would echo down the nineteenth century among Southerners who wished to see their region advance economically. It was an argument that Hinton Helper would push in 1860 and one that Henry Grady, prime exponent of the New South, would press in the 1880's. "What is most wonderful is that the forest and iron mines of the South supply in great part," wrote Ruffner, "the materials out of which these things are made." It was the standard protest of the colony against the metropolis, but the blame was being laid at slavery's door. Although a city like Richmond, Ruffner pointed out, enjoyed all sorts of advantages in materials and closeness to the sea, yet the whole state produced fewer manufacturers "than a third rate New England town" like Fall River.

The conflict between slavery and economic development was phrased even more succinctly by Cassius Marcellus Clay, perhaps Kentucky's most outspoken antislavery man. "Give us free labor," Clay exclaimed in 1840, "and we will manufacture much more than now. Slaves would not manufacture if they could; and could not if they would!" Clay went further than Ruffner, however, for he recognized that slavery inhibited the development of the economy for reasons other than the lack of skills or incentive. Manufactures were slow to develop in an economy in which a slave population was a large part of the potential market. "Lawyers, merchants, mechanics, laborers, who are your consumers?" Clay

7. Ruffner, *Address to the People of West Virginia*, p. 20.

asked. "Robert Wickliffe's two hundred slaves? How many clients do you find, how many goods do you sell, how many hats, coats, saddles and trunks do you make for these two hundred slaves, as two hundred free men do?" Under a system of free labor, "the towns would grow and furnish a home market to the farmers, which in turn would employ more labor; which would consume the manufactures of the towns; and we could then find our businesses continually increasing, so that our children might settle down among us and make industrious citizens" instead of emigrating to the free states.[8]

THE LION OF WHITEHALL

Cassius Clay's life was a testimony to Southern antislavery. A cousin of the more famous Henry Clay, Cassius was born into a slaveholding family and held slaves himself until 1844, when he emancipated them. As a youth he studied at Yale College, where he heard William Lloyd Garrison denounce slavery; this was the first time the youthful Clay had heard slavery attacked. It was also while in New Haven that Clay witnessed what he came to believe were the glaring differences between a society based on free labor and one which rested on slavery. In his writings Clay always made much of the industriousness of the North as compared with what he despised as the indolence of his own people, a defect he attributed to the influence of slavery.

Clay's antislavery convictions, formed early in life, outlasted the institution he opposed. He was especially unusual in that he never concealed his hatred of slavery even though he remained in the South. Indeed, in 1845, in pursuit of his goal of ridding Kentucky of slavery he began publishing the *True American* in Lexington. The paper was dedicated, as most of his speeches in behalf of the Whig party for the previous five years had been, to the denunciation of slavery. Although Clay had a formidable reputation as a

8. *Ibid.*, pp. 23, 27; David L. Smiley, *The Lion of Whitehall: The Life of Cassius M. Clay* (Madison, Wis., 1962), p. 47. I have relied heavily upon this excellent biography for the facts of Clay's life. Horace Greeley, ed., *The Writings of Cassius Marcellus Clay including Speeches and Addresses* (New York, 1848), p. 227.

bowie-knife fighter—he once literally cut pieces from the body of an opponent in a fight—he knew that his newspaper needed elaborate protection if it were to survive physically in the midst of slave territory. The year 1845 was long after the genteel debates in the Virginia legislature; after fifteen years of abolitionist agitation even Kentuckians were sensitive on the subject of slavery. Recognizing the situation, Clay transformed his brick publishing office into a small fortress. He had the doors and window shutters lined with sheet iron to prevent burning, and he placed two brass four-pounder cannons on a table near the door. They were kept loaded with shot and nails. The entrance to the building was protected by folding doors arranged in such a way that the cannon could be aimed through them, but that attackers would have only a small opening for returning the fire. The office was also stocked with firearms and lances. If the office was in danger of being overwhelmed by attackers, an escape hatch through the roof allowed Clay to escape, and a strategically placed keg of powder enabled him to blow up the whole building after he had left through the roof.

The elaborate—almost desperate—preparations were not as alarmist as they seem, despite Clay's proclivity for dramatics. These particular defenses were never brought into use, but the danger to his press on which they were premised was not imaginary. In August the *True American* published an article and a supporting editorial that proslavery men in Lexington thought went beyond their endurance. All of Clay's statements on slavery were attacks, but on August 12 Clay published an article by an anonymous correspondent entitled "What Is to Become of the Slaves in the United States?" Assuming that the unprofitability of slavery would soon end the institution, the writer went on to suggest that the proper course would be to prepare the freed people for eventual citizenship. One way to do this, the writer suggested, was to grant the vote to blacks already free. Needless to say, in a slave state that then denied the vote and many civil rights to free blacks, the essay was a provocative one. But when he began publishing the *True American,* Clay had promised to publish divergent views; this essay certainly qualified. It is true that at the time he approved the publication of the piece he was suffering from a high fever and may not have been as alert to the implicit dangers as when he was well. But Clay was also an impetuous, almost heedless man, so that it is not clear that the possibility of a violent reaction from the slaveholders would have deterred him, even if he had considered it. Besides, he published the article with an editorial that seemed not only to lend his support to the proposals in the article but also to go beyond them. At least one sentence in the editorial seemed to suggest that he favored a slave rebellion and even worse: "But remember, you who dwell in marble palaces, that there are strong arms and fiery hearts and iron pikes in the streets and panes of glass only between them and the silver plate on the board, and the smooth-skinned woman on the ottoman." Actually a close reading of the sentence makes clear he was appealing to nonslaveholding whites, but it could be misread, if one wanted to. When readers recalled that Clay had iron pikes in his newspaper office, his rhetorical flourish took on an ominous meaning. But he was not finished yet: "When you have mocked at virtue, denied the agency of God in the affairs of men, and made rapine your honied faith, tremble! for the day of retribution is at hand, and the masses will be avenged."[9]

Two days after that issue of the *True American* appeared, a group of influential citizens of Lexington met and determined to close Clay's paper. Respectfully, but firmly, they called on Clay to stop publishing what they called a paper dangerous to the public welfare. Clay at first categorically refused; he published a defense of his editorial and ridiculed the idea that a slave uprising was a likelihood in a state in which the whites outnumbered the slaves six to one. But he did repudiate the article that caused the commotion, and as days passed he even agreed to remove the firearms from his newspaper office. The consideration that caused Clay to make these concessions was a mass meeting scheduled for August 18, in which the slaveholders were determined to bring popular pressure to silence Clay's *True American*. His final concession to avoid the inevitable was almost total. Just before the mass meeting was scheduled to meet he offered to cease printing any comments on the slavery question until he was once again well enough to personally supervise the running of the newspaper.

9. Smiley, *Lion of Whitehall*, p. 91.

His enemies, however, were remorseless. On schedule the mass meeting was held, and it determined that, despite admitted constitutional guarantees of a free press, Clay had gone beyond the acceptable limits. The "community" must act to silence him. Clay was declared a "trespasser" in Lexington, and it was recommended that a committee of sixty be appointed to close the office and ship Clay's press out of the state. The mass meeting agreed to the recommendations without a dissent. The order was carried out, entirely by extralegal authority, of course, but with the tacit consent of the constituted authorities. Clay offered no resistance. His press was carefully crated, and Clay's personal effects were delivered to his home. This was vigilantism of the upper class—effective, calm, and careful of property, but nonetheless an unmitigated violation of constitutional principles.

Clay did not take his suppression without objection. Immediately, he began once again to publish the *True American,* though now the presses were located across the Ohio in Cincinnati, even if the dateline still read Lexington, Kentucky. He also brought members of the Committee of Sixty into court on charges of riot, but the jury exonerated them. Throughout Kentucky the slaveholding party organized mass meetings against him and his Emancipation party, so that by the end of 1845 Clay was losing supporters. The legislature also enacted stricter laws against attacks on slavery, especially in the press. But despite the setback, as we shall see later, Cassius Marcellus Clay was not out yet.

Like many other antislavery Southerners who deplored the economic impact of slavery, Clay had no moral objections to the institution. He could praise *Uncle Tom's Cabin* as an accurate depiction of slavery, but when John Fee, antislavery Kentuckian and minister, founded Berea College in 1858, Clay would not consent to being a trustee because the college accepted Negroes, though he himself had provided the land for the college. Slavery, Clay once said, "is not a matter of conscience with me. I press it not upon the conscience of others." Once in his *True American* he said that he would oppose suffrage for free blacks so long as they were unfit for it, though he conceded that in the future it might be possible. In short, despite the charges levied against him by his opponents, he did not believe in Negro equality. "We go for the abolition of slavery," he wrote in 1846 in the *True American,* "not because the slave is *black* or *white*—not because we love the black man best for we do not love him as well . . . but because *it is just.* . . ."[10]

BLAME SLAVERY FIRST

Clay's emphasis on the inability of slavery to develop sufficient markets to sustain an industrial economy did not exhaust the economic arguments marshaled against slavery by Southerners. Daniel Goodloe, for example, often contended that slavery absorbed capital which otherwise might have gone into manufacturing or commerce. He offered the instance of a cotton factory in Maine that employed more than a thousand men and women but was capitalized at only a million dollars. To run a business of comparable size with slave labor, Goodloe pointed out, would require more than $700,000 for labor alone if each worker was considered to cost $700—a not unreasonable estimate. When one also calculated that slaves worked less efficiently than free men, and therefore more slaves would be needed to do the same amount of work, Goodloe went on, it was clear that a million dollars in capital would be exhausted on the purchase of labor alone. It was for that reason, he contended, that capital invested in slaves was "unproductive. It may change hands, and the individual owner may exchange it for productive capital, but so long as it remains in the State or community, it is dead weight; it fetters, cripples, and sometimes destroys the energies of the community."

Like many historians who came after him, Goodloe was confused on the question of capital, however sound he may have been in other respects in writing about slavery. It is true that any individual who had invested in slaves to that extent lacked capital for investment in manufacturing or commerce. But since the purchase of slaves was done within the South, the foreign slave trade having been closed, the region lost no capital by the sale; it merely changed hands among Southerners. It was still available for investment, if the seller of the slave wished so to invest it. The problem

10. *Ibid.,* p. 48; Greeley, ed., *Writings of C. M. Clay,* pp. 293, 382.

of the slave South was not that its capital was tied up in slaves, but that most men with capital in the South preferred to keep reinvesting their profits and capital in slaves, rather than investing it in factories or ships. Goodloe was on sounder ground economically when he pointed out that the abolition of slavery without compensation would not reduce the wealth of the region, though it would reduce the wealth of individuals who held slaves. "The aggregate wealth of the community would be the same," he wrote. "It would have the same houses, land, stock, etc., as before, the same hands to work, and the same mouths to feed, as exist under the law of slavery."[11] What he did not mention was that abolition without compensation meant a redistribution of wealth from the slaveholder to the slave. And that is what defenders of slavery did not want to happen.

One of the favorite arguments of Southerners, especially during the 1820's and 1830's, was that the protective tariff was enriching the North at the expense of the slave South. John C. Calhoun, for example, carried this argument to the point of bringing his native South Carolina to the brink of war with the national government in 1832 when it nullified the tariff of that year. In subsequent years the tariff was lowered and its role in political disputes over slavery diminished. But in view of the emphasis that Southerners placed on the tariff as a source of their backwardness or lack of wealth, it is not surprising that antislavery Southerners would counter that argument by minimizing the tariff as a cause of Southern economic retardation. During the South Carolina nullification controversy, 1828–32, James Madison, the reputed "Father of the Constitution," told several of his correspondents that slavery was a greater detriment to the South than the tariff. He even took it upon himself to tell Thomas R. Dew, the proslavery writer from the University of Virginia, not only that the tariff had been in operation for a long time without objection but that a slave state like Virginia had lagged behind nonslave states long before the protective tariff came into operation.

Jesse Burton Harrison, another Virginian who, like Madison,

11. [Daniel R. Goodloe], *The South and the North: Being a Reply to a Lecture on the North and the South, by Ellwood Fisher, Delivered . . . [at] Cincinnati, January 16, 1849* (Washington, D.C., 1849), p. 6.

was interested in ridding the state of slavery through colonization, took up a similar argument in a pamphlet in 1833. Harrison's argument was also with Thomas Dew, for as an agent of the Colonization Society Harrison was charged with refuting Dew's attack upon colonization as a reasonable remedy for slavery. "For the ills which we have specified," Harrison wrote, "slavery seems to us an adequate cause. It seems at least reasonable to attribute no ills to the tariff except such as can be shown to have risen since 1824. None of those enumerated have had so late an origin."

Henry Ruffner was more direct. Writing in 1847, when the tariff had just been lowered, Ruffner denied any connection between the tariff and the South's lagging behind the North on the matter of manufactures and development. "It matters not to our argument," he wrote, "whether a high tariff or a low tariff be thought best for the country. Whatever aid the tariff may give to manufactures, it gives the same in all parts of the United States." To Ruffner's mind, intent upon economic development, the trouble with the tariff was not that it harmed the South, but that it did not stimulate the region's economy. "Under the protective tariffs formerly enacted, manufactures have grown rapidly in the free states; but no tariff has been able to push a slaveholding state into this important line of industry. Under the present revenue tariff, manufactures still grow in the North; and the South, as might be expected, exhibits no movement, except the customary one of emigration," he wryly observed.[12] Ruffner's comments on the tariff epitomize the alienation of Southern antislavery men from the values of most Southerners; unlike the proslavery advocates, the antislavery men simply did not like the overwhelmingly agricultural character of their region. What was wrong with the tariff was not that it hurt a primarily agricultural region, an injury they would deny or at least ignore, but that it did not encourage industry.

Ruffner's reference to the emigration of whites from slave states introduces another objection to slavery that seriously disturbed antislavery Southerners—that it retarded population growth. "In

12. [Jesse Burton Harrison], *Review of the Slave Question . . . With Particular Reference to Virginia: Though Applicable to other States where Slavery Exists* (Richmond, 1833), p. 24n.; Ruffner, *Address to the People of West Virginia,* p. 23.

the year 1800 Kentucky contained 221,000 in inhabitants, and Ohio 45,000," Ruffner noted, using the familiar comparative argument. "In forty years, the population of Kentucky had risen to 780,000; that of Ohio to 1,519,000. This wonderful difference," he concluded, "could not be owing to any natural superiority of the Ohio country. Kentucky is nearly as large, nearly as fertile, and quite equal in other gifts of nature." Ruffner recognized that there were two main causes for the South's falling behind in population. One was the emigration of whites from the region, especially from the upper South. To Ruffner and other antislavery men the cause of "this unexampled emigration is that no branch of industry flourishes, or can flourish among us, so long as slavery is established by law, and the labor of the country is done chiefly by men, who can gain nothing by assiduity, by skill, or by economy." The second reason in Ruffner's mind for the slow population growth in the South was the lack of foreign immigration. Ruffner readily admitted that much of the population growth of the North was clearly attributable to just that cause. But that did not absolve slavery of responsibility, for basically it was the lack of opportunity in an almost wholly agricultural South that prevented immigrants from entering the region in large numbers.[13]

Subsequent history, however, suggests that Ruffner was being overly simple in his analysis here. In the late nineteenth century and early twentieth century, when immigration reached new heights for the country at large, the South did not participate in the movement even though slavery ended in 1865. Ruffner, of course, was right that lack of opportunity played a large part in discouraging immigration into the South, but where he went wrong was in thinking that slavery was the only source of that dearth of opportunity. Basically it was the intensely agricultural and rural character of the Southern economy and society that caused the South to be unattractive to foreign immigrants. Abolishing slavery did not change that fact.

The rural character of the South always tempted antislavery Southerners to find a conflict between urban growth and slavery, if only because the contrast between free and slave states in urbani-

13. *Ibid.,* pp. 13, 17.

zation was so striking. Daniel Goodloe, for example, compared Missouri and Illinois in respect to cities; both were in the middle west, both came into the Union at about the same time, one with slavery and one without. Missouri, he noted, had "but one place deserving the name of town or city, while Illinois has thriving towns springing up in every direction, which are giving life and vigor to society, by furnishing markets—home markets—for the products of the farm, the dairy, and the workshop; and at the same time becoming the seats of learning, and the centers of intelligence." It was for this reason that in another pamphlet Goodloe referred to cities and slavery as being "at war with each other" and unable to *"thrive together.* If cities advance, slavery must recede; and if slavery advances, cities must disappear."[14] It is worth noting Goodloe's preference for an urban culture—the kind of society that the majority of Southerners of the nineteenth century rejected.

A BLIGHT ON CULTURE

Virtually all the antislavery Southerners ultimately came to attack slavery for its deadening effects on education and culture in general. Slaves as workers are inferior to free men because they are ignorant, George Summers asserted during the Virginia Debates. "Knowledge is incompatible with slavery," he said, "and without knowledge, many of the occupations of life would cease." Henry Ruffner compared the number of children attending school per white person in slave and nonslave states and found the striking differences to the advantage of the North. A similar comparison of literacy showed the North far in the lead. Although the figures were not precise, he went on, "they are sufficiently near to show . . . that slavery exerts a most pernicious influence on the cause of education. This it does," he quite realistically and accurately explained, "by keeping the white population thinly scattered and poor and making the poorer part of them generally indifferent about the education of their children." And it was a fact that

14. Daniel R. Goodloe, *Is It Expedient to Introduce Slavery into Kansas?* (Boston, 1855), pp. 53, 52.

popular education, which was well established in the North before the Civil War, did not come to the South until Reconstruction. Samuel Janney, the antislavery Quaker, worked for free schools in Virginia because he deplored the ignorance of the population as compared with that in the North. He thought it significant that Northerners were the teachers in Virginia schools, and characteristic that "seldom do we hear of a book being written by a Virginian! How few scientific discoveries we have made." Free schools, he thought, would not only enlighten the "governing class," but would promote "antislavery sentiment which was obstructed by ignorance and prejudice."[15]

For many antislavery Southerners, the very cultural level of the South suffered from slavery. The institution had so many economic and social disadvantages, George Tucker told his classes at the University of Virginia, that it could not exist in "the most advanced stages of society, where industry and economy are required. . . ." Daniel Goodloe showed, by his favorite device of statistics, that newspapers and libraries were fewer in number and smaller in circulation in the slave states than in the free states. Other opponents of slavery—among whom Thomas Jefferson, in a well-known passage in *Notes on Virginia,* may have been the first— deplored the moral insensitivity that slavery produced. George Summers at the Virginia Debates echoed Jefferson when he said that slavery made masters into minor tyrants and moral monsters. The slaveholder's "consciousness of superior destiny, takes possession of his mind at its earliest dawning, and love of power and rule, 'grows with his growth and strengthens with his strength,' " Summers contended. "When, in the sublime lessons of christianity, he is taught to 'do unto others as he would have others do unto him,' he never dreams that the degraded Negro is within the pale of that holy canon. Unless enabled to rise above the operation of powerful causes, he enters the world with miserable notions of self-importance, and under the government of an unbridled temper." To Thomas J. Randolph it was the rearing of slaves for market

15. Robert, *Road from Monticello,* pp. 85–86; Ruffner, *Address to the People of West Virginia,* p. 29; Samuel M. Janney, *Memoirs* (Philadelphia, 1881), pp. 95, 93.

that was morally offensive. "How can an honorable mind, a patriot, and a lover of his country," he asked his fellow legislators, "bear to see this ancient dominion, rendered illustrious by the noble devotion and patriotism of her sons in the cause of liberty, converted into one grand menagerie where men are to be reared for market like oxen for the shambles?"

A few antislavery Southerners made the moral wrong of slavery more specific than that even. They condemned it because it seemed to encourage interracial sexuality. In making a catalog of the evils of slavery one North Carolinian told of instances of miscegenation that came to his attention in bastardy proceedings while he had been an officer of a county court. In those proceedings, he wrote, "mulattoes are not a rare article and the wives and daughters of slaveholders are oftener the mothers of them, than are poor women. How far the sons of slaveholders are in the practice of manufacturing Negroes for their fathers, their brothers, and their own services, no one enquires—little yellow faced, tow-headed brats running about the kitchens is by no means a rare occurrence," he contended. That his concern was as much the interracial sexuality as the extramarital sex under slavery is shown by his shock at recalling three families in which one parent was black and the other white and "two cases where young white girls induced Negro slaves to steal horses and run away with them, wishing to find a place where they could live together as husband and wife."

Mary Blackford did not discuss the sexual side of the evils of slavery, but she was struck by the callousness with which otherwise moral white people could treat black people. "Many good and Christian people among us . . . would shudder at" the mistreatment accorded slaves if that same treatment were visited upon whites, she wrote in her diary. They can pass by "gangs of chained human beings going South with indifference. Why? Because property in human beings hardens the heart, dims, aye blinds, us to human rights and human suffering." But perhaps Cassius Marcellus Clay, in his headlong way, summed up the Southern slaveholder's indictment of slave society: "I declare then, in the face of all men, that I believe *slavery* to be an *evil*—an evil morally, economically, physically, intellectually, socially, religiously, politically . . . an unmixed evil."[16]

HATING BLACKS AS WELL AS SLAVERY

Probably the best-known antislavery Southerner then and today was Hinton Rowan Helper, whose book *The Impending Crisis of the South: How to Meet It* (1857) was certainly the most widely read tract against slavery ever written by a Southerner. Simply because it is so well known, a discussion of it and its author has been left to the end of this consideration of the Southern antislavery argument. As any perusal of the book makes evident, *The Impending Crisis* was primarily a summing up of the arguments we have already looked at in the writings of other antislavery Southerners. By an ingenious and relentless use of the census figures for 1850, Helper mounted the most elaborate comparison between Northern and Southern states ever undertaken by an antislavery man. He then went on to blame all the defects of Southern society on slavery: its dearth of cities, its lack of commerce, its absence of manufactures, its high rate of illiteracy and paucity of schools, libraries, newspapers, and general culture.

Helper himself can stand for more than merely a summing up of the classic antislavery argument. He represents, also, in its most extreme form, the man who hated Negroes as much as slavery. It is deceptively easy to make the case that Helper's objection to slavery actually derived from his Negrophobia. Certainly his racism antedated his public opposition to slavery. In his first book, *Land of Gold* (1855), which he wrote soon after returning from a visit to California, he indicated quite openly his disgust with people who were not Caucasian. The book was the tract of a disappointed gold seeker and was intended as a warning to others who might be tempted to seek their fortunes in the Golden State. Throughout the book whenever he encountered Latin Americans,

16. Tucker, *The Laws of Wages,* p. 48; Robert, *Road from Monticello,* pp. 85, 97; Ms. of Speech, B. Hedrick to B. S. Hedrick, April 10, 1862, Benjamin Hedrick Papers; L. Minor Blackford, *Mine Eyes Have Seen the Glory* (Cambridge, Mass., 1954), p. 39; Smiley, *Lion of Whitehall,* p. 49.

Chinese, Indians, or Negroes, Helper's reaction of disgust was the same. He also displayed a streak of anti-Semitism in the book which his recent and thorough biographer Jack Cardoso says he never lost. Certainly, his Negrophobia intensified *after* publication of *The Impending Crisis of the South.*

Nevertheless a close examination of *The Impending Crisis* does not support the argument that Helper's antislavery views derived principally from his hatred of Negroes. For one thing there are almost no references to blacks in the whole length of the book, and certainly slavery is emphasized as the evil, not blacks. For another, in several places he writes of the burden that slavery imposed upon Negroes as one of the many reasons for getting rid of the institution. It is true that when he speaks of slavery being "an oppressive burden to the blacks" he couples it with an equivalent statement of its evil for the whites. But when he comes to informing the nonslaveholders what advantages will accrue to them through abolition, one gain he advances is that they "will be restoring to them [the slaves] their natural rights and remunerating them . . . for the long and cheerless period of their servitude from the 20th of August 1620 [*sic*] when . . . they became the unhappy slaves of heartless masters."

On the other hand, Helper made no effort to conceal from his readers the belief that the Negroes ought to be removed from the country or that they were inferior to whites. At one point in the book, for example, he states as his preference that he "would ship them all within the next six months" to Liberia. He was somewhat more oblique in admitting that he did not consider blacks as equal to whites. Yet the context in which he raised the issue places him in opposition to those who rested their defense of slavery upon a racial argument. Let us look at the argument.

When Helper wrote, a small group of Northern and Southern ethnologists were insisting that Negroes did not have the same origins as white men and hence could be considered different and inferior. It is to this intellectual development that Helper referred when he mentioned "certain ethnographical oligarchs" who "proved to their own satisfaction that the Negro was an inferior 'type of mankind.' " With this information, he continued, "they chuckled wonderfully and avowed in substance, that it was right for the stronger race to kidnap and enslave the weaker. . . ." He rejected the defense of slavery on the ground that "Nature had been pleased to do a trifle more for the Caucasian race than for the African." It is worth noting that Helper did not deny that difference; he simply did not think it relevant. "No system of logic could be more antagonistic to the spirit of true democracy. It is probable that the world does not contain two persons who are exactly alike in all respects," he admitted. "Yet *'all* men are endowed by their Creator with certain *inalienable* rights, among which are life, *liberty* and the pursuit of happiness.' All mankind may or may not be the descendants of Adam and Eve," he conceded, referring to the conflict between the ethnologists and the religious thinkers on race. "In our own humble way of thinking, we are frank to confess, we do not believe in the unity of the races"—that is, he agreed with the ethnologists rather than the theologians. "This is a matter, however, which has little or nothing to do with the great question at issue." Even earlier in the book he had denied that it is "our business to think of man as a merchantable commodity; and we will not, even by implication admit . . . that the condition of chattelhood may rightfully attach to sentient and immortal beings."[17]

The point is not to deny Helper's Negrophobia, which was always present, and destined to intensify with time, but rather to recognize that his antislavery sentiments were not dependent upon it. Among antislavery people throughout the nation—North as well as South—hatred or fear of blacks could and did accompany opposition to slavery. James Pike, an ardent antislavery man from Maine—a locality about as remote from Southern slavery as an American could get—has been shown by his biographer Robert Durden to have been violently hostile to blacks. Like Helper he wished to confine them to an out-of-the-way place in the United

17. Hinton Rowan Helper, *The Impending Crisis of the South: How to Meet It* (New York, 1860), pp. 184, 185, 182–83, 184, 86. Undoubtedly the fullest and best study of Helper, and one to which I am beholden, is Joaquin Jose Cardoso, "Hinton Rowan Helper: A Nineteenth Century Pilgrimage," unpublished Ph.D. dissertation, University of Wisconsin, 1967. Cardoso's study will soon be published. Hugh C. Bailey, *Hinton Rowan Helper, Abolitionist-Racist* (University, Ala., 1965), lacks the thorough research of Cardoso's work; Bailey, for example, did not use the Hedrick Papers at Duke University.

States, if he could not send them abroad. On a wider canvas, Eugene Berwanger in a study of attitudes of Westerners toward slavery argues that the opposition of the frontier and Western states to slavery stemmed largely from fear of, and opposition to, Negroes rather than to the institution. Whether the anti-Negro roots of Western antislavery are any more clear than in the case of Helper does not really concern us here. The point is that in the North many antislavery men were also hostile to Negroes, slave or free.

If Helper's racism does not set him apart, his book *The Impending Crisis* did. As we have seen, the argument it presented was not new, but it became better known than any other antislavery tract by a Southerner because it was published and distributed in 1859 as a Republican campaign tract. As such it became entangled in a bitter fight for the speakership of the House of Representatives, which brought it to the attention of the nation. To help raise money to pay for the cost of the 100,000 copies to be printed, Helper obtained endorsements of his book from a number of Republican party leaders, including John Sherman, a prominent Republican congressman from Ohio. When Sherman was put up for the speakership, Southerners denounced him for the endorsement, while Northerners almost as automatically leaped to the defense of the tract. (Long after the struggle, which lasted almost two months, during which Sherman had to withdraw his candidacy, Sherman admitted that he had endorsed the book without even reading it.) As a result, Helper leaped from obscurity to notoriety as a Southern antislavery man.

Helper's notoriety was so great that after the election of Lincoln, in whose support *The Impending Crisis* had been reissued, Helper was viewed as a liability to the new administration. A number of antislavery men were given jobs by the first Republican administration, presumably as a reward for services in the past and perhaps to project abroad an image of antislavery. Thus Cassius Clay was sent as minister to Russia, Carl Schurz to Madrid, Charles Francis Adams to London, and John Bigelow, as consul general, to Paris. Antislavery and Republican Southerners, in addition to the prominent Cassius Clay, also received jobs from the Lincoln administration. Daniel Goodloe and Benjamin Hedrick, for example, received jobs early in the new government. (Hedrick, also a North Carolinian and a friend of Helper, gained some national notice in 1856 when he was removed as professor of chemistry at the University of North Carolina for saying he would vote for J. C. Frémont, the first Republican presidential candidate.)

Hinton Helper, though, was not so rewarded. Months after Hedrick had received his own appointment, he wrote to his wife, "Helper has not received his promised place, but is still trying. There is some rascality about it somewhere. Chase [Secretary of the Treasury] gave him a position promise and now backs out."[18] Helper undoubtedly had an inflated idea of what kind of job he deserved, but it is very likely that his notoriety as an antislavery Southerner slowed down action on his request for a job. In the first year of the war, the Lincoln administration concentrated on holding the border slave states in the Union, and it probably feared the impact upon that delicate campaign if the notorious Helper were rewarded with a job. Finally, at the very end of 1861, Helper was appointed consul at Buenos Aires, where he remained throughout the war.

As one might expect from even a cursory knowledge of Helper, his correspondence while in Argentina is heavily interlarded with comments on the illiberality of the Roman Catholic Church in Latin America and the general incompetence of the population. When war among Argentina, Paraguay, Uruguay, and Brazil broke out in the spring of 1865 he gave vent to his racism. That and other wars on the continent he attributed to "the unfortunate and disgraceful commixture of the first European settlers with certain grossly inferior races of mankind, who are totally undisciplined and undisciplinable, unschooled and unschoolable, unfitted and unfittable for civilization." The region could be improved, he believed, only if the population were to be "composed chiefly—all the better if entirely—of Germanic, of Anglo-Saxon, and of Anglo-

18. Benjamin S. Hedrick to his wife, Aug. 19, 1861, in B. S. Hedrick Papers. See also Ellen Hedrick to BSH, March 31, 1861, and April 3, 1861, in B. S. Hedrick Papers.

American origin."[19] By now, Helper was as pronounced a racist as any writer of his time.

Helper's dislike for Latin Americans, however, did not prevent his marrying an Argentine woman or his developing a consuming interest in the southern continent's economic development. For more than thirty years he busied himself with various projects in Latin America, the most notable of which was a campaign to build a railroad that would link North and South America. Into this project he sank whatever money he could get his hands on, and to it he devoted, it seemed, almost all his waking hours. When he died in 1909, a suicide, penniless, and nearly demented, in a cheap rooming house in New York City, his waning strength was still being directed to pressing his cause of a hemispheric railroad upon anyone who would give him attention.

The development or at least the expression of Helper's Negrophobia is a fascinating study in pathology. Even before he returned to the United States from Buenos Aires, Helper made clear to Republicans his feelings about Negroes, if they had not been obvious before. In October, 1865, he wrote to John Sherman, now a senator, identifying himself as "one who knows something of the lamentable unworthiness of the Negro." The purpose of the letter was to urge Sherman to oppose Negro suffrage. In the violent language that had made *The Impending Crisis* both hard to take and notorious, he expressed the hope that not many American statesmen "are afflicted with that new and disgusting malady which, for some time past, has been manifesting itself among us, and which in the irregular nomenclature of the day, is not inaptly designated Negro-on-the-brain—a sort of delirious accompaniment to the Black Vomit."[20]

After his return to the United States in 1866, Helper published in rapid succession three books on Negroes—all of which were vicious in their racism. *Nojoque: A Question for the Continent* (1867) had as its primary purpose, he wrote, "to write the Negro out of America and the secondary object is to write him . . . out

19. William Pratt Dale II, "Hinton Rowan Helper and Hispanic America," unpublished M.A. thesis, Duke University, 1934, p. 32.
20. Hinton Rowan Helper to Benjamin S. Hedrick, Oct. 18, 1865, in B. S. Hedrick Papers.

of existence." Although the book came close to calling for extermination, Helper made clear he intended no more than enforced emigration for all colored or non-Germanic peoples. By now, though, Helper had focused on the Negro as worst, for though the Indian was "a very miserable fellow indeed . . . yet he is a nobleman in comparison with the negro." The book's first chapter was devoted to showing, through quotations from the ethnological literature of the day, the physical inferiority of blacks and their tendency to die out as a race. Then in a remarkable tour de force he marshaled more than 150 pages of quotations to prove the obvious—the good connotations attaching to "white" and the bad associated with "black." The Old Testament was also ransacked to justify the removal of effete people from a country. In a travesty on his own earlier antislavery writings, he compared Massachusetts' and New York's progress to South Carolina's and Virginia's backwardness and attributed the difference to the presence of blacks in the South. "Great States are made up only of white men, white women, and white children . . . ," he concluded, savoring every opportunity to use his favorite adjective. By now he had lost his once healthy skepticism of the antebellum Southern press on the issue of slavery, for he quoted at length from it to show that blacks had been willing to remain in slavery or to be re-enslaved if free. Without questioning, he accepted reports in the Confederate press which described slaves buying Confederate bonds. Most Negroes had joined the Union army, he contended, not to fight slavery, but to avoid regular work![21]

A year later he brought out *The Negroes in Negroland,* and in 1871 he followed this paean to white supremacy with *Noonday Exigencies in America,* the last of his diatribes against blacks. The last book did not advance beyond *Nojoque,* and a single quotation from it is sufficient to expose the quality of his thought: "White communities, in whatever part of the world they exist, are at once suggestive of Knowledge, Truth, Virtue, Industry, Wealth, Progress and Honor; while black communities, whether in Africa, in America, or elsewhere, are as unerringly indicative of Ignorance, Falsehood, Vice, Idleness, Poverty, Retrogression, and Infamy."

21. Hinton Rowan Helper, *Nojoque: A Question for the Continent* (New York, 1867), Preface, pp. 221, 66–67, ch. II, ch.VI, pp. 78, 194–204.

As this caricature of thought makes evident, by this time Helper's Negrophobia was out of control. The ultimate measure of that loss of control is a letter from a friend that he included in *Noonday Exigencies,* as a self-advertisement. The friend told of having held at least "a thousand conversations" with Helper and "if he has ever expressed a pro-negro sentiment, orally or chirographically, I have neither heard nor seen it." Helper himself pointed out that recently in Philadelphia he had been served ice cream by a Negro and had been barely able to swallow the food. He boasted that for the previous seventeen years he had refused to patronize any place that hired blacks. Indeed, he went on, "every white American who is, by choice, or by preference, the employer in the United States of any servant or other person who is not white is a vile traitor to his race, and a sower of the seeds of immorality, dissension, strife, demoralization and ruin."[22]

Sadly enough, when his pathological hatred was pointed out to him, Helper could not recognize it. When his friend Benjamin Hedrick rebuked him for the violently anti-Negro statements in *Nojoque,* Helper replied smugly, "It is strange how you and others, who ought to know better, will persist in calling my preference for white men 'hatred' for the negro. Yet I flatter myself that some of you will learn what I am about, and see and acknowledge that I am right, in less than ten years from today."

Benjamin Hedrick, like Helper, was an opponent of slavery and a native North Carolinian. Unlike Helper, he was not a racist. Hedrick did not write anything for publication, but he certainly paid for his willingness to be known as an opponent of slavery in the South. As we have seen, he was fired from his job as professor of chemistry at the University of North Carolina in 1856 for saying he would vote for a Republican that year. He then went into "exile" in New York City, where he remained until the Lincoln administration in 1861 provided him with a government job in Washington. Hedrick must have been among the first Southerners to advocate suffrage for the former slaves. In a long letter in July, 1865, he explained his political beliefs, which led him to conclude that since Negroes were men, were compelled to obey the laws,

22. Hinton Rowan Helper, *Noonday Exigencies in America* (New York, 1871), pp. 155, 206, 27, 71.

and paid taxes, the suffrage could not be denied them. "If the negroes are excluded from the ballot box, it must be for some good reason," he contended. "I have never seen any good reason assigned for such exclusion." Nor would he take the Negroes' lack of education as a reason, since, as he rightly pointed out, uneducated white men possessed the vote.[23] After the war Hedrick returned to North Carolina as a Republican, along with his friend Daniel Goodloe. These two antislavery North Carolinians stand in sharp contrast to their friend Helper, since both of them became champions of Negro rights, while Helper grew ever more virulent in his hatred of blacks.

THE LIMITS OF SOUTHERN ANTISLAVERY

Where does this examination of the character and context of the Southern antislavery argument leave us? What broader conclusions might one draw? Perhaps the most obvious is the limited number of white Southerners who expressed *any* objection to slavery. Although, as we shall see later in this chapter, antislavery arguments were heard in the South right down to the moment of secession, the number of people who heeded them, much less uttered them, was always minuscule. This is true even when one defines opposition to slavery in the broadest possible way—that is, regardless of motive. When some discrimination is made between motives, so that opposition to slavery because of its impact upon whites is not seen as true antislavery, then the number of white Southerners who opposed slavery shrinks even more. Those who opposed slavery primarily because of what it did to the Negro were few indeed. It is true that in the antebellum South if one were interested in arousing men against slavery, an appeal to whites in the name of white prosperity was certainly the more practical line to take. Yet from the private statements of antislavery Southerners it is clear that the great majority of those who opposed slavery because of what it did to whites took the position for that reason and not because they thought the argument was a more practical tactic to follow.

23. Hinton Rowan Helper to Benjamin S. Hedrick, May 3, 1869; Benjamin Hedrick to Ulysses S. Rich, July 4, 1865, B. S. Hedrick Papers.

A second obvious conclusion is that the antislavery Southerners are conspicuously concentrated in the upper South. Of all the Southern antislavery advocates discussed in this and the previous chapters, only John McDonogh worked in the deep South—and his commitment to antislavery was through colonization only. Indeed, even a contemporary antislavery Southerner like Daniel R. Goodloe found it difficult to locate or identify significant antislavery men in the deep South. In 1858 he published a compilation of statements against slavery by Southern men of the previous generation, including some from the Virginia Debates of 1832. His purpose, of course, was to show that antislavery statements could be found among prominent Southerners. Proudly he pointed out that Northerners were, at that time, less opposed to the institution than "the leading minds of the South, except those of South Carolina and Georgia. . . ."[24]

There were individuals, to be sure, here and there in the deep South who opposed slavery. Professor Anne Scott in a recent book on Southern women has collected a number of statements from wives and daughters of planters to show that women, even in the deep South, expressed dissatisfaction with the institution. Best known in this regard, of course, is Mary Chesnut of South Carolina, who claimed, in her well-known diary, that she had been an abolitionist from age nineteen. Kate Stone of Louisiana recalled that she had been "born and raised in the South. . . . Yet . . . my first recollection is of pity for the Negroes and the desire to help them. . . . Always I felt the moral guilt of it, felt how impossible it must be for an owner of slaves to win his way into Heaven." Mary Chesnut objected to slavery because of the extramarital sexuality it encouraged among the white men; other women simply saw it as un-Christian. One Northerner who opposed slavery told of talking about the institution with women in Charleston and seeing "their eyes fill with tears when you talk with them about" slavery.[25]

There were men, too, in the deep South who gave expression to

24. Daniel R. Goodloe, comp., *The Southern Platform: or, Manual of Southern Sentiment on the Subject of Slavery* (Boston, 1858), p. 2.

25. Anne Firor Scott, *The Southern Lady, from Pedestal to Politics, 1830–1930* (Chicago, 1970), pp. 48–53.

opposition to slavery. Joel Poinsett, the prominent South Carolina politician and Unionist, wrote his cousin in England in 1847, for example, that he looked "forward to the gradual extinguishment of slavery. . . . Within my recollections, it has become extinct in 8 opulent states, and in several others it is becoming burdensome to retain them. In the region of the country where I now am, it is only moderately profitable to cultivate the soil by slave labour. Where I reside in the summer, it is ruinous to do it. We are a shrewd people and if let alone will consult our own interest and employ that labor which is most profitable. We are humane, too, for the slave; the black slave is far better off in the Carolinas than the white slave in the North of Europe. Both are evils, I acknowledge, and I have long been convinced that a free State has greatly the advantage over one that admits of slavery."[26] Poinsett may have been expressing his true views, but he did not do so in public, and his cousin was obviously pricking his conscience. Yet there were other expressions of antislavery sentiment in the deep South, some of which derive from a broader base than merely individual idiosyncrasy. In January, 1849, for example, the Columbia, Georgia, *Times* published a statement by an Alabamian in which the writer asserted that "the South has the germ of a special and unknown anti-slavery party." The party, he went on, would contain not only the nonslaveholders "who regard the slave as a rival in production," but also people of all backgrounds "who are wearied out with the struggle of unproductive labors . . . and those who desire more populous white communities for the purposes of trade and education." The author thought that "this combination of opinion against slavery had prodigiously increased within a few years and is now increasing at a rapid pace."

Five months later, the Augusta *Chronicle,* also in Georgia, answered an attack on slavery from a Boston newspaper by candidly admitting that "slaveholders must demonstrate in a large way and by visible results that slave labor in Georgia is as profitable to you and as useful to the world, as free labor is at the North or can be at the South—that it is not inimical to common schools, the improvement of the soil and the progress of manufactures."

26. Copy of letter by Joel Poinsett to his cousin "Miss Tyrrell," Jan. 18, 1847, in Charles Chandler Papers, Folder 55.

Obviously, to that newspaper at least, the value of slavery was not proved beyond doubt. "The whole matter will turn in the end on the pivot of dollars and cents," the paper concluded matter-of-factly. "We can only prove our view by attaining prosperity."[27]

But no matter how tantalizing and suggestive these isolated statements from the deep South may be, they are no more than exceptions to the general rule. In those regions of the South where Negroes constituted more than 30 percent of the population *and* where cotton could be grown in profitable amounts, opposition to slavery never achieved any significant expression during the nineteenth century. (The figure of 30 percent is arbitrary; it is meant to include those places in which large numbers of blacks were present, but still falling short of a majority. Historically, a clear majority of blacks has never been necessary in order to strike fear in the hearts of white North Americans that they would be "overrun.") Virginia and Kentucky, with their small-scale agriculture and relatively small number of slaves, might produce a small antislavery movement, but the booming cotton states of Mississippi, Louisiana, Alabama, and Texas could not; and though South Carolina found itself in trouble economically by the 1850's, its black majority made emancipation for a society of white men who feared black men, slave or free, a dangerous doctrine to express.

It must not be forgotten that antislavery sentiment was dangerous—as Cassius Clay, Hinton Helper, and Benjamin Hedrick, to name only three examples, certainly found out. That danger also explains why some Southern antislavery men forsook their principles as the pressure mounted. John Letcher, and Samuel McDowell Moore of Virginia Debates fame, for example, endorsed Henry Ruffner's pamphlet when it was published in 1847, only to be hounded for years for that endorsement. By 1850 Letcher was explaining why he had done so, and by 1860 he was declaring his earlier act a mistake. When Moore was challenged in 1860 to defend his endorsement yet another time, he asked plaintively, "When [will] the act of limitation for signing the Ruffner Pam-

27. Richard Harrison Shryock, *Georgia and the Union in 1850* (Philadelphia, 1926), pp. 36–37, 34–35.

phlet commence?"[28] Several of the outspoken opponents of slavery during the Virginia Debates eventually recanted—Charles Faulkner and Thomas Jefferson Randolph among them.

THE ATTACK CONTINUES

The fact that Southern antislavery people were relatively few in number and limited to the upper South does not, however, justify another conclusion often drawn about antislavery in the South. The standard judgment has been that after the great debate in the Virginia House of Delegates in January, 1832, a blackout descended like a pall upon the South, killing off further discussion of the issue. As the quotations from Poinsett and the two Georgia newspapers cited above make evident, even in the deep South antislavery sentiments continued occasionally to be heard and even read. To be sure, as we shall see, it made a difference who uttered the sentiments—white or black, Northerner or Southerner—and under what circumstances, but that criticisms of slavery continued to be heard after 1832 there can be no doubt. Expression of that sentiment, to be sure, was largely confined to the upper South— Missouri, Kentucky, Tennessee, Virginia, and North Carolina. And the dominant argument was economic, rather than moral. It was an argument in behalf of the white man's prosperity rather than in behalf of the black man's freedom. And it was true that the antislavery agitation prior to 1832 had been so peripheral and minor in the life of the region that it did not take much to continue it at the same level. Yet throughout the remainder of the antebellum years after 1832 antislavery propaganda was heard in the upper South. There was no blackout.

Two years after the close of the Virginia Debates, when a constitutional convention was in the offing in Tennessee, some thirty memorials were presented to the convention, asking for the abolition of slavery in the state. Of more than 1,800 persons who signed the thirty petitions, the majority lived in eastern Tennessee,

28. William Gleason Bean, "The Ruffner Pamphlet of 1847: Some Antislavery Aspects of Virginia Sectionalism," *Virginia Magazine of History and Biography*, LXI (1958), 279–81.

where slaves were almost unknown; no petitions came from western Tennessee, where cotton was cultivated and slaves were numerous. Although the committee of the convention that reported on the petitions made a plea for noninterference in the issue by those who live in areas of the North "where slavery does not now exist," it denominated slavery an evil and predicted its end. An unambiguous vote on emancipation was not taken in Tennessee in 1834 any more than it had been in Virginia in 1832. Individual members of the convention, however, usually from east Tennessee, denounced slavery and slaveholders at some length. At least one delegate, for example, even accused slaveholders of being inhumane. Significantly, too, none of the defenders of slavery argued that it was anything better than a necessary evil.

Instead of moving to end slavery, however, the convention voted to strengthen it against future attacks. By a vote of 30 to 27 the new constitution provided that slavery could not be abolished without the consent of slave owners. When the convention failed to make any step in the direction of emancipation, the antislavery men then rallied to resist threats to the suffrage rights of free blacks. Ever since the first constitution in 1796, free Negroes had been able to vote on the same basis as whites. The convention of 1834, however, now inserted the word "white" into the suffrage clause of the new constitution by a vote of 33 to 23. When some of the delegates tried to soften the blow to Negroes who already exercised the ballot by excluding them from the operation of the new clause, they lost by almost the same vote, 34 to 22.

Although these roll calls in the Tennessee convention suggest that the men who sought to protect slavery also opposed Negro suffrage, they should not be interpreted as meaning that those who opposed slavery also favored Negro suffrage. The fact is that in east Tennessee, where there were few slaves, but where the state's antislavery sentiment was centered, there was little sympathy for the free Negro. Virtually all the antislavery delegates to the convention were agreed that if emancipation took place it must be accompanied by deportation or colonization. The hostility toward slavery in Tennessee after the convention of 1834 died down, though there were occasional public criticisms after 1834. Tennessee, as we shall see in Chapter 4, harbored a large number of dissenters from the traditions of the Majority South, but that dissent took the form of support for the Union rather than outspoken opposition to slavery.[29]

There is stronger evidence in Kentucky for the persistence of antislavery expression after the Virginia Debates. Cassius Clay and Robert Breckinridge, as we saw, continued their public opposition to slavery in Kentucky all through the 1830's and 1840's. Kentucky's response to the threat of servile insurrection in the 1830's was the enactment of a law in February, 1833, forbidding the further importation into the state of slaves intended for sale. By design the law did not interfere with a white migrant's bringing his own slaves into the state or the inheritance of slaves from outside. The law apparently had some of the intended effect, for the proportion of slaves in the population in 1830 was lower than it had been for several decades. To some Kentuckians the prohibition was a first, if small step toward emancipation. Indeed, one legislator in 1835 waxed enthusiastic on the subject. "The spirit of emancipation is abroad in the land," he said, "and you had as well to resist electricity or control the lightnings of heaven as to attempt to check its onward march. . . ." Proslavery men, of course, sought to repeal the prohibition, but without success. The issue became a major question in the elections of 1840–41, with candidates being asked their views on the subject. Robert Breckinridge, Cassius Clay, and Thomas Marshall, the leading antislavery men of the state, spoke widely and successfully against repeal. At least one Kentucky newspaper linked the opposition to importation of slaves to antislavery. "There are thousands upon thousands of the citizens and themselves slaveholders, too," wrote the Frankfort *Commonwealth* in 1840, "who look upon slavery as an evil. . . . They have considered that an act which operates to keep down

29. For the meager history of antislavery in Tennessee see James W. Patton, "The Progress of Emancipation in Tennessee, 1796–1860," *Journal of Negro History*, XVII (1932), 67–102, and Chase C. Mooney, "The Question of Slavery and the Free Negro in the Tennessee Constitutional Convention of 1834," *Journal of Southern History*, XII (1946), 487–509. Two general studies emphasize the weakness of the movement in the South, even before 1832: Gordon E. Finnie, "The Antislavery Movement in the Upper South Before 1840," *Journal of Southern History*, XXXV (1969), 319–42, and Kenneth M. Stampp, "The Fate of the Southern Anti-Slavery Movement," *Journal of Negro History*, XXVIII (1943), 10–22.

the increase by excluding foreign supply" would also help the "growth of the white race."[30]

Public opposition to slavery in Kentucky continued through the 1840's. In 1845 in Fayette County, where citizens insisted upon questioning candidates about their stand toward emancipation, an old proslavery candidate for the legislature who refused to respond to the question was defeated. That year, too, Cassius Clay began publishing the *True American,* which was, as we have seen, dedicated to the ending of slavery in Kentucky. Within two months of its founding it had 700 subscribers in Kentucky alone. The *Christian Intelligencer,* a Methodist weekly in the state, supported Clay's program. In the Green River region, the most proslavery part of the state, the Democratic newspaper reprinted excerpts from Clay's *True American* and wrote about the competition of slavery with white workers. Clay himself organized an Emancipation party, and at least one candidate stood for the legislature under the party's banner. Actually, the August 18 affair in which Clay's press was silenced finished off the Emancipation party in Kentucky, though four years later a few candidates were still running under its name.

The antislavery movement, although never very widespread in Kentucky, put what popularity it had to the test in 1848 when the legislature, after repeated refusals, finally repealed the prohibition on the importation of slaves. Recognizing that this move would eliminate the one slim promise that slavery was on its way out, however slowly, the emancipationists pressed for a constitutional convention to settle the issue. Reluctantly, the legislature agreed to convoke one in October, 1849. The emancipationists organized themselves ahead of time with county committees actually meeting in about a fourth of the state's counties. Their state party convention took a conservative position on the ending of slavery. Emancipation was to be accompanied by compensation to the slaveholders and would affect only Negroes born in the future—the approach that had been taken in many Northern states a half-century earlier. Cassius Clay thought the program much too

30. Asa Earl Martin, *The Anti-Slavery Movement in Kentucky* (Louisville, 1918), p. 102; Smiley, *Lion of Whitehall,* pp. 44–45.

gradual considering the lateness of the historical hour, but to preserve a united front he went along.

The campaign for the election of delegates to the convention would be a test of popular attitudes on slavery. Because the proposals of the emancipationists were conservative, the antislavery forces had expectations of winning the support of the mildest antislavery people. The antislavery advocates also enjoyed the support of some of the most influential and renowned men in Kentucky politics. The two United States senators, Henry Clay and J. R. Underwood, for example, spoke in behalf of the election of emancipationist candidates. Clay, who was then the national president of the American Colonization Society, published a long letter in which he detailed his view on slavery. Conspicuous in Clay's Pindell letter was the explicit rejection of the so-called "positive good" defense of slavery that Calhoun and the proslavery men of the deep South had been elaborating ever since the 1830's. "I am aware that there are respectable persons who believe that slavery is a blessing, that the institution ought to exist in every well-organized society and that it is even favorable to the preservation of liberty," he began. "Happily, the number who entertain these extravagant opinions is not very great, and the time would be uselessly occupied in an elaborate refutation to them." But it is worth pointing out, he went on, that if that kind of argument were to be followed logically, then when no Africans were obtainable it would be justifiable to enslave one portion of the white race to serve the other. His logical objections also extended to the argument that slavery was justified by virtue of the racial inferiority of the African. "But if this argument be founded in fact (as it may be, but which I shall not now examine), it would prove entirely too much. It would prove that any white nation, which had made greater advances in civilization, knowledge, and wisdom than another white nation, would have a right to reduce the latter to a state of bondage. Nay, further: if the principle of subjugation founded upon intellectual superiority be true, and be applicable to races and to nations, what is to prevent its being applied to individuals? And then the wisest man in the world would have a right to make slaves of all the rest of mankind."

Clay went on to say that he thought the "vast majority of the people of the United States" regretted the introduction of slavery into the colonies, "regard the institution as a great evil to both races," and would like to see it removed. But since black men and white men cannot live in equality and freedom together, the ending of slavery must mean the removal of blacks to Africa.[31] Clay's position was not only that of a national statesman of great stature; it was also an example of the continuation of Jeffersonian thought, for Jefferson's view was identical with Clay's—even to the kind of logical argument against the racial defense of slavery that Clay advanced in his Pindell letter. Abraham Lincoln's own later argument against justifying slavery on grounds of race may well have been borrowed from Clay, whom Lincoln greatly admired. Clay's program for emancipation is virtually identical, also, with that which Lincoln preferred while President when he advocated compensation to slaveholders and the removal of the freed blacks from the United States.

The publication of Clay's letter understandably led to his denunciation in the deep South. He told his son that though he anticipated the unpopularity that would ensue, "I nevertheless wish it published. I owe that to the cause, and to myself, and to posterity."[32]

Although Henry Clay was undoubtedly the most famous of the advocates of emancipation prior to the election of delegates in Kentucky, he was far from alone. His nephew C. M. Clay, Robert J. Breckinridge, one of the old warhorses in the Southern antislavery movement, Thomas F. Marshall, and T. J. Boyle also stumped the state in behalf of the emancipationists. It is striking that virtually all of the prominent emancipationists were slaveholders themselves. The principal exception was Cassius Clay, who had emancipated his last slaves in 1844.

Strenuous as the effort and broad as the emancipationists' platform was, the response was pitifully inadequate. Not a single one of the twenty-nine candidates who ran on an emancipationist platform was elected to the convention. About 10,000 votes were cast for them—a number that probably measured the full extent

31. The text of the Pindell letter can be found in *Works of Henry Clay* (Federal Edition, New York, 1904), III, 346–52. It is dated Feb. 17, 1849.
32. Martin, *Anti-Slavery . . . in Kentucky*, pp. 128–29.

of antislavery sentiment in the state. It is true that to vote for an emancipationist, a Kentuckian would have had to repudiate his party, since both Whig and Democratic parties officially opposed emancipation. Yet to do so was hardly unrespectable if Henry Clay could support emancipation. Moreover, in Kentucky non-slaveholders must have outnumbered the slaveholding voters by nine to one. The implications of this fact will be examined at the end of this chapter.

Instead of ending slavery, the Kentucky convention—like the Tennessee convention fourteen years earlier and the Virginia legislature sixteen years before—moved to strengthen the legal supports of slavery. Article XIII of the new Kentucky constitution of 1850 placed slave property in an especially sacred category—in effect, beyond the constitution. Section 3 of the article read: "The right of property is before and higher than any Constitutional sanction; and the right of the owner of a slave to such slave, and its increase, is the same, and is as inviolable as the right of the owner of any property whatever."[33]

The convention of 1849 was undoubtedly a defeat for the anti-slavery forces in Kentucky. And though opposition to the institution continued to be voiced right down to the Civil War, it was weaker than ever. Cassius Clay, for example, ran for governor in 1851. During his campaign he spoke in some eighty counties without molestation, but sometimes without an audience. As always, though, his attacks on slavery were in behalf of the non-slaveholder. He received 3,621 votes. Never again after 1849 would emancipation attract the support it had then. Indeed, although Kentucky remained in the Union during the Civil War, it clung almost desperately to slavery, refusing to ratify the Thirteenth Amendment. Slavery ended within the boundaries of Kentucky only with the promulgation of the adoption of the Thirteenth Amendment in December, 1865—almost eight months after Appomattox.

Virginia, too, offers evidence to show that the debates of 1832 did not usher in a blackout on antislavery expression. The legislature, it is true, never again took up the question of emancipation,

33. Francis Newton Thorpe, comp., *The Federal and State Constitutions* . . . (Washington, D.C., 1909), III, 1312.

but the subject was publicly discussed throughout the 1840's. Samuel McPherson Janney, who lived his whole life in Virginia working against slavery, talked openly against slavery even in Richmond. Moreover, he was heard with a certain amount of sympathy. According to his private letters, Janney thought that during the 1840's antislavery sentiment in Virginia was actually rising.

In 1845 John Hampden Pleasants, the editor of the influential Richmond *Whig,* opened his newspaper's columns to antislavery sentiment, including a series written by Samuel Janney. In his last article, Janney sought to argue that the blacks need not be removed from the state once emancipation had been achieved. When Pleasants read the piece he lost his nerve; he refused to publish it without major revision. The article never appeared. Instead the *Whig* carried another article by Janney on Yankee immigrants who lived in Fairfax County, Virginia, and who had restored the worn-out plantations through the introduction of new and invigorating methods of agriculture without slave labor. In the months that followed Janney's series the *Whig* published a number of letters from others opposing slavery. The paper itself at one point declared that unless slavery was removed, Virginia will "continue to sink, sink, sink! In the scale of nations!"[34] By this time John Pleasants was so involved in opposing slavery that he resigned the editorship of the *Whig* in order to begin an antislavery paper. His intended paper presumably was to be modeled after Cassius Clay's *True American,* which was then in its first year of publication. But in early 1846 Pleasants was killed in a duel with Thomas Ritchie, the editor of the *Whig*'s Democratic rival, the Richmond *Enquirer.*

Although the death of Pleasants ended the possibility of an antislavery newspaper in Virginia, other writers continued to express in print their hostility to slavery. Robert R. Howison, in his *History of Virginia,* published in 1848 in Richmond, asserted that the people of the state "hold slavery to be an enormous evil, bearing with fatal power upon their prosperity. This sentiment," he noted, "has been gaining ground during many years."[35] About the

34. Patricia P. Hickin, "Slavery in Virginia, 1831–1861," unpublished Ph.D. dissertation, University of Virginia, 1968, p. 177.
35. *Ibid.,* pp. 167–68.

same time, of course, Henry Ruffner of western Virginia published his *Address,* which we have looked at already. Ruffner's pamphlet was also published in the Lexington *Gazette,* a Whig newspaper. Ruffner was so pleased with the favorable response he received from the appearance of his *Address,* especially in the eastern, or slaveholding, part of the state, that he resolved to put out a new edition. Apparently the illness and death of his wife precluded his carrying out that decision.

The 1840's are a special decade in the history of the antebellum South, for that was a period of low prices for cotton. Inasmuch as many of Virginia's slaves were sold to the cotton regions, even Virginia would feel the effects of a fall in the price of cotton. One of the sources of antislavery sentiment was undoubtedly the declining state of the economy, especially since many Southern antislavery proponents believed that the principal argument against slavery was that it impoverished the South. Thus when the economy declined, the interest in abolishing slavery (and removing blacks) rose. Conversely, when the Southern economy picked up in the 1850's, bringing slave prices up with it, the antislavery sentiments of the previous decade in Virginia fell off.

During the 1850's the public expression of antislavery attitudes in Virginia was largely confined to the panhandle (now West Virginia) and other western areas where no slaves existed. Patricia Hickin, while noting that historians have underestimated the extent of the antislavery movement of the 1840's, attributes the decline of antislavery sentiment in the 1850's to the rising prices for slaves rather than to the abolitionist attacks on slavery. Indeed, the evidence for the 1830's and 1850's on the expression of antislavery views in the South as a whole suggests that fear of abolition, as an explanation for the weakness of Southern antislavery sentiment, is exaggerated. As we shall see a little later in this chapter, that fear operated quite selectively.

Even during the 1850's some Southerners continued to speak out against slavery within the strongholds of the institution. During those years, for example, Daniel Worth and Alfred Vestal worked as antislavery missionaries in North Carolina, usually without molestation, right down to the days of John Brown's raid at Harpers Ferry in 1859. Worth, a former Quaker, had lived for a number of years in Indiana, but he decided to preach against slavery in North Carolina as an agent of the American Missionary Association. In 1858 Worth wrote the Association, "I am in constant and daily intercourse with slaveholders: sometimes I tarry a night with one, and then I always call in the slaves and pray with them and their masters; and it is worthy of remark, that in many conversations on the slavery subject, several of which have been with slaveholders, not a man has seemed to take offense; and yet I have maintained the principles of an ultra school, for I am an abolitionist of the Gerrit Smith type."[36] (Smith was a well-known Northern abolitionist who in 1859 provided financial support to John Brown and his scheme for a slave uprising in the South.) On the other hand, Worth never talked to a slave without a master's being present, and apparently he never took the risk of helping a slave to run away. That same year and the following year, Worth was bold enough to distribute more than a hundred copies of Hinton Rowan Helper's *Impending Crisis,* which he undoubtedly felt was an appropriate book for Helper's native state. Worth also felt free to accept subscriptions to Horace Greeley's antislavery New York *Tribune.*

The situation changed radically after John Brown's raid at Harpers Ferry in October, 1859. The slave South became alarmed that other insurrections were in the making. Soon thereafter Worth was arrested and convicted for circulating Helper's book. He appealed his sentence of one year in prison, but, while out on bail, left the state for good.

The sudden closing in on Worth suggests how the modern idea of a blackout on antislavery discussion in the South got started. For despite the examples of suppression throughout the antebellum years, it was always possible, at least in the upper South, to discuss the disadvantages, if not the outright evil, of slavery, as long as two conditions were met. One was that the person making the criticism be a native Southerner—not an outlander or, worse, a Northerner. The point is made neatly in a novel *The Kentuckian in New York* (1834) by Virginian William Alexander Caruthers. A

36. Clifton H. Johnson, "Abolitionist Missionary Activities in North Carolina," *North Carolina Historical Review,* XL (1963), 309.

character addresses a fellow Southerner: "You know I am no *abolitionist,* in the incendiary meaning of the term; yet I cannot deny from you and myself, that they [slaves] are an incubus upon our prosperity. This we would boldly deny, if a Yankee uttered it in our hearing; but to ourselves, we must e'en confess it." A non-fictional antislavery Southerner made the same point on the floor of Congress. In 1841, Kenneth Rayner of North Carolina admitted that even though he was a slaveholder he was no believer in the blessings of slavery; indeed, he thought slavery a misfortune. "But if it were ten times greater an evil than it is," he went on, "we will never suffer those who are uninterested in the matter to interfere with us."[37]

The second condition was that the criticism must not be made in the context of a threat to the slave system, such as during a national election in which the outcome might affect the future of slavery. The elections of 1856 and 1860 fall into these categories, since a frankly antislavery party had candidates in the field. John Brown's raid was an even stronger threat to the institution. Benjamin Hedrick, it will be remembered, was an antislavery Southerner who was hounded out of the South because of his favoring Frémont, the Republican candidate, in 1856. The upper South, at least, could tolerate criticism of its peculiar institution as long as that criticism did not appear to incite the "enemy within."

Daniel Worth, for one, was quite convinced that his success in preaching and talking against slavery for many years in the South was dependent upon his own special characteristics. He prided himself, in a letter to his nephew in 1858, on preaching "as strong and direct against slavery as ever you heard me in the north." The reasons he could do this, he said, were complex, but "are mainly my southern birth on the very spot where I preach," his age (sixty-two), which won him some reverence, his influential connections—that is, slaveholding relatives and popular personages—and his widespread acquaintance in the area.[38]

37. William Alexander Caruthers, *The Kentuckian in New York* (Ridgewood, N.J., 1968, reprint of 1834 ed.), I, 76–77; Clement Eaton, *Freedom of Thought in the Old South* (Durham, N.C., 1940), p. 267.
38. Noble J. Tolbert, "Daniel Worth: Tar Heel Abolitionist," *North Carolina Historical Review,* XXXIX (1962), 290.

A TIMID ANTISLAVERY

It comes as no revelation to observe at this point that the Southern opponents of slavery and their arguments were generally conservative and cautious. They did not rest upon a very strong belief in the potentiality of the Negro; on the whole the antislavery argument in the South was dominated by a concern for white men and their prosperity. When Jesse Burton Harrison undertook to answer Thomas Dew's contention that colonization was no way to end slavery, he began by assuring his readers that "there is not the slightest moral turpitude in holding slaves under existing conditions in the South. We *know* too that the ordinary condition of slaves in Virginia is *not* such as to make humanity weep for his [*sic*] lot. Our solicitations . . . are founded but little on the *miseries of the blacks*. We direct ourselves almost exclusively to the injuries slavery inflicts on the whites."[39] And, when slavery was done away with, those Southerners contended, it would be accompanied by the removal of the free blacks. Most of these white Southerners—though not all, it should be said—were not interested in radically altering society, certainly not in changing the traditional relations between the races. Patricia Hickin in her study of Virginia antislavery observes that of all the native Virginians who professed opposition to slavery, Samuel Janney was unique in his willingness to speak of emancipation without removal. Daniel Goodloe of North Carolina was another. Even clergymen who opposed slavery were never prepared to make slaveholding a matter of church discipline, as the Quakers did. Antislavery attitudes in the South, in short, were limited in outlook or ideology as well as in extent.

To draw such a conclusion is but to observe that Southerners— even when they were antislavery—differed from Northerners. Among the Southern antislavery people there was no William Lloyd Garrison or Lydia Maria Child, though there certainly were some who expressed concern for blacks as well as whites in the slave South. On the whole, however, antislavery in the South has

39. Harrison, *Review of the Slave Question*, p. 9.

that realistic, down-to-earth, particularistic, even personal quality that distinguishes Southerners in general from Northerners. To believe in the potentiality of Negroes when they were known only as slaves required a great deal of idealism and of imagination, for the everyday life of the slave seemed to deny that blacks could be like free white people. In the culture of the antebellum South there was little to encourage that belief in perfectibility and potentiality upon which the Northern abolitionists drew. Southerners generally had little use for theorizing or speculating about what might be; it was the here and now that concerned them and has ever since. It is not accidental that there were no Transcendentalists in the antebellum South.

The contention that the nature of the Southern antislavery thought also revealed the difference between Northerners and Southerners is borne out, too, by the background of many of the antislavery Southerners. The number of them who had some first-hand contact with the North is suggestive. Cassius M. Clay attended Yale, Benjamin Hedrick and Jesse B. Harrison were educated at Harvard, and Charles Fenton Mercer and E. W. Caruthers were graduated from Princeton. John Fee, the Kentucky abolitionist, was educated at Miami University and Lane Seminary in Ohio. Daniel Worth, although a native Southerner, spent his formative years in Indiana, where he became a minister before returning to the South to preach his antislavery principles. That it required exposure outside the South to bring Southerners to an antislavery stance suggests again that Southerners lacked that idealistic, reform imagination necessary to press against slavery on their own. The conservative character of the antebellum South is illustrated, in short, not only by the small number of the region's antislavery advocates, but also by the narrow conception of its antislavery ideology and by its dependence on outside influence.

POTENTIAL BETRAYERS OF SLAVERY

On the face of it, in a society in which most men did not own slaves, but in which all adult white males could vote and hold office, one would expect some conflict between slaveholders and nonslaveholders. As James McDowell said during the Virginia

Debates, "the slaveholding interest of the country, will and can coalesce with no other interest and must, as a consequence, be separate and hostile to all others. . . ." During the debates other antislavery members were even more explicit in referring to class conflicts over slavery. The nonslaveholders, one speaker pointed out, provided the force to maintain the system. "In the character of PATROLS, they are made to perform onerous and disagreeable duties—not to protect themselves and their property, but to protect the slaveholder in the enjoyment of that which it is the interest of non-slaveholders should not exist. He is thus made to fold to his own bosom and protect the adder which stings him." Thomas Jefferson Randolph, a slaveholder himself, could not help but notice the irony. Who paid for the maintenance of the system? he asked. The burden falls "not upon the lordly masters of their hundred slaves, who will never turn out except to retire with their families when danger threatens. No, Sir, it is to fall upon the less wealthy class of our citizens; chiefly upon the non-slaveholders. I have known patrols turned out when there was not a slaveholder among them. . . . I have slept in times of alarm quietly in bed without having a thought of care, while these individuals owning none of this property themselves, were patrolling under a compulsory process, for a pittance of seventy-five cents per twelve hours, the very curtilage of my house and guarding that property, which was alike dangerous to them and myself. . . ." Those who had to patrol had a natural objection, too, as the petition of twenty-two citizens of Henrico County, Virginia, in 1836 revealed. The petition asked for the end of slavery because it encouraged idleness and "the disagreeable hoars [sic] of knight [sic] watch we have to labor under besides the awful frights our companions undergo. . . ."[40]

Cassius Clay's efforts in the 1840's to end slavery in Kentucky were based upon this same assumption of a natural antagonism. For example, in an article in the *True American* in 1845 he noted that printers refer to those who work at less than the usual rates as "rats." Well, using that terminology, he said, the slaveholders have

40. Robert, *Road from Monticello*, pp. 103, 86, 97; James Hugo Johnston, "Antislavery Petitions Presented to the Virginia Legislature by Citizens of Various Countries," *Journal of Negro History*, XII (1927), 671.

"ratted us" with their 180,000 slaves. "They have *ratted* us till we are unable to supply ourselves with the ordinary comforts of a laborer's life. They have *ratted* us out of the social circle. They have *ratted* us out of the means of making our own schools. . . . They have *ratted* us out of the press. They have *ratted* us out of the legislature. They have *ratted* us out of *all the offices of honor and profit.*" To add insult to injury, he noted at another time, the slaveholders refer to the nonslaveholders as "white negroes" and "tame Indians." "How much longer will slaveholders add insult to their other crimes against us?" he wanted to know.

Clay's deliberate and persistent effort to drive a wedge between the slaveholding and nonslaveholding classes was echoed, too, by Hinton Rowan Helper in his *Impending Crisis*. Like Clay he played upon the dominance of the slaveholders in places of power and prestige. "Nonslaveholders of the South: farmers, mechanics, and workingmen, we . . . assure you that the slaveholders, the arrogant demagogues whom you have elected to offices of honor and profit, have hoodwinked you, trifled with you, and used you as mere tools for the consummation of their wicked designs. They have purposely kept you in ignorance, and have, by moulding your passions and prejudices to suit themselves, induced you to act in direct opposition to your dearest rights and interests."[41] And Helper was only the most vociferous of still other antislavery Southerners who voiced the conflict between slaveholders and those who held no slaves.

Yet what is most significant in the literature and history of Southern antislavery is the small part class hostility plays in sparking antislavery statements or actions. Historians are prone to point to Helper as spokesman of the nonslaveholder, but the fact is that Helper's origins are almost unique among those of the two dozen or so well-known antislavery advocates one can point to in the South. A much more common pattern was for the antislavery advocate to be a slaveholder or to come from the slaveholding class. Certainly this was true of Robert Breckinridge, Cassius Clay, and Henry Clay of Kentucky, as it was of Thomas Jefferson Randolph, Henry Ruffner, and Mary Blackford of Virginia and

41. Greeley, ed., *Works of C. M. Clay,* pp. 268, 404; Helper, *Impending Crisis,* p. 120.

William Gaston of North Carolina. In fact exactly half of the fifty-eight men in the Virginia House of Deputies in 1832 who voted to have the legislature move ahead toward emancipation were slaveholders. Moreover, at the convention of emancipationists held in Frankfort, Kentucky, prior to the constitutional convention of 1849, three-quarters of those who attended were slaveholders. The point is not to emphasize the liberalism of slaveholders or even to call attention to their possible guilt over the institution, a feeling that cannot be established by such a small and unrepresentative sample in any event. Rather it is to notice that despite whatever class antagonisms might seem to have been justified regarding slavery, the fact of the matter is that few nonslaveholders complained about the institution. Put another way, the slaveholders, given their minority status in the society, were greatly overrepresented among the antislavery men. Evidence in the same direction is also provided by recalling that antislavery Southerners who left the South, like James Birney, Angelina and Sarah Grimké, and Edward Coles of Virginia, who became the antislavery governor of Illinois, were all from the slaveholding class, too.

Nor can the lack of nonslaveholders among the leaders of antislavery in the South be explained simply by referring to the fact that nonslaveholders, as a class, lacked the wealth or education necessary to become leaders or spokesmen against slavery. For when nonslaveholders had opportunities to oppose slavery without reference to wealth or education—as in the vote in Kentucky in 1849—they refused to do so, though the issue had been discussed openly, and the adult males possessed the ballot to record their views. Cassius Clay's whole compaign against slavery was predicated on the fact that nonslaveholders outnumbered slaveholders by six to one and that servile insurrection was effectively ruled out by the additional fact that slaves were outnumbered nine to one. But despite his hope and his considerable efforts he could not convince the mass of nonslaveholders that on the question of black bondage they had a significantly different interest from that of the slaveholders. If class hostility toward slave owners by nonslaveholders could not catch fire in Kentucky, then it was weak and undeveloped indeed.

Some recent writers on the proslavery argument in the South

have contended that the published defenses of slavery, though ostensibly directed to Northerners, were really directed to the nonslaveholders of the South. That interpretation may well be accurate, for in the middle of the nineteenth century slavery was increasingly a social and political anomaly. Only Cuba and Brazil, outside of the United States, still retained the institution in the New World. Those who did not have a direct stake in slavery might well have turned against the anachronistic institution. But whatever the motivation behind the proslavery argument, there is really no reason to believe that it was necessary insofar as the nonslaveholders were concerned. When contemporary Southern publicists like James D. B. De Bow or David Hundley asserted that the yeoman farmers saw no conflict of interests with the slaveholder they were right. Perhaps a conflict ought to have been there, as slaveholders themselves occasionally pointed out, but one thing that the nature of the antislavery argument and the character of the proponents of that argument reveal is that few nonslaveholders actually saw in the society or felt within themselves that supposedly obvious conflict of interest.

Also striking among antislavery Southerners is the high proportion of Whigs. Henry and Cassius Clay were Whigs, of course, and so were Robert Breckinridge, Daniel Goodloe, John Pleasants, and William Gaston. On a broader level, Patricia Hickin has concluded from her study of antislavery Virginians that Whigs, in both the eastern and the western parts of the states, were "less wedded to slavery" than Democrats. For example, a Whig organ, the Lexington *Gazette,* republished in its columns Ruffner's antislavery *Address* of 1847, and the Richmond *Whig* published the antislavery writings of Samuel Janney and others. That such sentiments appeared in Whig newspapers suggests that at least many of the party faithful were not hostile to such ideas. At the convention of emancipationists held in Frankfort, Kentucky, in 1849, the great majority of delegates were Whigs.

The association between Whiggery and antislavery in the South reinforces an earlier observation about the character of antislavery Southerners. The party most often associated then and now with the planters—the so-called aristocratic party—was also the party that contributed a disproportionate number of antislavery leaders in the South. If the Democratic party is taken, in a general way, as the party of the common man—which statistically must be the nonslaveholder—then we have another reason for believing that nonslaveholders apparently did not see a serious conflict of interest with slaveholders. By the late 1850's, after all, it was the Democratic party that became the great defender of slavery and the interests of a slave South.

That opponents of slavery in the South should more often than not be Whigs is not so surprising once the class explanation for antislavery is abandoned. The Whig party, after all, both nationally and regionally stood for economic development. Henry Clay's so-called American Plan for a tariff, a national bank, and internal improvements was intended for just that purpose. Constitutionally and politically the Whig party was also more nationalistic than the Democratic party. As we shall see in the next chapter it was more favorable to Southern Unionism as well as to antislavery than the Democratic party. The cause of economic development was central to the ideology of Southern antislavery. It is therefore quite natural that Whigs should be antislavery and that antislavery advocates should be Whigs. The two were mutually supportive. It was considerably less dangerous to be a Whig than an antislavery man in the South, but it is conceivable that a man's Whig principles would make him susceptible to antislavery arguments. Undoubtedly a man's antislavery sentiments, from whatever source they were derived, would incline him to being a Whig. Certainly the Democratic party provided a poor haven for those who had doubts about slavery.

By logic and fact, both Whiggery and antislavery predisposed Southerners to a nationalist view. Whiggery did so by its principles of economic development; antislavery did so through its demand that the labor system of the South be made over in the image of the North's. It is not surprising, therefore, that many Whigs and antislavery people were also opponents of secession. But not all those who opposed secession were opposed to slavery or were even Whigs. Hence if we seek to understand the nature of dissent in the antebellum South we must now turn to those Southerners who opposed secession and supported the Union.

BOOK

II

SOUTHERNERS
FOR THE UNION

4

"The Union Now and Forever"

As a region, the South had never been antislavery however incisive or well known some of its antislavery advocates had been. The situation was quite different with that other great dissenting cause of the antebellum years—the opposition to secession. Although there is no way of measuring the degree or even the extent of Unionism among Southerners in the early nineteenth century, it is not unreasonable to argue that in the era of Jefferson and Madison, the Southern people as a whole were Unionist. A large part of this question of loyalty depends upon definition, to be sure. But if one means by "Unionist" that the South perceived no sharp division between its sectional interests and future and those of the nation, then the generalization is quite true. Those were the years, after all, when Southerners occupied the White House almost without interruption and Congress was dominated by the South. In these same years Southerner Thomas Jefferson doubled the size of the Republic with his purchase of Louisiana, and Southerners eagerly supported the unprecedented act. Madison, another Virginian, led the nation into a war, which, whatever its unpopularity in New England may have done to Unionist sentiment there, did not cause a rift between the South and the nation. In the years immediately after the War of 1812, Southerners were among the leaders of national consciousness, as they had been in the famous Twelfth Congress, which had declared war on Great Britain because it threatened the national honor on the high seas. Henry Clay of Kentucky and John C. Calhoun of South Carolina were only the best-known of the War Hawks, who continued to be nationalists after the war. As late as 1817 Calhoun was deploring those New Englanders and other disunionists who treated the Constitution as a lawyer's document to be construed narrowly where the powers of the federal government were concerned.

In the broadest view, then, the history of Union sentiment in the South is quite unlike the story of Southern antislavery. The South began as a Unionist section and gradually lost its commitment until that fateful moment when it forsook the Union completely. Another way of saying the same thing is that the Unionism of one era is not always equal to the stresses of another. Yet always in the South there were those whose Unionism was unqualified, even when tested against loyalty to region; these Southerners would not be revealed—often not even to themselves—until the Civil War, when a final and painful choice in loyalties had to be made. Although eleven states of the South eventually repudiated the Union, it is worth recalling that the shift from the Unionism of Thomas Jefferson to the Secessionism of Jefferson Davis required a half-century. Furthermore, as we shall see, as late as 1861 it was not at all clear that the majority of Southerners, even then, were ready to repudiate the Union and opt for the Confederacy.

In the course of that half-century there were three great tests of Southern Unionism. The first was during the nullification crisis of 1832, the second was at the time of the so-called Compromise of 1850, and the third and most searching was during the secession winter and spring of 1860–61.

SOUTH CAROLINA AGAINST THE SOUTH

The first test came as a result of a decade of mounting dissatisfaction in the state of South Carolina with various policies of the federal government in the course of the 1820's. The ostensible cause that propelled the Palmetto State into "calculating the value of the Union," as President Thomas Cooper of South Carolina College advised, was the growing Northern demand for a protective tariff. Since the publication in 1965 of William Freehling's

Prelude to Civil War, however, historians no longer accept at face value the nullifiers' insistence that the tariff was their primary concern. Behind the hostility to the tariff lay the deeper fear, as John Randolph of Roanoke warned, that the constitutional power that permitted Congress to enact a protective tariff could also be used to free the slaves. The motives of the men who led South Carolina in its nullification of the Tariff of 1832 are obviously more complex than Randolph's remark might suggest, but the fact is that the continuity between nullification in 1832, disunionist efforts in 1850, and secession in 1860–61 is established by more than a common constitutional interpretation of the Constitution. All three movements were linked by the desire to protect the South's "peculiar institution," slavery. But it is not the cause of South Carolina's nullification of the tariff in 1832 that concerns us here so much as the reaction of those Southerners who could not accept an abrogation of the Union.

When South Carolinians, meeting in convention in 1832, voted to nullify the tariff, the Unionists within the state who had fought hard to prevent that decision did not cease their opposition. Joel Poinsett, James L. Petigru, Daniel Huger, and Hugh S. Legaré of Charleston and the low country, and Benjamin F. Perry of the upcountry continued their uncompromising attacks on the doctrine and the practical effects of nullification and secession. But the most influential native South Carolinian in the nullification crisis to uphold the Union was the President of the United States, Andrew Jackson. In his public message to the citizens of South Carolina, Jackson shrewdly invoked that nativity. "Fellow citizens of my native State, let me not only admonish you as the First Magistrate of our common country, not to incure the penalty of its laws, but use the influence that a father would over his children whom he saw rushing to certain ruin." He then appealed to their patriotism, asking them to recall that "we too are citizens of America. Carolina is one of these proud States; her arms have defended, her best blood has cemented, this happy Union."

On a more practical level Jackson was in close and almost constant communication with the Unionist leaders in Charleston and elsewhere in the state. From the outset Joel Poinsett, an upcountry man who by then was an established lawyer in Charleston, prodded Jackson to support the Unionists in South Carolina. In November, 1832, he told Jackson that some friends were advocating that South Carolina be permitted to "go out of the Union if she will go." But Poinsett was adamantly against that. "If such a course should be opted," he wrote the President, "the union must be dissolved in all its parts and foreign and domestic wars necessarily ensue." But if the rebellion is stopped, he continued, "the union will be cemented by their conduct and by the vigour of the government, and you will earn the imperishable glory of having preserved this great confederacy from destruction." Because the President moved too cautiously for him, Poinsett in mid-January was asking for federal military forces to support the Unionists on the spot. "Some of us never will submit to the tyranny and oppression of these arrogant and presumptuous men," he wrote, "but we shall have to contend against fearfull [*sic*] odds, if the federal government folds its arms and looks on without taking part in the contact."[1]

Jackson had not been idle. He asked for and received from Congress authorization to use the army in carrying out the tariff law, though he cautiously arranged things in such a manner that the nullifiers would have to attack deliberately the U.S. Customs ships or officers if they would carry out their decision to refuse to obey the law. Simultaneously, Jackson worked with another Southern Unionist, Henry Clay of Kentucky, to have the tariff reduced, thus providing an opportunity for the outgunned and outnumbered nullifiers to recede from their exposed position with some dignity.

Less physically powerful but no less intellectually committed in his opposition to nullification was the aged former President James Madison of Virginia. In an important sense, Madison was heavily, if reluctantly, involved in the controversy over nullification, since the Kentucky and Virginia Resolutions, which Jefferson and he had published in 1798, were important intellectual supports of the nullification doctrines, especially as propounded by John C. Cal-

1. William W. Freehling, ed., *The Nullification Era: A Documentary Record* (New York, 1967), pp. 161–62; Joel Poinsett to Andrew Jackson, Nov. 24, 1832; Poinsett to Jackson, Jan. 16, 1833, copies in Charles Chandler Papers. The indispensable work on Poinsett is J. Fred Rippy, *Joel R. Poinsett: Versatile American* (Durham, N.C., 1935), which I have used.

houn. The Kentucky and Virginia Resolutions against the Alien and Sedition laws had advanced a states' rights position that stopped just short of actual nullification, but which the impetuous logic of Calhoun had subsequently transmuted into full support. In Madison's mind, his own Virginia Resolutions, whatever might have been said about Jefferson's Kentucky Resolutions, had never asserted the right of a single state to nullify a national law. Calhoun's frequent reference to the support he found in the writings of '98 was a source of embarrassment to Madison, as his correspondence in the early 1830's makes clear.

Madison was also brought into the nullification controversy, despite his advanced age—he was eighty-one in 1832—because of his central role in the writing of the Constitution. Known even in his own lifetime as the "Father of the Constitution," Madison was importuned to expound the document which Calhoun and the other nullifiers construed as a compact, an interpretation that meant a sovereign state was capable of abandoning the Union any time its interests would be served. Not only did Madison deny that the resolutions of 1798 carried any such intent, but he went on to say that a doctrine which permitted a state to overrule a majority "would overturn the first principle of free government and in practice necessarily overturn the government itself." Madison's Unionism was only a little less emotional than Jackson's. The idea that a constitution and government, which have been so "fruitful of blessings," should be "broken up and scattered to the wind without greater than any existing causes is more painful than words can express," he wrote to a friend. Always faithful to the idea that the majority could be counted on to know its own interest, he could understand the popular acceptance of such an idea only by thinking that the people had been deliberately misled. "It is impossible that this can ever be the deliberate act of the people, if the value of the Union be calculated by the consequences of disunion."[2]

From the viewpoint of power, the reactions of the other Southern state legislatures to South Carolina's nullification were undoubtedly more important than Madison's and probably as important as Jackson's. In 1860, when South Carolina seceded, it

2. *Writings of James Madison,* ed. by Gaillard Hunt (New York, 1900–10), IX, 399, 480.

was soon followed by other states, but in 1832, when it nullified an act of the national government, no other Southern state emulated its example. In fact, all of the Southern states denounced, with varying intensity, the very theory on which nullification rested. Virginia's resolution of February 8, 1833, was the mildest. It proclaimed itself friendly to South Carolina, but it "earnestly and respectfully requested and entreated" that state to rescind its action. It went on to say that Virginia still believed in states' rights "as set forth in the Resolutions of 1798," but that they were not considered as "sanctioning the proceedings of South Carolina." More forthright were the reactions of North Carolina's legislature. It proclaimed nullification "revolutionary in its character, subversive of the Constitution of the United States and [leading] to a dissolution of the Union." South Carolina's southern neighbor, Georgia, was no less hostile: "We abhor the doctrine of Nullification as neither peaceful, nor a constitutional remedy, but, on the contrary, as tending to civil commotion and disunion; and while we deplore the rash and revolutionary measures, recently adopted by a Convention of the people of South Carolina, we deem it a paramount duty to warn our fellow citizens against the danger of adopting her mischievous policy."

Freighted with greater significance, as well as providing some of the strongest statements against nullification, were the reactions of Alabama and Mississippi. States of the deep South, they were already heavily committed to cotton, slavery, and the plantation. In fact, black slaves already constituted 48 percent of the total population in Mississippi and 40 percent in Alabama. Both states admitted in their responses that the tariff was bad for the agricultural South in general, just as it was bad for South Carolina in particular. But, as the Alabama legislature phrased it, "nullification . . . is unsound in theory and dangerous in practice . . . as a remedy it is unconstitutional and essentially revolutionary, leading in its consequences to anarchy and civil discord, and finally to the dissolution of the Union." Mississippi was equally hostile. The legislature proclaimed itself as not wanting to be associated with the "disorganizing doctrines recently promulgated in South Carolina. . . . We are opposed to nullification. We regard it as a heresy, fatal to the existence of the Union." The legislature therefore resolved that the "doctrine of Nullification is contrary to the letter and spirit of the Constitution, and in direct conflict with the welfare, safety and independence of every State in the Union; and to no one of them would its consequences be more deeply disastrous, more ruinous than to the State of Mississippi. . . ."[3]

Between the steady pressure exerted by its native son in the White House and its isolation in the South, South Carolina had little recourse but to rescind its ordinance of nullification. The compromise reduction in the tariff provided the necessary concession to justify the retreat.

In the crisis of nullification the vast majority of Southerners were clearly Unionist. The decade of the 1820's may have transformed South Carolina into a stronghold of anti-Unionists, but it had not produced that effect in the South as a whole. The first test of Southern Unionism found the majority more than adequate. The disunionists, however, had learned a lesson they would not forget: do not act without support in the rest of the South. From 1833 to 1861, South Carolinians and other Southerners who feared the effects upon their society of a too powerful Union would seek to build support across the South in order to avoid a repetition of the humiliating retreat of South Carolina in February, 1833. For the victory of Unionism converted few nullifiers to Unionism; it simply frustrated their determination to free themselves from federal control.

THE UNIONISM OF SOUTHERN WHIGS

The second great test of Southern Unionism did not come for almost a generation. When it came in 1850 many things had changed. Madison was long since dead, as was that other great Southern Unionist, Andrew Jackson. Calhoun, the author of nullification, still lived, but he would be dead before the test would be concluded. Clay, still opposed to Calhoun on the question of the Union, as he was on slavery, would participate in the settlement of 1850. But he, too, would be dead within another year.

3. The replies of the Southern states can be found conveniently in Herman V. Ames, ed., *State Documents on Federal Relations: The States and the United States* (Philadelphia, 1902).

The significantly new element in the constellation of forces in 1850, as compared with 1832, was the Whig party. There is no need here to go into the origins or history of that party other than to observe that it began in 1833–34 as a response to the charisma and authority of Andrew Jackson, especially in regard to the Bank of the United States. The Whigs proclaimed their hostility to the excessive authority of Jackson, but in practice they were more a party of national authority than was Jackson's own democracy. For the fact was that on certain national issues, such as the Bank of the United States, internal improvements, and the tariff, Jackson was hardly a nationalist. Since, at least in its inception, the Whig party derived its main principles by reversing Jackson's, the party attracted supporters of a nationalist cast of mind on economic affairs. Probably the greatest of all Whigs—certainly the greatest of Southern Whigs—was Henry Clay. It was Clay, with his American Plan of Bank, tariff, and internal improvements, that infused the Whig party with economic nationalism. Significantly, it was Henry Clay who worked out the compromise tariff in 1833 that helped to settle the nullification crisis, and it was Clay who would be in the forefront in fashioning the Compromise of 1850. Clay's nationalism, like his antislavery view, was neither strident nor insistent, but it was reliable. His Whig party, as we shall see, provided a shelter as well as a vehicle for Southern Unionists in the crisis of 1850, and even after the party was no longer fielding candidates its influence in behalf of Unionism was still to be felt. Ironically, it was the party's very Unionism that would bring down the party in the South when the slavery controversy whipped up the winds of disunion to hurricane strength.

The sources of the crisis that resulted in the Compromise of 1850 need only be touched on for our purposes. As a result of the territorial acquisitions from the war with Mexico (1846–48), slavery in the new territories became a burning national question. Over the years the Southern states had become increasingly prone to identify their future with the institution of slavery, especially as cotton cultivation became the primary economic activity of the states of the deep South. Thus when certain Northerners sought to prevent the movement of slaves into the new territories, Southern politicians and publicists took this to be not only a denial of the

Southern right to take their property into what was called the common territory of the Union, but also an attack upon the central or peculiar institution of the South itself. The issue came to a head in 1850 when the newly acquired territory of California petitioned for admission as a state from which slavery would be barred. Should California be accepted as a free state? What would be the future of the remainder of the western territories, which stretched between the Rockies and the Pacific coast? Northern antislavery men and women insisted that all of it must be free of slavery, while Southern defenders of slavery insisted it must be open to slavery, for had not the whole area been acquired by a war waged in common by all Americans, from all sections? Southerners were also keenly aware that the Mexican war had not been popular in New England, where so many of the abolitionists and antislavery people lived, while the vast majority of volunteers, who had won the war against Mexico, were from the South and the West.

When Congress met in December, 1849, Southern rights men, led by the already dying, but indefatigable John C. Calhoun, worked to line up Southern congressmen to vote against any limit on slavery in the territories. Calhoun and other extremists among the group were bold enough to suggest acts of disunion if such should prove necessary to protect the South's peculiar institution. By the time the great debate began which resulted in the famous Compromise of 1850, the threat of secession had been heard many times. Not until the summer of 1850 was the exhausted Senate able to hammer out the various measures that made up the final Compromise. And even when the agreement between the sections was accepted by President Millard Fillmore, it was not at all clear that the Southern people would accept the work of their representatives. The Compromise was put to a popular test in the elections of 1850 and 1851 when candidates in the South ran for office on their views of the Compromise. Throughout the South the Whig party accepted the terms of the Compromise, if only because the great Southern Whig, Henry Clay, had been so influential in their formulation, even if Democrat Stephen A. Douglas had been indispensable for their final passage. The Compromise measures also enjoyed the support of the Whig national administration. But the principal reason the Whig party in the South carried the fight for the compromise was that the Whigs were the closest thing to a party of Unionism in the region.

Historians have not been in agreement as to the social basis of the Whig party of the South, however much they may be in agreement on its chief principles. Given its doctrines and the general conservative tone that pervaded the rhetoric of its leaders, the party has often been spoken of as the party of the rich and the well born. Efforts to be more precise and to show a statistical correlation between sociological background and party leaderships have been neither rewarding nor convincing. At least two historians, for example, have correlated the social background of Whigs and of Democrats in the Alabama legislature to test whether the two parties differed significantly in social character.[4] The results show the Whigs to be a little wealthier and a little more business-oriented than the Democrats, but the contrast is hardly significant. The fact of the matter is that most leaders of American political parties tend to come from the same middle and upper classes, and so, if the social background of leaders is examined, the differences between parties does not show up as significant.

If instead one examines voting patterns across the South, the coincidence of Whig majorities in certain states with counties where slaves were concentrated is striking. And counties with 50 percent or more slaves can be taken as wealthy counties. This correspondence between Whig voting and wealth is especially noticeable in the counties along the Mississippi River in Mississippi, Arkansas, and Louisiana. The heavily slave counties of central Georgia, south central Alabama (Black Belt), and the Louisiana sugar delta also produced Whig majorities in the 1840's. This kind of evidence, which was first advanced in Arthur Cole's *Whig Party of the South* more than half a century ago, has been one of the principal reasons for identifying the Whig party as the organization of the great planters and their clients.

A moment's reflection, of course, reminds us that no party in a society in which universal white male suffrage prevailed could win

4. Grady McWhiney, "Were the Whigs a Class Party in Alabama?" *Journal of Southern History,* XXIII (1957), 510–22; Thomas B. Alexander, et al., "The Basis of Alabama's Ante-bellum Two-Party System," *Alabama Review,* XIX (Oct., 1966), 243–76.

anything but local elections from such a narrow social base. And the Whig party was often a statewide winner in the South before 1852. As one might expect from the Whig position on banking and credit, the Whigs made strong showings, too, in the cities of the South. The South, to be sure, was the most rural region of the nation—as it still is today. Cities were small and few in number. Arkansas did not have a city of 2,500 in 1850; Mississippi had only two, and neither of them reached 5,000. Indiana and Illinois, which came into the Union at the same time as Alabama and Mississippi, counted in 1850 more cities over 3,000 than all nine states south of Virginia and Kentucky. The urban vote, in short, was not large in the antebellum South, but what there was of it tended to be more Whiggish than Democratic. According to the census of 1850, in the South there were twenty-three cities of 2,500 population or more (today's census definition of a city). In the presidential elections of 1844 and 1848 these twenty-three cities voted Whig 65 percent of the possible votings. Seventy-seven percent of the cities voted for Whigs either in 1844 or in 1848.

Perusal of election maps for the 1840's reveals a more numerically significant source of Whig voting than the planters, cotton factors, storekeepers, and urban dwellers. Whig strength was particularly noticeable in eastern Tennessee, western North Carolina, western Virginia, and in Kentucky. Whigs, in short, were well represented in the backcountry of Appalachia. Indeed, most counties in the mountainous regions of North Carolina and Tennessee were Whig in every national election during the 1840's, the heyday of the Whig party. One can easily understand that planters, cotton factors, and storekeepers, with their interest in banks, internal improvements, trade, and property, would be Whigs; it is not easy, however, to explain why mountain men, without slaves or other property and little interest in banks, paper money, or the protection of property, would be Whigs. Sometimes, as in Kentucky, the charisma of Henry Clay might be a large part of the explanation, but that would not account for Tennessee, where the popular Andrew Jackson was a Democrat, or for North Carolina, where the Whig leaders were lackluster personalities, and hardly charismatic. One suspects the chief appeal of the Whig party to small farmers was state sectionalism, rather than issues. Since the slaveholding regions in these states were strongly Democratic, the small farmers who felt they were being ignored because they were not slaveholders or cotton planters would naturally gravitate to the opposition party. Whatever the explanation, the Whigs in the South on the eve of the Compromise of 1850 were a diverse group, socially. They could hardly be called the party of the slaveholders, for though many slaveholders were Whigs, the party counted many more nonslaveholders among its adherents, especially in the upper South.

The diversity of the social character of the Whigs suggests that the old historiographical debate over which was the party of wealth and which the party of the small farmer may be irrelevant when talking about the region or the nation. More important is to notice the continuity of Whiggish voting with Unionism. For whatever reason, Southern Whigs were more Unionist than Democrats. In the next chapter we shall have an opportunity to examine some statistical evidence of this correlation between Whigs and Unionism, but for the moment let us look at another kind of evidence to suggest a correlation between Whiggery and Unionism.

ROUND NUMBER TWO

One measure of that correspondence is the important role that the Whigs played in having the Compromise of 1850 accepted in the South. Although party labels often became irrelevant as Unionism and Southern rights became the important divisions between candidates, the Whigs were prominent among the defenders of the Compromise and the Union, especially in Georgia, Alabama, and Louisiana. In Georgia, for example, Alexander Stephens and Robert Toombs, two prominent Whigs, made a concerted effort to have their state support Howell Cobb, a Democrat, who was running for governor on a platform of support for the Compromise. Cobb, in fact, said in August, 1851, that he did not believe that the right of secession existed at all. To believe such a doctrine, he contended, "we are called upon to admit that the framers of the Constitution did that which was never done by any other people possessed of their good sense and intelligence—*that is to provide in the organization of the government for its own dissolution.* It seems to me that such a course would not only have been an anomalous proceeding, but wholly inconsistent with the wisdom and sound judgment which marked the deliberations of those wise and good men who framed our Federal Government." Like the conservatives they were, the Unionists in the South of 1851 were not about to debate abstractions. As Alexander Stephens advised Cobb earlier that summer: "Treat the right of secession as an abstract question. It is but a right to change the Government, a right of revolution, and maintain that no just cause for the exercise of such rights exists. And keep the main point prominent that the only question now is whether we should go into revolution or not. South Carolina is for it. This is the point to keep prominent," he emphasized.[5] By making secession equivalent to revolution Stephens hoped to hold in line conservatives, who naturally feared change or what he called "revolution."

The strategy and Unionism of Stephens and Cobb won handily in Georgia; Cobb received 56,000 votes to his opponents' 37,000. The legislature also went strongly Unionist, with 101 members of the House classified as Unionist and only 26 as Southern rights men. Alabama by then had already shown its support of the Union in its election of five Unionist congressmen to only two Southern rights men. The prosecessionists had never even nominated a candidate for governor, so popular was the Compromise in the state. The Southern rights men had great expectations for Mississippi, even if Georgia and Alabama could not be relied upon. But in that state, too, Unionist Senator Henry S. Foote, while a Democrat, put on a whirlwind campaign in behalf of the Compromise and his own election as governor. Although pilloried and denounced for allegedly betraying his region for supporting the Compromise measures in the Senate, Foote and the other Unionists carried the state. Foote himself defeated Jefferson Davis, the leading Southern rights Democrat in the state. In the election to the convention that would have considered secession, the Union ticket won by more than 7,000 votes out of 50,000 cast.

5. Ulrich Bonnell Phillips, ed., "The Correspondence of Robert Toombs, Alexander H. Stephens, and Howell Cobb," in *Annual Report of the American Historical Association for the Year 1911* (Washington, D.C., 1913), pp. 251, 238.

Even in secession-minded South Carolina, the Unionists showed remarkable strength. Joel Poinsett, now an old man of seventy-one, but as staunch a Unionist as he had been in nullification days, wrote a powerful public letter in November, 1850, to his fellow Carolinians. Once again he refuted the pretensions of secession and denied the existence under the Constitution of any right of secession. Calling upon his long years as a diplomat in Latin America, he warned that to disrupt the Union every time there was a conflict between the sections would soon cause the United States to "exhibit the miserable aspect of the Spanish American States." Moreover, he pointed out, the European powers would hardly be sympathetic to slavery as a cause for disruption. And as for South Carolina's seceding by itself, he thought that would be like throwing oneself "from a precipice in the expectation of injuring his enemy by the fall."

Other old stalwarts from nullification days, like James Petigru and Benjamin Perry, were also active, but the Unionists this time also enjoyed the support of men like James Chesnut, Robert Barnwell, and James Hammond, who were cooperationists rather than strict unionists. They opposed unilateral secession—having learned the lesson of 1833—and so joined with the Unionists to defeat the secessionists in the elections to the state convention. The secessionists lost in South Carolina itself by almost 8,000 votes out of 43,000 cast. The Unionists, of course, acknowledged the limited character of the cooperationists' loyalty to the Union. For, as Petigru wrote Poinsett soon after the election, the "opposition to disunion had been made under the cover of the same principles that the secession people profess. . . . But the co-operationists . . . with the Union men have taken the state from Rhett [a leading fire-eater] and broken as I think the spell that Calhoun left."[6]

In 1851 *Harper's Weekly* totaled up the vote in South Carolina, Georgia, Mississippi, and Alabama in order to measure the Unionist strength in the strongholds of cotton and slavery. The vote in the four states for secessionists was 111,000 as compared to 151,000 for their opponents.

6. Rippy, *Poinsett*, pp. 240–42.

In the remainder of the South, Unionism was never in doubt. Louisiana's Whig-dominated lower house prevented the Democratic senate from even naming delegates to the disunionist Nashville Convention. In that state there simply were few prominent politicians who were identified at all with secession. In the upper South, Unionists were victorious in all states. The Virginia legislature passed a resolution in April, 1851, announcing itself "unwilling to take any action . . . calculated to destroy the integrity of this Union." It passed with only one vote in opposition. As one Whig-Unionist in North Carolina summed up the sentiment of his state after the election of August, 1851: "I do not believe there is in this county, Hereford, a sympathiser with South Carolina in her present position in regard to seceding from the Union. Every man here and I may, I think, say throughout the State, is a Union man with perhaps one or two mad exceptions. . . ."[7]

Clearly it was the Unionism of the vast majority of Southerners that prevented a breakup of the Union in 1850–51, especially those in the crucial states of South Carolina, Georgia, Alabama, and Mississippi. The price of the Unionist victory, however, was high. Ironic as it may sound, the Whig party was destroyed in the South and the nation because of its great success. In state after state, the fight over the Compromise and secession strained, beyond the breaking point, the cohesion of the Whigs as a national party. For the fact was that in the North the Whig party was being increasingly identified with antislavery sentiment. Daniel Webster might eloquently contend that there was no reason to prohibit slavery in the western territories because the soil and climate were not suitable to plantation agriculture and slavery. But there was now a new generation of Northern Whig leaders, men like Joshua Giddings of Ohio, William Seward of New York, and Charles Sumner of Massachusetts. They were not prepared to stake their commitment to antislavery and to free labor on the ability of inhospitable topography and climate to contain slavery. They in-

7. William D. Valentine diary, Aug. 9, 1851, in Valentine Diaries. The Southern electoral response to the Compromise can be followed in Allan Nevins, *Ordeal of the Union* (New York, 1947), pp. 364–78, which I have used. Also useful are the political articles in *Harper's Weekly* for 1851, vols. II–IV.

sisted on legislative prohibitions on slavery in the territories. Moreover, the traditional Whig party principles of the Bank, the tariff, or internal improvements did not carry much appeal to Southerners, whose economy was overwhelmingly agricultural. Finally, with the deaths of Clay and Webster by 1852, the party no longer possessed a truly *national* leader and certainly none who could fill Clay's place in the South. The party did nominate General Winfield Scott to run against Franklin Pierce in 1852, but Scott's defeat was an accurate measure of the party's moribund character. As one ardent North Carolina Whig wrote immediately after the election, "Scott's minority is so small as hardly to amount to the dignity of a competition. . . . This result is disastrous to what I deem the good cause. I had thought the Whig party was so large and respectable as to be at least formidable. . . . It is or used to be large in intellect if not in members." The defeat, he thought, was so great "that there seems no probability of its rising again for many long years, if ever."[8]

The prophecy was truer than the North Carolinian probably imagined. All over the South, Whigs began to drift into the Democratic party and to such an extent that by 1854, when the controversy over the Kansas-Nebraska bill broke over the nation, the Whig party was well on the way to its dissolution. It did not even enter its own presidential candidate in the 1856 contest. The rise of the sectional Republican party in the North after the passage of the Kansas-Nebraska Act only hastened the flight of erstwhile Southern Whigs into the Democratic party.

Yet there were always some old Whigs who could not stomach membership in the hated Democracy. The party battles of the 1840's, after all, had often been harsh and wounding, and the differences in principles ran deep. Moreover, the taint of disunion that the Democratic party had earned from the powerful Southern influence in its national councils made it difficult for old supporters of Clay and Webster to move easily into the party of John C. Calhoun. The Democratic party in the South was the home of a new generation of so-called fire-eaters, men like Robert Rhett of South Carolina, William Lowndes Yancey of Alabama, and Albert

8. Valentine diary, Nov. 10, 1852.

Gallatin Brown of Mississippi, who were pressing for the breakup of the old Union if the South's interests were not respected.

Faced with such an alternative, many former Southern Whigs joined the American party, which sought to avoid the slavery issue and its threat to nationalism by concentrating on the immigrant and his alleged threat to national integrity. Among the prominent Southern Whigs who took this course were Benjamin Hill of Georgia and Kenneth Rayner and Zebulon Vance of North Carolina. The Know-Nothings, as the members of the American party were called by their enemies, were more than an anti-immigrant party, especially in the South. In fact, in the South immigrants were so few that if the presence of aliens had been the party's principal reason for existence, Southerners would have had small reason to join it. A few cities like New Orleans, St. Louis, Baltimore, and Louisville, located on the periphery of the region, recorded substantial proportions of aliens, to be sure, but the great German and Irish immigration of the 1850's largely by-passed the South. And even as late as 1860 only ninety-three counties, out of roughly a thousand in the whole South, counted more than 10 percent of the population as foreign-born. About 83 percent of Southern voters in 1860 lived in counties in which foreigners constituted less than 10 percent of the population. Yet, despite the absence of an obvious "foreign threat," many thousands of Southerners, principally former Whigs, voted the American ticket in 1856. The party's candidate that year was the former Whig President, Millard Fillmore of New York, whose candidacy was endorsed by what was left of the Whig national party when it met in convention at Baltimore. The closeness of the vote in a number of Southern states betrays the movement of Whigs into the American column. In Alabama, for example, Fillmore lost by only 1,800 votes out of 75,000; in Arkansas by 1,100 out of 33,000; in Georgia by 12,000 out of 98,000; in North Carolina by 12,000 out of 85,000.[9]

One of the chief reasons for the movement of so many Southern Whigs into the American party in 1856 was their desire to avoid

9. James H. Broussard, "Some Determinants of Know-Nothing Electoral Strength in the South, 1856," *Louisiana History*, VII (Winter, 1966), 16–17; W. Darrell Overdyke, *The Know-Nothing Party in the South* (Baton Rouge, 1950), p. 154, gives the election figures for various states.

making a decision in the conflict in loyalties between section and nation, which the polarization of the other two major parties demanded. The American party did not require a stand on slavery in the territories or anywhere else. This is not the proper place in which to examine the continuity between the Whig party, the Know-Nothings, and the Constitutional Unionists—that will be canvassed in the next chapter. It is pertinent here, however, to observe that 1856 was not the last time that Southern Unionists would seek to resolve a conflict in loyalties by evading the issue of slavery. That conflict in loyalties was peculiarly Southern, and for that reason it is worth pausing to compare Northern and Southern Unionism before continuing the story of Southern Unionism.

A PECULIAR UNIONISM

Because the South was the region that disrupted the Union through secession, it is common to view attitudes and actions prior to 1860 that were in behalf of the South as sectional and antinational. At the same time, attitudes and actions by the North that favored its interests are usually taken as expressions of nationalism. Thus the assertion of Northern antislavery men that the Union possessed the constitutional power to control slavery in the territories is considered an expression in favor of national authority, while the statements of Southerners that denied the legitimacy of such authority are considered sectional or antinational. On the level of abstract power, that formulation of the issues is correct enough. Northerners were indeed defending an enlarged degree of national power that was denied by Southerners. But placed in the context of a rivalry between sections, the so-called nationalism or Unionism of the Northern spokesmen shrinks to a sectional principle supported by abstractly nationalist means. For the fact is that the exclusion of slave property from the territories was no more a truly national goal than the insistence that they be allowed in the territories. In the former the national government gained a power to control a species of property, which in the latter it would be denied. But that was only a difference in means, not a difference in national sentiment. In fact, the tendency to view Southern aspirations as sectional, and Northern as national or Unionist, is really the result of the South's minority position within the United States. It was that position that caused the South to deny the use of national authority, for it was through the national power that its central interest—slavery—could be injured or destroyed. Insofar as the South was a *permanent* minority, to that extent it could not use the national power in its own behalf. Hence its hostility toward the exercise of national power. On the other hand, the North, by virtue of its numerical power in the government—it was the majority—could exploit national authority in behalf of its sectional interests while calling that usage "Unionist" or "nationalist."

Let us look at two concrete issues to see how this worked out in practice. The North had an obviously sectional interest in the protective tariff, as its industry began to develop. But those who argued for a tariff could employ the argument of nationalism because in theory a protective tariff would also benefit the South if or when that section should develop manufactures. The protection of slavery, on the other hand, could not be justified on the ground that some day the North might want such protection. Slavery was ended there and not likely to return. The only reason why the North might accept or support legal protections for the South's special interest was as a favor to, or as a quid pro quo with, the South. This might be done, for example, as a party measure, a fact that makes clear why the breakup or polarization of the political parties was an unsettling omen for the South.

"A Northerner could, and many Northerners did, support the Union for sectional reasons," David Potter has correctly pointed out. But the concluding half of Potter's remark is not equally accurate. Potter concluded his sentence with: "no Southerner could possibly support it [the Union] for any other than national reasons."[10] That conclusion is true only if one assumes that Southern interests were *never again* to be supported by national power—that is, that the South was a permanent minority. To John C. Calhoun and certain other Southern rights advocates that seemed to be the case even before 1850. In historical fact, however, it was not yet true in 1850, if it ever became true. On the issue of slavery—the South's peculiar interest—the South was still

10. David M. Potter, "The Historian's Use of Nationalism and Vice Versa," *American Historical Review,* LXVII (1962), 942.

being supported by non-Southerners and with national power as late as 1850 and after. The Fugitive Slave Law of 1850 is a concrete example. At the time, in fact, the example was so obvious that Northern legislatures and courts began to react to *that* use of national power just the way Southern ones did when the situation was reversed. They began to deny the authority of the national government. A state court in Wisconsin, for example, declared the Fugitive Slave Law unconstitutional. A number of other states passed "personal liberty laws," which sought to impede the authority of the national government in retrieving runaway slaves—that is, they expanded state powers at the expense of the federal government. Moreover, even after secession occurred there were many Southerners, as we shall see in the next chapter, who firmly believed that slavery would be better protected in the Union than outside it. Those Southerners certainly did not think of the South as a permanent minority even in 1860.

The point here, however, is not to suggest that both the Northern pot and the Southern kettle are black, but rather to show that a sentiment or attitude like loyalty to the Union was not unambiguous. Simply because the North was in the majority, its interests, no matter how sectional in character, could easily be passed off as national. But issues that were no more sectional in nature, but were Southern in origin, could not as easily be labeled as national. And the reason was that the South was generally in a minority position and, moreover, hastening down the road toward being a permanent minority at that. Men and women in both sections, to be sure, had conflicts in loyalties, as they always do. But the conflict between section and nation, which culminated in civil war, was obscured in the North or never tested, while in the South the conflict was increasingly exposed and tested by events.

As David Potter has pointed out, in the North a man could speak of himself as a New Yorker and an American without anyone asking him which came first or accusing him of an unresolved conflict in loyalties. For a while Southerners spoke the same way, but as the decade of the fifties wore on, the question of which loyalty was prior became more insistent. For the South's minority status brought it increasingly into conflict with the national authority. And the reason for the conflict is that slavery was not an issue on which Northerners had anything in common with the South. As long as the matter of slavery was morally neutral, the North could cooperate with the South in protecting it as a favor to the South. The North, however, had no more than that very limited involvement with slavery; the Fugitive Slave Law would never be of value to it. Or, put another way, no interest in the North would be injured directly by restrictions on slavery. At the same time, however, in the South slavery was becoming increasingly identified with the section since it was in fact not only an institution that set the South apart from the rest of the nation but a substantial material interest as well. Not surprisingly, slavery and its protection became the one issue on which the South tested its friends in the North. For the South to view the Union as useful and valuable, it needed to know that slavery would be protected. Yet that was the precise issue on which no group in the North had an interest in common with the South. Since by the 1850's it was clear that slavery was immoral in the eyes of the western world, it was not likely that it would ever be accepted again in the North, as it once had been. The North, in sum, found itself not only without an interest in slavery, but with no reason to believe it would ever have an interest in it—as, for example, Whiggish Southerners could expect they might have an interest in the protective tariff some time in the future. Furthermore, since few moralists outside the United States could justify Negro bondage, the North even had a moral justification for *refusing* to protect the South's interest.

From the foregoing it follows that the root cause for secession was the belief on the part of those Southerners who supported secession that by 1860 their region was a *permanent* minority within the nation. Since its status was permanent, the secessionists reasoned, then their section could no longer remain in a Union that was hostile to its interests. For, by definition, a permanent minority was one that could never expect to be supported by non-Southerners in the federal government, or, put another way, one which would never be a part of a majority on the question of primary interest to the region.

By this definition too, Southern Unionists were those Southerners who did not think the South's minority status was permanent and that, therefore, the rest of the nation could be trusted to consider and respect the interests of the South. In fact, that was the precise argument that Southern Unionists made when they sought to dissuade secessionists from their drive to disunion. In the secession Convention of Virginia in April, 1861, for example, delegate Chapman Stuart conceded that he thought slavery morally right and worth defending, but he denied that secession was the best way to achieve that goal. "We find a large portion of the people of the Northern States standing up also to vindicate and support our rights. I believe," he went on, probably correctly, "that at this day there is a majority of the people of the free states in favor of the right of the Southern portion of the Confederacy to the institution of slavery."[11]

Since the matter was largely subjective, at what point a particular Southerner ceased to be a Unionist varied according to his own fears, hopes, and experiences. These hopes and fears, of course, were alternately aroused and deflated by successive tests of loyalty —an experience which a Northerner did not have to undergo. Some Southern Unionists mentally abandoned the Union even before secession occurred, some did so only during the secession conventions, others did not do so until secession was a fact, and still others waited until Lincoln moved to use force against the seceded states. The range of reactions is broad, extending right down to those who, in the end, deserted their section entirely and put the Union above region.

As we shall see in a subsequent chapter, the number of Southerners who placed the Union above section was not negligible; nevertheless Southern Unionism as a whole has always seemed more tentative and pallid than Northern Unionism. One of the principal reasons, as has already been suggested, was the minority position of the South. It was easier to be a Unionist in the North than it was in the South. Thus in 1851 William Seward of New York could give expression to what Paul Nagel has rightly called absolute Unionism. "We are in the Union for richer or poorer, for better or worse," Seward said, "whether in a majority or in a minority, whether in power or powerless, without condition, reser-

11. George H. Reese, ed., *Proceedings of the Virginia State Convention of 1861* (Richmond, 1965), III, 169.

vation, qualifications, or limitation, for ever and aye."[12] Seward may have been quite sincere in defining his highly nationalistic position, but he was never put to the test which many Southern Unionists had to face when war occurred between their section and the Union. There were Southerners, to be sure, who acted out the position that Seward advocated. But that position was indeed the absolute expression of Unionism; to follow it out meant abandoning not only the abstraction of national loyalty, but the dearer concrete loyalties as well, which underlay that abstraction: familiar surroundings, esteem of friends, long associations, and not infrequently, love of family itself.

Seward's definition of Unionism, it is necessary to observe, was not typical by any means among Northerners. Many of them saw the Union in more conditional terms, as an agreed-upon relationship, not one resting upon coercion or compulsion. Millions of Northern Democrats, for example, denied the validity or value of a Union held together by force. Many felt so strongly about the invalidity of a coercive Union that they resisted and defied the Lincoln government during the Civil War in order to proclaim their views. Even nationalists of an antislavery point of view could have doubts about a Union maintained by force. In 1801 when John Quincy Adams feared that Aaron Burr might break up the recently created union he was not sure that it ought to be held together by force. "If they break us up—in God's name, let the Union go," he wrote. "I love the Union as I love my wife. But if my wife should ask and insist upon a separation, she should have it, though it broke my heart." Sixty years later another son of Massachusetts and an abolitionist, Wendell Phillips, used the wifely metaphor again—this time in confronting an actual breakup of the Union. Phillips spoke after secession had taken place. "A Union is made up of willing states not of conquered provinces," he said. "There are some rights, quite perfect, yet wholly incapable of being enforced. A husband or wife who can only keep the other partner within the bond by locking the doors and standing armed before the door had better submit to peaceable separation."[13]

12. Paul C. Nagel, *One Nation Indivisible: The Union in American Thought, 1776–1861* (New York, 1964), p. 107.
13. *Ibid.*, pp. 253, 257.

One further caveat in thinking about Southern Unionism. Virtually all historians, including this one, are agreed today on the centrality of slavery in explaining the road to secession. Yet if we would understand the nature of Southern Unionism we cannot stop there in accounting for the abandonment of Unionism by sufficient Southerners to create the Confederacy. Human motivation and loyalties are more complex than that. A concern about the future of slavery was more often in the background than in the forefront of Southerners' thinking about the Union. Certainly it is difficult to show a clear causal line between direct involvement with slavery and attitudes toward secession. For one thing, too many unconditional Unionists, as we shall see, were slaveholders. For such persons the ownership of slaves was not sufficient reason for supporting secession. For another, most of the Southerners who made up the Confederacy were not directly connected with slavery at all. The majority of white Southerners, after all, did not own a single slave. Their concern for the institution of slavery could at best have been only an indirect motive for supporting secession and later the Confederacy.

It makes much more sense to see slavery as a shaper of Southern civilization and values than as an interest. The anxiety about the future of slavery was there because the future of the South was intimately tied up with the institution. But the role of slavery in moving individual Southerners from Unionism to secession was neither simple nor obvious. Precisely at what point an individual Southerner decided that he or she could no longer support the Union when it came into conflict with region depended upon many things, not only upon his or her immediate relationship to slavery. For some, of course, their direct interest in slavery was paramount and decisive; for others, equally interested in the institution, it was not at all clear, and for some, as we shall see, slavery was sacrificed to the cause of the Union. For still others, slavery was at best an abstraction or symbol, representing the central concern, which was the region. And these varieties still do not exhaust the many motives that shaped the choices of Southerners during the winter and spring of 1861.

One way of appreciating the complicated process whereby Southerners moved from Unionism to secession—or failed to move—is to examine individual decisions. In that way the personal dilemmas and anguish that often accompanied those decisions can be concretely witnessed. That will be the task of the next chapter. Then, in Chapter 6, we can once again broaden our view and take a measure of the extent and impact of Unionism in the South by examining Unionists collectively, rather than individually and personally.

5

The Civil War Within

By the spring of 1861 each Southerner had to make his or her own choice among loyalties; no longer could loyalty to region be comfortably subsumed under loyalty to nation. There is no analogue in all of American history for the intensely personal experience that secession was for Southerners. Of all Americans, only Southerners have had to make a choice between birthplace and nation. (The most nearly comparable experience was during the American Revolution when Englishmen in North America were called upon to choose between the Empire and a new nation. At that time the Tories were the equivalent of the Southern Unionists, for, like the later Unionists, they chose the larger loyalty over the smaller.)

Some Unionist Southerners dropped their allegiance to the United States without much discomfort, perhaps even without much thought, and they did so early. Others did so slowly, often painfully, and at the last moment. Some never did at all. How and why each person arrived at the choice he or she did is not possible to rediscover now, if it ever was. But if we examine closely a series of individual, personal decisions perhaps we can obtain some understanding of the broad range of responses as well as a sense of the commitment, anguish, and courage that often accompanied Unionism in the South. The series of cases is arranged in the form of a spectrum, running from the weakest to the strongest commitment to the Union. And it ought to be seen as a continuum, for the decisions were indeed many and various in content as well as in number.

A CONDITIONAL UNIONISM

Howell Cobb can stand as a representative of those Southern Unionists who shifted early. Although a Democrat, Cobb, it will be remembered, had deserted his party in 1851 to support the Compromise of 1850 in Georgia. Because of the support from the Unionist Whigs in his campaign for governor, Cobb's victory had been a victory of Unionism in the state. During the campaign Cobb publicly and resolutely repudiated secession. Yet, like most Unionists in the South, Cobb was not an absolute Unionist, nor did he conceal the conditional character of his Unionism. At his acceptance of the nomination for governor he said, "Should the time ever arrive when the condition of her [Georgia's] remaining in the confederacy [the Union] are *degradation* and *inequality,* I should be prepared with her 'to resist, with all the means which a favoring Providence may place at her disposal' even (*as a last resort*) 'to a disruption of every tie which binds her to the Union,' any and every power that seeks to put her upon such debasing terms."[1] In December, 1860, when South Carolina seceded, Cobb's Unionism evaporated. He resigned from Buchanan's cabinet, where he was Secretary of the Treasury, and went home to urge secession upon the people of Georgia.

Cobb's abandonment in 1860 of his Unionism of ten years before was not unusual after the election of Lincoln in November, though some conditional Unionists of 1850 were less enthusiastic than Cobb. James Henry Hammond of South Carolina had been a cooperationist in 1850–51, who had worked with Unionists to resist successfully secession in South Carolina that year. A great planter and man of broad culture, Hammond won election to the U.S. Senate over Robert Rhett, the most outspoken and fiery Southern rights man in the state, if not in the whole South. Ham-

---

1. Ulrich B. Phillips, ed., "The Correspondence of Robert Toombs, Alexander H. Stephens, and Howell Cobb," in *Annual Report of the American Historical Association for the Year 1911* (Washington, D.C., 1913), p. 241.

mond deliberately set himself against Rhett's disunionism by telling his constituents as late as 1858 that "an overwhelming majority of the South" would prefer to stay in the Union if the Constitution were upheld. At another time Hammond observed that the South could "control its actions in all the great affairs" if it remained in the Union. In the late 1850's and in South Carolina such words were sufficient to have Hammond labeled a Unionist, though he described his own position more accurately as a Unionism "of policy, not principle."[2]

It was largely because Hammond lived in secessionist-minded South Carolina that his Unionism is noticed, for it was certainly not strong. Yet he dragged his feet as his fellow Carolinians demanded dissolution of the Union. Almost immediately after the election of Lincoln in early November, Hammond's colleague in the U.S. Senate, James Chesnut, resigned his seat, at which point the president of the South Carolina Senate inquired rather testily whether Hammond was not going to follow Chesnut's example. On November 12, Hammond complied. The same day he wrote to his brother: *"C'est fini.* I have resigned. I heard yesterday that Chesnut and Toombs [of Georgia] had resigned—Why I know not. . . . People are wild. The scenes of the French Revolution are being enacted already. . . . God knows the end." In the light of these troubled remarks it is not surprising that Hammond, unlike Cobb, refused all of the many invitations he received to speak throughout his home state, as it prepared for possible war with the United States.[3]

All over the deep South, Lincoln's election was a signal to abandon the Union. As the Troy, Alabama, *Advertiser,* which had supported Stephen A. Douglas in the election, put it: "We for one throw off the garb of Democracy [Democratic party] and go for secession at once. Before Lincoln's election we were against disunion . . . but now the die is cast, the last feather has been placed on the camel's back, and our only salvation is in secession. We have fought long to the best of our humble ability to preserve the Union. Now the battle is fought and the victory won and none

2. Lillian A. Kibler, "Unionist Sentiment in South Carolina in 1860," *Journal of Southern History,* IV (1938), 346–47.
3. *Ibid.,* p. 358.

but the most cowardly will submit to the cursed domination of a Republican majority."[4] To some stauncher Unionists, such a quick transition by a Douglas Democrat seemed to confirm the suspicion that Southern support of Douglas was merely a device for splitting the true Unionist vote between Douglas and John Bell's Constitutional Union party and thus ensuring the victory of John C. Breckinridge, the Southern Democratic candidate. If that motivation lay behind the shift of the Troy *Advertiser* it was not true of Alexander Stephens of Georgia, who had also been a Douglas supporter.

A UNIONISM OF ANTI-REVOLUTION

Stephens had long been one of the leading Whigs of his state, and as we have seen, during the great Unionist upswell of 1850–51, he was a central figure in the victory of Cobb and Unionism. With the dissolution of his beloved Whig party, Stephens went directly into the Democratic party, scorning the way station of the ephemeral American party. Although certainly a believer in and defender of states' rights, Stephens was sufficiently conservative to find contemplation of a disruption of the Union exceedingly painful. Two weeks after the election of Lincoln, whom he knew personally when both served in Congress more than a decade earlier, Stephens still believed the Union was worth sustaining. Writing to a friend in New York, he conceded that the South might well be in trouble with the new administration. "But candor compels me to say that I am not without hopes that our rights may be maintained and our wrongs be redressed in the Union. If this can be done it is my earnest wish. I think also that it is the wish of a majority of our people."

After South Carolina seceded in December, 1860, Stephens's optimism, wan as it was, paled still further. At the close of the year he wrote, "I have now for two years been impressed with the conviction that we are approaching 'the beginning of the end' of this great republic. . . . All is now dark and gloomy. I see no ray of hope. What is to become of us I know not." He went on to say that

4. Durward Long, "Unanimity and Disloyalty in Secessionist Alabama," *Civil War History,* 11 (1965), 261.

the election of delegates to a convention to consider the secession of Georgia would be held in two days. "It will be over before you get this. I now feel almost confident that this State will go for secession. I think it unwise and have done what I could to prevent it; but it is beyond my control, and the movement will, before it ends, I fear, be beyond the control of those who started it."[5]

Like most prominent former Whigs of the South, Stephens was a slaveholder and a conservative socially. He talked states' rights, but was clearly reluctant to abandon the Union, not only because he had a long and sentimental attachment to it, but because disruption would bring in its train unforeseen and, most likely, dangerous changes. Even before any state had actually seceded, Stephens voiced his innermost fears. Writing to a friend in New York in late November, 1860, he said, "Revolutions are much easier started than controlled, and the men who begin them, even for the best purposes and objects, seldom end them. The American Revolution of 1776 was one of the few exceptions to this remark that the history of the world furnishes. Human passions are like winds; when aroused they sweep everything before them in their fury. The wise and the good who attempt to control them will themselves become the victims." The conclusion to be drawn from these observations was clear to Stephens and provided a succinct statement of the conservative source of his Unionism. "To tear down and build up again are very different things; and before tearing down even a bad government we should first see a good prospect for building up a better."

Once the revolution was begun, however, that same conservatism would cause Stephens to support the new order. "We are now in the midst of a revolution," he wrote in early February, 1861, as the Confederacy was being formed. "It is bootless to argue the causes that produced it, or whether it be good or a bad thing in itself. The wise men—the patriot and statesman in either section—will take the fact as it exists, and do the best he can under the circumstances."[6] In the end, of course, Stephens became vice-

5. Phillips, ed., "Correspondence," pp. 504, 527.
6. *Ibid.*, pp. 504–5; Hubert J. Doherty, Jr., "Union Nationalism in Georgia," *Georgia Historical Quarterly*, XXXVII (1953), 37–38.

president of the Confederacy, but even before that took place, it is clear he had mentally thrown in his lot with the new order.

CAROLINIANS AGAINST SECESSION

Alexander Stephens's public stance in favor of states' rights—a position he continued to support publicly under the Confederacy, too—obscured the depth of his Unionism, which his private letters reveal. There were, however, even in secessionist South Carolina, Unionists who had never hidden their Unionism behind public assertions of states' rights. As we have seen already, in 1832 South Carolina could boast of Unionists like Daniel Huger, Joel Poinsett, James L. Petigru, and Benjamin F. Perry. All of these men stood against secession and the leadership of John C. Calhoun in 1850, and those who still survived in 1860 once again battled against secession. Petigru, for example, never made a secret of his Unionism, but his image among most Charlestonians, if only because he was a member of the Carolina aristocracy, was that of an eccentric. His Unionism, regardless of the depth of conviction with which it was held, was tolerated rather than influential. The day after the secession ordinance was signed, he was asked where he stood. "I have seen the last happy day of my life," he replied.[7] Significantly, however, he did not leave the state or oppose the Confederacy. He died in 1863.

More vigorous and influential among the old Unionists of South Carolina was Benjamin Perry of Greenville, which was located in the western, mountainous part of the state. A longtime Whig and opponent of Calhoun, Perry had been a tower of strength during all of the crises of the Union in his state. He was especially active in the weeks before secession in December, 1860. Yet, when the great decision had been made by his fellow Carolinians, Perry told Petigru, "I have been trying for the last thirty years to save the State from the horrors of disunion. They are now going to the devil, and I will go with them." When the Confederacy was orga-

7. Kibler, "Unionist Sentiment in South Carolina," pp. 352–53, 356. On Petigru see also Clement Eaton, *The Freedom-of-Thought Struggle in the Old South* (New York, 1964), p. 386, and James Petigru Carson, *Life, Letters and Speeches of James Louis Petigru* (Washington, D.C., 1920).

nized in February, 1861, its marking of the end of his cherished Union struck Perry anew. "It is the destruction of my country," he wrote in his journal on February 10, 1861, "the dismemberment of that great and glorious Union, cemented by the blood of our fathers. The American people seem demented. Nothing in History equals it. They are exulting over the destruction of the best and wisest form of Government ever vouched by God to man. Fools and wicked fools they know not what they do and may God forgive them." To his son, a Harvard graduate, a month later Perry made quite explicit his ultimate commitment to South Carolina. "You must volunteer your service in defense of your state," he wrote. (Willie said that he had done so already.) Yet in the older Perry's mind the conflict was still incompletely resolved. "That my son should ever fight against the Union," he wrote in his journal, "is what I never expected. But I may have to do so myself. The dire necessity of self defense [has] fallen on South Carolina and we must defend our independence and liberty."[8]

The fact is that despite the good fight Unionists in South Carolina put up, right down to the decision to secede, once that decision had been made, they all stayed with the Confederacy. Perry even went so far as to recruit troops for the Confederacy and serve as a Confederate official.

A STIFFENING UNIONISM

The secession of South Carolina in early December, 1860, brought the Unionism of many in other parts of the deep South to the point of decision. Just as South Carolina was deciding its course, a meeting in Greene County, Alabama, where the Constitutional Union party had carried the vote the previous month, resolved no longer to wait for the South as a whole to secede. It was thought to be "unsafe, impolitic, and ruinous to our safety to wait or advise such cooperation. We favor concert of action after secession," the meeting concluded. Congressman Jeremiah Clemens of Alabama, a strong supporter of Bell in the election, waited until the end of January, 1861, before accepting secession by his state.

8. Lillian Adele Kibler, *Benjamin F. Perry, South Carolina Unionist* (Durham, N.C., 1946), pp. 347–48.

He had wanted to wait for the border states, he wrote a friend. "I resisted the secession of Alabama to the last moment not because I doubted that it must come sooner or later but because I preferred to wait until you in Tennessee were ready to go with us." Clemens's decision was not as firm as he thought, and his subsequent behavior provides some insight into the turmoil which many Unionists in the deep South must have experienced.[9]

After making his decision in late January, Clemens put up a strong front. In February, for example, he wrote publicly that nine-tenths of Alabamians "sustain the action of the convention and before the 4th of March there will not be one man in a thousand to raise his voice against it." Yet in 1862, Clemens himself turned around and swore allegiance to the Union, to which he remained faithful for the rest of the war.

Other northern Alabamians were not as quick as Clemens to concede the triumph of secession. As late as March 8, 1861, a Tuscumbia, Alabama, newspaper approved of waiting or joining Tennessee. "We speak from the record, when we say that the great body of the people of this county, who voted the cooperation ticket at the late election, for members to the State Convention, would rather see North Alabama attached to Tennessee, *in the Union,* than to see Alabama, *out of it.*" Yet the kind of subtle but effective pressure that would weaken Unionism, even in north Alabama, had been suggested in the previous month by a secessionist writing to the governor. "The secession movement is not popular with Union savers," he conceded, "but the ambitious who expect to be known throughout the state are not only becoming reconciled, but are preparing their followers to be reconciled and will support the measure as soon as they can do so." By early April, a Huntsville newspaper observed that "so great a revolution has taken place in the public sentiment of Limestone [County], that a Unionist is hard to find."[10] As we shall see in the next chapter, and as the example of Jeremiah Clemens makes evident, the decline of Unionism in northern Alabama was more a function of its impracticality at the moment than a change of heart. Once some Union

9. Long, "Unanimity and Disloyalty . . . Alabama," pp. 265, 259.
10. Elbert L. Watson, "The Story of Nickajack," *Alabama Review,* XX (1967), 24–25; Long, "Unanimity and Disloyalty . . . Alabama," p. 271.

troops invaded the area the situation was once again transformed.

A considerably more enduring example of Unionism in the deep South is provided by Sam Houston of Texas. Of all the governors of the states of the lower South as the secession crisis neared, Houston stood alone in making clear that he would not entertain any moves for a convention, even if Lincoln were elected. And when the secessionists in his state legislature pressed him to call a convention, he refused. And even when the convention was called, he opposed it, and when the convention not only voted secession but applied for admission to the Confederacy as well, Houston denied its power to do so. In return, the convention prescribed an oath of allegiance by all state officers to the Confederacy. When Houston refused to take the new oath he was declared deposed. He protested his deposition to the legislature, but without effect.

Houston declared that he would not abandon his oath of allegiance to the United States in order to swear allegiance to the Confederate states. The voice of the people, he rather sadly observed, was not always the voice of God. Earnestly he reminded his fellow Texans of the Unionist performances in office of Southern Presidents Washington, Jefferson, Jackson, and Polk. Moreover, he added, "All our Northern Presidents have been equally patriotic and just to the South. Not a single Southern right has been violated by any President or by any Federal Administration." Many strong secessionists, of course, could have easily agreed with Houston here. It was not the past actions of the North that aroused the fears or hostility of the secessionists. It was what might happen in the future to the South and its distinctive and important institution of slavery that really worried them and propelled them to secession.

But as Houston made clear in that same speech, slavery in his eyes did not merit a higher priority than the Union. Secessionists, he shrewdly pointed out, "forget or else are ignorant of the fact that the best sentiment of Europe is opposed to our system of negro slavery." Outside of the Union, Texas might not find Europe so responsive to the power of cotton.

As a nationalist, Houston also ridiculed the overblown, self-serving rhetoric of secessionists in which they asserted the natural superiority of Southern military courage and prowess over Northern. "Never was a more false or absurd statement ever made by designing demagogues," Houston contended. Civil war he thought inevitable and near at hand. "When it comes, the descendants of the heroes of Lexington and Bunker Hill will be found equal in patriotism, courage, and heroic endurance with descendants of the heroes of Cowpens and Yorktown." For this reason, "I predict that the civil war which is now near at hand will be stubborn and of long duration." Houston detected in the Confederacy "the germs and seeds of decay which must and will lead to its speedy ruin and dismemberment if it can ever secure any real existence. Its seeds of ruin and decay are the principle of secession which permit any one or more of the Confederate states to secede from the parent Confederate Government and to establish separate government. Can any well-informed man doubt that the time will soon come when several of the Confederate States will secede and establish separate governments?" he asked. "Within ten years we would have ten or more separate Confederate governments, which would in time fall an easy prey to foreign governments."[11]

Houston stood his ground longer and more firmly than men like Perry in South Carolina or the Cooperationists in Alabama and Mississippi. But the determination of his fellow Texans to leave the Union overbore him, too. On May 10, 1861—almost a month after Sumter, but before Bull Run—Houston publicly confessed that "the time has come when a man's section is his country. I stand by mine. All my hopes, my fortunes are centered in the South. When I see the land for whose defense my blood has been spilt, and the people whose fortunes have been mine through a quarter of a century of toil, threatened with invasion, I can but cast my lot with theirs and await the issue. . . . I have ever been conservative," he went on. "I remained conservative as long as the Union lasted; I am now a conservative citizen of the Southern Confederacy, and giving to the constituted authorities of the country, civil and military, and to the Government which a majority of the people have approved and acquiesced in, an honest obedience. I feel that I should do less than my duty did I not press upon others the importance of regarding this the first duty of a good

11. Edward R. Maher, Jr., "Sam Houston and Secession, *Southwestern Historical Quarterly,* LV (1952), 456; Amelia W. Williams and Eugene C. Barker, eds., *The Writings of Sam Houston* (Austin, 1943), VIII, 295–98.

citizen." And when four months later a Northern newspaper report asserted that Houston did not truly support the Confederacy, the Texan publicly stated that the story was false. Once secession was voted, he pointed out, he had "performed all the acts of a dutiful and loyal citizen of the Southern Confederacy." Moreover, he added, "If there is any Union sentiment in Texas, I am not apprised of it."[12]

A MORE PERSISTENT UNIONISM

The tide of secessionist sentiment ran so strongly in the lower South that within three months after the election of Lincoln all seven of the Gulf states had seceded and formed the Confederate States of America. In the process the small number of Unionist leaders in those states were overwhelmed. In the upper South, however, Unionism was more widespread and of greater endurance. As one Virginia Unionist wrote in 1860, he did not see "any cause existing or probable" that could justify civil war, "but I have unbounded faith," he went on, "in the stupidity and recklessness of the Belials of South Carolina and the Molochs of Mississippi. I cannot tell, between these qualities, what they might not do." Indeed, as we shall see in more detail in the next chapter, until Lincoln called in April, 1861, for volunteers to suppress the "rebellion," Union sentiment in the upper South was demonstrably more popular than secession. In Virginia, Tennessee, North Carolina, and Arkansas the popular hostility to secession brought the secession movement to an abrupt halt. So effective was the resistance that Northern observers often misread its character, assuming that refusal to secede at that point was equivalent to unconditional unionism. Thus in February, when the slave states of the upper South refused to follow the deep South into the Confederacy, the legislature of Minnesota tendered its thanks to the "patriotic citizens of the Southern states who have nobly and manfully exerted their utmost efforts to prevent the catastrophe of disunion." And the legislature of Wisconsin offered its thanks to the "Union-loving citizens" of the upper South for their resistance to secession.

12. *Ibid.*, VIII, 301–2, 305, 310–14.

Southern Unionists, however, knew that the unionism of many of their fellow Southerners was limited, rather than absolute or unconditional. As a Nashville newspaper of conditional Unionist persuasion put it on February 10, 1861, "We would not have the people of the Free States misunderstand our position, and we take the occasion to remind them that the continued loyalty of Tennessee to the existing Government will depend upon the spirit with which her earnest and patriotic efforts to save that Government are received by them. They must not suppose . . . that the majority are for coercion," that is, holding the Union together by armed force. Northerners must not assume from the recent vote of the people of Tennessee against immediate secession, the paper added, that Tennesseans are willing to submit "to the Republican electioneering dogma that the people of the Southern States are to be excluded by legislation from the privilege of settling in the Territories with their slaves."[13]

On a more private level, Unionist Charles Phillips of Chapel Hill, North Carolina, wrote in a similar vein to his fellow Carolinian and Unionist, Benjamin Hedrick, the antislavery man, who was then living in the North. Hedrick was now a Republican and as staunch in his Unionism as in his antislavery convictions, which had compelled him to leave his native state. "You seem to think that we Unionists are playing 'a game,'" Phillips wrote on February 1, 1861. "I do not know what you mean by Unionists or by a game. Only this I know, if the Northerners do not quit their folly about our fugitive slaves—and their policy about the territories— we will not sail in the same ship with them, even if our two shallops are both wrecked. I associate only with Unionists—those branded as submissionists—yet I know of no one who [does] not endorse what I write."[14] Of course, those who warned of the limited nature of the Unionism of the majority of the people of the upper South were proved correct when Lincoln's call for troops after the fall of Fort Sumter in April, 1861, provided the ultimate test of loyalty between region and nation.

13. L. Minor Blackford, *Mine Eyes Have Seen the Glory* (Cambridge, Mass., 1954), p. 140; Dwight Lowell Dumond, *The Secession Movement, 1860–1861* (New York, 1931), p. 246 and n.

14. Charles Phillips to Benjamin Hedrick, Feb. 1, 1861, in B. S. Hedrick Papers.

No Southern man was more prominent throughout the nation for his resistance to secession than John Bell of Tennessee. A lifelong Whig, Bell placed himself at the forefront of Southern Unionists in 1860 when he ran as the presidential candidate of the hastily constructed Constitutional Union party. Capitalizing upon his old Whig ties and his reputation in his state and region as a responsible defender of slavery, his candidacy offered an alternative to the extremes of Breckinridge and Lincoln. In the election of 1860 he virtually divided the popular vote of the South with Breckinridge. When it became clear that Lincoln would be the new president, Bell still refused to see that as a reason for secession or even alarm. He insisted that "secession is but another name for an organized resistance by a State to the laws and constituted authorities of the Union, or, which is the same thing, of *revolution.*"[15] Bell's leadership was an important force in keeping Tennessee from following the states of the deep South into Confederacy in January and February, 1861.

When Lincoln called for troops to suppress the rebellion, however, Bell reached the end of his Unionism. On April 18 he joined with ten other Tennessee conservatives to praise the indignant refusal of the secessionist governor of Tennessee to provide militia to the United States government, even though Tennessee was still in the Union. Five days later a Nashville newspaper quoted a public speech in which he said, "The time for action in the South had arrived and he was for standing by the South, all the South, against the unnecessary, aggressive, cruel, unjust wanton war which is being forced upon us." He advocated "a strong and effective military league or union among all the slaveholding states for the successful prosecution of the war" but would not declare himself in regard to any political connections with the recently established Confederacy.

Bell's switch, however ambiguous and reluctant it may have been, came as a surprise and an outrage to Unionists in both sections of the country. John Minor Botts, an old Whig and Unionist in Virginia, later wrote that when he learned of Bell's abandonment of his Unionist position, he begged God's forgive-

15. Joseph H. Parks, *John Bell of Tennessee* (Baton Rouge, 1950), p. 391.

ness for having voted and worked for Bell in the campaign of 1860. The Louisville *Journal* thought that Bell's defection "must excite unspeakable mortification, and disgust, and indignation, in the breast of every true and enlightened lover of his country." And in the North the Republican New York *Tribune* mockingly spoke an elegy for Bell: "Alas that such should be the ignominious close of the long public life of John Bell."[16]

The inner explanation for Bell's change will probably never be known, for few of his intimate papers have survived. Some historians have argued that the shift stemmed from chagrin in being ignored by the new Lincoln administration. Others attribute it to weariness in fighting for so long in behalf of a cause that increasingly seemed hopeless. It is true that he was now an old man and had never been a very quick one, mentally. Yet he had always doubted that the future of Tennessee could ever be bright in league with the deep South. He had preferred a confederacy of the Southern and Northern border states, one in which the extremes in his view—New England and the deep South—would be shorn off. Even at the time this solution of a central confederacy seemed remote, for it won little support outside Tennessee and North Carolina. It was, after all, anathema to the nationalist Lincoln administration as well as to the disunionist lower South.

The only reply that Bell ever gave to criticisms of his shift was in a speech he made in east Tennessee, in June of 1861. No one should ever have thought, he said, "that when this great contest had become, as it had done, a *war between the North and the South,* he could be found occupying any other position than that of *for the South.*" Nevertheless, he added, secession was still heresy. During the war, when his beloved middle Tennessee was invaded by Union armies, Bell fled to the deep South, where his frail health deteriorated. His return to Tennessee after the war brought neither happiness nor power. He died a sick and broken man in 1869.[17]

Less prominent and younger Unionists of the upper South made

16. Mary Emily Robertson Campbell, *The Attitude of Tennesseans Toward the Union 1847–1861* (New York, 1961), p. 194; Parks, *John Bell*, pp. 400–1.

17. *Ibid.*, pp. 400, 403, 406; for further information on Bell after 1861 see James Welch Patton, *Unionism and Reconstruction in Tennessee, 1860–1869* (Chapel Hill, N.C., 1934), pp. 16–17.

somewhat better adjustments to events that stretched their Unionism, like Bell's, beyond the breaking point. North Carolina, with its strong Whig tradition and its geographical situation—as wits put it, that of being "a valley of humility between two mountains of conceit"—provided a solid base for Unionism. Expressions of strong Unionism were elicited by President Buchanan's soft response to South Carolina's secession. Wrote North Carolina Unionist Richmond Pearson to his wife: "So the president says a state has no right to secede, but if she does I can't help it—poor old man he is not fit to govern in these sad times." The important point, Pearson went on, is to defeat the move to call a constitutional convention for the purpose of voting on secession. "If we can't put out the fire, our policy it to draw a line around it, that is let the border states stand off and see if it won't go out of itself." Ten days later another Unionist of North Carolina, W. C. Kerr, a professor at Davidson College, took a harder line. "I am in favor of their collecting the revenues even if S.C. takes the forts at Charleston. . . . Let the revenue be collected even if two or three states go along with South Carolina. If we just had a president at Washington now . . . and if a determination had been shown to collect the revenue and execute the laws on all offending individuals, everywhere without asking or caring whether he was backed by his state—why then I could see our way out of these troubles."[18]

Such statements were not typical, however, for most North Carolinians were not unconditional Unionists. A Unionist meeting at Raleigh at the end of November resolved that the election of a sectional president did not justify secession and so North Carolina must remain faithful to the Union "as long as the Constitution is respected and maintained—*but no longer.*" Its conditional Unionism was underscored by its call for the repeal of all laws in the Northern states that nullified the Fugitive Slave Law and for the reorganization of the North Carolina militia.[19]

A prominent North Carolina Unionist like Zebulon Vance, who was a fledgling congressman, also revealed early the conditional

18. Richmond M. Pearson to wife, Dec. 16, 1860, R. M. Pearson Papers; W. C. Kerr to Benjamin Hedrick, Dec. 26, 1860, B. S. Hedrick Papers.
19. Quoted in Joseph Carlyle Sitterson, *The Secession Movement in North Carolina* (Chapel Hill, N.C., 1939), p. 194.

character of his Unionism. At the end of December, before any state except South Carolina had seceded, Vance wrote privately, "The Union is dissolved, of course, S.C. has already gone and I make not a doubt but every Gulf State will be with her by the 4th March." He did not think that his own state would or ought to go, for like John Bell and some other Tennesseans, Vance saw the interests of the upper and lower South as divergent. "I think the only way that the Union can be reconstructed, and these cotton states brought to treat us with proper respect," he wrote, "is this idea of a great Central Confederation." Georgia would join such a scheme, he thought, and New England could be induced to stay out.[20] Vance's Unionism, in short, had been eroded away more than a month before the Confederacy was established at Montgomery.

Publicly he still fought against secession in North Carolina down to April, 1861, when Lincoln's call for troops to suppress "the rebellion" altered the situation. It is not surprising, therefore, that once his own state seceded, Vance went along rather easily. He became first an officer in the Confederate army and then a wartime governor. But if his Unionism seemed to be overborne by his state's secession, Vance never gave the same loyalty to the Richmond government that he had to the one in Washington. As Confederate governor of North Carolina, Vance is best known for his strong states' rights position vis-à-vis the central government of Jefferson Davis. No governor of a Southern state, with the possible exception of Joseph E. Brown of Georgia, cooperated less with the Confederacy than Zebulon Vance.

THE AGONY OF JONATHAN WORTH

The Unionism of Jonathan Worth, also an old North Carolina Whig, was less volatile than Vance's. An older and more prominent figure than Vance, Worth was probably the state's most outspoken public opponent of secession. As a member of the state senate he did his utmost to prevent the convening of a secession

20. *The Papers of Zebulon Baird Vance,* ed. by Frontis W. Johnson (Raleigh, 1963), I, 77–78; Sitterson, *Secession Movement . . . North Carolina,* p. 179n.

convention, even after Lincoln's call for troops. Worth was convinced that once a convention met it would vote for secession. When it became evident that a bill calling for a convention would pass, Worth tried to amend it so that any action of the convention would be subject to the vote of the people before it could take effect. If Worth's amendment had been adopted, the process of secession in North Carolina would have been slowed down and perhaps even stopped. The Senate, however, voted down his amendment and went on to pass the call for a convention. Worth was one of the three senators who voted against the call; in the lower house no one at all voted against the convention.

Worth's consistent and unyielding public fight against secession, however, concealed his inner turmoil over Lincoln's resort to military coercion. All his life Worth had been convinced that the Union of the states was the ideal government. His deep emotional attachment to the Union comes through clearly in a letter in March, 1861, after hearing the news of the surrender by General David Twiggs of the United States military installations in Texas to the new Texas government. "Twiggs ought not to be shot," Worth wrote his brother. "He ought to be hanged and his name for all time to be written in connection [with] and immediately after Benedict Arnold." When Lincoln called for troops to suppress rebellion, Worth was confronted with a choice he dreaded and was clearly ill-equipped to make. Always he had prided himself on the use of reason and reasonableness in arriving at political decisions. But now reason was little help, though he sought to use it however weak its support. Detesting both civil war and secession, he now had to choose one. For, as he told his constituents, he still believed that secession was unconstitutional and wrong. Moreover, he was convinced that the federal government had "the right and duty . . . to execute the laws to protect the public property by military forces in such seceding states. . . ." Yet he was not prepared to support Lincoln's efforts to do so, for now the rebellion was so widespread that its suppression would require full-scale war. Under those circumstances, he explained, "I deemed it highly inexpedient for the Government to attempt coercion by military force." Civil war he thought would bring bloodshed, but it could not restore the Union. Since Congress, he went on, had refused over the previous months to authorize force against the seven seceded states, Lincoln's effort to do so was usurpation of presidential authority.[21] This was good Whig doctrine, but it came with poor grace from a man who had never made clear how secession could be stopped without force. Clearly Worth was grasping at straws to explain his inability to find ways to defend the Union without war.

Privately, he gave vent to his dissatisfaction with himself and the inapplicability of the principles of a lifetime. That same month he confessed to a friend that "my mind became so painfully embarrassed with the conditions of our country" that he forgot to carry out their common business. "I am still painfully impressed with my total impotence to accomplish anything tending to the preservation of our country from the calamities of civil war." As a public official he felt it was his duty to provide guidance and leadership, but none of his old arguments or principles seemed to apply. His personal objection to secession meant little, apparently, to most of his fellow Southerners. Indeed, his sense of inadequacy was so great that at one point he considered resigning his public office. Then, yielding to the drift of public opinion, he resolved that "the best chance I see is to present a united front," by which he meant military resistance to Lincoln's threat. With "unity among ourselves" he reasoned, peace might be preserved if only because the Lincoln administration might be prevented from imposing its will if confronted by a united South. "In this view," he told friends, "I shall take to the stump tomorrow to urge our young men to volunteer."[22]

Emotionally Worth may have cast his lot with his region, but intellectually he knew that the course was wrong in principle as well as self-defeating for the South. Deep down he still hoped secession could be stopped, for it endangered not only the South, but the North and the principles of good government as well. "Popular government is proving itself a fallacy and delusion. Virtue and order are unequal to a contest with ambition and selfishness." The evils of war may have made him accept a

21. J. G. deRoulhac Hamilton, ed., *The Correspondence of Jonathan Worth* (Raleigh, 1909), I, 135–37.
22. *Ibid.*, I, 140–41.

Southern confederacy as the only basis for peace, as he admitted, "but I confess . . . that the evils growing out of the recognition of secession and the immeasurable petty governments which must spring from it, will probably overbalance the loss of life and property which the war will occasion. Will not the Northwest submit to self-immolation if they [*sic*] recognize secession?" he asked. Almost desperately he was hoping that the North would be able to come up with the miracle that would end secession without war.

Two days later his doubts and agony were still so strong that he again wrote his son, trying to explain to him and justify to himself why he was abandoning the principles of a lifetime. "I have been forced by surrounding facts to take sides, or rather front, with my section," for secession was preferable to civil war. Yet the new government that the South was constructing, he recognized, would not be the equal of the old. "I think the South is committing suicide, but my lot is cast with the South and being unable to manage the ship, I intend to face the breakers manfully and go down with my companions." Once more he lamented the nagging sense of inadequacy, of being unable to avert what he clearly saw as a calamity for his people. "I have become resigned from conscious impotence to do anything to impede the evils upon us, and have concluded to drift with the current" to wait for something to turn up. To a close friend, in a strictly private letter, a few days later, he poured out his frustration in finding that his familiar, reasonable way of dealing with political problems no longer worked. "The whole nation has become mad. The voice of reason is silenced. Furious passion and thirst for blood consume the air. . . . Nobody is allowed to retain and assert his reason. The cartridge box is preferred to the ballot box. The very women and children are for war." In such circumstances, no one could avoid the painful choice of picking a side. "I think the annals of the world furnish no instance of so groundless a war," he complained. Yet the people want war; therefore "let us fight like men for our own firesides."[23] Feeling and sentiment, not reason, were now the guides, and Worth, along with many other Southern Unionists, knew it, and they blamed themselves.

But if the decision was settled in his viscera, it was not quite

23. *Ibid.,* I, 141–42, 144–45, 149.

settled in his mind. A week later he was still justifying secession on the ground that there was "no alternative to the South, only between independence and humiliation." And for a moment some optimism about the future crept into his mind. "I have feelings that we cannot be conquered." But then his realism flooded back. Will the secessionists really work with old Unionists and Whigs or will they demand "absolute vassalage to them?" He was not sure at all. "Their unmanly course toward us thus far is only less galling than submission to Lincoln." Once again his thoughts turned to the "good sense of the free states . . . to arrest the war before rage and passion shall have ruined the land."

When North Carolina on May 21 finally took the plunge into secession, Worth went along, as he knew he must. A year later he remembered the decision a little differently from the way it happened. Now the agony and the sense of inadequacy were purged, the course clearer. "Being thus forced into war, I had no hesitation on which side I would fight," he recalled. The personal forces that shaped his decision were familiar to all Southern Unionists who faced the same choice that spring of 1861. "My home, my wife and children, my property, are all here, and when forced to fight, I never had hesitation, embracing the side of the South, and wishing it to be victorious."[24]

UNIONISM FOR PEACE

Worth's Unionism was not forgotten, and after the war he was elected governor on the basis of his support of the old Union. Interestingly enough, Worth's opponent in that postwar election campaign was William Woods Holden, also a prewar Unionist. Personally, however, Holden was the opposite of Worth; he had little in common with the almost compulsively conservative and consistent Worth. Holden, an illegitimate child, was an intensely ambitious man who changed his political affiliations several times in the course of his life. Beginning his political life as a Whig, he

24. *Ibid.*, I, 151, 172. Richard L. Zuber, *Jonathan Worth: A Biography of a Southern Unionist* (Chapel Hill, N.C., 1965), is useful but not illuminating, and somewhat misleading on the nature of Worth's opponents like Albion W. Tourgée, the carpetbagger.

then became a Democrat when he bought a Raleigh newspaper of Democratic persuasion. In the capacity of editor of the *North Carolina Standard,* Holden became a power in the state. It was Holden's attacks on Benjamin Hedrick in 1856 that impelled the University at Chapel Hill to fire Hedrick for his antislavery and Republican views. (After the war and another change in principles, Holden apologized to Hedrick after the latter returned to the state. "I met yesterday Holden," Hedrick wrote his wife in May, 1865, from Raleigh. "He expressed himself as very sorry for his past course toward me.")[25] As late as December, 1859, the *North Carolina Standard* was proclaiming secession as the only protection for the South, but in 1860 Holden became increasingly identified with a Unionist position. The switch is not easy to account for, except as an act of opportunism, as his biographer has remarked. But from then on, his position was consistently and increasingly Unionist. As a delegate to the Democratic convention at Charleston, he refused to bolt with the lower South, and within his own delegation he strenuously opposed disunion. Although he personally favored Douglas in the election of 1860, he supported Breckinridge because of local candidates who favored an ad valorem tax on slaves, a working-class cause that Holden was actively supporting. After South Carolina seceded, Holden counseled patience in avoidance of any precipitant action. During the campaign for the election of delegates to the convention in February, Holden took command of the Unionist forces, which defeated secession. During the Civil War, Holden and his newspaper became the center of dissenting and peace sentiment in the state. In 1862 he managed the successful campaign of Zebulon Vance for governor, a victory that was viewed in the North as a continuing sign of Unionism in the Old North state. Calling his organization "the Conservative party," Holden continued to work for the withdrawal of North Carolina from the Confederacy and for the return to the Union. So outspoken was his Raleigh *Standard* in opposing the war that in 1863 its offices were sacked and Holden had to flee temporarily to the countryside. By this time, Holden's hostility

25. Benjamin S. Hedrick to his wife Ellen, May 12, 1865, B. S. Hedrick Papers.

toward the war and the Confederacy had caused a break between him and Vance, who remained the war governor of the state.

When the war ended, Holden ran against Jonathan Worth for the governorship, with the tacit support of another Southern Unionist, Andrew Johnson, who was by then President of the United States. Worth's victory in that contest was clearly a disappointment to the President, who wrote Holden that the "results of the recent election in North Carolina have greatly damaged the prospects of the State in the restoration of its governmental relations."[26] Johnson undoubtedly warmed not only to Holden's staunch Unionism during the war, but to his humble origins as well. Ironically enough, Holden went on to become the leader of the Radical Republicans in the state and a sharp thorn in the side of the President, while Jonathan Worth as governor revealed himself to be just the kind of conservative old Unionist that Johnson valued and sought in the South.

Another example of Southern Unionism for peace, but one more resistant to the Confederacy than even Holden's, was represented by John Minor Botts of Virginia. An old Whig and lawyer who came from a prominent family in Virginia, Botts was well known in politics, having been a congressman and delegate to the state constitutional convention of 1850. There was no question of his support of the Union or of his conviction that secession was unconstitutional. He fought against secession in the public prints after the Confederacy was established, hoping to keep Virginia from seceding. The turning point came for Botts when Lincoln called for volunteers in April, 1861 to suppress the Southern resistance. Botts was not prepared to support Lincoln, yet he could not condone secession. His immediate solution was a famous series of letters to Edward Bates, Lincoln's Attorney General and a native of Virginia, urging the calling of a national constitutional convention as a result of which the seceded states would be permitted to leave unmolested. Botts, like Worth, had decided that the most important issue was to avoid bloodshed. "You may *overrun,*

26. Horace Wilson Raper, "William Woods Holden: A Political Biography," unpublished Ph.D. dissertation, University of North Carolina, Chapel Hill, 1951, p. 175. Raper's study is the only full-length treatment of Holden, and I am indebted to it.

but cannot *subjugate* the united South," he told Bates. The seceded states would soon find out that they would be better off in the Union than out. Moreover, "what possible good is expected to be accomplished by a war among ourselves? . . . After 500,000 lives have been lost and $1,000,000,000 of money has been spent, must it not at last end in a severance of the ties that have heretofore held us together as one people?" A government has the right to suppress rebellion, he admitted, but is a Union held together by force worth anything? "I would give millions this night (if I had them) to have the power of Mr. Lincoln for one moment, that I might say, 'Brethren, depart in peace; let there be no more quarrel between us,' and then what a bright sunshine would spread over the land at once!" The course he advocated, however, was rejected by the nationalist Lincoln administration.

Soon thereafter, Botts retired to a farm he bought a mile outside of Richmond. He entertained visitors but left the premises only three times in nine months to go to Richmond to attend funerals of his friends. He made no secret of his continued Unionism, and on March 1, 1862, when martial law was declared around Richmond by the Confederate government, Botts was arrested and lodged, as he put it, in "a dirty, filthy negro jail." There he remained for almost two months, until he was allowed to leave on the understanding that he would not speak against the Confederacy. He moved to Culpeper County, where he stayed throughout the remainder of the war—still a Unionist, but a silent one.[27] Not all Southern Unionists, however, could be silenced so easily.

AN ENDURING DEMOCRATIC UNIONISM

Probably the best-known and most outspoken Southern Unionist was Andrew Johnson of Tennessee. Unlike some well-known Southern political figures of the antebellum years, Johnson had long championed the small farmer and nonslaveholder of the South. As first a congressman and then senator from Tennessee, Johnson emphasized his own humble origins as the source of his

27. John Minor Botts, *The Great Rebellion: Its Secret History, Rise, Progress, and Disastrous Failure* (New York, 1866), pp. 257–59, 262–64, 282. Despite the publication date, the book contains earlier documents.

concern for the nonslaveholders. "Sir, I do not forget that I am a mechanic," he once said, recalling his early career as an illiterate tailor in east Tennessee. "I am proud to own it. Neither do I forget that Adam was a tailor, and sewed fig-leaves or that our Savior was the son of a carpenter." One of his most cherished causes in the Senate was a homestead bill that would provide free land in the West for poor farmers. Yet for all Johnson's known distrust of the slaveholding class, he was unassailable on the slavery issue. As he pointed out in 1860 from the floor of the Senate, if slavery should ever be threatened in the South, all white men, regardless of class, would be united. "When there was agitation in Tennessee, in 1856," he recalled, "I saw that the non-slaveholder was the readiest man to rise up and join the master in extirpating, if necessary, this race from existence, rather than see them liberated and turned loose upon the country." As a lifelong Democrat, Johnson supported Breckinridge in the election of 1860, contending that the election of Breckinridge would save the Union by protecting slavery.[28]

When South Carolina seceded after the election of Lincoln, Johnson pronounced it a mistake from the Senate floor, asserting that "the continuance of slavery depends upon the preservation of this Union, and a compliance with all the guarantees of the Constitution. I believe an interference with it [slavery] will break up the Union; and I believe a dissolution of the Union will, in the end, though it may be some time to come, overthrow the institution of slavery." Before he was through, however, it was clear that his real concern was the Union, not slavery. "Sir, I will stand by the Constitution of the country as it is, and by all its guarantees. . . . It was good enough for Washington, for Adams, for Jefferson, and for Jackson. It is good enough for us." He even tried to shame the secessionists by trivializing their reasons for breaking up the Union. "Does not every man, Senator or otherwise, know, that if Mr. Breckinridge had been elected we should not be to-day for

28. LeRoy P. Graf, "Andrew Johnson and the Coming of the War," *Tennessee Historical Quarterly,* XIX (1960), 210; *Congressional Globe,* 36th Cong., 1st Sess. (Washington, 1860), part 2, p. 1368; Verton M. Queener, "East Tennessee Sentiment and the Secession Movement, November 1860–June 1861," East Tennessee Historical Society, *Publications,* No. 20 (1948), p. 79.

dissolving the Union? Then what is the issue? It is because we have not got our man. If we had got our man, we should not have been for breaking up the Union; but as Mr. Lincoln is elected, we are for breaking up the Union! I say no. Let us show ourselves men, and men of courage." Although Johnson's speech in the Senate did not halt the mass resignations of his fellow Southerner senators, he was proud of the fact that he was "the first man south of Mason and Dixon's line who entered a protest or made an argument" in that body against secession.[29]

Unlike most other senators from the seceded states, Johnson did not resign his seat. Instead he reminded the Senate of his origins as a supporter of Jackson in the days of nullification and his consistent Unionism ever since. After the attack on Fort Sumter and Lincoln's call for troops, Johnson went back to Tennessee to speak against secession, although by this time popular sentiment was heavily against the Union. An eyewitness reported his reception at Jonesboro, in east Tennessee, in May, 1861, just before the election of delegates to the convention. "Such a time has never been since I have lived in the place," the witness wrote to a friend immediately after the event. "Johnson rose to speak. The crowd at once commenced *booing, booing,* until it finally deafened you. He gave back for a little while, and then came forward and commenced. Such groans and cursing you never heard. They cursed him for a *God Damed* [sic] *Traitor*—told him he was hired by Lincoln to make speeches, and asked how much he got—he again sat down." Then Johnson moved to a small basement room, where he began to speak to a small crowd. "The boys would occasionally thrust through the window a secession flag, and ball [sic] for him. When he went to start out to Nelson's [another Unionist] they raised the shout, groaned and booed him out of town. . . . You never saw such a time. Men on horses ripping up and down the streets, screaming upon the top of their voices, 'you damed traitor, you damed traitor.' "

When Johnson's usefulness in the South ended with the secession of his state, he preached his unbending Unionism in the North. In June, 1861, he told an audience in Cincinnati that "this

29. Frank Moore, ed., *Speeches of Andrew Johnson* (New York, 1970, reprinted from 1865), pp. 148, 162, 168, 178.

odious doctrine of secession should be crushed out, destroyed, and totally annihilated."[30] Johnson remained in his seat in the U.S. Senate, continuing to represent Tennessee for almost another year.

The courage of his convictions was apparently unlimited. In 1862 he returned to Tennessee as its first military governor after Union troops conquered the major portion of the state. Indeed, his defiant Unionism made such an impression on the North and the Republican party that in 1864 he was selected as Lincoln's running mate to demonstrate the nonsectional character of the party and the war. (For the purposes of the election, the Republicans dropped the party name that was so offensive in the South. In 1864 Lincoln and Johnson were the candidates of the Union party.)

AN ENDURING WHIG UNIONISM

Also of strong, unyielding Unionist sentiment was William "Parson" Brownlow, who, like Johnson, was from east Tennessee. Brownlow, too, considered himself a spokesman of the nonslaveholders of east Tennessee and, by extension, of the whole South. He also resembled Johnson in his defense of slavery, though, characteristically, Brownlow set no limits on his defense of the institution in the antebellum years. "When the angel Gabriel sounds the last loud trump of God," he wrote in his newspaper, "and calls the nations of the earth to judgment—then, and not before, will slavery be abolished south of Mason and Dixon's line." For all their superficial similarities, however, Johnson and Brownlow were political enemies in Tennessee, since Brownlow was a Whig of the most partisan variety.

The newspaper he edited, the Knoxville *Whig,* prided itself on the quantity as well as the quality of its vitriol. For example, the paper branded Harriet Beecher Stowe *"a deliberate liar"* for her *Uncle Tom's Cabin* and later went on to say that "she is as ugly as Original sin—an abomination in the eyes of civilized people. A tall, course [*sic*], vulgar-looking woman—stoop-shouldered with a long yellow neck and a long peaked nose—through which she

30. Patton, *Unionism . . . in Tennessee,* p. 53; Moore, ed., *Speeches of . . . Johnson,* pp. 318–19.

speaks." Indeed, Brownlow's defense of slavery was so intense that it obscured the depths of his Unionism. During the campaign of 1860 he declared that if Lincoln as President should so much as interfere with the domestic slave trade he "would take the ground that the time for Revolution has come—that all the Southern States should go into it; AND I WOULD GO WITH THEM."[31]

Yet, when Lincoln was elected, Brownlow saw no reason for secession. Correctly, he pointed out that Lincoln would not have a Republican Congress or a Supreme Court favorable to whatever abolitionist intentions he might harbor. The secession of South Carolina did not weaken Brownlow's Unionism, either, if only because he had long held Carolinians in contempt. Thirty years before, as a young itinerant Methodist preacher, he had been in South Carolina during the nullification crisis and had been disgusted with that state's threat to the Union. Tracing the causes of disunion to the Tories of the Revolutionary era, he contended that South Carolina was prone to secession because of its large number of loyalists. (As was his impetuous wont, Brownlow blithely ignored the fact that during the American Revolution the Tories were the loyalists and the patriots the "secessionists" of the time.)

In the weeks of campaigning for and against secession in Tennessee, Brownlow's *Whig* took the lead in opposing secession. And when departure from the Union was voted—Tennessee was the last state to join the Confederacy—Brownlow still refused to countenance disunion. Having lived all his life in east Tennessee among its nonslaveholders, Brownlow was something of an anomaly in his total defense of slavery. But when the choice came between his local region and the South with slavery, he chose to abandon slavery and the South.

Unlike Johnson, however, Brownlow stayed in Tennessee to organize resistance to the Confederacy, which he denounced almost daily in his newspaper. His mail overflowed with denunciations of his betrayal of the South and with threats on his life. Along with other last-ditch Tennessee Unionists, Brownlow organized a separate government for east Tennessee, refusing to recog-

31. E. Merton Coulter, *William G. Brownlow, Fighting Parson of the Southern Highlands* (Chapel Hill, N.C., 1937), pp. 102, 95, 137.

nize the Confederacy and electing representatives to sit in the United States Congress in Washington, D.C.

The Confederacy, of course, recognized the anomaly, not to mention the danger to its cause, of disloyal east Tennessee. It acted to silence the dissenters. Confederate troops were sent to the area to hold it for the Richmond government. Nevertheless, Brownlow continued to publish the Knoxville *Whig,* filling it with denunciations of the Confederacy. As his biographer notes, "if there were any limits to the freedom of the press in the Confederacy, Brownlow had not been able to discover them."[32] The limits were soon discovered, however. In October, 1861, Brownlow was arrested and his paper closed. Vilified and mistreated, he asked to be released from jail and sent North. His request was granted. Until September, 1863, when General Burnside's reoccupation of Knoxville made his return safe, Brownlow remained in the North, principally in Philadelphia, speaking and writing in behalf of the Union cause. After his return to the South he began publishing a newspaper again. This time it was called *Whig and Rebel Ventilator,* but the denunciations of the rebels and the Confederacy were as vehement and heedless as ever.

Ultimately, Brownlow's Unionism altered his defense of slavery and even silenced his hatred of Negroes, an emotion that underlay his antebellum defense of slavery. As with everything else in which he believed, Brownlow had made no secret of his dislike for Negroes. Once, during the antebellum years, he had refused to debate the Negro abolitionist Frederick Douglass simply because of Douglass's race. And as late as 1861 he was applauding the North's refusal to enlist blacks in the army, saying, "We abhor Negroes and Whites mingling in a white man's war." He could quote with approval in 1862 remarks that he had made thirty years earlier to the effect that those who cared decently for their slaves and "instruct them in religion are better friends to them than those who set them at liberty."[33]

As the war transformed itself from a war for the Union into one to end slavery as well, Brownlow accepted the new war aim.

32. *Ibid.,* p. 178.
33. Patton, *Unionism . . . in Tennessee,* pp. 68–69; Queener, "East Tennessee Sentiment," p. 68; Coulter, *William G. Brownlow,* p. 138.

Indeed, he went further than many Northerners were prepared to go; he followed the example of William Holden rather than that of conservative Unionist Jonathan Worth. Brownlow became a Republican and a supporter of Negro suffrage in Tennessee, just as Holden did in North Carolina. As Radical Republican governor of Tennessee in 1866, Brownlow virtually compelled the legislature to ratify the Fourteenth Amendment. As a result, the state escaped Radical Congressional Reconstruction, though it had Radical Brownlow Reconstruction instead.

Whether it was his personal ambition to be governor—he had tried to run in 1860 without success—or his longstanding hatred of Andrew Johnson, who was now President, Brownlow had permitted his Unionism to go to the farthest limit. If Unionism was not the cause of his transformation on slavery and the Negro, it was at least the vehicle of that sea change.

FROM STATES' RIGHTS TO UNIONISM

Still another pattern of Unionism was that represented by J. F. H. Claiborne, the famous historian of Mississippi. Claiborne came from an old Mississippi family of considerable wealth. He himself was a great slaveholder and a remarkably successful planter. Moreover, before the war he was not only an active Democrat but a states' rights advocate as well. In 1853 he was a chief lieutenant of Albert Gallatin Brown, the most prominent Southern nationalist and secessionist in the state. Claiborne also contributed thousands of dollars to Democratic political campaigns. In 1860 he apparently accepted secession, at least in theory. His son died fighting for the Confederacy.[34]

Yet when secession and then war came, Claiborne could not go along. Why he could not, given his political, not to mention his social, background, is not clear. It is interesting, nevertheless, that in his *History of Mississippi* he defended the loyalists of the

34. For my conception of Claiborne's Unionism I have relied upon Herbert H. Lang, "J. F. H. Claiborne at 'Laurel Wood' Plantation, 1853–1870," *Journal of Mississippi History*, XVIII (1956), 1–17; William C. Harris, "A Reconsideration of the Mississippi Scalawag," *Journal of Mississippi History*, XXXII (1970), 27–28; and J. F. H. Claiborne Papers.

Revolution for their "sense of loyalty and duty [which] forbade them to fight." But refusal to fight, as we shall see, was not Claiborne's only reaction to disunion, even if it was his first. When the war began he withdrew to his plantation, Laurel Wood, on the Gulf coast and busied himself with its operation and his historical writing. On the surface he was a loyal Confederate. He even bought several thousand dollars' worth of Confederate bonds and became a Confederate commissioner of oaths. In actuality, however, as early as December, 1862, he was corresponding with Union commander Nathaniel Banks in New Orleans. In the course of the correspondence, which went on for months, Claiborne reported on the activities of Confederate saltworks and tanneries in the vicinity of his plantation. On at least two occasions he warned General Banks of Confederate sympathizers in his New Orleans headquarters, and once he recommended that Banks bombard the saltworks. He also intercepted letters for Confederate sympathizers in Union-occupied New Orleans and copied them for Banks's information. At still another time he brought to Banks's attention a Confederate employee who was prepared to reveal diplomatic secrets of the Confederacy. Thanks to Claiborne, the man went on to Washington, where he told of Confederate secret negotiations with England to President Lincoln and Secretary of State William A. Seward. Claiborne, in short, acted as a spy for the Union.

His actions were not without risk. Although Confederate authorities apparently never suspected his spying, they did think he was selling cotton and other commodities to the enemy, a surmise that was completely accurate. But the Confederates never obtained sufficient evidence to prosecute him. When the war ended he made clear his Unionism, though he did not become active in postwar Southern politics. He wrote President Johnson within three weeks after the war ended, for example, that the Republicans must win in Mississippi or the spirit of rebellion would surely revive. He himself took the oath of allegiance to the United States in July, 1865.

Claiborne remained in Mississippi during Reconstruction, generally approving of the new order. He resumed his correspondence with his old chief, Albert G. Brown, the secessionist, who was now a supporter of the new dispensation of Reconstruction, too.

AN ABSOLUTE UNIONISM OF THE DEEP SOUTH

Claiborne was of the deep South, but his Unionism seems to have been a product of the war, rather than of the past. Unlike Andrew Johnson or William Brownlow, Claiborne had not been conspicuous in the fight against secession. He did remain in the South, as Brownlow and Johnson could not simply because they did not hide their Unionism. Yet there were literally thousands of Southerners who neither concealed their Unionism nor left the South. These men and women were indeed the hard-core Unionists. On them fell the full brunt of Confederate hostility, and in them there was no doubt that nation came before region. The activities and numbers of such Southerners we will examine in more detail in the next chapter. For now, let us look at a striking example of a Unionist who stayed, James Madison Wells of Louisiana.

When the war broke out, Wells was a wealthy planter in Rapides Parish, the same parish in which he had been born. According to the census of 1860, Wells owned a plantation of 3,000 acres with 96 slaves. His personal property was listed as $236,000, a very large fortune in those days. Wells's biographer writes that Wells's wealth increased tenfold between 1850 and 1860, suggesting that he had not always been a great planter. It is not without significance in evaluating his Unionism that although Wells was a slaveholder he had attended schools in Connecticut and Ohio as well as Kentucky. At the Cincinnati law school he attended he came under the influence of Charles Hammond, a Federalist editor, abolitionist, and strong Union man.

Prior to secession Wells was a Unionist, and remained one after secession as well. Publicly he denounced the war as a rich man's war and a poor man's fight. When his verbal opposition proved insufficient to stem secession, he turned to guerrilla warfare, burning Confederate equipment, and then going into hiding. He deliberately placed himself at the head of the nonslaveholders in his parish. At least once he was arrested, but later released. Subsequent efforts by Confederate authorities to arrest him proved futile; his old hunting preserve, Bear Hollow, where he hid out, was apparently impenetrable to the Confederates. In November, 1863, after the federal navy had gained control of the Mississippi River and New Orleans, he fled from his parish to the Union gunboats and thence to New Orleans.

In that city he became immersed in the new politics of Reconstruction, being elected lieutenant governor in 1864 under Unionist Michael Hahn. While lieutenant governor he raised eight companies of U.S. troops—about 450 to 500 men—in Rapides Parish, suggesting something of his influence in his home territory. When Hahn resigned from the governorship in order to take a seat in the U.S. Senate in March, 1865, Wells became governor, first by succession and then by election. He was the only native Louisianan to serve in that office throughout the whole Reconstruction period.

Although Wells was of a quite different social class from Holden or Brownlow, his Unionism propelled him through a similar progression in attitudes. While he served under Hahn, who was cautious on the Negro question, Wells made no appeals to blacks, although they constituted a majority of the people. In fact, for a while in 1865 he apparently thought that the political force of the future in the state would be the returning Confederates. As a consequence he tried to influence the national administration to withdraw the federal army and General Nathaniel Banks and to repudiate the local Radical Republicans. He announced that he was not in favor of Negro suffrage, and most of his appointments to office were locally popular because the men he chose were often former Confederates. Wells's opponents contended that some of his appointees still wore their gray uniforms when they assumed office. Down to the middle of 1866, in short, Wells was a conservative Unionist, a supporter of President Johnson, and a believer in the possibility of a quick and painless reconstruction.[35]

Then, in July, 1866, Wells virtually repudiated his old policies and began to speak out against the "rebellious spirit," which he now saw all around. The President's "pacific policy," he now contended, was causing the rebels to become "arrogant, intolerant,

35. The principal authority on Wells is Walter McGehee Lowrey, "The Political Career of James Madison Wells," *Louisiana Historical Quarterly,* XXXI (1948), 995–1123, to which I am greatly indebted. J. K. Menn, *The Large Slaveholders of Louisiana—1860* (New Orleans, 1964), pp. 335–36, is the source of my figures on Wells's wealth.

and dictatorial." He also came out in support of Negro suffrage. He publicly declared that the states were dead constitutionally and that Congress had the right to treat them as territories until equal rights for all, regardless of color, had been established. Unlike most of the other governors of the Southern states, Wells recommended the ratification of the Fourteenth Amendment when it came before the legislature in the fall of 1866. He went on to tell the legislature: "I regard establishing of free Negro schools . . . as the most important recommendation I can make to you. . . ."[36]

Wells's transition from extreme Unionism to radicalism on the Negro question was not a common pattern, as we shall see in Chapter 7. But a shift to the Republicans often coincided with a new view of the future of the South, as the war came to an end. Wells's willingness during the war to follow his Unionism to the point of carrying on war against the Confederacy was more widespread than is often thought. Even the fact that Wells and Claiborne were members of the planter class is not as anomalous among Southern Unionists as conventional history might suggest. As we shall see, thousands of planters in the South, especially in Mississippi and Louisiana, quite materially supported the Union cause.

As the activities of Wells make evident, the spectrum of Southern Unionism was indeed wide. It extended from the conditional Unionism of James Hammond and Alexander Stephens through the sullen but passive Unionism of Sam Houston and Jonathan Worth to the enduring Unionism of Andrew Johnson and Madison Wells. Wells, Brownlow, and Johnson represent the extreme of Unionism—those who were prepared even to fight against section, if necessary, in the name of a loyalty to the Union which William Seward had described as sacred and as binding as the vows of marriage.

That there was a wide spectrum there can be no doubt, and that the abandonment or retention of Unionism posed hard and often painful choices for individual Southerners is equally certain. What we want further to know about Southern Unionism is how significant it was in the history of the South. Examination of representative individuals provides some insight into the variety of motives

36. Lowrey, "Career of Wells," pp. 1072–75, 1085.

and circumstances that shaped individual decisions as well as revealing something of the human dimensions and individual cost of Southern Unionism. Yet these particular examples cannot be more than illustrations. We need broader and more inclusive evidence than a handful of personal histories of Unionists. Therefore, in the next chapter we will examine the quantitative evidence that is available for an evaluation of the extent of Southern Unionism. We can begin with the results of the election of 1860.

6

Southern Unionism Tested

In the election of 1860, Abraham Lincoln, a Republican, and Stephen A. Douglas, a Democrat, may have been the chief Unionist candidates in the North, but in the South, neither counted for much. To begin with, Lincoln was not on the ballot in any of the seven states of the deep South, nor in North Carolina, Tennessee, or Arkansas. Where he was capable of being voted for, the Republican organization was negligible. Douglas was on the ballot and able to be voted for, but he had little attraction for Southerners. What votes he received were concentrated in the upper South where they constituted about 15 percent of the region's total. The South, after all, had its own Democratic candidate, John C. Breckinridge. In the course of the campaign, Breckinridge emphasized that he was not a disunionist candidate, but everyone knew that he was the candidate of the strongest states' rights or Southern rights men in the South. The real alternative to Breckinridge in the South was not Lincoln or Douglas, but John Bell of Tennessee, the candidate of the newly formed Constitutional Union party.

A PARTY OF SOUTHERN UNIONISTS

It is customary for historians to ignore when they do not ridicule outright the Constitutional Union party, if only because it deliberately sidestepped the burning issue of the time—the future of slavery in the territories. Yet the Constitutional Unionists provide one of the most useful measures of the extent of Unionism in the South on the eve of the Civil War.

The Constitutional Union party was a Southern party. One gauge of that Southern character was that its first and only party convention was dominated by Southerners, particularly those from Kentucky, Virginia, North Carolina, and Tennessee. Moreover, its platform appealed deliberately to the ambivalent Unionism of the South, and particularly that of the middle and upper South. It is true that the basic plank of the party was support of the Constitution, yet that was not an unqualified endorsement of the Union. For the platform went on to say that if the Constitution were supported "the just rights of the people and of the states" would be "reestablished and the Government again placed in that condition of justice, fraternity, and equality" which the Founding Fathers had intended. In short, in the eyes of the party, the Union was in jeopardy from the North as well as from the South. Furthermore, the platform remained silent on the question of slavery not only to avoid a vexing issue, but also because that would permit local organizations to write their own planks on the issue. And in those circumstances, local state organizations might well adopt, as some did, a much stronger stand in behalf of slavery in the territories than others. And finally, its particularly Southern flavor was also shown by the fact that Breckinridge attracted more votes than Bell in every Northern state except Ohio, Illinois, and Iowa, but in those states Breckinridge's vote was negligible.[1]

Nevertheless, the Bell candidacy testified to the persistence of a strong Southern resistance to secession, if not to Unionism. Southerners who voted for Bell might not have been willing to embrace the absolute Unionism of Lincoln, but they were not prepared, as many Breckinridge followers apparently were, to advocate secession if Lincoln were elected. For many Breckinridge supporters, a Republican victory was to be the signal for secession. On the eve of the election, for instance, every governor of the seven states of the lower South, except for Sam Houston of Texas,

1. Dwight Lowell Dumond, *The Secession Movement, 1860–1861* (New York, 1931), pp. 93–94; David Y. Thomas, *Arkansas in War and Reconstruction, 1861–1874* (Little Rock, 1926), p. 39.

and almost every senator and representative in Congress from those states, were already on record as favoring secession in the event Lincoln won. Three state legislatures had already provided for arming their states on the assumption that force might be used to prevent secession.

Yet, as the election returns make clear, the statements and actions of the fire-eaters and secessionists did not always represent the attitudes of the mass of Southern voters. Breckinridge himself sensed this during the campaign when he denied he was a disunionist and said further that he was not connected with any organization whose aim was disunionist. When the ballots were counted, Breckinridge received only 55 percent of the total vote in the slave states. This general figure, however, is misleading, for it does not discriminate among the states. If the Bell, Douglas, and Lincoln votes are counted together as Unionist, then Breckinridge won a majority in the popular vote in only five of the fourteen slave states. (There was no popular vote in South Carolina, where the legislature cast the state's electoral votes.) Put another way, when the Confederacy organized itself in February, 1861, and prepared to fight a defensive war, 49 percent of its voting population had just voted for candidates (Bell or Douglas) both of whom had opposed the formation of a Confederacy.[2]

Who were those Southerners who were reluctant to take an extreme position even as late as 1860? What were their political and social characteristics? If the results of the election of 1860 are plotted on a map of the South, the pattern is both familiar and startling. It is familiar because the pattern of Bell counties is similar to that for Whig candidates in 1852, 1848, and 1844. Professor John Mering of the University of Arizona has carried out a statistical analysis that neatly summarizes the correlation between Constitutional Unionists and Whig voting.[3] Mering statistically

2. Dumond, *Secession Movement,* p. 99; Avery O. Craven, *The Growth of Southern Nationalism, 1848–1861* (Baton Rouge, 1953), p. 341; Thomas Alexander, "Persistent Whiggery in the Confederate South, 1860–1877," *Journal of Southern History,* XXVII (1961), 307.

3. John Mering, "Who Were the Southern Whigs?" unpublished paper presented at Southern Historical Association meetings, 1969. See also his article "Persistent Whiggery in the Confederate South: A Reconsideration," *South Atlantic Quarterly,* 69 (1970), 124–43. Mr. Mering has generously given me access to his unpublished paper as well as to other data he has

correlated the percentage of votes for Whigs in 1848 with the percentage of votes for Bell in 1860 in 550 counties of the South. The coefficient of correlation was .72, which is very high. (The figure is based upon a system in which 1.00 equals perfect correlation and 0.00 represents no correlation at all.) Put in ordinary language, this meant that the proportion of the Whig vote in 1848 in any given Southern county was a fairly good predictor of the proportion of Constitutional Unionist vote in 1860. Mering also studied the continuity between the vote for the Know-Nothing party in 1856 and Whig voting in 1848 and found a coefficient of correlation of .70. This conclusion supports the view that much of the support for the Know-Nothing party in the South came from Whigs unwilling to join the Democrats. In the upper South alone the continuity between the vote for Whigs in the 1840's and 1852 and the vote for Bell in 1860 was amazingly high. Mering's correlation coefficients ran to .90 and above, that is, close to perfect correlation. In the deep South the correlation was considerably reduced. In 255 counties in the seven states of the lower South the correlation coefficient between Whigs in 1848 and Bell in 1860 was .59—not high, but respectable. A comparison of the vote for Know-Nothings in 1856 with that for Bell in 1860 yields a coefficient of .62. In short, Constitutional Unionists were largely old Whigs, who, in turn, had often been Know-Nothings in 1856. As late as 1860, then, the South was still a two-party region, with a substantial proportion of the electorate unwilling to accept the Democratic doctrine of secession or extreme states' rights.

Socially, who were these Southern opponents of secession in 1860? This is more difficult to get at, but the *geographical* distribution of the vote gives some clues to the *social* character because of what we know of the social nature of local areas. A large number

---

accumulated in his own study of the Constitutional Union party. I am deeply indebted to him for his help and his criticism. It is important to point out, too, that he draws a somewhat different conclusion from his statistics than I do. As his published article makes clear, he does not think that coefficients of correlation of .70 are significant in showing continuity in party affiliations. He denies, in short, that Whiggery persisted, but I do not think he denies what is of interest to my argument, that the old Whig areas were also areas of Unionism in 1860 and after. He would emphasize the Democratic sources of Unionism after 1861 more than I do.

of planters along the Mississippi River, in Arkansas, Mississippi, and Louisiana, must have been voting for Bell, since these heavily black counties, which earlier had voted Whig, now voted for Bell. Central Georgia and Black Belt Alabama also showed support for Bell, as they had shown strong Whig allegiance earlier. These were the plantation areas, where cotton and slaves were concentrated. But, as we have seen already, the Whig party had not been simply a planter party; it had been strong in east Tennessee, western North Carolina, and western Virginia, where the mountains precluded plantation agriculture and slaves were consequently rare. Here, too, Bell was strong. In the deep South, however, the non-slaveholders more commonly voted for Breckinridge, since they were Democrats, while the planters were often Whigs. As one student of the election of 1860 has remarked, in Georgia "the whiter the county the surer it was to vote for Breckinridge." In Arkansas, too, he goes on, "the fewer slaves there were in the county, the more likely it was to support the radical candidate, Breckinridge." A similar pattern was apparent in Mississippi, though in Alabama and Louisiana the heavily slaveholding counties were as likely to go for Breckinridge as for Bell.[4]

There are several things that can be said about the pattern of voting in 1860. The first is that a continuity in voting patterns over the previous fifteen years or more suggests that the election was still a party election, despite the formal disappearance of the Whigs after 1856. In 1860, in sum, most Southerners were still voting their traditional party affiliations, though the Whigs were voting under a new name. That Southerners should still be doing so, despite the excitement of the previous decade, not to mention the agitations on the hustings in 1860, all of which talked of dangers to the South, is remarkable testimony in itself to the persistence of old ways, which included loyalty to the Union. Furthermore, we know from our knowledge of the character and activities of the Whig party during its heyday that it was the party of the Union in the South. All members of the Whig party and all voters for Bell in 1860 were not unconditional Unionists, to be sure, but

4. David Y. Thomas, "The Southern Non-Slaveholders in the Election of 1860," *Political Science Quarterly*, XXVI (1911), pp. 230–31; Thomas, *Arkansas in War*, p. 39.

if a man was an unconditional Unionist he was likely to be a Whig rather than a Democrat. And more important, if he was opposed to secession, however conditionally, he was more likely to be a Whig than a Democrat. In that sense, the vote for Bell was a measure of Southern Unionism, though it was a Unionism that was not yet tested outside of the traditional party context.[5]

UNIONISM ON THE DEFENSIVE

A clearer test came after Lincoln's election in November, 1860. Within six weeks after the election, South Carolina seceded, as it had promised to do, and called upon its fellow slave states to follow its example. Two months later, six other states had also seceded, though not without an amount of haste that betrayed concern and even fear that secession could not be carried through without the immediate and temporary excitement of Lincoln's election. As David Potter has pointed out, only one of the seven states that created the Confederacy in early February permitted the voters to be heard directly on the action of the secession conventions. And that exception was Texas, where secession came after six other states already had left the Union. Potter has argued on this ground as well as on others that most people in the Gulf states did not desire secession. He points out, additionally, that the vote was considerably reduced from the election of 1860, a fact that casts a shadow of doubt, at the very least, on the contention that the calling of the conventions was a popular act. Even in secession-prone South Carolina the secessionists recognized that it was necessary to strike while the excitement of Lincoln's election was high. "I do not believe that the common people understand" secession, wrote a secessionist to James Hammond in late Novem-

5. In an elaborate statistical analysis Seymour Lipset argues that there was a significant shift in sentiment between the election of 1860 and the votes for the secession conventions a few months later, "The Emergence of the One-Party South—the Election of 1860," in Seymour Martin Lipset, *Political Man* (New York, 1960). There is now increasing evidence that there was not much shifting, but very much of a fall in turnout. See Thomas Alexander, *et al.*, "The Basis of Alabama's Ante-bellum Two-Party System," *Alabama Review*, XIX (1966), pp. 267–76; and Ralph A. Wooster, *The Secession Conventions of the South* (Princeton, 1962), p. 263.

ber, 1860. "In fact, I know that they do not understand it; but whoever waited for the common people when a great move was to be made. We must make the move and force them to follow."[6]

It is true that the strong resistance to secession in the conventions of Georgia, Florida, Alabama, and Louisiana did not stem from a resolute Unionism. The vast majority of the opponents in the secession conventions of the deep South were cooperationists, that is, men who did not wish to see their own states secede individually, but who had no philosophical objection to secession. Generally they wished to see their states secede only in conjunction with other Southern states, hence their name of cooperationists. Yet Potter is correct when he says that cooperation was a difficult goal to achieve, and while it was being engineered, the excitement and alleged threat of Lincoln's election was passing. If the cooperationists could have won their point in the conventions they might have forestalled secession for good. That they came close in four of the seven states of the lower South supports the point Potter is making: most Southerners in the lower South did not support secession even after the election of Lincoln.

The remainder of the South was even less willing to view the election of Lincoln as a reason for secession. Under pressure from the fire-eaters in their midst and from the seceded states, each of the states of the upper South consulted its voters. The results all told the same story. In early February, 1861, the voters of Tennessee by a vote of 68,000 to 59,000 turned down the legislature's recommendation for a constitutional convention to consider secession. East Tennessee, where slaveholders and slaves were few, voted against a convention by five to one; west Tennessee, where cotton was grown and slaves were concentrated, voted for a convention by a majority of 15,000. At the same time that the people were asked to vote on the question of a convention they were asked to vote for delegates to the convention in the event it were held. The tally here was even more strongly antisecessionist.

6. David M. Potter, *Lincoln and His Party in the Secession Crisis* (New Haven, 1942), p. 208. Ralph A. Wooster, "The Secession of the Lower South: An Examination of Changing Interpretations," *Civil War History*, VII (1961), 117–27, disagrees with Potter's conclusion that a majority of the voting population of the lower South did not want secession in early 1861; I still think Potter is right.

The votes of those delegates pledged against secession topped that for the secessionist delegates by 67,000. As one east Tennessee Unionist said, "If we had to choose between the government on one side without slavery, and a broken and dissevered government with slavery, I would say unhesitatingly, 'Let slavery perish and the Union survive.' "[7]

Later the same month, the voters of North Carolina turned down, albeit by a closer vote, the call for a convention. There, too, the vote on delegates revealed a strong resistance to secession; out of 120 delegates elected, only 42 were secessionists and as many as 50 were unconditional Unionists. Although Unionist sentiment was strong in the mountains, it was also considerable in the piedmont. As the historian of North Carolina secession has written, "a secession county was likely to be a slaveholding county, but a slaveholding county might not necessarily be a secession county."[8] Planters and slaveholders were still opposing secession, even after the election of Lincoln and the secession of the lower South. The old Whigs of North Carolina, planter and mountaineer, were still sticking to the Union.

Arkansas and Virginia were not as unambiguous as North Carolina and Tennessee in resisting secession, but they, too, refused to abandon the Union when the Gulf states seceded. The people of Arkansas voted 27,000 in favor of a call for a convention to 16,000 against. But the vote on delegates, based on the actual stand they took in the convention, was against secession by 6,000 votes. Moreover, some 20,000 people who had voted in 1860 did not vote for delegates. A secessionist newspaper estimated that two-thirds of the nonvoters were pro-Union. When the Arkansas convention met on March 4, it indicated its political complexion by electing an antisecessionist as president. Finally, when the convention voted on a motion to secede, the motion was lost 39 to 35. The convention then adjourned, three weeks before the firing on Fort Sumter.

In Virginia the secessionists succeeded in having the bill for a

7. Mary Emily Robertson Campbell, *The Attitude of Tennesseans Toward the Union, 1847–1861* (New York, 1961), p. 201.

8. Joseph Carlyle Sitterson, *The Secession Movement in North Carolina* (Chapel Hill, N.C., 1939), p. 224.

convention passed without requiring a vote by the people on whether they wished it to convene. Nevertheless, when the delegates were elected on February 4, the Unionists were in the majority. Of the 152 delegates only about 30 actually said they wished immediate secession, and out of 145,000 votes cast only 45,000 were cast against referring the decision of the convention to the people. Actually, the strength of the Unionists was somewhat less clear than those figures suggest. Among the so-called Unionists were a number who are more accurately categorized as conditional Unionists, that is, those who would stand with the Union, but only if certain conditions were maintained. Nevertheless, it is significant as a measure of Unionism in Virginia in the spring of 1861 that 85 of the 152 delegates had favored Bell in the recent presidential election; 37 had supported Douglas, and only 30 had been for Breckinridge. The historian of Virginia secession estimates that about 50 of the delegates were true Unionists and that almost all of them were former Whigs.

The Virginia convention, however, unlike Arkansas's, did not vote on secession at once. Instead it stayed in session, marking time as events in Washington and at Fort Sumter came to a head. By April 1 the drift in sentiment within the convention, thanks to the pressure from the states already seceded and the impact of Lincoln's words and actions, was toward secession. But as late as April 4, on a test vote, it was evident that the moderates and Unionists were still in control of the convention by two to one.

SOUTHERN UNIONISM BECOMES A MINORITY

The whole Unionist front in the South came apart, however, when Lincoln, after the fall of Fort Sumter on April 14, called for troops to suppress what he called a rebellion. Unionists were now forced to say whether they would stand by the Union even if coercion were used to hold it together. As we have seen, not even all Northerners thought a Union held together by force was worth saving. Yet even in this extremity, Unionist sentiment in the South was not entirely dissipated. The Virginia convention, which was still in session, on April 17 voted to secede by a vote of 88 to 55. Half of the dissenters, of course, came from the west. Within two years the western part of the state would itself "secede" to become the state of West Virginia. (The ratification of secession which was held in May in Virginia is useless as a measure of popular sentiment, since there was so much coercion on both sides.) Arkansas hastily called its convention back into session, and it quickly voted 65 to 5 in favor of secession. All but one delegate responded favorably to the request that the decision be made unanimous. In North Carolina, too, the Unionists collapsed in the face of Lincoln's determination. The legislature hastily called for a convention, with only three dissenting votes in the senate (one was Jonathan Worth's) and none in the lower house. The convention, when it met two weeks later, unanimously voted secession. The swift change in outlook was evident on the lowest level of society. As one North Carolina woman wrote in May to her sister, "You asked me if Henry was a Union man? There are no union men here now. Those that were, have changed, and every one is determined to resist to the death rather than submit."[9]

Considering the large Unionist sentiment concentrated in east Tennessee, it is not surprising that the state never did secede; it invoked the right of revolution rather than the so-called constitutional right of secession, which was the legal basis of all the other states' actions. The Tennessee legislature passed "A Declaration of Independence and Ordinance Dissolving the Federal Relation" between Tennessee and the United States. The Declaration was submitted to a vote of the people, which showed two to one in favor of separation, but with east Tennessee casting about 70 percent of the negative vote. In fact, in that stubborn stronghold of unconditional Unionism the vote went against leaving the Union by 2,000 votes even at the height of the excitement aroused by Lincoln's clearly coercive intentions.[10]

Confronted by Lincoln's determination to hold the Union together by force, most Southern Unionists elected to go along with their states, making the best adjustments they could. But not all,

9. S. D. Thompson to Ellen Hedrick, May 20, 1861, in B. S. Hedrick Papers.
10. J. Milton Henry, "The Revolution in Tennessee, February, 1861 to June, 1861," *Tennessee Historical Quarterly*, XVIII (1959), 117; James Welch Patton, *Unionism and Reconstruction in Tennessee, 1860–1869* (Chapel Hill, N.C., 1934), pp. 17, 20–21.

by any means. Some chose to leave the South. John G. Winter, a well-to-do businessman in Georgia, for example, and a strong Unionist, left for England. "The border States will be lost if Government dont [*sic*] prove that it has strength enough to protect its adherents," he wrote Andrew Johnson in late March, 1861. " 'Moral suasion' is not the treatment for lunatics and robbers— Stripes until they *see* the Stars, is the only medicine which will answer," he advised. "I dare not write my name in full—*I wish to live* for my country, and see the Rascals out to the bitter end." A. P. Dostie of Louisiana, who later returned to become prominent as a Radical Republican during Reconstruction, left New Orleans for Chicago in 1861 because he would not sign the oath of allegiance to the Confederacy. The Texas Unionist James P. Newcomb, who left for California in 1861, would return in 1867 to become a leader of the Republican party. In January, 1862, a North Carolina Unionist wrote from Indiana that "some hundreds of Carolinians have arrived in Indiana and hundreds of others desirous to come when opportunity offers." He said, too, that nine-tenths of the refugees were antislavery as well as pro-Union.[11] But our interest here is not with those Southern Unionists who fled the South, but with those who stayed. For them, in 1861, the severest tests were still ahead. The most painful would come when a Unionist chose to support the nation rather than region in time of war.

Although time, successive crises, and internal pressures of many kinds had eroded Unionist sentiment in the South, not even a war in self-defense could weld all Southerners into the united nation that Jefferson Davis and his government aspired to. Always there were contrary pulls of history, of tradition, and of principle. After all, the South had never been a homogeneous region economically or socially, and certainly it had not been a one-party region. These divergences and conflicts inevitably carried over into the era of the Confederacy, as they would into the era of Reconstruction. In fact, as one looks back upon the social and political divisions and

11. LeRoy P. Graf and Ralph W. Haskins, "The Letters of a Georgia Unionist: John G. Winter and Secession," *Georgia Historical Quarterly,* XLV (1961), 390, 396; Jesse Wheeler to Benjamin Hedrick, Jan. 20, 1862, in B. S. Hedrick Papers.

conflicts within the antebellum South, the remarkable thing is that the Confederacy was able to hold together as long as it did.

The persistence of Unionist feelings and principles was probably not a primary cause for the ultimate defeat of the Confederacy. Yet it would not be too far wrong to say that in the short life of the Confederacy, Unionist attitudes and activities not only weakened its fight for life, but always stood as an internal alternative to which deserters, the faint-hearted, and the despairing could turn. And as time passed and the Union armies pressed relentlessly into the heartland of the South, such people became more and more numerous. Certainly they, in conjunction with the Unionists, if not the Unionists alone, were a primary weakness of the beleaguered Confederacy. For as Benjamin Hill of Georgia recalled in 1877, "We had a class of native men in the South who were always called Union men—they were opposed to secession and to the war and willing at any time to make terms with the United States and come back." Of the fourteen Confederate congressmen who consistently voted for peace measures in the congress at Richmond, for example, twelve had been Union Whigs before the war. Eleven of them had opposed secession until Lincoln's call for troops. By the time the Second Confederate Congress was elected in 1863, old Unionists were coming to the fore. In that year, according to the recent study by Thomas Alexander, two-thirds of the newly elected members were old Unionists and most of them were old Whigs.[12]

MOUNTAINEER UNIONISTS

The lowest common denominator of the Unionism that was strong enough to withstand the pressure of accomplished secession was the conviction that secession would not improve things. Those Southerners who owned no or few slaves and lived where topography or climate made the prospect of becoming a cotton planter

12. Frank W. Klingberg, *The Southern Claims Commission* (Berkeley and Los Angeles, 1955), p. 13; Thomas B. Alexander and Richard E. Beringer, *The Anatomy of the Confederate Congress: A Study of the Influences of Member Characteristics on Legislative Voting Behavior, 1861–1865* (Nashville, 1972), pp. 44, 293.

remote had little incentive to support the new order. For all Southerners, as Lincoln would later say, knew that slavery "was somehow the cause of the war." Thus it is not surprising that Unionist sentiment within the Confederacy was most obvious in those regions of the South where neither the slave nor the plantation flourished. The red clay counties of north Georgia and the sand hills of northern Mississippi had voted Unionist in 1861, and there Unionist sentiment persisted after the war had begun. In Jasper County, Georgia, for example, some Unionists refused to lower the United States flag for weeks after secession was declared. But Governor Joseph E. Brown, a shrewd judge of his people, did not press the issue, and gradually he won them over to acquiescence in, if not support of, secession. Probably because Brown was never an enthusiastic supporter of the Davis government in Richmond, Unionist activity in his state was weak. Nevertheless, north Georgia did resist conscription in 1863. Besides, Sherman's famous march through the state in 1864 did little to cause friendship for the Union to flower, even though the Confederacy's doom was fast approaching.

Northern Alabama, however, presented a different picture. It, too, had been strongly opposed to secession. All of the seventeen counties of the northern part of the state had sent cooperationist delegates to the secessionist convention, and a majority of them voted against secession. Thirty-three of the delegates from north Alabama refused to sign the Ordinance of Secession. (North Alabama, unlike strongly Unionist areas in the upper South, had been overwhelmingly Democratic in the antebellum years, as had northern Georgia.) Although the decision to secede seemed to silence the Unionists of north Alabama for a while, by the summer of 1862 Union troops operating in the area learned that many native whites were interested in joining the United States army. By October, 1862, the First Alabama Cavalry, U.S.A., was organized. More than 2,000 white Alabamians joined it in the course of the war. The unit served with Sherman in his march through Georgia and the Carolinas. By October, 1862, too, reports from north Alabama to the Confederate authorities spoke of open defiance of the government, of trading with the enemy, and of informing to the Union army. Confederate General Gideon Pillow estimated that there were 8,000 to 10,000 "Tories," as he called them, in north Alabama in the fall of 1862, of whom some, at least, were deserters from the Confederate army. With the Union army operating in the area, Unionists became bolder, and the governor of the state complained that the Confederate conscription laws could not be enforced in several northern counties. From 1862 on, a Peace Society, with handgrips and recognition signs, was active in northern Alabama and northern Georgia. By the time the war was drawing to a close, northern Alabama was a well-known refuge for Confederate deserters and stragglers, who came and went without fear of arrest, and Confederate army enrolling officers could expect to be ambushed and killed.

The mountain regions of Arkansas had also been opposed to secession in 1861 and remained a focal point of Unionism during the war. Van Buren County in the Ozark Mountains was the locale in the fall of 1861 for the founding of the Peace and Constitutional Society, probably the first of several such organizations in the South. Within a month 27 men were arrested by the authorities, at which time it was ascertained that there were about 1,700 members in the state. Each member was sworn to encourage desertion from the Confederate army, to recruit for the United States army, and to help that army when it invaded. Later in the year, 78 more were arrested and marched to Little Rock for trial, where they were given the choice of jail or service in the Confederate army! One historian who studied the background of 181 members of the Peace Society who could be identified found that none of them held slaves and that they were generally even poorer than their poor neighbors. As many as 115 out of the 181 were born in Tennessee, and of 21 leaders, all were born in the South except one who had resided in Arkansas for the previous eighteen years. In September, 1863, Colonel W. F. Cloud of the U.S. army reported that in one day he had assembled six companies from among the native whites. "The people come to me by hundreds and beg of me to stand by them," he reported to Washington. Other officers echoed his report.[13] One measure of the Unionism

13. Studies of Alabama Unionism are abundant. See, for example, Georgia Lee Tatum, *Disloyalty in the Confederacy* (Chapel Hill, N.C., 1934), the standard study for the whole South; William Stanley Hoole,

of Arkansas, and perhaps of the effectiveness of its Peace Society, is that more than 8,000 white men from the state served in the United States army during the war, a figure that was larger than that for Arkansas Negroes in the U.S. army.

The most striking instance of the correspondence between Unionism and mountain people, of course, is West Virginia. There the disaffection of the nonslaveholding whites from the rest of Virginia went back a generation, as we have seen already in regard to attitudes toward slavery. Soon after Virginia seceded, the western mountainous counties began to form into a separate state, a goal that was achieved in 1863. The mountainous region of Virginia had the advantage of bordering on the North; its active dissent from secession could be quickly supported, as it was, by Northern military power.

This advantage was not available, however, to the mountain people of North Carolina and Tennessee, many of whom resented as well as rejected secession. At the beginning of the war it was hoped that the Union army would be able to penetrate southern Appalachia to support the Unionists there. The New York *Tribune* in July, 1861, for example, called for a military campaign to support Southern Unionists, so that they could form a state "in the very heart of the slave-holding country."[14] And for months Lincoln endeavored to push a Union army into eastern Tennessee, but it was not until 1863 that the aim was accomplished. Neverthe-

---

Alabama Tories: The First Alabama Cavalry, U.S.A., 1862–1865 (Tuscaloosa, Ala., 1960); Hugh C. Bailey, "Disaffection in the Alabama Hill Country, 1861," *Civil War History,* 4 (1958), 183–194; Walter L. Fleming, *Civil War and Reconstruction in Alabama* (New York, 1905), and Durwood Long, "Unanimity and Disloyalty in Secessionist Alabama," *Civil War History,* 11 (1965), 257–73, which disputes Bailey's earlier piece with new evidence; Donald Bradford Dodd, "Unionism in Confederate Alabama," unpublished Ph.D. dissertation, University of Georgia, 1969, pp. 80–83.

The statement from Colonel Cloud is quoted in Robert F. Smith, "The Confederate Attempt to Counteract Reunion Propaganda in Arkansas, 1863–1865," *Arkansas Historical Quarterly,* XVI (1957), 55. For other studies on Arkansas Unionism see Jack B. Scroggs, "Arkansas in the Secession Crisis," *Arkansas Historical Quarterly,* XII (1953), 179–224; and Ted R. Worley, "The Arkansas Peace Society of 1861: A Study of Mountain Unionism," *Journal of Southern History,* XXIV (1958), 445–56, which contains an analysis of members' economic background.

14. Klingberg, *Southern Claims Commission,* p. 2.

less in the mountainous counties of western North Carolina Unionist sentiment persisted without federal troops. The Order of the Heroes of America had its locale in North Carolina and eastern Tennessee. Like the Arkansas Peace Societies, the Heroes was a secret organization of Unionists with passwords, handgrips, and rituals. By 1863 Unionist groups in western North Carolina were so numerous and dangerous because of their guerrilla attacks on Confederate property and installations that six companies of cavalry were dispatched against them. In the fall of that year the Confederate assistant secretary of war, with a pardonable exaggeration, said that the disaffection in the mountain regions of the South was as dangerous to the Confederacy as either of the two Union armies that were then invading the South. At that time in western North Carolina alone the Unionists controlled 240 square miles of territory. Individual Unionists like William Holden through his defeatist newspaper the Raleigh *Standard* and Thomas Settle, a prominent politician, preached peace and reunion whenever possible. The judiciary, which under the leadership of Chief Justice Richmond Pearson was strongly Unionist, so weakened the conscription laws that the western part of the state became a haven for draft dodgers and deserters. In 1864 Judge Pearson held that resisting arrest for desertion was not a crime and a member of the State Home Guard could not be forced to arrest deserters or conscripts unless the accused was liable for militia duty.[15] Significantly, Pearson, Settle, and Holden became prominent Republican leaders in North Carolina after the war.

TENNESSEE UNIONISM

East Tennessee was undoubtedly the most spectacular example of the persistence of Unionism in the heart of the Confederacy. After the state had officially committed itself to the Confederacy, what amounted to civil war broke out in the eastern part, which had voted Whig before 1856, for Bell in 1860, and against disunion in June, 1861. When the Confederate authorities moved troops into the area, the population resorted to guerrilla warfare,

15. A. Sellew Roberts, "The Peace Movement in North Carolina," *Mississippi Valley Historical Review,* XI (1924), 194–95.

striking at Confederates from ambush, burning bridges, and derailing trains. Unionists who were caught were summarily executed, their bodies left hanging in conspicuous places to remind other Unionists of the fate that awaited overt opposition.

Despite the Draconian measures, by 1862 the Unionists had brought Confederate conscription in eastern Tennessee to a halt. In April of that year Confederate General E. Kirby Smith described the situation to his superiors in Richmond. "Every effort made by the state authorities to call out the militia of East Tennessee has proved unavailing. The county officers chosen in the recent state elections are generally open advocates of the Federal Government. The people only await the appearance of a Northern Army to range themselves under their [*sic*] banner." He went on to observe that "open and avowed supporters of the Federal Government have been elected to almost every office and they will be installed on Monday next."[16] Indeed, throughout the war, representatives from eastern Tennessee sat in both the United States and the Confederate Congresses.

The ultimate measure of Tennessee Unionism was that the state provided more white troops to the U.S. army than any other state of the Confederacy. More than 31,000 men from Tennessee, formed into 51 regiments, fought under the United States flag in the Civil War. Most of them undoubtedly came from east Tennessee, but certainly not all. Not surprisingly, Tennessee was one of the four Southern states in which the number of white men who served in the U.S. army outnumbered the number of Negroes.

UNIONISTS IN BLUE

The severest test of Unionism in the South was willingness to serve in the invading army. Although this was the most demanding test to meet, literally thousands of white Southerners demonstrated their Unionism by passing it. More than a hundred officers of general or admiral rank in the U.S. armed forces were born in

16. Patton, *Unionism in Tennessee*, pp. 66, 51–52; also useful are Verton M. Queener, "The Origin of the Republican Party in East Tennessee," East Tennessee Historical Society, *Publications*, No. 13 (1941), pp. 66–90; and E. Merton Coulter, *William G. Brownlow, Fighting Parson of the Southern Highlands* (Chapel Hill, N.C., 1937).

what became the Confederate states. Some of them, like Generals Winfield Scott and George Thomas of Virginia, and Admiral David Farragut of Tennessee and Virginia, are well known. All told, about 54,000 white Southerners native to the Confederacy fought in the invading Union armies, contributing 89 regiments. The distribution by states provides a rough indication of the relative strength of Unionist sentiment among the Confederate states.

White Southerners in U.S. Armed Forces During the Civil War

Alabama	2,578	Mississippi	545
Arkansas	8,289	North Carolina	3,156
Florida	1,290	Tennessee	31,092
Louisiana	5,224	Texas	1,965

Despite the apparent precision of these figures, they ought to be accepted as only generally accurate. In this particular list, for example, Virginia, Georgia, and South Carolina are not depicted as contributing any white soldiers to the Union forces. Another list, equally "official," credits Virginia with 880 and Georgia with 160, though it also counts none for South Carolina. Under the circumstances prevailing at the time, the discrepancies are certainly understandable. Moreover, the two lists are in general agreement as to the three states in which enlistments in the U.S. army were minimal, that is, Virginia, Georgia, and South Carolina. Virginia and Georgia officially were counted as having one white regiment each in the Union army, but it is not always clear that the complements of those regiments were actually from the state of their banners.[17]

UNIONISTS WITH SLAVES

The weakness or absence of slavery in a given area of the South was undoubtedly one of the primary reasons for the persistence of

17. For a list of high officers of Southern birth in the Union forces see Charles C. Anderson, *Fighting by Southern Federals* (New York, 1912); on number of Southerners in federal service see Frederick H. Dyer, *A Compendium of the War of the Rebellion* (New York, 1959, orig. ed. 1909), pp. 11–12; also Klingberg, *Southern Claims Commission,* p. 43, which reprints the official table.

Unionism in the Confederacy. But there were other reasons why Southerners would refuse to relinquish their attachment to the old Union. Jason Niles of Kosciusko, Mississippi, was a Union man who simply refused to change his political views. A prewar Whig, he ultimately became a Republican leader in Mississippi and congressman. During the war he and his family reread Webster's reply to Hayne and still judged it "unsurpassable." In Columbia, Mississippi, a Presbyterian minister named James A. Lyon also retained his Unionist sympathies, even though he lived in a county in which 48 percent of the population in 1860 were slaves and despite harassment for his Unionism. His son was court-martialed for his disloyalty to the Confederacy, but still managed to run for the legislature in 1863. Although physical violence was used to keep men from voting for young Lyon, when the ballots were counted, about 25 percent of the voters of Marion County had selected a candidate who ran on a platform of reconciliation with the North.

Some insight into the sources of James Lyon's enduring Unionism is provided by the three consequences he saw emerging from the war in 1864. The people, he said first, will be punished for having allowed "the great trust of free government" to pass into the hands of demagogues. The second change will concern "slavery, a great and peculiar trust committed to their hands for the civilization and Christianization of the African, but which they have vilely abused, and used only for selfish and sordid purposes, regardless of the natural rights of the slaves." He thought slavery would be reformed "if indeed it is not abolished altogether." The third improvement he saw coming out of the war was that the government in Washington "will be strengthened, and *consolidated* (not centralized) and made what the framers of the Constitution intended it to be." Obviously a Unionist of the nationalist school, Lyon went on to say that states' rights had "been the *sand* in the machinery, the *friction* in the cogs" of government. Getting rid of states' rights, he thought, was "one of the providential designs of this war." From the beginning, he said in another connection, he had opposed secession "not only as a great political heresy, but as an egregious blunder that would bring war and ruin upon the land." Lyon lived to see the war end, and he remained in his pastorate at Columbus until 1870, at which time he left to become a professor at the University of Mississippi.[18]

Mississippians with more social standing were also Unionists before and during the war. Many of the planters and former Whigs who lived in the rich river counties had opposed secession in 1861. Twenty-three counties along the Mississippi River, which contained only 29 percent of the state's white population, but 57 percent of the slaves, produced 56 percent of the cotton. These twenty-three wealthy counties were conspicuous for their strong support for cooperationists in the secession convention. In the state at large, cooperationists captured 42 percent of the total vote, but in these twenty-three river counties cooperationists gained 55 percent of the vote.

During the war individual planters in the river counties were prominent in support of the Union. William L. Sharkey, for example, who before the war had been chief justice of the High Court of Errors and Appeals and a prominent Whig, disdained having anything to do with the Confederate government of his longtime enemy and fellow Mississippian Jefferson Davis. Sharkey adamantly refused to sell supplies to the Confederate forces, and during the first Union siege of Jackson, he freely turned over the first floor of his house to the federal commander. In August, 1863, Sharkey and other Mississippians took the oath of allegiance to the United States. About the same time a newspaper correspondent estimated that half of the inhabitants of Natchez, most of whom were wealthy planters and slaveholders, were Unionist in sympathy.

When United States General Lorenzo Thomas occupied Natchez, Mississippi, in the fall of 1863, he found many of his old friends from prewar army days still friendly to him and the cause of the Union. Many of them were prominent former Whigs and planters. "They are extremely desirous of bringing this state back into the Union," he wrote Secretary of War Edwin Stanton. "The strong undercurrent of Union feeling is daily growing, and the time

18. Entry in Jason Niles's diary, Oct. 16, 1864, in Diaries and Journals of Jason Niles; John K. Bettersworth, "Mississippi Unionism: The Case of the Reverend James A. Lyon," *Journal of Mississippi History,* I (1939), 49, 41.

is not far distant when it will rise to the surface and assert its proper sway," Thomas concluded.[19]

One of the most forward of the Unionist planters, as well as one of the wealthiest, was William Minor. He freely associated with the occupying authorities, advising them and supplying their troops. Minor's son John, also a Unionist, risked his fortune as well as his neighbor's approbation for the Union cause. After the war his widow presented a claim for $64,000 for young Minor's contribution to the military support of the Union, but the cautious Southern Claims Commission allowed her only $13,000—still a substantial amount for those days.

The wealthy planters of Louisiana also found that their traditional Whig Unionism led them into passive and sometimes overt opposition to secession and the Confederacy. One student of the Louisiana secession convention found that delegates to that convention from the old Whig parishes tended to be more cooperationist or conditional Unionist than those from the usually Democratic parishes. During the war William Bailey, one of the wealthiest planters in all of Louisiana—he owned 1,300 acres of cleared land and scores of slaves—supplied the Red River army of Union General Nathaniel Banks when the troops' regular supplies were cut off. Bailey, a veteran of the War of 1812, was joined in his active Unionism by another planter and veteran of the war with England, James B. Sullivan. Sullivan was arrested by the Confederates for refusing to sell them cotton. Although the Union troops destroyed his plantation, Sullivan was, nevertheless, tried for treason by the Confederacy.[20]

Some of the leading political figures of Texas, too, were active in support of the Union forces during the war. Edmund J. Davis, prominent politician and judge, joined the U.S. army and recruited for the Union. The Hamilton brothers, Andrew and Morgan, had been active in Texas politics before the war, but both

19. *Official Records of the Union and Confederate Armies,* Ser. III (Washington, D.C., 1900), III, 916–17.

20. Klingberg, *Southern Claims Commission,* pp. 110–113; James W. Garner, *Reconstruction in Mississippi* (Baton Rouge, 1968, orig. pub. 1901), p. 53; Frank Wysor Klingberg, "The Case of the Minors: A Unionist Family Within the Confederacy," *Journal of Southern History,* XIII (1947), 27–45; Wooster, *Secession Conventions,* pp. 262–63.

risked all for the Union. Eventually Andrew Hamilton fled to Mexico to escape Confederate arrest.

Examples of wealthy Unionists were not difficult to locate in North Carolina, either. When one North Carolina Unionist returned with the U.S. army to his native state in 1863, he wrote that "there are quite a number of persons in town, who are loyal and were men of respectability and influence before the war. I do not know any place in North Carolina where there are as many men of wealth who are truly loyal as in Washington [North Carolina]."[21]

Individual examples of wealthy men or women who supported the Union cause are informative, but by themselves they do not tell us much about the importance of that class of Unionists. Fortunately, there is a source that does fill in some of the gaps in our knowledge of this aspect of Southern Unionism. It is the records of the Southern Claims Commission, which have been admirably analyzed in a study by Frank Klingberg of the University of North Carolina.

During the war the Lincoln administration had promised Unionist Southerners that they could expect to be recompensed for any costs they incurred while assisting the Union cause. Obviously this was a way of encouraging their loyalty and eliciting their support. But once the war was over, the Radical Republicans were less interested in recompensing Southerners, even Unionists. It was not until 1871 that Congress got around to carrying out the promises made during the war. It provided for a commission that would receive and evaluate claims of Southern Unionists against the United States. As might be anticipated, the standards that had to be met for reimbursement were high. Not only was it necessary to show receipts for supplies furnished to the army (mere damage by the U.S. army was not covered under the law), but the recipient also had to show that he had never aided the Confederacy. If he had voted in a Confederate election or paid taxes to the Confederacy, or given a horse to a Confederate, he was not eligible, even though he held receipts from the U.S. army for goods he had supplied. One claim was disallowed, for example, because the claimant, a clothier, had once supplied uniforms to the Confeder-

21. John A. Hedrick to Benjamin Hedrick, Dec. 9, 1863, in B. S. Hedrick Papers.

ate army. Another claim was rejected even though the claimant had refused to make cartridge boxes for the Confederacy; it turned out that he had made saddles and other cavalry equipment, which were judged as helpful to the enemy as cartridge boxes.

To assist in making its judgments on claims, the commission received affidavits, and for claims over $10,000 the claimants were required to appear in person in Washington, D.C., to be personally interrogated. The commission also employed agents who checked records and visited the area to ascertain the extent of the claimant's Unionism as well as the accuracy of the claim. The agents in their quest for information checked with former slaves as well as with white neighbors. The procedures of the Court of Claims were followed by the commission, and virtually all of the decisions of the commission, when later brought before the claims court, were upheld.

Given the stringent nature of the commission's standards, it is somewhat unexpected that more than 22,000 persons submitted claims, for a total of $60 million. Not all of the claims were allowed, of course; in fact, only about $4.6 million was paid to almost 7,000 successful claimants. Yet the difficulties and expenses involved in even filing a claim, much less carrying it through, make it evident that the 22,000 claims represent the hard core of Southern Unionism rather than its outer limits. Many a Unionist who might have had some claim was undoubtedly discouraged from even entering a claim by the expense or time involved, or the fear of hostility from Northerners, or he may simply have lacked the necessary documentation, such as receipts. Undoubtedly there were fraudulent claims, but they probably were more than balanced off by those that were legitimate but unfiled. What is most important about these claims is that they reveal a class of wartime Southern Unionists who are quite different from the Unionists of the mountain areas. These are Unionists of property, for that is what they gave to the Union cause.

If the claims are broken down into classes of amounts, an indication of the extent of planter support for the Union emerges. Almost 1,500 claimants asked for $5,000 or more as their contributions to the Union cause. In 1860, $5,000 was a substantial sum. The annual wage of a good skilled worker in New York City was about $600; the yearly salary of the Chief Justice of the United States was then $6,500, that of the Vice-President of the United States $8,000. Of those 1,500, about 700 filed claims of $10,000 or more. These higher claims need to be evaluated against the fact that the law placed additional burdens on those who filed claims of $10,000 or more; they incurred the added expense of a personal appearance before the commission in Washington. Therefore, it seems reasonable to assume that the number of claims over $10,000 is a minimum rather than a maximum number of persons who made such large contributions to the Union cause. More than 80 percent of those who entered claims of $10,000 or more, as one might expect, were planters who owned, on the average, 54 slaves. The range of slave ownership ran from 15 to 310. For comparison purposes it can be noted that only about 68,000 persons in the whole South owned as many as 15 or more slaves.[22] These Unionist claimants, therefore, were not a negligible part of the planter class. Actually almost 200—191 to be exact—of those who claimed $10,000 or more had their claims approved. And 224 of 786 who claimed between $5,000 and $10,000 had their claims accepted. In short, there were literally hundreds of great planters in the South who carried their Unionism through to the end, even in a war that was supposed to save the slave system of which they were the principal beneficiaries.

An examination of where the claimants came from reinforces what we already know about the distribution of Unionists. If all the 22,298 claims are counted, then claimants came from 655 counties across the Confederacy. As one might expect, Tennessee recorded the highest number of claims. Virginia and Georgia came next, even though very few volunteers for the Union army came from these two states. They were sites of extensive military operations, however, and aid to the military forces of the United States was the primary basis of claims. The 701 claimants for $10,000 or more each are heavily concentrated, as again one might expect, in Louisiana, Mississippi, and Virginia. These three states alone accounted for 436 of the 701. Louisiana and Mississippi, as we have observed already, were conspicuous for the concentration of Whig planters living in the counties along the Mississippi River.

22. Klingberg, *Southern Claims Commission,* p. 158.

Virginia, too, had a large number of wealthy Whigs who had resisted secession.

On one level the large number of planters and slaveholders who remained Unionists even after 1861 comes as something of a surprise. The surprise comes principally because we are accustomed to think of secession as undertaken in behalf of slavery and the so-called Southern way of life, in which well-to-do or successful planters obviously had a heavy stake. And, at bottom, they did have a stake in the perpetuation of slavery and the society on which it was built. But it is a long way to the bottom. Many motives and concerns intervened before the bottom was reached. As a result, many large slaveholders reacted to secession on something short of simple self-interest, or even of class interest, one must add. Many of them, for example, were old Whigs, an affiliation that meant they were not disposed to accept association with a Democratic policy. Others simply thought secession could not work. Unionist Francis A. Owen of Mississippi, for example, told the Southern Claims Commission: "I had no confidence in the success of the South and I did not desire it. I believed it to be an effort to establish an oligarchy, and we would have been a little handful of men just there, and we would have had to have pocketed the insults of the North and every other nation that was disposed to insult us." A few had philosophical objections. James G. Taliaferro of Louisiana told the secession convention of his state: "I believe that peaceable secession is a right unknown to the Constitution of the United States," and secession would bring war, anarchy, and loss of property. Secession "is a revolutionary act that this Convention," he contended, "is, of itself, without legitimate power to perform." Taliaferro, a judge and Whig who refused to support the Confederacy during the war, went on to become a Republican after the war.[23] Some of the slaveholding Unionists who resisted the Confederacy, though probably not very many of them, were ambivalent, when not outright unhappy, about slavery anyway. Jonathan Worth, who was a slaveholder, apparently fell into this category. The sister of Confederate General

23. *Ibid.*, p. 194; Roger Wallace Shugg, "A Suppressed Co-Operationist Protest against Secession," *Louisiana Historical Quarterly,* XIX (1936), 199–201.

Gideon Pillow owned 120 slaves, but she supported the Union. She refused to take the oath to the Confederacy and accepted the Emancipation Proclamation. Even before the war she remarked on "the inconsistency of the people of the South shouting for liberty and freedom while they themselves held four millions of human beings in severe servitude." Harriet J. Carey of Mississippi opposed both secession and slavery, too, but she did not speak out against slavery until later. "I owned slaves and concluded if I was merciful and humane to them, I might just as well own them as other persons. . . . [But] I had an instinctive horror of the institution," she later told the Southern Claims Commission. "We did not dare call ourselves an abolitionist—but those were my sentiments, always." Some Whig planters were willing to accept compensated emancipation if that would avoid the disruption of an antislavery army of invasion. As early as 1862 a North Carolina Unionist reported that around Greensboro there were many "unqualified Union men, including many large slaveholders who say that they would willingly give up every negro they had if it would restore peace. . . ."[24]

Some planters, too, believed—and rightly so, as events turned out—that slavery would be protected better inside the Union than out. Men who were not planters, it is true, like Andrew Johnson, made this argument. But so did John S. Carlile, a slaveholder and admitted believer in the morality of slavery. "How long, if you were to dissolve this Union," he asked in the Virginia Secession Convention, "would African slavery have a foothold in this portion of the land? I venture the assertion that it would not exist in Virginia five years after separation, and nowhere in the Southern states twenty years after. How could it maintain itself, with the whole civilized world, backed by what they call their international law, arrayed for its ultimate extinction?" Within the Union, he pointed out, the North was committed to stand by the South in the defense of slavery. It is significant, too, that in the end Carlile voted in the convention against secession—his argument was not simply concocted for the occasion; he acted on it. A delegate from the western part of the state, where there were few slaves, made a

24. Klingberg, *Southern Claims Commission,* pp. 196, 108; Jesse Wheeler to Benjamin Hedrick, Jan. 20, 1862, B. S. Hedrick Papers.

similar argument. His constituents believed that slavery "is right, legally, morally, and in every sense of the word." But outside of the Union, it would not be protected, so he urged opposition to secession.[25]

Finally, many planters and upper-class Southern Unionists must have opposed secession because it was radical. If there is one characteristic that stands out in the remarks and explanations of Southern Unionists it is their conservatism. Sam Houston, as we have seen, quite frankly applied that term to his beliefs. So did John Bell, and so very likely would have the Natchez nabobs who were friends of General Lorenzo Thomas during the war. The long and complicated anguish of Jonathan Worth was a witness to his conservatism, his fear of what change would bring.

By its very nature Unionism in the South was conservative. The Union, after all, was the going situation; those who sought to disrupt it, to change the status quo, were the radicals, the innovators. By and large, men of wealth have always and everywhere approved of the status quo, if only because they have done so well within it. To change it is fraught with the threat of the unknown. What other social disorders or disruptions might follow? As Alexander Stephens pointed out, to make a revolution is to open up the floodgates, for when the traditional controls are gone, anything may happen. Revolutions have a way of slipping away from those who begin them. Such thoughts must have underlain the decisions of a number of great planters when they refused to accept the political solution of secession though it was offered for their benefit.

AN UNDERLYING LINK

Though it is certainly true that virtually all antislavery Southerners were Unionists, the converse is not true. Most Unionists were certainly not antislavery in sentiment. In fact, as the examples of "Parson" Brownlow or Andrew Johnson make evident, even if a Unionist lived in a nonslaveholding region of the South, his Unionism did not automatically make him hostile toward, or

25. George H. Reese, ed., *Proceedings of the Virginia State Convention* (Richmond, 1965), I, 458–65; III, 168–69.

even critical of, slavery. And, furthermore, as we have observed, a large number of slave owners were strong Unionists. Was there no linkage, then, between dissenters in the antebellum South?

One link was certainly their common love for the region. Antislavery and Unionist Southerners may have rejected some of the values of their region, but it would be a mistake to assume, as many Majority Southerners at the time did, that this meant these dissenters were betrayers of their region. It is true that the values both of them espoused were values that were often dominant in the North, such as nationalism, economic development and diversification, and opposition to slavery. Hinton Helper, the Southern abolitionist, put the combination succinctly when he wrote in *The Impending Crisis of the South,* "Our motto . . . is *the abolition of slavery, and the perpetuation of the American Union.*" Yet Helper made quite clear that his advocacy of Northern or national values was for the advancement of the South, and not for an assimilation of the South into the nation or submission to the North. At the very opening of his most famous book he pointed to the South's shameful misuse of its abundant resources for economic development. "Instead of cultivating among ourselves a wise policy of mutual assistance and cooperation with respect to individuals, and of self-reliance with respect to the South at large, instead of giving countenance and encouragement to the industrial enterprises projected in our midst, and instead of building up, aggrandizing and beautifying our own States, cities and towns, we have been spending our substance at the North, and are daily augmenting and strengthening the very power which has us so completely under its thumb." Later he returned to the same point of emphasizing his Southern orientation. "We are all spend thrifts," he said, referring to Southerners; "some of us should become financiers. We must learn to take care of our money; we should withhold it from the North, and open avenues for its circulation at home."[26]

Those Unionists who were not opposed to slavery also considered themselves as guardians of the South's best interests. Adherence to the Union, they were convinced, would save the

26. Hinton Rowan Helper, *The Impending Crisis of the South: How to Meet It* (New York, 1860), pp. 186, 23–24, 357.

South from a devastating war, which, in the end, the South would lose. The South would also lose, as Jonathan Worth said, the best government in the world, and one, moreover, as Sam Houston reminded his fellow Texans, that had served the South well.

But this common concern for the future of the South was not the only link between Southern Unionists and antislavery people. They also shared a conservative outlook. Within the South, Unionism may have been a form of dissent, but it was also a defense of the old order. It could stand only in sharp contrast with secession, which was daring, disruptive, and radical. It was not accidental that secessionists were called "radicals" while during the war Unionists in the South were called "Tories." Antislavery sentiment, to be sure, was subversive of the slave South, but among most antislavery Southerners, as we have seen, it was cautious, conservative, and realistic. The opposition to slavery in the South lacked that moral and idealistic incandescence that is traditionally associated with abolition in the North. Even the Unionism of Sam Houston or Andrew Johnson did not compare in imagination or nobility with the democratic nationalism of Abraham Lincoln. It is not accidental, in short, that there were no Transcendentalists in the antebellum South, no advocates of women's rights, no Elihu Berritt preaching world peace, no New Harmony experimenting with new schemes of social organization. Instead there were only conservative Unionists and cautious antislavery advocates. For the antebellum South was indeed a different society from the North, divided as it may have been, and one of the reasons we know that is because its dissenters were different, too. Paradoxically enough, despite their dissent, they wore the stamp of their region. They were Southerners, too.

On one level the dissent of the antebellum and war years came to a natural and, one would have thought, conclusive end. The Union was saved and slavery was abolished. The dissenters had become the winners, after all. But since the sources of the South's divisions had derived from more than the issues now settled, and since the very conflicts between Southerners had reinforced their past differences, the South after Appomattox was not likely to be any more free of dissenters than before. Moreover, there were now new sources of division. There were no longer any slaves, to be sure, but the Negroes were still present. Their future, like that of the South itself in the restored Union, was yet to be decided. Here there would be ample occasion and cause for division and dissent.

A generation, if it is lucky, may solve its principal problem with which history has confronted it, but that very solution usually only lays bare a new set of problems. Thus it was that the abolition of slavery and the preservation of the Union provided new sources of dissent in the South without eliminating the old bases of division. Let us turn now to a consideration of those Southerners who dissented from their region in the era of Reconstruction—those people still called, to this day, Scalawags.

SOUTHERNERS FOR A DIFFERENT SOUTH

7

"Taking a New
Start in the World"

"Our scallawag is the local leper of the community," wrote the
Tuscaloosa, Alabama, *Independent Monitor* in 1868. "Unlike the
carpetbagger, he is native, which is so much the worse. Once he
was respected in his circle; his head was level, and he would look
his neighbor in the face. Now possessed of the itch of office and
the salt rheum of Radicalism, he is a mangy dog, slinking through
the alleys, haunting the Governor's office, defiling with tobacco
juice the steps of the Capitol, stretching his lazy carcass in the sun
on the Square, or the benches of the Mayor's court."[1] The native
white who cooperated with congressional Reconstruction of the
South after 1867 and joined the Republican party was excoriated
in this manner long after Reconstruction was just a memory.
Northern as well as Southern historians did little more than tone
down the strong language of the Tuscaloosa editor, and even when
they did, the condemnation itself stood.

Only recently, since the 1940's at the most, has a more favorable interpretation of the Scalawag been advanced by professional
historians. For most Americans, the native white Southerner who
cooperated with the North during Reconstruction—unlike the

1. Sarah Van Voorhis Woolfolk, "The Role of the Scalawags in Alabama
Reconstruction," unpublished Ph.D. dissertation, Louisiana State University, 1965, p. 2.

native white Unionist—remained not only a rather nondescript figure but usually a disreputable one as well.

If any date can be selected for marking the shift in the professional historians' conception of the Scalawag, the best is probably 1944, when a young historian, David Donald, published an article on the native white Republicans in early Mississippi Reconstruction. The burden of the article was that, far from being disreputable figures, the leaders of the Republican party in Mississippi, at least in the years immediately after 1865, were drawn from among the prewar leaders of the state. The article examined the background of several of the major personages in the party.

Since Donald's article appeared, other historians have looked into the question of the nature of the Scalawags. Some have emphasized, as Donald did, the upper-class character of the native Republican leaders, while others have merely pointed to the contributions that the native whites made to the South in the course of Reconstruction. Donald's emphasis on the Whiggish background of the Scalawags has subsequently been criticized for ignoring the lower-class composition of the Scalawag rank and file. Actually, of course, the question of whether the Scalawags were wealthy or poor cannot advance us very far in ascertaining the social character of the native Republicans. A political party by its very nature cannot be either effective or important if its membership is drawn only from the wealthy, who, by definition, are few in number. In short, there are really two questions we want to examine in looking at the social nature of Scalawags: the character of the leaders and the social origins of the voters who supported them. Let us begin an examination of these questions by looking at numbers.

HOW MANY WERE SCALAWAGS?

From the beginning to the end of Radical Reconstruction, that is, from 1867 to 1877—and in a number of Southern states the period was shorter than that—the Republican party was everywhere dependent upon Negro votes. Indeed, as we shall see, it was only the enfranchisement of the former slaves that made feasible the formation of the Republican organization in the Southern states. Consequently, the number of white Southerners who voted with that party was always a minority. No one knows for sure how many whites joined the Republican party or voted its ticket in the South, but probably the number went no higher than 20 percent of the white male voters, or about a fifth of the total Republican vote.

A general figure like that, however, does not do justice to the importance of the white Republican vote in making Reconstruction possible, nor does it recognize the uneven distribution of Republican whites in the former Confederate states. In the Reconstruction years, three of the eleven former Confederate states contained a majority of blacks: South Carolina, Mississippi, and Louisiana. In those states, the mere enfranchisement of blacks—all other things being equal—guaranteed Republican political dominance. But in the other seven states, the blacks were less than a majority, though in Alabama, Florida, and Georgia they were 40 percent or more. In sum, in seven states enduring Republican rule depended upon converting whites to the Republican party. (Although disfranchisement of whites is often said to account for the Republican domination of the Southern states during Reconstruction, not enough Southern whites were disfranchised to make a significant difference in elections. The truth of this observation is shown by the fact that Radical Reconstruction came to an end in most of the Southern states through the ballot box, that is, by white Democrats coming out in sufficient numbers to outvote the blacks and the Scalawags. In Mississippi, Louisiana, and South Carolina, where blacks were in a majority, terror and intimidation of blacks were indispensable for Democratic victory; in the other states intimidation was just helpful.)

To speak of white Republicans as making up a fifth of the voters is still not quite the full story. In some states like Florida or Georgia, the Scalawags barely reached 10 percent of the total. On the other hand, in Tennessee, North Carolina, and Virginia they ran as high as 25 to 30 percent. Tennessee and North Carolina counted the highest number and proportions of white Republicans, with Arkansas and Virginia following, in that order.

But if Scalawags were a distinct minority among the voters and even among the party faithful, they were very well represented in the offices held by Republicans under the Reconstruction governments. Contrary to the myth of Reconstruction, the Northerners who came South, the so-called carpetbaggers, were always too few in number to play a numerically significant role in the exercise of political power. Even in Florida, where the state was dominated by a carpetbagger governor, the native white Southerners held the preponderance of offices, both elective and appointive. All of the supreme court justices, for example, were Southerners. Of the almost 200 whites appointed by the carpetbag governor down to August, 1868, some 148 were born in the South. In Alabama, where carpetbaggers were of some importance, too, the native whites were clearly dominant. Only nine out of thirty-eight congressional candidates during Reconstruction were of non-Southern birth. Native whites were appointed or elected to 82 percent of state offices. In Mississippi, in both houses of the legislature, the Scalawags always outnumbered the carpetbaggers. Although the picture varied in detail from state to state, the pattern is clear: white Southerners dominated Radical Reconstruction, even though in Arkansas, Florida, and Louisiana the governors were usually Northerners.[2]

Who, then, were these native white Southerners who played such an important part in carrying out Radical Reconstruction? What connection, if any, was there between them and the dissenters who had preceded them in the antebellum South? To what extent were they betrayers of the South to the Northern conquerors? How radical in fact were they? Some of these questions can be answered only by looking a little later at individual explanations or justifications for becoming a Republican. First it is useful to try to generalize about their social background.

2. Allen W. Trelease, "Who Were the Scalawags?" *Journal of Southern History*, XXIX (1963), 445–68; David Donald, "The Scalawag in Mississippi Reconstruction," *Journal of Southern History*, X (1944), 447–60; Joe M. Richardson, *The Negro in the Reconstruction of Florida 1865–1877* (Tallahassee, 1965), pp. 199–200; William Warren Rogers, *The One-Gallused Rebellion: Agrarianism in Alabama, 1865–1896* (Baton Rouge, 1970), p. 34; Woolfolk, "Scalawags in Alabama," p. v; David Gaffney Sansing, "The Role of the Scalawag in Mississippi Reconstruction," unpublished Ph.D. dissertation, University of Southern Mississippi, 1969, p. 113.

THE SCALAWAG AS A "NOBODY"

Several historians have attempted to draw some general conclusions from an examination of either election returns or large samples. Allen Trelease, for example, sought to identify the Scalawag vote in the election of 1872 by noting those counties in which the Republican vote exceeded substantially the number of adult male Negroes. The difference he assumed to be the number of white Republicans. The trouble with this method is that it does not reveal white Republican strength when it is combined with large numbers of blacks. It cannot disprove, for example, the argument of David Donald and others that well-to-do whites who lived in the Black Belt counties of Mississippi or Louisiana voted Republican during Radical Reconstruction. In those counties the Republican vote rarely exceeded by much the adult male Negro population. Trelease's statistics do show, however, that white Republicans were strong in the white counties of the South. There were 125 counties in the former Confederacy in which the Republican vote in 1872 was at least 30 percentage points greater than the proportion of blacks. In short, those counties were very strongly Scalawag. When they were examined as to their per capita wealth, it was evident that these counties were among the poorest in the South. Trelease shows, in fact, that the higher the proportion of white Republicans in a county, the lower the per capita wealth. Although these counties were located all over the South, they were especially conspicuous in the mountain regions of Tennessee and North Carolina, and in northeastern Arkansas and northern Alabama. These were not the cotton planting areas of the South, which had produced the principal leaders of the region before the war. Trelease's election statistics thus support the general argument that Scalawags were new men to come to power, to be charitable, or just "nobodies," to be blunt.

Support is also given to that view by a study of a large group of Scalawags by a young historian, Richard Hume.[3] Hume attempted

3. Richard L. Hume, "The 'Black and Tan' Constitutional Conventions of 1867–1869 in Ten Former Confederate States: A Study of Their Membership," unpublished Ph.D. dissertation, University of Washington, 1969, pp. 655–74 and passim; William C. Harris, "A Reconsideration of the

to identify all of the 1,010 individuals who participated in the constitutional conventions held in ten Southern states by congressional acts from 1867 to 1869. Those were the conventions that drew up the constitutions under which Radical Reconstruction was carried out. The convention delegates were elected by manhood suffrage, which included blacks. The largest single group elected were Southern whites, who made up 47 percent of the total. For our purposes at the moment, the significant point is that 14 percent of them were unidentifiable, except that they were white. It seems reasonable to conclude that most of these unidentifiable delegates were men so obscure that election to the convention was their first and last political experience. In three states, the proportion of unidentified white delegates was strikingly high: 50 percent in Texas, 31 percent in Mississippi, and 30 percent in Louisiana.

Now it is true that not all of the native white Southerners who served in the Radical constitutional conventions were themselves politically radical. A majority were, however. Hume determined whether a particular delegate was radical or conservative by how he voted on a series of issues. Votes in favor of Negro rights and of disfranchisement of former Confederates were taken as Radical. He found 232 of the Southern whites to be "Radical." (The vast majority of the 258 black delegates also voted the same way.)

The 232 native white delegates analyzed by Hume constitute the largest sample of identified white Republicans ever compiled. It is not possible to reduce the myriad of occupations and activities of so many delegates to a few categories, but it is striking that when they are compared with their Southern white colleagues who voted on the other side of the same issues, the Radicals often are revealed as less wealthy and more lowly in occupational background. The "typical" radical delegate in the conventions of North Carolina, Virginia, Georgia, and Arkansas was poor and a farmer as compared with white conservative members of the same conventions. In South Carolina, Alabama, and Texas, the Radicals were as likely

Mississippi Scalawag," *Journal of Mississippi History,* XXXII (1970), 27; Thomas S. Staples, *Reconstruction in Arkansas, 1862–1874* (New York, 1923), p. 339. *See also* Richard L. Hume, "The Arkansas Constitutional Convention of 1868: A Case Study in the Politics of Reconstruction," *Journal of Southern History,* XXXIX (1973), 183–206.

to be business or professional men as the conservative whites. (Mississippi and Louisiana had so many unidentifiable delegates that Hume could not make a general statement about their backgrounds. But he does note that in Mississippi the Radicals had little political experience as compared with the conservative delegates, who were typically "professionally trained individuals.")

More narrowly based studies also suggest the newness of the Scalawags. An examination of some 140 active Republicans in Reconstruction Mississippi turned up only eight who were large landowners or slaveholders before the war. Twelve more, however, were physicians. Thomas Alexander's examination of more than 500 members of a Union convention in Tennessee in 1865 revealed that three-fifths of them had not served in any civil or military office before that convention and were not notable in politics between 1835 and 1890. And if holding office outside of the period of Radical Reconstruction is eliminated, then probably 80 percent of them were without political significance before or after Reconstruction.

Opponents of the Radicals at the time, of course, made the same point. And so did the Radicals themselves. One carpetbagger wrote to Northerner Benjamin Butler in 1871 that it was not wise to confine the jurisdiction of judicial commissioners to one county because "in the Republican party South, you will scarcely find persons in Every County competent for the work." Or as one Republican wrote from Duplin County, North Carolina, "The Republicans in this county are very weak so far as Property are concerned."[4]

Yet it would be misleading to dwell unduly upon the white Republicans as "nobodies," for in the years of Reconstruction the white conservatives were not always men of political prominence, either. As one student of the Virginia convention of 1868 observed, most of the conservatives were young Confederate veterans without political experience: "Old Virginia's solons were absent,"

---

4. Thomas B. Alexander, *Political Reconstruction in Tennessee* (Nashville, 1950), p. 18; W. S. Ball to B. F. Butler, Feb. 16, 1871, in James A. Padgett, ed., "Reconstruction Letters from North Carolina, Part IX, Letters to Benjamin Franklin Butler," *North Carolina Historical Review*, XXI (1944), 347; Amos McCullough to Daniel L. Russell, Oct. 10, 1874, Daniel Russell Papers.

comments Jack Maddex.[5] Those were novel, even shattering times, and the men who answered the call to politics under such strange and novel rules were not likely to be old-timers or well-known leaders. Moreover, in the early days of Reconstruction, a number of the old leaders were temporarily disfranchised. Furthermore, many of the antebellum leaders in Virginia and elsewhere had come from the Black Belt constituencies; they often had a hard time competing with carpetbaggers for the votes of their former slaves.

THE SCALAWAG AS ANTEBELLUM LEADER

But the principal reason for not dwelling upon the obscure origins of the native white Republicans is that among the leaders of the Scalawags was a startling number of imposing figures from the society of the antebellum South.

In every one of the eleven states of the former Confederacy, the new Republican party could point to leaders who had been prominent politically or socially before the war. The radical leader of the Republicans in Virginia, for example, was James W. Hunnicutt, a native of South Carolina and a slaveholder before he migrated permanently to Virginia in 1847. There he settled in Fredericksburg, editing a newspaper and espousing the cause of the Union. Unlike the vast majority of his fellow Southerners, Hunnicutt was a college graduate. The Republican leader of Florida who became governor during Reconstruction, Ossian B. Hart, had held public office in the state since 1849. In Louisiana, J. Madison Wells, who was the only native Louisianan elected governor during the Reconstruction period, had been a large planter before the war, as we have seen. The president of the Louisiana Constitutional Convention of 1868 was James G. Taliaferro, who had been a judge of the state courts in the antebellum years. Although Confederate General James Longstreet did not remain in New Orleans throughout Reconstruction, when he first became a Republican he lived in Louisiana. An even better-known figure from the antebellum years who became a Republican was Joseph E. Brown, the prewar governor of

5. Jack P. Maddex, Jr., *The Virginia Conservatives 1867–1878: A Study in Reconstruction Politics* (Chapel Hill, N.C., 1970), p. 57.

Georgia. Amos T. Akerman, lawyer, Confederate officer, and old Whig in prewar Georgia, became Attorney General in Grant's cabinet. South Carolina Republicans counted James L. Orr, elected governor of the state by white suffrage in 1865–68, and Dr. Albert G. Mackay among their several distinguished leaders from prewar years. Mackay was a Charleston physician of recognized culture and head of the Freemasons of the state. Although Franklin J. Moses, Jr., earned notoriety as a corruptionist in South Carolina Reconstruction, he was a man of education and came from one of the most distinguished families in the state. Even the party in Arkansas, which came closest to fitting the stereotype of a party of "nobodies," carpetbaggers, and Negroes, contained some leaders of prewar distinction. John M. Bradley, for example, was a minister, lawyer, and Confederate officer, and Oliver P. Snyder had been a member of the lower house of the legislature during the war. Asa Hodges, a Radical member of the convention, owned 64 slaves before the war.

The states of Mississippi, Alabama, Texas, and North Carolina were in a class by themselves when it came to men of prewar prominence in the Republican party leadership. The party in Mississippi could boast of James Lusk Alcorn, one of the wealthiest planters in the state before the war and levee commissioner, an office whose high prestige was measured by the fact that its salary was greater than the governor's. Alcorn became the first Republican governor of the state in 1869. Other Republicans were former U.S. and Confederate congressman John A. Orr, Hiram Cassedy, former speaker of the Mississippi House of Representatives, and C. C. Shackleford, president of the Mississippi Central Railroad during the war and a member of a prominent Whig family. Something of the quality of the native Republican leaders in Mississippi is also shown by the esteem in which the state courts were held during Reconstruction. Of the eighty-six judges who sat on the three courts of record in those years, fifty-five of them were Republicans. Yet no branch of Mississippi government was held in higher esteem than the judiciary.[6]

The native white Republicans of Alabama during Reconstruc-

6. Sansing, "Scalawag in Mississippi," pp. 156–57; Harris, "Reconsideration of . . . Scalawags," p. 28.

tion were equally distinguished. Indeed one student, Sarah Wool-folk, has pointed out that the five most prominent Republican leaders during the Reconstruction had all been highly visible in politics before the war. Moreover, three of the five held substantial property, a good portion of which they lost with Emancipation; all five were lawyers, and all had held public office before becoming Republicans. Woolfolk goes on to generalize about the several score of Scalawag leaders in Alabama she has identified, observing that "an overwhelming number" of them were lawyers who had college education or some other formal legal training; "many were members of outstanding families and some were men of consider-able property. . . . Most of these men had had active public careers in a wide variety of elective and appointive offices."[7]

In some ways the high place of Scalawags in Texas before the war surpassed that of the Republican leaders in Alabama. The count can begin with the brothers Andrew J. and Morgan C. Hamilton, both of whom had come to Texas from Alabama. Both were active in founding the Republican party in Texas, though eventually Andrew led the conservative wing of the party, while Morgan was a leader among the Radicals. Morgan had been secre-tary of war under the Texas Republic, and Andrew had been a member of the state legislature and a member of Congress before 1860. Andrew's strong Unionism caused him to flee to Mexico during the war. James Flanagan and his son Webster were also important figures in the party, with Webster serving as lieutenant governor and United States senator under the Radicals. James Flanagan had been a land speculator and merchant as well as a lawyer and friend of Sam Houston before the war. Edward Degener and George W. Whitmore were two other prominent Texans who became Republicans. Degener, a German immigrant, had been a member of the Frankfort Assembly and a Forty-eighter before coming to Texas and starting life over as a grocer. He was a delegate to the constitutional conventions of 1866 and 1869. George Whitmore was born in Tennessee, but lived in Texas after 1848. He had been a member of the Texas House of Representa-tives for three terms during the 1850's; he served as a Radical in Congress after 1869.

7. Woolfolk, "Scalawag in Alabama," pp. 61–66.

The leader of the Radical Republicans in Texas was Edmund J. Davis. A native of Florida and scion of a wealthy planting family there, Davis migrated to Texas after service in the Mexican War. A graduate of West Point, he became a lawyer, district attorney, and judge in prewar Texas. During the war, his fervent Unionism caused him to join the Union army and to recruit Texans. At one point he was captured, along with his men, by Confederates, but because the incident took place on Mexican soil, the Mexican authorities insisted on Davis's release. For a while he left Texas, but the end of the war found him back in the state, leading Union troops.

In later years his friends liked to tell the story of a meeting between Davis and Robert E. Lee on the eve of the war. Lee was on his way back to Virginia from service in Texas, just after U.S. General David E. Twiggs had surrendered federal installations to the Texan government. Davis reminded Lee, in the course of the conversation, of their common West Point training and reviewed the legal arguments against secession. At the same time he stressed his own thoroughly Southern derivation from a South Carolina family that went back before the Revolution. Lee, the story goes, was visibly moved by Davis's eloquent appeal, but he still would not desert his native Virginia.[8]

Since the North Carolina Republican party contained the largest white contingent of any in the South, it is appropriate that the leaders in that state should also count many distinguished political leaders from the prewar years. Certainly one of the best-known Democrats in the state before 1860 was William W. Holden, whose secessionist newspaper was one of North Carolina's most influential. During the war, as we have seen, Holden had a change of heart, and after 1865 he became a leading Republican and eventually the Radical Republican governor. Behind Holden in organizing the party in that state were prominent jurists from the antebellum years like Richmond Pearson and William Bynam and political leaders like Robert P. Dick and Thomas Settle.

8. W. C. Nunn, *Texas Under the Carpetbaggers* (Austin, 1962), pp. 19–24; Paul Casdorph, *A History of the Republican Party in Texas, 1865–1965* (Austin, 1965), pp. 1–2, 14–17; Hume, " 'Black and Tan' Conventions," pp. 641–43.

The point to be drawn from these examples is not that all Scalawags were prominent figures prior to their becoming Republicans, but rather to show that whatever might be concluded about the kinds of Southerners, in general, who became Republicans, there were many leaders who were drawn from the elite of the prewar South. When put in that fashion, especially when it is recognized that such an elite had a stake in the society inherited from the antebellum years, the question immediately rises as to why such people would elect to join a party that was designed to serve the conquerors' purpose of revolutionizing Southern society. Some of these leaders, moreover, like many of the rank and file, had only recently worn the gray uniform of the Confederacy and had been fighting against not only the United States but the policies and principles of the Republican party as well. In short, even when one has identified who the Scalawags were, the more interesting question is why did they become Scalawags?

Here, too, the answers are many. In fact, they are so complex and varied that though the historian may categorize and analyze individual reasons, the actuality was rarely that neat. A single person might become a Republican for several reasons, or have primary and secondary reasons for joining the party—or not be entirely aware of or candid about his true reasons. Therefore, any analysis of motives always does some violence to the complexity of the springs of human decisions and actions. The types of motives that will be examined here, then, should be seen as more analytical devices than as full or entirely faithful representations of the way the individual human beings made up their minds to act. The Scalawags themselves will be permitted to express their reasons in their own words, to be sure, but it should be assumed that their motives were probably more mixed, less fixed, and certainly less sharply defined than they appear to be when placed in categories. Yet these categories provide some idea, at least, of the range of reasons that impelled some white Southerners to dissent from the majority of their fellows. Furthermore, an examination of the reasons illustrates once again the diversity of the South and the remarkable continuity in Southern history, even across the chasm of civil war and emancipation.

A UNIONIST FOUNDATION

The most obvious sign of this continuity as well as a major source of support for the Republican party in the reconstructed Southern states was the Unionists, those men and women who had resisted secession and sometimes even fought against the Confederacy. The Loyal League of northern Alabama, for example, brought thousands of white Unionists into the party in the early years of Radical Reconstruction. The Heroes of America, a Unionist secret organization that had been strong in western North Carolina, was another source of Republican votes. "The Heroes of America is destined to be a big thing," commented one Tarheel to another in early 1867. Another North Carolinian pointed out to a Northern Republican in 1868 that "nearly one-fourth of the Voters" who cast a Republican ticket in his precinct in the previous election "wore the Blue during the war." One Mississippian joined the Republican party because otherwise the state would fall back into the clutches of those whose "hands were still red with the blood of Union victims."[9]

The Unionist foundation on which much of the Radical Republican party in the South rested is best observed in a general way through the ten constitutional conventions in the Southern states. Richard Hume's comparison of the Radical with the Conservative Southern white delegates reveals that in at least six of the eight conventions for which there is information on their members, the Radical members were clearly stronger in their Unionism. Many Conservatives, it is true, had been reluctant to accept secession, but the Radicals were not only opponents of secession, but frequently opponents of the Confederacy, and some had even been soldiers in the Union army. Florida's convention, for example, contained only four native white Radicals, but three of the four had deserted the Confederate army. In the Alabama convention,

9. J. L. Johnson to Benjamin Hedrick, March 18, 1867, in B. S. Hedrick Papers; W. B. Siegrist to W. E. Chandler, Oct. 16, 1868, in James A. Padgett, ed., "Reconstruction Letters from North Carolina, Part VI, Letters to William E. Chandler," *North Carolina Historical Review,* XIX (1942), 64–65; Harris, "Reconsideration of . . . Scalawags," p. 15.

five of the Radical white Southerners had served in the Union army. A similar pattern was true of Radical members of the conventions in Arkansas and Texas.

The Unionists were not always content merely to vote their Unionist beliefs. In northern Alabama, for instance, the Unionists clamored so strenuously for reprisals against former Confederates that even the occupying authorities were embarrassed. The vehemence stemmed naturally enough from the losses in property, power, and prestige that many Unionists had sustained before and especially during the war because of their beliefs. Now that the secessionists had been defeated, the Unionists hoped to gain the political power which they had long been denied. Their very hardships under the Confederacy inured them against pleas for mercy from the defeated. *"Now* is the time to build up the Republican party," wrote one radical in May, 1867, to Thomas Settle, a North Carolina Republican leader. "Negro suffrage connected with the fear of confiscation has knocked secession out of traitors. The highest duty of a Christian patriot is to oppose the works of the devil and the democratic party." On another occasion Settle himself observed that although he did not like disfranchisement of former Confederates, "let me tell you that if I live till grief kills me because of disfranchisement, history will record one older man than Methuselah." John Pool, another North Carolina Republican, wrote in 1868 that the former secessionists must learn that Union men will not be "again tyrannized over by men whose morality was not shocked by robbery, whose humanity was not aroused by either murder or the most atrocious cruelty, and whose insane hatred can now be neither opposed nor limited."

Given this wish to control the secessionists, many Unionists in the South welcomed the imposition of military rule by Congress. "The loyal people of North Carolina," wrote one citizen of the state to Radical Congressman Thaddeus Stevens immediately after the passage of the first Reconstruction Act, "hail the passage of the Reconstruction bill with feelings of joy and look to it as fully adequate to protect the loyal Men of the rebel States." If implemented, he went on, it should "purge the Government of disloyalty, Provided the Authorities will not enfranchize the rebels too soon."

The intense Unionism that was felt by at least some Southern Republicans is evident in a letter sent to a number of North Carolina Republicans as late as 1876. The letter invited the recipients to "attend the decoration of the graves of the Union soldiers in the National Cemetery" at Salisbury, North Carolina, which was in the old Unionist, western end of the state.[10] These North Carolina Republicans were not sunshine patriots. Their loyalty to the Union and their vehemence against secessionists drew upon a long history of internal conflict within the South which was continuing in the new arena of Reconstruction.

BRIDGING THE CHASM OF WAR

One consequence of the persistence of Unionism was that the issues of the past often dominated the years of Reconstruction. That was particularly true where Unionists felt that they had suffered harshly at the hands of the secessionists. Tennessee was the most conspicuous example of prewar Unionism's being not only a source of Republican strength but a basis of division and vindictiveness after the war as well. Under the lash of William Brownlow, the Unionists of Tennessee, most of whom lived in the eastern end of the state, quickly moved to disfranchise as many former rebels as necessary to put themselves in power. Even before the national government moved to disfranchise rebel leaders, the Unionist-Republicans in Tennessee had made disfranchisement a basis of their political power. One Tennessee Radical wrote to a Northern Republican in early 1868 that "the great aim of the radical politicians of Tennessee of all classes is to exclude as many white conservatives from voting as possible and to control the negro vote. With universal suffrage," by which he meant no disfranchisement of former Confederates, "neither they nor the blacks would stand much chance."[11]

10. Jonathan B. Odom to Thomas Settle, May 18, 1867, Settle Papers; Speech of March, 1867, Folder 4, Settle Papers; J. G. deRoulhac Hamilton, *Reconstruction in North Carolina* (New York, 1914), p. 288n.; William F. Henderson to Thaddeus Stevens, March 4, 1867, in James A. Padgett, ed., "Reconstruction Letters from North Carolina, Part XII, Other Letters," *North Carolina Historical Review*, XXI (1944), 242; Letter from Committee, Folder 18, James Graham Ramsay Papers.
11. Alexander, *Reconstruction in Tennessee*, p. 201.

The hostility of Unionists toward those who had led Tennessee out of the Union was shown, too, in the refusal to allow former Confederates to sit on juries as well as to deny them the ballot and the right to hold office. Violent acts against persons and property of former Confederates were common, especially in the early years of Reconstruction, if only because the war in Tennessee had been a guerrilla struggle inside the more conventional one.

A similar carry-over from the divisions and rivalries of the prewar South was evident among Republicans in Arkansas, where, as in Tennessee, the state had long been split between slaveless hill people and slaveholding planters in the river valleys. Before Radical Reconstruction began, the Unionists were already complaining that they were being overwhelmed by the return to power of the old Confederates. "The unpleasant part is that Union men must take back seats," wrote one Unionist to Charles Sumner in 1866, "whilst rebels fill the offices of Government, with purjury [sic] in thier [sic] throats." Not surprisingly, therefore, when the Radical convention met to draw up a new constitution, it enacted the strictest disfranchisement clause passed by any of the ten conventions of the Reconstructed states. It was estimated that 40,000 were disfranchised by the constitution. The Unionist-Republican vindictiveness toward former Confederates persisted in Arkansas for years. By 1872 all of the Southern states had reduced significantly whatever disfranchisements they may have insisted upon in the early days of Reconstruction—but not Arkansas. Indeed, one of the major conflicts within the Republican party of the state throughout Reconstruction and a source of the party's decline there was the old Unionists' insistence on keeping the former Confederates out of government as long as possible.[12]

In Georgia, Texas, and Virginia, where Unionism was also a prime source of Republicans, the Republicans were not as vindictive in outlook and so did not insist upon widespread disfranchisement. Indeed, in some states Unionists could be quite generous, like one in the Virginia convention who wrote to Thaddeus Stevens asking for his opinion on disfranchisement. "I am a

12. William A. Russ, Jr., "The Attempt to Create a Republican Party in Arkansas During Reconstruction," *Arkansas Historical Quarterly*, I (1942), 210–211, 222.

radical Republican, but don't believe in the policy of heavy disfranchisement because I believe it would result injuriously to the colored race and poor whites."[13] That the efforts at severe disfranchisement were a result of prewar Unionism and not Radicalism in general is shown by the lack of interest and sometimes disapproval that black delegates to the state convention showed toward such measures. In the Louisiana convention, for example, where an effort was made to bar a large number of white Confederates, P. B. S. Pinchback, the black Republican leader, said that Negroes did not want such an extreme measure, though in the end the blacks there, unlike blacks in other conventions, did support disfranchisement. It is also significant that where a sharp prewar division between whites was lacking, as in Mississippi or Florida, there was no severe disfranchisement of former Confederates.

If Unionism could render white Radicals vindictive toward fellow whites, it did not necessarily make them into friends of blacks or supporters of Radicals. Even strong antislavery Unionists, like Daniel R. Goodloe and Benjamin Hedrick, found it difficult to go along with the Radicals in North Carolina. In fact, Goodloe became the principal opponent of William W. Holden, the Radical governor and self-styled friend of blacks. And in 1875 when Mississippi Democrats were girding themselves to launch the reign of terror that would result in the overthrow of the Radical regime, Cassius M. Clay, the old antislavery Kentuckian, came into the state to speak against the Republicans. (Clay had been a Republican in the 1850's and 1860's.) After his visit to the state one of the leaders of the Conservatives wrote him offering his "thanks for your kind assistance which you rendered us [in] our hour of need. We will remember the favor."[14]

A CONTINUITY OF INTERESTS

Some white Southerners, it appears, became Republicans because they found in the party an answer to certain economic problems, of either personal or regional interest. Sometimes the

13. Hume, " 'Black and Tan' Conventions," p. 145.
14. David L. Smiley, "Cassius M. Clay and the Mississippi Election of 1875," *Journal of Mississippi History,* XIX (1957), 259.

problems were very personal, as with a Mississippian who wrote frankly, "I am in need of employment, which would give me some remuneration." Others were less personally but no less financially involved. Major R. W. Millsaps, also of Mississippi, became a Republican because he thought the party's program would advance his financial and commercial interests. One recent student of Mississippi Reconstruction, William C. Harris, has pointed out that eight of the ten white Republican counties in the state clustered along two railroad lines, which were then bringing in a new lumbering industry to the previously undeveloped region. Significantly, the piney woods counties, which also had a history of wartime Unionism but no new development through railroads or lumbering, did *not* support Radical Reconstruction.[15]

Radicalism among north Georgia whites seems also to have been sparked by their special economic situation. In the constitutional convention of 1868 the white north Georgia delegates pressed strongly for debt relief measures and homestead exemptions, which appealed to their poor farmer constituents. They showed little interest in, and a good deal of hostility toward, disfranchising Confederates or opening public offices to Negroes. In the elections of 1868, for example, north Georgia was a stronghold of Republicans, principally for economic reasons and because former Governor Joseph E. Brown—a hero of the area—had become a Republican.

Economic issues of interest to small farmers also came up in the North Carolina convention of 1868, where protection of debtors was strongly supported by radical whites, though there the same group was prepared to go along with black officeholding as well as black voting. Leading Republicans, too, in North Carolina made clear their commitment to economic development. As Thomas Settle said at the outset of Radical Reconstruction, "the object of my ambition now is to see this country developed. I have witnessed the first great step. I have seen freedom take the place of slavery. I wish now to see vice give way before virtue, ignorance, poverty and want to intelligence, happiness and wealth."

15. Harris, "Reconsideration of . . . Scalawags," pp. 30–32; 37n.; Vernon Lee Wharton, *The Negro in Mississippi 1865–1890* (Chapel Hill, N.C., 1947), p. 157.

Scalawags in Alabama too showed a keen interest in economic development. "Unite north and south Alabama by railroads," urged one Scalawag editor, "and do it by state aid, as a great State necessity." Alexander White, who became a Republican after 1868, was motivated to do so because he was deeply interested in the economic development of the state. "We need capital and we need labor," he wrote, and it is folly to denounce Northerners who might bring those factors of production to Alabama. Northern Republicans had already pointed out to Southerners that only through Republican rule would the resources of the South be adequately developed. Samuel Rice, another Alabamian who left the Democrats to join the Republicans, gave as one of his reasons for the shift his expectation that the new party would bring about "the revival of industry and prosperity, the lightening of debt and taxes. . . ."[16]

THE PERSISTENCE OF CLASS

If a previous Unionism or an economic purpose brought a number of native whites into the Republican party, there was another incentive that lay behind both of them. It deserves to be identified as an attraction in its own right. Class conflict was not conspicuous in American politics during the nineteenth century, and it certainly was not in the antebellum South. But at times of crisis the natural divisions of class in any society come to the surface, and the South during the crisis of Reconstruction was no exception. It is clear, for example, that many of the so-called economic demands of the Radicals in the conventions were really class demands, for they were coming from small farmers in the undeveloped areas. The unsettled state of government and society that was the Reconstruction South provided opportunities for other, franker expressions of class antagonism by men who saw in the new Republican party a vehicle for righting wrongs, real or imagined, visited upon their class in the antebellum years.

16. Settle Speech, March, 1867, in Settle Papers, Folder 4; Woolfolk, "Scalawag in Alabama," pp. 180–81; Sarah Van V. Woolfolk, "Alabama Attitudes Toward the Republican Party in 1868 and 1964," *Alabama Review,* XX (1967), 28–29; Sarah Van V. Woolfolk, "Five Men Called Scalawags," *Alabama Review,* XVII (1964), 49.

In some areas of the South, the appeal to class came during the war itself, usually, however, in those places where the Union armies had already penetrated. Thus Michael Hahn, who would become a Republican senator from Louisiana during Radical Reconstruction, denounced the state constitution of 1852 as unfair "to the small planters, and farmers, and adventurous frontiersmen, the honest mechanics." He thought a new constitution was needed, not only to get rid of slavery, but also to reduce "the power of the aristocracy" in order to give to "the poor man that which he has never had—an equal voice in the state." A North Carolinian from the nonslaveholding western part of the state denounced those "bombastic, high falutin, aristocratic fools" who have been "driving negroes and poor helpless white people until they think they can control the world of mankind." When Northern troops occupied portions of eastern North Carolina in 1862–63, many nonslaveholding whites joined the Union army and denounced slavery as a part of the "aristocracy" that had oppressed them.[17]

In the early months of Radical Reconstruction the appeal that the Republican party had for the poor and the nonslaveholders seemed so obvious that conservatives commented on it, either to express their fear of what it portended or to use the fact as a basis for ridicule. One Georgian, for example, urged "the intelligence and Patriotism of the State" to control the upcoming constitutional convention, for otherwise the Unionists and Negroes will "form a government for us. If they have control—Repudiation—the abolition of poll tax—a general division of lands—and disfranchisement of Rebels will probably follow with laws regulating the price of labor and the rent of lands—all to benefit the negro and the poor." About the same time a Tennessee conservative was making a similar point, though with less premonition of danger. The Radicals, he said, were the "party paying no taxes, riding poor horses, wearing dirty shirts, and having no use for soap."[18]

17. Roger W. Shugg, *Origins of Class Struggle in Louisiana* (Baton Rouge, 1939), p. 199; Otto H. Olsen, "Reconsidering the Scalawags," *Civil War History,* XII (1966), 310; Norman D. Brown, "A Union Election in Civil War North Carolina," *North Carolina Historical Review,* XLIII (1966), 391–92.
18. Alan Conway, *The Reconstruction of Georgia* (Minneapolis, 1966), p. 148; E. Merton Coulter, *William G. Brownlow, Fighting Parson of the Southern Highlands* (Chapel Hill, N.C., 1937), p. 337.

The Radical leaders did not repudiate these descriptions; rather they gloried in their implications. At the Mississippi Constitutional Convention the president opened the proceedings with the observation that "this hour brings to a final end that system that enriches the few at the expense of the many. . . ." In North Carolina the official Republican appeals in behalf of ratification of the constitution of 1868 were frankly directed to the lower classes, saying that in the past the working people of the state had been "imposed upon socially, politically, and pecuniarily by southern aristocrats and secession oligarchs." One poor white Republican wrote that "if we could have had as good a constitution for the past 40 years" as the one just produced by the North Carolina convention "we should now have been quite a different people from what we are. . . . It seems to me," he continued, "that those who have heretofore ruled in the South ought to begin to realize the change which has been made. . . . The contest which we have in North Carolina now is one of the struggles in the 'irrepressible conflict' of which Seward spoke in 1855. It will go on til right shall finally prevail. . . . The old, rotten, pro-slavery aristocracy must go under." Unionist James P. Newcomb, when he returned to Texas in 1867, after having fled the state in 1861, considered the triumph of the Republicans in the South as indispensable for peace and order. The Republicans which he denominated "the party of liberty and progress" would ensure not only "equality of citizens" but would prevent the Southern states from falling under the control of "the wealthy landowners," who are "in opposition to all that has cost the nation so much of its precious blood and treasure."[19]

The class appeals of Republicans were sometimes reflected in the actions of Radical governments. In 1866, for example, Radical Governor William Brownlow of Tennessee said that he thought that a quarter of the prisoners in the state penitentiary had been put there unjustly because of their color or social background. During the early months of 1868 he pardoned about 250 pris-

19. Sansing, "Scalawag in Mississippi," p. 42; Olsen, "Reconsidering . . . Scalawags," p. 315; David Hogbin to Benjamin Hedrick, April 2, 1868, in B. S. Hedrick Papers; Dale A. Somers, "James P. Newcomb: The Making of a Radical," *Southwestern Historical Quarterly,* 72 (1969), 465.

oners. Brownlow also called upon the dirt farmers of the old nonslaveholding counties of the state to join the militia to suppress the Klan; the conservative whites, he knew, could not be counted on in that job.

Occasionally a white Republican recognized that Democratic appeals to the color line were ways of obscuring class differences between whites. "The democrats have used the poor white man to hold the negro down," a North Carolinian wrote in 1875, "and now the axe is raised to inflict a mortal wound, but the cross-eyed democracy is looking the poor white man squarely in the face, and I for one say turn the negro loose before the blow has fallen."[20]

WHIGS AND DEMOCRATS

Prewar Unionism was undoubtedly more widely influential in accounting for native Southerners becoming Republicans than class antagonisms inherited from the days of slavery. Both, however, testified to the continuation of prewar conflicts into the era of Reconstruction. Another example of that persistence across the chasm of war was the large number of Southerners who were attracted into the party by their memories of prewar political rivalries. Many of the new Republicans were conservative old Whigs. They had often opposed the war because it was anti-Union and because it was, in their judgment, brought about by the Democrats. One former Whig, now a Republican, emphasized his conservative roots. "I was never in favor of anything that was radical," wrote Judge Edwin G. Reade to a correspondent in 1868. "I was opposed to abolition because it was radical. I was opposed to secession because it was radical." The Republican party offered these conservative former Whigs an alternative to the hated Democrats and the promise of an appreciation for their Unionism, for which, during the war, they had often paid dearly in social ostracism, or in exclusion from politics.[21]

In few states was the continuity between antebellum Whiggery and Republican support more evident than in Mississippi. In a

20. W. McKee Evans, *Ballots and Fence Rails: Reconstruction on the Lower Cape Fear* (Chapel Hill, N.C., 1967), p. 234.
21. E. G. Reade to M. B. Clarke, July 20, 1868, in W. J. Clarke Papers.

recent, ingenious study of elections in Mississippi, Warren Ellem has shown that in the black counties along the river, where the old Whig strength had been concentrated, a majority of whites voted Republican. He found that more than half of the Scalawags in the state were located in the twenty-four counties in which Negroes constituted 60 percent or more of the population. These delta or river counties were the most consistently Republican between 1869 and 1875. Contrary to Allen Trelease's findings for the South as a whole, in Mississippi the white counties were not the center of Scalawag strength, just as they had not been the center of Whig strength in the early 1850's. In Mississippi, at least, the Republican party drew a good deal of its white support from former anti-Democrats: Whigs, Constitutional Unionists, and American party members.

With its long history of rivalry between western Democrats and eastern Whigs, Tennessee is a prime instance of prewar Whiggery's being a basis for the new Republican party. In the early years of Reconstruction, as Thomas Alexander has shown, the Reconstruction government under the leadership of Governor William Brownlow was overwhelmingly Whig. The lower house of the legislature in March, 1865, for example, was composed of almost all native Tennesseans, of whom a great majority were former Whigs. Forty-six of the seventy-six members were former slaveholders, and some of them had owned many slaves. As one Nashville editor explained in 1869, the Whigs of Tennessee "were never reconciled to the faith of the faithful. . . . They regard the Democratic party as author of all their troubles, and . . . hold the very name of Democracy as a synonym of disaster and defeat."[22]

Throughout the South one could find individuals like Judge W. W. Chrishold of Mississippi, who hated Democrats so much that he became a Republican, or W. C. Wickham of Virginia, who had been a Confederate general, friend of Robert E. Lee, and a Whig senator before the war. A few weeks after Appomattox, Wickham

22. Warren A. Ellem, "Who Were the Mississippi Scalawags?" *Journal of Southern History* XXXVIII (1972), 217–40; see also the rejoinder by Allen W. Trelease, *Journal of Southern History* XXXVII (1972), 703–5; Harris, "Reconsideration of . . . Scalawags," pp. 40–42; Alexander, *Reconstruction in Tennessee,* p. 221.

joined the Republican party because he considered it the legitimate successor of the old Whigs. A more obscure Republican in North Carolina conceded in 1877 that he had "been voting the Republican ticket for the last seven years—do not intend to vote any other unless that Old Whig party should be revived. . . ."

Hatred or distrust of the Democratic party, however, was not always sufficient to make an old Whig into a fervent Republican. The principal reason was that the conservative social philosophy, which had brought men to the Whig party in the first place, was often affronted by the novel and reformist tendencies of the Republican party. The old Whig editor of the Hinds County, Mississippi, *Gazette,* after half a decade of trying to cajole old-line Whigs into the Republican party, wrote in 1870, "Republicanism and modern Democracy are the same in principle; Both are for tearing down all Constitutional restraints and opening a high-way to the role of mobocracy or despotism."[23]

Some more conservative Unionist-Whigs in Mississippi, as elsewhere in the South, could have told the editor the same thing years earlier. William Sharkey, as we saw in Chapter 6, was so fervent a Whig-Unionist that during the war he refused to have anything to do with the Democratic-dominated Confederacy. He even entertained Northern invaders in his home. After the war he was recompensed to the extent of $2,000 for his contributions to the Union war effort by the United States Southern Claims Commission. Under no circumstances would he join the Democratic party, as many of his planter friends had done, however reluctantly, during the secession crisis or during the course of the war. But neither would Sharkey accept the new Republican party, despite its Unionism. Because of Sharkey's wartime loyalty to the Union, President Andrew Johnson appointed him provisional governor of the state during early Reconstruction. As governor, Sharkey refused to accept Negro suffrage, the Fourteenth Amendment, or Radical Congressional Reconstruction. Once he was again a private citizen, Sharkey instituted lawsuits to have Radical Reconstruction declared unconstitutional. In short, the inflexibility of his

23. James A. Washington to Thomas Settle, Aug. 25, 1877, in Settle Papers; Harris, "Reconsideration of . . . Scalawags," p. 24n.

Whiggery and Unionism, which had made him a hero when the Confederacy was the enemy, now made it impossible for him to accept the social and political changes that the Republican party was insisting upon in the conquered South.[24] There must have been many Sharkeys among the old-line Whigs of the South.

James Lusk Alcorn of Coahoma County, Mississippi, was of the same social and economic class as Sharkey. He, too, was a partisan prewar Whig who could not accept the Democracy and who opposed secession and the war. Unlike Sharkey, however, Alcorn was not as inflexible in his Unionism, nor, therefore, in his later attitude toward the Republican party. When war did come, Alcorn managed to stifle his opposition long enough to become a Confederate general. Halfway through the war, however, he resigned his commission. During the remainder of the war he was one of those few Southerners who managed to *increase* his fortune, by selling cotton to the Union army. When the war was over, Alcorn was ready to accept the new order. Although he has often been instanced as an example of the transition made by many Whig leaders, especially in Mississippi, from Whiggery to Republicanism after the war, he brought few upper-class Whigs with him. To many of them, Alcorn was overly ambitious and politically unreliable, if only because of his wartime compromise with the Confederacy. Moreover, Alcorn's frank acceptance of Negro suffrage and his willingness to work with Radical Northerners in the Mississippi party organization made him suspect. Most of the Whigs in the Republican party of Mississippi, it appears, voted against Alcorn when he ran for governor in 1869, preferring to vote for his opponent, a Northern moderate Republican.

Some old-line Whig leaders in northern Alabama were no more united in their willingness to go along with Radical Reconstruction than Mississippi Whigs. All three candidates for governor in Alabama in 1865, for example, were old-line Whigs from the northern part of the state, but it is significant that none of them

24. L. Marshall Hall, "William L. Sharkey and Reconstruction, 1866–1873," *Journal of Mississippi History*, XXVII (1965), 1–17; Wharton, *Negro in Mississippi*, p. 157; Richard Grady Lowe, "Republicans, Rebellion, and Reconstruction: The Republican Party in Virginia, 1865–1870," unpublished Ph.D. dissertation, University of Virginia, 1968, p. 326n.

was an active Republican after 1867, when Radical Reconstruction began.[25]

If in some states Whigs were divided about becoming Republicans, the same could be said about Democrats. In certain areas of the South prewar Democrats were as conspicuous among the new Republicans as Whigs. The white counties in the South, for example, that Allen Trelease identified as voting overwhelmingly Republican in 1872 were as likely to have been Democratic in the past as Whig. In the five presidential elections between 1832 and 1852, about half the counties had voted Democratic and half had voted Whig. Another student of Scalawags identified eighty-three active, native Republicans in Mississippi, of whom twenty-four had been Democrats and twenty-five Whigs in the antebellum years (twenty-six were of unknown past political affiliation). An examination of the eighteen Radical native whites in the constitutional convention of Alabama in 1868 revealed that seven were former Whigs and four had been Democrats.

Former Democrats were also plentiful among Republican leaders in other states. Even in an old Whig state like North Carolina, Republican leaders William Woods Holden, Thomas Settle, Robert P. Dick, and Curtis H. Brogden had all been Democrats before the war. Significantly, of the twenty-seven counties in North Carolina that had supported Holden in 1858, when he was a Democrat, twenty went on to give large majorities to the Radical Republicans after Holden became Radical Republican governor in 1868. Former Democrats were conspicuous among Republican leaders in South Carolina too. Six of the thirty-six whites who sat in the South Carolina Constitutional Convention of 1868 had been secessionists. Indeed, Franklin J. Moses, Jr., who became the Radical governor of the state, had been a red-hot secessionist before the war. One of his prides was to have lowered the Stars and Stripes from over Fort Sumter at its surrender in April, 1861. Robert Hughes, a leader of the Virginia Republicans, was also an old Democrat. The Republican party in Alabama counted David P. Lewis, who became governor in 1872, and Alexander McKinstry among the prominent former Democrats in its leadership.

25. On Alcorn's career see Lillian A. Pereyra, *James Lusk Alcorn* (Baton Rouge, 1966); Woolfolk, "Scalawag in Alabama," p. 39.

Samuel Rice, another leader of Alabama Republicans, had been a secessionist Democrat and a member of the Alabama Senate during the war.

That Democrats were also prominent in the membership and leadership of the Southern Republicans suggests that prewar political allegiances were by no means the complete explanation, any more than Unionism was the full explanation for becoming a Republican. Equally important with these, it would seem, was the willingness to accept change. The contrasting experiences of William Sharkey and James Alcorn in Mississippi illustrate the point. Both had been Unionists, both had been Whigs, and both were members of the planter class, yet Alcorn became a Republican and Sharkey did not.

There were a number of reasons why one would accept change in the South. It might be because of a certain opportunistic realism, as seems to have been the case with Samuel Rice of Alabama or Joseph Brown of Georgia. But it could also be because of a genuine interest in change, not only that imposed from without, but that generated from within as well. A Southern Republican party would facilitate reform by Southerners themselves.

THE PROMISE OF REFORM

Whatever reputation the Republican party may have today as a party of reform, in the middle of the nineteenth century it was certainly the party of change. That had been its principal appeal to the country in the days of its meteoric rise in the North as an antislavery party. It was still its chief appeal during Reconstruction. The party emphasized its reformist nature, if only because reform was its reason for being in the postwar South. It was, after all, the agency entrusted with revolutionizing the region.

Southern Republicans made the point again and again. In Georgia, for example, the party united its class and reformist character in a single message. "Poor White men of Georgia: Be a man!" one of its handbills said. "Let the slave-holding aristocracy no longer rule you. Vote for a constitution which educates your children free of charge; relieves the poor debtor from his rich creditor; allows a liberal homestead for your families; and more than all, places you on a level with those who used to boast that for every slave they were entitled to three-fifths of a vote in congressional representation." The Republicans of Arkansas in the fall of 1867 similarly advertised themselves as the party of "progress and reform." The party asked, "Do you want good roads throughout your state? Do you want free bridges? Do you want free schools and the advantages of education for your children?" At the conclusion of the constitutional convention in South Carolina the Scalawag patrician and president of the convention, Dr. Albert G. Mackay, said in his valedictory, "We do not claim a preeminence of wisdom or virtue, but we do claim that we have followed in the progressive advancement of the age; that we have been bold and honest enough and wise enough to trample obsolete unworthy prejudice underfoot."[26]

It is clear, too, that many of the white Southerners who joined the Radicals during Reconstruction had been interested in reform before the war. Several of the leaders of Radical Reconstruction in North Carolina, for example, like John Pool, Tod Caldwell, and Alfred Dockery, had been active in behalf of better roads and a public school system. Thomas Settle, another North Carolina Republican, said in early 1867 that he envisioned the Republicans as the "party of progress, of education, and development." How can it be called the "nigger party," he asked, when it had done so much for the white man of the North? "It is the party of humanity," he concluded, because it helped to feed the hungry and clothe the naked after the war.

A former Democrat and Confederate veteran explained publicly that his conversion to Republicanism derived from its reformist nature. The new constitution of North Carolina, Edward Cantwell wrote, "embraces all the cardinal principles for which the Democratic party in Europe and this country have so long and so successfully contended, viz.: universal suffrage; civil and religious liberty; universal amnesty; universal education; the equality of all

26. C. Mildred Thompson, *Reconstruction in Georgia, Economic, Social, Political, 1865–1872* (New York, 1915), p. 204; Staples, *Reconstruction in Arkansas*, p. 173; Francis Butler Simkins and Robert Hilliard Woody, *South Carolina During Reconstruction* (Chapel Hill, N.C., 1932), pp. 95–96.

men in the sight of the law . . . no property qualifications for office, and a frequent recourse to the source of power at the polls." The new Radical constitution's innovations, Cantwell contended, will "enable us to keep step with the advance of civilization and the progress of the human race."[27]

Throughout the South, the constitutions produced by the Radical conventions testified to the strong commitment of Republicans to reform. Each of the states adopted free public education for the first time, many increased the number of insane asylums and prisons, expanded the rights of women over their property, provided for greater popular control over local government, and generally democratized politics and government in the South. The Florida convention went so far as to provide for representation for the Seminole Indians in each house of the legislature and required that the representatives be Indians, not whites!

A concrete insight into the reformist side of the white Southern Radical in power is provided by the activities of an obscure North Carolina legislator, David Hogbin. He was an old Unionist and in such poor circumstances that he could not run for the legislature under the old constitution because, by his own admission, he did not own sufficient land. But under the new Radical constitution he was elected to the legislature. In 1869 he wrote to his old friend Benjamin S. Hedrick, the old Unionist and antislavery man, now a Republican, "Well, we are jogging along here in the 'scalawag' legislature trying, or at any rate a large number of us, to do what we can to restore the 'waste places.' True, there may not be as much profound learning to be found here as in days of yore," he conceded, "but I assure you the intention of the majority is to do the best they can." He then went on to tell of the various reforms in penal and tax matters that the legislature was engaged upon. Speaking of the prison reform, he said that once that was arranged, "we can dispose of the numerous inmates in our jails which are now crowded." Then the legislature could turn to the school bill, which he expected to be a good one. Yet he admitted that even a reform supposedly as popular as free schools could still run up

27. Olsen, "Reconsidering Scalawags," pp. 308–9; Speech of Thomas Settle, March, 1867, Settle Papers, Folder 4; Olsen, "Reconsidering Scalawags," p. 315.

against the conservatism of Southern farm people. "Our people are less inclined to start and support schools than I like to see them," he lamented.[28]

That some changes would occur as a result of the war and emancipation most Southerners undoubtedly recognized. And once Radical Reconstruction had opened up the possibility of more fundamental change, particularly through the constitutional conventions, white Southerners braced themselves for innovations from within. What could not be clear, however, was whether any of the imposed changes, particularly Negro equality, would endure. It was not only quite possible that Southerners might successfully resist the innovations, but that the Northern people themselves might not sustain the Radical Republican Congress in its design to work a revolution upon Southern society. As we know today, most white Southerners never accepted the Radical program for the South, and that fact turned out to be determining for the future of Southern Republicans. But in the early years of Radical Reconstruction that result could not be known. In fact, as we shall see, at the time there was sound reason for expecting the changes and reforms to stick. Hence, many white Southerners came to the conclusion that Radical Reconstruction was the wave of the future. As a result they became Republicans. Why they did, and when in the course of the Reconstruction the decision was taken, varied greatly. Each person viewed the future through his or her own experience and hopes. For some, the decision flowed naturally from the defeat of the Confederacy itself.

A WAR DECIDES THINGS

That was the view taken by James Longstreet, the Confederate general and associate of General Robert E. Lee in the Army of Northern Virginia. Longstreet publicly announced his becoming a Republican in early 1867, but he always gave as his reason, both in public and in private, the arbitrament of war. In 1867 he wrote to General Lee urging his former commander to speak out in support of sectional reconciliation. In the course of his letter,

28. David Hogbin to Benjamin Hedrick, Jan. 16, 1869, in B. S. Hedrick Papers.

Longstreet carefully explained his own reasons for joining the political party of the conquerors. Some concessions, he contended, must be made by the conquered to the conqueror or else "we shall ere long be on the same road that Mexico has pursued for the last twenty-five years. . . . I fancy that few of our brave men that have fallen in the late struggle would have risked their lives if they had supposed that the war was to settle nothing. And yet," he pointed out, "if the claims of both sides are good, nothing has been settled." Two years later, in another letter to a fellow Confederate officer, Longstreet added that once Southerners admitted that some reconstruction must follow the laying down of arms, then they could not "escape the corollary that reconstruction in full recognition of the law and the changed status of affairs was a necessity."[29] Longstreet, in short, thought that defeat meant accommodation to the conquerors.

The Radical Republicanism of another Georgian, Amos Akerman, also began with the defeat. "There was a choice between acting in politics upon ideas which had prevailed in the war and upon the ideas which had been overcome," Akerman explained to a fellow Georgian in 1871. "The former, I thought, was the part of wisdom and of honor, too: of wisdom because it would soonest quiet the war, and whether we liked it or not would bring us speedily to the shore on which we are bound ultimately to land; and of honor, because a surrender in good faith really signified a surrender of the substance as well as the form of the Confederate cause." Albert Gallatin Brown, the old secessionist leader of Mississippi Democrats, put the same reasoning more succinctly. "I am and have been from the moment of Surrender," he wrote in 1880, "in favor of reconciliation on the best terms we can get. In my judgment it was never the right of the conquered to dictate terms." Brown never became a Republican, but his turnabout from

29. Unaddressed letter in pencil, June 8, 1867, in James Longstreet Papers. Longstreet's biographer T. R. Hays identifies the letter as being addressed to Robert E. Lee; James R. Longstreet to E. P. Alexander, Aug. 9, 1869, in Edward Porter Alexander Papers. On Longstreet see also Donald Bridgman Sanger and Thomas Robson Hay, *James Longstreet* (Baton Rouge, 1952); William L. Richter, "James Longstreet: From Rebel to Scalawag," *Louisiana History,* XI (1970), 215–30; and his own work, James Longstreet, *From Manassas to Appomattox* (Philadelphia, 1896), particularly pp. 636–37, where he explains his decision.

a fiery Southern nationalist in 1861 to an advocate of reconciliation on Northern terms, including Negro suffrage, makes him a dissenter in the Reconstruction on a par with any Republican. He ceased to be a Democratic leader as soon as his view became known in March, 1867. He never did repudiate secession, however.[30]

COMMITMENT WINS CONVERTS

No Republican party, however, could be built on the number of Southerners who became Republicans because of the Surrender. Nothing makes this clearer than a bare recital of the beginnings of the Republican party in the South. Two years after Appomattox the party had formal organizations in only three states of the former Confederacy. Moreover, every one of the three states—Tennessee, Virginia, and Louisiana—had been occupied in part or whole by the Union army for some time. The organization of the Republican party in the remaining eight states of the formerly Confederate South did not begin until the passage of the Reconstruction Acts in March, 1867. In short, it was the throwing of the power of the federal government behind Radical Reconstruction that pushed many white Southerners into the new party. (For all his talk of the decisions of war, even Longstreet did not commit himself publicly to the Republicans until June, 1867, that is, after the passage of the Reconstruction Acts.)

The power of the federal government catalyzed popular support in the South for the Republican party in two ways. By requiring under the Reconstruction Acts that new constitutions be drawn up, and within the context of Negro suffrage, the federal government provided at one and the same time a reason and an electoral base for the formation of Republican organizations in each of the Southern states. One further consequence was that some white Southerners now joined the party to control its excesses. Joseph

30. Amos Akerman to James Jackson, Nov. 20, 1871, in Akerman Letterbooks. I am indebted to Elizabeth S. Nathans for this and other references from the Akerman Letterbooks; Albert G. Brown to J. F. H. Claiborne, April 27, 1800, in J. F. H. Claiborne Papers; James Byrne Ranck, *Albert Gallatin Brown, Radical Southern Nationalist* (New York, 1937), pp. 253–75.

Bennett of Mississippi, for example, admitted that he became a Republican in order "to make the burden of his people light" and to temper the impact of the party's program on his state. Joseph E. Brown of Georgia was of a similar mind when he joined the Republicans in 1867. Brown, as the wartime governor of the state, was undoubtedly the most prominent white Georgian to join the Republicans. He defended his decision on the ground that it was wise to "agree with thine adversary quickly." He counseled popular acceptance of Negro suffrage and the calling of a convention to write a new constitution, that is, immediate acquiescence in the Reconstruction Acts. To Brown it seemed clear that the power of the federal government was behind the new order in the South. "If we reject the terms proposed," he told his fellow Georgians, "I confess I see no hope for the future." Brown's public decision brought not only old political friends like O. A. Lochrane and H. I. Kimball into the party, but a good part of the electorate of north Georgia as well. Elizabeth Studley Nathans has shown, through a statistical analysis of voting patterns in 1868 and in the prewar years, that the strongest correlation between the Republican vote in the north Georgia counties in 1868 was with the vote for Brown in the gubernatorial election in 1858.[31]

As the formation of party organizations makes clear, the commitment of the federal government to a new Southern order was important in bringing white Southerners to think the new order would last. Yet there were others who were not yet certain that the revolution in constitutional power and society would endure. Northern voters might well reject it or fail to support it. To Southerners of that view the presidential election of 1868—the first after the imposition of Radical Reconstruction—came as a final persuader. Not only did the party win overwhelmingly in the South, but Ulysses S. Grant was elected President with enormous majorities throughout the nation and the Republicans captured both houses of Congress. Even before the votes were counted, the crucial role of the election was appreciated. One Mississippi

31. Sansing, "Scalawag in Mississippi," p. 57; Elizabeth Studley Nathans, *Losing the Peace: Georgia Republicans and Reconstruction 1865–1871* (Baton Rouge, 1969), pp. 39, 94, and appendix; Louise Biles Hill, *Joseph E. Brown and the Confederacy* (Chapel Hill, N.C., 1939), pp. 269–71, 288.

Republican wrote just before election day that "if Grant is elected, white Republicans will be as thick as leaves in Val Ambrosa, and they will not be 'carpetbaggers' either, but gentlemen 'to the manor born.' "[32]

And sure enough, soon after the election, large numbers of whites did enter the party, not only in Mississippi but across the South. For some new Republicans the obvious lesson from the election was that for a future in politics, membership in the Republican party was indispensable. Samuel Rice of Alabama, an old secessionist Democrat, joined the Republicans soon after the election because he thought the disastrous defeat of the Democrats doomed them and him to political inactivity and frustration. He did not believe, he said, in "sullen inaction." Another well-known Scalawag in Alabama, Lewis Parsons, joined only after the election, too. He later said that he had stayed out of the Republican party "as long as it was worthwhile" but that by early 1869 he had become convinced that "it would be better to make terms with them [sic], work along with it, and in that way acquire their confidence." He saw "no use in any further opposition to the reconstruction policy which the Government had adopted." Sarah Woolfolk in her study of five prominent Alabama Scalawags (two of whom were Parsons and Rice) notes that each of them joined the Republican party only *after* digesting the results of the election of 1868. Alexander White, for instance, issued a public address "to Old Union Men," in which he advised them to follow his example. The recent election, he argued, had decided the permanence of the Union, Reconstruction, and Negro suffrage. Woolfolk further points to the increase in native officeholders in Alabama as a result of the shifting of many former secessionist Democrats into the Republican party after the 1868 presidential election.[33]

A Northern white man living in Virginia also commented on the sudden interest among native white Southerners in the Republican party. "Republicans are increasing since the election of Grant," wrote Samuel Armstrong, the founder of Hampton Institute, "and several southern gentlemen about here are much more radical than

32. Harris, "Reconsideration of Scalawags," p. 15.
33. Woolfolk, "Five . . . Scalawags," p. 49; Woolfolk, "Alabama Scalawag," p. 112; Woolfolk, "Alabama Attitudes," p. 29.

I. . . . Scores are getting down off the fence and rushing wildly to the Republican lines and already beginning to talk of what they have suffered for their principles."

After the election, the essence of realism seemed to be acceptance of Reconstruction as permanent. "Whether we approve or not," wrote Judge William B. Wood of Alabama in April, 1869, "the fact is still the same that the Reconstruction Acts are the terms and the only conditions" for a state government in the South. Even Negro suffrage, he thought, ought to be accepted, since it seemed beyond reversal. "Looking at the situation then as it really and emphatically exists, it is the part of wise men to make the most of it, and try by every effort to turn it to a good account." Wood had arrived at his assessment of the future considerably later than Longstreet or even Joseph E. Brown, but his reasons were the same. The Hinds County, Mississippi, *Gazette* similarly thought it made no sense in 1869 to continue resistance or foot-dragging on Reconstruction. It was impressed with the power and persistence of the federal government. Mississippi, the paper pointed out, is "unarmed and naked" while the United States has the state "by the throat, with the bayonet just entering the skin of the left breast. The government tells us to do so and so, and if we don't do it, it will do it for us!"[34] Like Wood, the *Gazette* wanted white Southerners to work to contain the revolution from within rather than to resist it ineffectually from without. Even a Democratic paper, the Jackson *Clarion,* thought that the recent victory of Grant and General Longstreet's open support of the Republicans had made a moderate Republican party acceptable in Mississippi.

RECONSTRUCTION AS OPPORTUNITY

Not all those who joined the Republicans did so simply because they resigned themselves to the inevitable; some welcomed the opportunity for change that the new order promised. This was true

34. Edith Armstrong Talbot, *Samuel Chapman Armstrong* (New York, 1904), p. 144n.; Woolfolk, "Alabama Scalawags," pp. 48–49; Thomas B. Alexander, "Persistent Whiggery in Mississippi Reconstruction: The Hinds County *Gazette," Journal of Mississippi History,* XXIII (1961), 79.

of Thomas B. Manlove, a Confederate colonel from Mississippi, who explained his rejection of the Democratic party in just those terms. His old party, he said, sought "to evoke from a dead nation's tomb the shadowy phantoms of an irrevocable past," while the Republican party "meets the living issues of the time in which we live. . . . Permitting the 'dead past to bury the dead,' it looks with unfaltering trust to the future, wherein its grand mission is to be accomplished, and peace and liberty become the portion of all." The Scalawag president of the Mississippi Constitutional Convention of 1868 was more specific in making the same point. As the convention began its work he told the delegates that they were now bringing to an end "that system that hindered the growth of towns and cities, and built up large landed aristocracies—that system that discouraged agricultural improvements and mechanic arts—that destroyed free schools and demoralized church and state. . . ."[35]

In a speech before whites and blacks in North Carolina, Republican Thomas Settle described the new order under the Radicals as "a general breaking up of the old ideas . . . taking a new start in the world. . . . If we are to have any prosperity," he warned, "we must make up our minds to look at several things in a very different light from that in which we have been in the habit of viewing them." Negroes must be educated, he asserted, and Yankees must not be excoriated, but accepted for what they could do for the South. "I tell you Yankees and Yankee notions are just what we want in this country. We want their capital to build factories and work shops, and railroads. . . . We want their intelligence, their energy and enterprise to operate these factories, and to teach us how to do it." But this acceptance of Yankee ways was not simply to be a making over of the South, for he went on to say that once Southerners learned how to produce, the importations from the North would no longer be necessary.[36] Settle did not say so, but his argument was a direct descendant of those advanced by Southern antislavery advocates in the prewar years when they

35. Harris, "Reconsideration of Scalawags," p. 30; Sansing, "Scalawag in Mississippi," p. 42.
36. Speech of March, 1867, in Settle Papers, Folder 4.

urged the end of slavery in the name of Southern economic independence.

To some white Southern Republicans, it was the party's inclusion of the black man as citizen and voter that was the central tenet—even if it was not the primary reason for a Southerner to join the party. "Men are Republican or Democratic according as they are or are not attached to the last three amendments of the Constitution [the 13th, 14th, and 15th]," contended Amos Akerman. As a Georgian who had fought for the Confederacy, he explained his transition to Republicanism as beginning with the decision made by war. After the Surrender, those who had served the Confederacy "felt it our duty . . . to let Confederate ideas rule us no longer. . . . Regarding the subjugation of one race to the other as an appurtenance of slavery, we were content that it should go to the grave in which slavery had been buried." At first, he conceded, "the extension of suffrage to colored men was . . . an alarming proposition on account of the supposed ignorance of the class to be enfranchised. But on reflection we considered that if ignorance did not disqualify white men, it should not disqualify black men." Negroes, like white men, could tell whether the government was doing its job and therefore could be trusted with the ballot. Moreover, "we considered that those who most objected to their ignorance, had opposed every proposition for removing it by public education and that as a class they would never get education until they could force it by the ballot. . . . These views reconciled us to the suffrage of colored men and carried us into the Republican party."[37]

Thomas Settle of North Carolina also saw the party's emphasis on "Liberty, Union, and Equality before the law" as its central principle. It was a party, he said early in Reconstruction, "that purposes to elevate mankind of all races and colors, and to develop the country." Occasionally the implicit social radicalism in Republican ideology carried a native white Southerner to extremes, as in the case of Miles L. Langley of Arkansas. In the constitutional convention of 1868 he defended female suffrage and de-

37. Unaddressed letter, undated, in Amos T. Akerman Letterbooks, 1871–76.

clared that there was no need for a legal ban on interracial marriage. On neither subject did the convention agree with him. Langley, however, had a record of "extremism," since he had been an antislavery man before the war.[38]

THE ENDURING SCALAWAG

The reasons why individual white Southerners became Scalawags obviously constitute a wide spectrum. That the power of the federal government had much to do with bringing about the shifts in allegiance is clear. It is also true that conversions made under coercion are not always the most enduring. The best-known example of the principle in practice is Joseph E. Brown of Georgia, who moved into the Republican camp in 1867 after consulting his political future and then moved out in 1872 after he had consulted it again. At both times he brought a good number of north Georgia dirt farmers with him. Throughout the South, as the difficulties of carrying out Radical Reconstruction mounted, whites who had joined the Republicans at a time when the future seemed likely to be of that political persuasion now began to drift back to more familiar positions. Some, in time, would even deny that they had ever been Republicans.

It would be untrue to the courage of many Scalawags, however, to place too much emphasis upon those who followed Brown's example. There were many others, whatever their original reason for becoming a Republican may have been, who stayed in the party, even when the future no longer looked bright. Indeed, on a popular level it is worth noting that Republican voters were being counted by the thousands in the eastern white counties of Tennessee and North Carolina right into the twentieth century. Furthermore, many of the leaders who entered the party in Reconstruction remained within its fold for years after a Republican South was only a fantasy. James L. Alcorn was a Republican until 1890; William Holden of North Carolina stayed with the party until the late 1880's, when he rejoined the Democrats. Apparently Albert

38. Speech by Thomas Settle, March, 1867, Settle Papers, Folder 4; Paul C. Palmer, "Miscegenation as an Issue of the Arkansas Constitutional Convention of 1868," *Arkansas Historical Quarterly*, XXIV (1965), 108–9.

Gallatin Brown, at his death in 1880, was still supporting Grant for the presidency. Of the five Alabama Scalawags studied by Woolfolk, only David Lewis returned to the Democrats before the end of Reconstruction in 1876. Thomas Settle and Daniel Russell of North Carolina continued to be Republicans for the rest of their lives.

One relatively obscure Reconstruction Republican from North Carolina continued to act on his Radical principles right down to the end of the century. Samuel F. Phillips did not become a Radical until 1870, but in 1895 he was acting as a lawyer for the Negro plaintiff in the case of *Plessy* v. *Ferguson* then before the United States Supreme Court. Plessy was protesting the Jim Crow accommodations on Louisiana railroads. Associated with Phillips in the case was Albion W. Tourgée, a former North Carolina carpetbagger. It was in the Reconstruction South that the Southerner and the Northerner had become friends in joint support of Negro rights. Twenty years later they were fighting the same cause before the U.S. Supreme Court, where their efforts proved to be as fruitless as in the Reconstruction South.[39]

The association of Phillips and Tourgée, however, was not typical. In the Reconstruction South, as we shall see in the next chapter, Scalawags and carpetbaggers were not usually in harmony. Nor did the question of the Negro usually have the effect on white men in the South that it had upon these two men. Whites usually agreed on the question, to be sure, but generally it was on the opposite side from that taken by Phillips and Tourgée. Indeed, what makes the Reconstruction period in the South striking as well as important is that it was a time when Southern white men divided over the black man. That division was not easy to achieve, nor was it as deep as it might have been. Yet it was more extensive and profound than at any time in Southern history down to the middle of the twentieth century. It is to the unlikely story of Southern white men confronting each other because of the black man that we now turn.

39. Otto H. Olsen, *Carpetbagger's Crusade: The Life of Albion Winegar Tourgée* (Baltimore, 1965), p. 132.

8

Black Suffrage
and White Dissenters

From the outset and all through Reconstruction, Negro suffrage was at once the hope and the burden of the Radical Republicans in the South. If Negro votes made possible Republican victories, the advocacy of the franchise for former slaves threatened to eliminate the white support that other principles had won for the party.

UNIONISTS AND BLACKS

Some of the Southerners most hostile to blacks and Negro suffrage were dedicated Unionists. Whitelaw Reid, a Northern journalist who toured the South immediately after Appomattox, wrote that "few Union men in the South, who have political aspirations, can be safely expected to advocate justice, much less generosity to the negro. . . ." At the Louisiana Constitutional Convention of 1864, W. T. Stocker, whose Unionism had been strong enough at the secession convention in 1861 to make him one of the eight delegates who refused to sign the ordinance of secession, publicly announced his hostility toward blacks. "My sympathies are with the white man and not with the negro," he told the convention in 1864. "My hand is against the African, and I am for pushing him off the soil of this country." Another wartime Unionist, Robert S. Tharin of Alabama, similarly expressed the hostility toward blacks that often accompanied a love for the Union. *"Let the niggers be confined to the cotton field,"* he wrote in 1863; "let no more negro blacksmiths, and negro carpenters, and negro bricklayers, and negro wheelwrights be used to drive the poor white man to poverty and to idleness." From Goldsboro, North Carolina, John Robinson wrote in 1866 to Thaddeus Stevens to warn him about the dangers of mixing Unionism and black suffrage in a single political party. "While I must acknowledge myself vindictive enough to see the arch rebels of the South humiliated," he said, "yet our country is for posterity; and I believe I am sufficiently conversant with the habits of both races to Know that they cannot live together in harmony. . . ." Three months before the beginning of Radical Congressional Reconstruction, another North Carolinian told a Northern Republican congressman that it was fortunate that blacks were moving southward, out of Virginia and the Carolinas, for "our people have been oppressed with *fear* and *not hate* of or from negroes," he explained. "This emigration Southward has done more to relieve and cheer our people than all else. . . . Let the Republicans keep up this move—encourage and aid the Negroes to move South," he advised, and the party will have a bright future in the region.[1]

The fear of what the inclusion of blacks would do to the prospects of a political party in the South was also evident in Tennessee, where Radical Congressional Reconstruction was never imposed. There was no question of the radical Unionism of the government of Governor William Brownlow, but neither was there any question of its hostility toward Negro political equality. When Brownlow asked that blacks be enfranchised in order to ensure

1. Whitelaw Reid, *After the War: A Tour of the Southern States 1865–1866* (New York, 1965; orig. pub. 1866), p. 45; Roger W. Shugg, *Origins of Class Struggle in Louisiana* (Baton Rouge, 1939), p. 196; Robert S. Tharin, *Arbitrary Arrests in the South: Scenes from the Experience of an Alabama Unionist* (New York, 1863), p. 75; John Robinson to Thaddeus Stevens, Feb. 22, 1866, in James A. Padgett, ed., "Reconstruction Letters from North Carolina, Part I, Letters to Thaddeus Stevens," *North Carolina Historical Review*, XVIII (1941), 182; D. F. Caldwell to John Sherman, Jan. 18, 1867, in Padgett, ed., "Reconstruction Letters from North Carolina, Part II, Letters to John Sherman," *North Carolina Historical Review*, XVIII (1941), 290–91.

Unionist dominance in the state, his Unionist constituents in east Tennessee went along only reluctantly. The Radical legislature, for example, refused to permit blacks to hold office or to serve on juries, though both activities had normally gone hand in hand with the conferring of the franchise upon classes of whites in the past. In time, when Congress insisted upon full political rights for blacks in the reconstructed states, the Republicans of Tennessee had to repeal the laws denying officeholding and jury service to blacks. The repeal, however, changed few minds in east Tennessee. In the elections of 1868, for example, no black candidates appeared on the Republican slate for state offices in Tennessee.

Even when political equality for blacks was imposed on the Southern states by Congress under the Reconstruction Acts of March, 1867, some Southern Republicans dragged their feet. Former Governor Joseph E. Brown of Georgia, a public convert not only to the Republican party but to Negro suffrage as well, never committed himself to the correlative principle that Negroes could hold office in Georgia. (Two years later, Conservatives were able to expel black representatives from the Georgia legislature on the basis of the Radicals' ambiguity on the question.) During the campaign in Georgia to ratify the Reconstruction constitution of 1868, Radicals campaigned in north Georgia, where there were few blacks, on a platform of no officeholding for blacks, and in middle Georgia, where there were many black voters, on a platform accepting blacks in state offices. And they were never caught! To minimize black influence in Florida, the Republicans in the constitutional convention there so arranged things that no county was to have more than four representatives in the legislature regardless of the population. The provision was intended to keep down the number of blacks, since only a few counties in the state had black majorities.

The lament of Benjamin Hedrick's brother in early 1868, "It is hard . . . to carry the eternal nigger," summed up the worries of white Republicans in the South. William H. Bagley was an old Whig, but he was unable to join the Democratic party, because he did not feel he could "vote to disfranchise Bartholomew F. Moore, and *enfranchise* 'Boots' the Barber—the one, life long Union man, and one of the ablest lawyers in the whole Union; and the other a dirty barber as *dishonest* as he is *dirty,* and as *ignorant* as he is *dishonest.*" One North Carolinian commented that he thought the Republicans had a chance in the upcoming election in 1868, but that "should the negros [*sic*] insist upon having a negro on the ticket it will kill it dead." The safest practice, of course, was not to put Negroes on the ticket at all, as was done by the Republicans of east Tennessee. The Republican organization in Wilmington, North Carolina, even though the blacks had been active in the party and constituted a majority of the voters, also fielded an all-white slate in its first election in 1868.[2]

THE SHOCK TREATMENT

The imposition of Radical Reconstruction by Congress acted as a kind of "shock treatment" for many white Southerners, especially in changing their minds about black participation in politics. In Virginia, for example, the governor had recommended in 1866 that the legislature ratify the Fourteenth Amendment, but the legislature refused to do so. At that point, it was evident, only a minority of legislators were prepared to accept the principle that the federal government would have jurisdiction over civil rights or to acquiesce in raising the question of Negro suffrage even in the indirect fashion contained in the Fourteenth Amendment. Yet by 1868 these very same conservative legislators, as Jack Maddex has argued, had accepted black political equality as a fact of their society. Unionists in north Alabama had never been friendly toward black suffrage, if only because such voters might be used by former slaveholders in central and southern Alabama to vote them out of office. Yet after March, 1867, a north Alabama Unionist was saying that Unionists must "look this Negro question directly in the face" and do justice to their new "unwelcome allies."

2. John A. Hedrick to Benjamin Hedrick, March 2, 1868; William H. Bagley to Benjamin Hedrick, June 2, 1868; H. C. Thompson to Benjamin Hedrick, March 5, 1868, all in B. S. Hedrick Papers; W. McKee Evans, *Ballots and Fence Rails: Reconstruction on the Lower Cape Fear* (Chapel Hill, N.C., 1967), p. 120.

Some Radical white Southerners recognized the necessity of such shock treatment. We "have been denounced in unmeasurable terms," wrote one Republican from the South to Thaddeus Stevens, "as being 'free Negro equalizers' and 'radicals' " and everything else. The recently passed Reconstruction Act, he went on, "has had a salutary effect upon the country, and has caused cesech in some measure to cease to dictate their own terms of" restoration.

Once the shock had been administered, a new atmosphere prevailed; now blacks possessed the power of the vote. This fact in itself opened eyes, changed minds, and helped to move some white Southerners to assume a Radical Republican outlook. A part of the shock was the great interest that blacks themselves showed in politics. In elections in 1867, for example, in New Hanover County, North Carolina, some Negroes walked more than thirty miles to vote, "their faces radiant with smiles," one white Republican commented. They reminded him of the song "There's a Good Time Coming." Another report at the same election told of a Negro arriving at the polls in an ambulance, with a leg missing, it having been amputated only half an hour before. One Radical congressman in Tennessee said that he witnessed a column of Negroes voting; they had come as a group so that the illiterate ones would not be tricked by the opposition into voting the wrong ticket. (Throughout the nineteenth century the "ballot" was actually a "ticket" provided by the party, not the government. There was always a danger that an illiterate voter of either color would be deliberately given the wrong ticket to cast since he could not verify its correctness.) The blacks did not arrive at the polls until an hour after they opened so that they would not interfere with whites who may have wanted to vote early. They broke off their own voting whenever a number of whites wanted to vote. "The anxiety on the part of the colored men to vote was intense," the congressman recalled. "Many reported that they had been solemnly warned not to vote; others that their farm contracts would end; some feared bodily harm. The night before, a general meeting had been held when it was agreed after voting that they would return to their churches and offer prayers of thanksgiving for having been allowed the freeman's privilege to vote. . . ."[3]

Not all white Southerners were as enthusiastic about black voting. Raphael Semmes, the Confederate naval raider and by then the editor of a newspaper in Memphis, did not conceal either his sense of novelty or his distaste. "To our eyes," he wrote, "the long procession of dusky figures, making their way slowly to the judge's stand, bore the semblance of a funeral procession. Liberty was dead we thought, and those were her pall-bearers." (The Radical Republican had concluded *his* observation of black voters with the remark: "the chattel had become a human creature.") White observers commented on the novel presence of blacks in the visitor galleries of the state conventions and legislatures. In fact, one white said that he found only Negro men and women in the gallery at the North Carolina convention. When black suffrage was voted for the first time in the Reconstruction South in Tennessee in February, 1867, the galleries were filled with intense, black faces.[4]

ACCEPTING THE HITHERTO UNACCEPTABLE

For some white Southerners the prejudices of a lifetime and the blinders born of slavery fell away even before Congress compelled Negro equality. James Lusk Alcorn told his wife in 1864 of a Kentuckian, a Union general, whose ideas on blacks had changed greatly under the impact of association with freedmen. Although the general had been opposed to the Emancipation Proclamation, Alcorn related, he is now "its present warm advocate, believes the negro equal to the white; while not the advocate of miscegenation, is willing to yield to the necessity—and looks for some American Toussaint L'Overture [sic] to appear and give the black his proper

3. William F. Henderson to Thaddeus Stevens, March 4, 1867, in James A. Padgett, ed., "Reconstruction Letters from North Carolina, Part XII, Other Letters," *North Carolina Historical Review,* XXI (1944), 242–43; Evans, *Ballots and Fence Rails,* p. 165; Thomas B. Alexander, *Political Reconstruction in Tennessee* (Nashville, 1950), p. 155.

4. E. Merton Coulter, *William G. Brownlow, Fighting Parson of the Southern Highlands* (Chapel Hill, N.C., 1937), pp. 340, 330; Otto H. Olsen, *Carpetbagger's Crusade: The Life of Albion Winegar Tourgée* (Baltimore, 1965), p. 93.

position on this continent." Alcorn himself accepted a qualified Negro suffrage as early as 1865.

Presumably, change came for the Kentuckian from association with blacks; for others it resulted from more practical considerations. No Southern politician had been more hostile toward blacks, as we have seen earlier, than the Tennessee Unionist William Brownlow. But as early as 1865, as governor, he recognized that Negro-baiting could no longer be tolerated; nor could his favorite remedy of deportation be counted upon. He told the legislature that he hoped that blacks would leave the country voluntarily, "but if the colored man, after looking over the whole ground, shall still ask to stay in the land of his birth, to till the soil and labor in the work shop . . . under the bright skies that smiled on his infancy," Brownlow concluded, "I say, in all conscience, let him remain. . . ."[5] In time the prospect of black votes helped to make Brownlow an exponent of Negro suffrage.

The most outspoken white friend of blacks in the Radical party in Virginia was James Hunnicutt. Yet during the war Hunnicutt had made quite clear that the black man's welfare was far from his concern. "Let the *Negro question* in this great struggle be forgotten," he advised in the early days of the war, "and let the whole race be transported to Africa when the proper time comes, where they now ought to be, and from whence they should never have been brought." William Holden of North Carolina was another leader of blacks in the Radical Reconstruction who went through a similar metamorphosis from being indifferent or hostile to blacks to accepting them as allies.

Occasionally we get a glimpse into the mind of a white Southerner who made such a radical shift. After mingling with blacks, one white Republican in 1867 said that "my opinion is that there is but little if any difference in the talents of the two races and I am willing to give them all an even start in the race." Even opponents of the Republicans could gain a new insight into blacks from observing the revolutionary spectacle of black men participating in politics at election time. One Democrat wrote in his diary after election day in 1867: "I must say that Fletcher McNeill (negro)

5. James Lusk Alcorn to wife, March 22, 1864, James Lusk Alcorn Papers; Alexander, *Reconstruction in Tennessee,* p. 100.

behaved pretty well—must praise him some for his good conduct."[6]

Robert Somers, an English traveler in the South in 1870, thought he saw the alteration in attitude on a broader scale. The *Reform Union* of South Carolina, Somers reported, which was an organ of the native white conservatives, "recognizes fully the civil and political equality of the negroes not only as an election platform, but as the fundamental law of the United States. . . ." We may doubt whether Somers read the situation completely accurately, since he was prone to take conservatives at their word. Yet there could be no question that Southern Republicans spread before the South a new conception, a new ideal of race attitudes and practices. As Thomas Settle told a group of whites and blacks early in Reconstruction: get rid of the idea that Southerners are better friends of the Negro than Northerners. "That is all foolishness, first because you can never make the colored man believe it, and secondly if you could it would be wrong to do so. Sectional appeals of that character are unpatriotic," he insisted. "If they [conservative whites] are going to prove what they say to be true, let them at once freely and cheerfully, not grudgingly accord to the colored man the full fruits of his freedom." In 1870 a Republican paper in Charleston reprimanded Democrats for suggesting that the whites would one day overthrow the blacks. "Such talk is as wickedly idle as for colored men to say that their race should have complete control. It is not to be a matter of race at all." Men ought to gain political power because of citizenship, the paper concluded, "not because they are white, not because they are colored, but because they are American citizens." The paper then spelled out the long-term objective that the Republicans were trying to bring to the South: "By-and-by we shall stop talking of the color of a man in relation to citizenship and power, and shall look at his wealth of mind and soul."[7] Few Northern Republicans of the time were prepared to say as much.

6. James W. Hunnicutt, *The Conspiracy Unveiled: The South Sacrificed; or The Horrors of Secession* (Philadelphia, 1863), p. 452; Olsen, *Carpetbagger's Crusade,* p. 81; Nov. 19, 1867, Washington Sanford Chaffin Journal.

7. Robert Somers, *The Southern States Since the War, 1870–1* (London and New York, 1871), p. 51; Speech of March, 1867, Settle Papers, Folder 4; Allen W. Trelease, *White Terror: The Ku Klux Klan Conspiracy and Southern Reconstruction* (New York, 1971), p. xxviii.

Of necessity, the Republicans in the South could not simply preach acceptance of blacks. They had to practice acceptance as well. Indeed, one of the truly revolutionary aspects of Reconstruction was the amazingly open relationships that obtained between whites and blacks in the course of organizing the Republican party. Here, too, is a measure of the Other South. When William "Pig-Iron" Kelly of Pennsylvania spoke in Mobile, Alabama, in the spring of 1867, a hundred "respectable" whites were present among two thousand blacks. All meetings throughout the South in that astonishing year found blacks present in the audience—and on the platform. "The assemblage about the Court House presents every shade of color from the jet-black to the fair at skin," remarked a Conservative white North Carolinian in September, 1867. When the North Carolina Republican party held its founding convention in March at Raleigh, two of the vice-presidents were black and two were white. A Republican newspaper wrote at the time that black and white met "upon the same floor on the same footing and cooperated together in the most cordial and harmonious manner." Choosing its words carefully in order not to suggest the tabooed *social* equality, the newspaper went on: "The former master met his former slave as his equal in all that pertains to manhood and the rights of self-government." In Mississippi the Hinds County *Gazette* used almost the same words to describe the meeting of white and black in Lowndes County, saying that prominent whites met "with their former slaves. . . . Old prejudices were laid aside and the utmost harmony prevailed." (The references to "harmony" suggest something of the foreboding the editors must have felt about the meeting of former masters and slaves.) At the meetings, blacks as well as whites spoke. In Mississippi old secession Democrat Albert G. Brown spoke beside a man whom he had recently tried to keep in slavery. Blacks were also later elected to the constitutional conventions and state legislatures.[8]

8. Sept. 7, 24, 1867, Washington Sanford Chaffin Journal; Richard Lee Hoffman, "The Republican Party in North Carolina, 1867–1871," unpublished M.A. thesis, University of North Carolina, Chapel Hill, 1960, pp.

SPREADING THE MESSAGE

The mere presence of black voters exerted an influence beyond the Republicans, for no sooner did it become clear that blacks would be voting than Conservatives wooed them. And in so doing they acted out a conception of race relations that was novel for Southern whites. Blacks were to be sought after, perhaps even flattered. In Tennessee, for example, the Conservatives in 1867 actually endorsed black officeholding before the white Radicals in power had accepted the principle. Some Conservatives in Virginia tried so hard for the black vote that they were accused by some Radicals of being Negrophiles! One young Conservative banker got into the newspaper because at a barbecue that he sponsored for blacks in Richmond, he himself was drowned in the course of the jollification. The Conservative Richmond newspaper *The Whig* urged its readers to vote for certain black candidates under the heading, "Whites and Blacks Shoulder to Shoulder." Some diehard Virginians, it is true, could not stomach what they referred to as "Big Black Buck negroes" being in the legislature, occupying the seats of the great Virginians of the past, but the younger Conservatives took the new racial order in their stride. They mingled easily and courteously with the two dozen or so black legislators. It was reported in Georgia during the campaign of 1868 that Democrats not only sponsored barbecues for black voters, but that the candidates even sat down to eat with Negroes.[9]

One Conservative, campaigning in the backcountry of North Carolina, recorded in his journal without comment the mixing of the races that became commonplace under the new political order.

25–26; Thomas S. Staples, *Reconstruction in Arkansas, 1862–1874* (New York, 1932), p. 166; Otto H. Olsen, "Reconsidering the Scalawags," *Civil War History*, XII (1966), 312; Vernon Lee Wharton, *The Negro in Mississippi, 1865–1890* (Chapel Hill, N.C., 1947), pp. 143–44; James Welford Garner, *Reconstruction in Mississippi* (Baton Rouge, 1968; orig. pub. 1901), p. 180.

9. Jack P. Maddex, Jr., *The Virginia Conservatives, 1867–1879: A Study in Reconstruction Politics* (Chapel Hill, N.C., 1970), pp. 81, 199; Elizabeth Studley Nathans, *Losing the Peace: Georgia Republicans and Reconstruction, 1865–1871* (Baton Rouge, 1969), p. 87.

November 11, 1867: Met a small number of persons white and colored at Lumber Bridge and delivered a speech of almost one hour in length.
November 12, 1867: Met the people at Randolsville [*sic*] & spoke of the great questions of the day. The people of both colors listened with marked attention.
November 13, 1867: Came to Floral College, and addressed quite a number of persons of both colors, with some apparent effect.

As late as 1870 even the platform of the Democratic party in Louisiana reflected the new insistence upon black equality. "The interests of both white and black men are identical. . . . Whatever rights and privileges either enjoy under the constitution are sacred, and it is the duty of every citizen to see that they are maintained." At their rallies in Louisiana the Democrats welcomed blacks.[10]

Probably the most striking example of the way Republican insistence on Negro rights affected white attitudes and behavior occurred in Louisiana in 1873.[11] Louisiana was not blessed with an honest or effective Reconstruction regime, yet it was also a state in which blacks were a majority. Under such circumstances, the corrupt carpetbagger regime could not be overthrown at the ballot box through the mobilization of whites, as had already been done in some other Southern states. To vote out the Republicans, the whites would have to attract black votes, and that would require that they recognize the political equality of Negroes. By this time even some of the Democratic newspapers of New Orleans acknowledged, however reluctantly, that acceptance of the war amendments to the Constitution and the "reasonable demands of the negroes" was necessary if carpetbag government was to be ended.

The impetus behind the Unification Movement, as it was called, was a group of fifty prominent black and fifty well-known white citizens. Isaac N. Marks, a prewar Whig and leading merchant,

10. Washington Sanford Chaffin Journal; T. Harry Williams, *Romance and Realism in Southern Politics* (Athens, Ga., 1961), p. 27.
11. My treatment of the Unification movement is based upon Williams, *Romance and Realism*, pp. 33–41; T. Harry Williams, "The Louisiana Unification Movement," *Journal of Southern History*, XI (1945), 348–69, which contains documents, and Joe Gray Taylor, "New Orleans and Reconstruction," *Louisiana History*, IX (1968), 189–208.

presided at the first public meeting, with former Confederate General Pierre G. T. Beauregard as chairman of the resolutions committee. (Beauregard had received the surrender of Fort Sumter in the spring of 1861.) Marks was convinced that peace and order would come to the state only when all citizens were accorded their just rights; Beauregard spoke out publicly and privately in behalf of Negro equality, too, even though, like his fellow Confederate, James Longstreet, he was denounced roundly for his stand. In its public platform issued in the spring of 1873, the movement announced that it stood for political and civil equality for both races, and equal division of state offices between black and white, and an end to segregation in schools, trains, steamboats, and other public accommodations. The platform, which was printed several times in the newspapers over a period of a month, also pledged its members "to exercise our moral influence, both through personal advice and personal example, to bring about the rapid removal of all prejudices heretofore existing against the colored citizens of Louisiana, in order that they may hereafter enjoy all the rights belonging to citizens of the United States."

The promise of that spring, however, was gone by summer. Opposition from whites in the countryside and distrust of white promises by some Negro leaders in New Orleans ended the movement. While it lasted it was a concrete example of that openness to change that is so striking during Reconstruction. At no other time in the nineteenth century was the white South so receptive to change on the question of the black man. It is true that the white leaders of the Unification Movement accepted black political equality as a means—to overthrow the carpetbag regime—rather than as an end. The fact, to be sure, shows the important role played by outside pressure in initiating change in the South on matters of race. But it also shows that white Southerners could differ among themselves when the intervention of federal authority provided an opportunity for difference. Even on the question of race, in short, the white South has not been a monolith. Indeed, the recurring divisions, even on this sensitive question, have required the Majority South over the years to take Draconian measures in an effort to create a monolithic regional outlook on race.

EQUALITY UP TO A POINT

However much Conservatives and Radicals may have competed for black votes or been forced to change their minds about Negro rights, it would be a mistake to conclude that the imposition of Negro suffrage caused white Radicals, much less Conservatives, to accept blacks as full equals. Throughout Reconstruction the great preponderance of white Radicals were always careful to draw the line between social and political equality. It was a line that old Whig and new Republican James L. Alcorn was demarcating as early as the summer of 1865. He told his wife that granting the suffrage to a Negro—an act that he thought was inevitable—"by no means implies his social equality; we don't recognize the social equality of the low and base of our own color who enjoy these prerogatives," he pointed out. And when William Brownlow was attempting to explain why east Tennessean whites ought to accept black suffrage he, too, was careful to deny that it would mean social equality. "Think of some low white man in your community you would not dine with," he advised. "Does his casting of a ballot make him your social equal?" Besides, he went on, great Tennesseans like John Bell, Davy Crockett, and Andrew Jackson all had sought black votes back in the days before 1834, when free Negroes enjoyed the ballot in Tennessee. Then he clinched his case by observing that blacks could be counted on to vote against secessionists and former slaveholders.[12]

Whenever the Conservatives taunted Southern Radicals with encouraging "amalgamation," the standard Republican reply was to deny that they ever intended to "trench on the social rights or status of the white race," as the Raleigh *Standard* put it several times in 1867. Thomas Settle, about the same time, tried to allay white fears that laws in behalf of political equality would soon lead to laws compelling social equality between the races. "Social equality does not exist now among the whites," he pointed out, "and no law has ever attempted to regulate that matter in this or

12. Alcorn to wife, Aug. 26, 1865, in James Lusk Alcorn Papers; Alexander, *Reconstruction in Tennessee*, p. 130.

any other country. Every man chooses his own company. The virtuous form one association, and the vicious another. This matter regulates itself, law cannot do it." In the mouth of one white Republican the principle came curiously close to a formulation that would make Booker T. Washington famous half a century later: "Equality in all things political; distinctions, according to the personal rights of each, in all things social." (In his famous Atlanta Address in 1895, Washington said, "In all that is purely social we can be as separate as the fingers, yet one as the hand in all things essential to mutual progress.")[13]

It is easy enough to find deficiencies today in the distinction the Southern Republicans drew between political and social equality. As a racial ideology it undoubtedly fell short of full acceptance of blacks by whites.[14] Radical Southern Republicans not only condoned segregation in schools and in the militia, they often urged it themselves. Furthermore, they opposed in law as well as in social practice intermarriage between the races. Sometimes, despite their talk about political equality, they went so far as to discourage or prevent blacks from running for certain offices because it might arouse the hostility of the majority of white voters. And it is also true that the distinction between social and political equality smacks of an opportunistic attempt to gain black votes without fully accepting blacks. William Brownlow is undoubtedly an example of a Scalawag who exemplified this motivation. Yet even in the case of less opportunistic Republicans, like James Alcorn or Thomas Settle, it is difficult to know whether their deploring of social equality was a deeply felt objection or simply a tactic to be used in seeking the votes of whites who feared too great a departure from traditional racial practices. Since few white Radicals espoused social equality even in private correspondence, it seems likely that the distinction was a real one in their minds. But as we shall see in the last chapter, where this rather complicated question is taken up again, the distinction has more the earmarks of a

13. Olsen, *Carpetbagger's Crusade,* p. 85; Speech, March, 1867, Settle Papers, Folder 4; James A. Padgett, ed., "Reconstruction Letters from North Carolina, Part IX, Letters of Benjamin Franklin Butler," *North Carolina Historical Review,* XXI (1944), 54.

14. A fuller comment on the significance of this cardinal and crucial distinction will be offered in Chapter 10.

device than a significant or defensible distinction. Yet in the context of Radical Reconstruction the distinction was undoubtedly important, for it at least provided a way station between the complete subordination of blacks to whites that obtained before the war and the new order of black participation in Southern society. The importance of it is mirrored in the simple fact that before Negro suffrage was imposed by the North very few white Southerners were prepared to advocate it. James Alcorn was one of the few, incidentally.

A measure of the limits on Scalawag acceptance of Negro equality was the so-called Wilmington Opera House case. The case was decided in 1873 and concerned an attempt by some Negroes to occupy first-class seats in the opera house in Wilmington, North Carolina. They were arrested for violating segregated seating and convicted before a Republican judge, Daniel Russell. (In 1896 Russell was elected governor as a Republican.) Russell found them guilty on grounds of breach of the peace, but then went on to say that since the opera house was a public place, licensed by the state, it should be open to all people. Access, he wrote, cannot be denied on grounds of color or race without flying in the face of "the Constitution and the laws according to their true intent and meaning." The manager of the establishment may have been right, Russell conceded, "to separate different classes of persons whose close association is not agreeable to each other," but the accommodations must be equal for all in "comfort, the style, convenience and all other considerations," he insisted.[15] Russell was here enunciating, of course, a form of the doctrine of "separate but equal" which the United States Supreme Court would set forth in the case of *Plessy* v. *Ferguson* in 1896. Russell, however, was permitting it by private fiat, not by state action, it is worth noting.

Even when we have noticed the compromises with full equality that Southern Republicans accepted during Reconstruction, it is worth recognizing that in the context of the times even a distinction between social and political equality was radical. After all, there were few Northern Republicans who would have pushed for

15. I have taken the facts of the Opera House case from a clipping in the C. W. Broadfoot Papers, Folder 46, from *Tri-Weekly Gazette* of Fayetteville, North Carolina, July 21, 1874.

acceptance of blacks in all social situations. Indeed, it had taken several years after the war before most Northern states accepted black suffrage. Even Northern antislavery people could be doubtful about accepting civil equality between the races. An Ohio girl, then living in North Carolina, for example, wrote in 1873 to her former teacher, James Garfield, then a congressman from Ohio, inquiring about the pending civil rights bill. Does the bill "really contemplate mixed schools, churches, etc., etc.!" she wanted to know. "For my part I protest against an attempt to compel blacks and whites to mingle more together. I would not consent to our children's attending a mixed school; for as the blacks are now, their society would be degrading."[16]

Moreover, white Southern Republicans, unlike Northern, were on the firing line of race relations. Ninety percent of the Negroes lived in the South, and that was where slavery had been their characteristic status only a few years before. Any change in the direction of equality between the races was not only new, but threatening to whites as it could hardly be in the North. Hence if today Daniel Russell's decision in the Wilmington Opera House seems conservative and compromising, in the South of the late nineteenth century it brought him years of attacks from outraged whites.

To expect the Southern Republicans to have been accepting of Negroes is not only anachronistic, it is to commit the even more heinous historical crime of failing to appreciate what was done. For white men in the South to support Negro suffrage was not only a personal act of courage, but an opening to the future that promised a truly new relationship between the races in the South. Why that promise was not fulfilled is the substance of the remainder of this book.

In the backs of the minds of most white Republicans was the hope expressed by W. W. Holden in his inauguration as Republican governor of North Carolina: "The repugnance to Negro suffrage which exists among many of our people, will gradually subside when they shall be convinced by actual experience that

16. Mary Neely to James Garfield, March 14, 1873, in James A. Padgett, ed., "Reconstruction Letters from North Carolina, Part X, Letters of James Abram Garfield," *North Carolina Historical Review,* XXXI (1944), 146.

none of the evils they anticipated have resulted from it." But the realization of that expectation was much more glacial and much more fraught with race baiting than Holden and other white Republicans foresaw. Benjamin Hedrick's brother Adam could write four years after the beginning of Radical Reconstruction, "I am still a republican but not a Mr. Sumnar man that believes that the negro should have equal rights in scools hotels etc for it would spoil some of them that does prety well now." One Georgia Republican told a congressional committee in 1870 that "if you talk about equality, they at once conclude that you take the negro into your parlor or into your bed—everywhere that you would take your wife. They seem to be diseased upon that subject," he reported. "They do not seem to consider that he is merely to be equal before the law, but take it, I suppose designedly, to mean equality in the broadest sense: and hence they stir themselves up and lash themselves in a fury about it."[17]

In view of such fears, it is not surprising that right down to the end of Reconstruction Republicans were drawing the distinction between social and political rights for blacks. Joshua Morris argued in a Mississippi court in 1873, for example, that the war decided that Negroes were "brought up to a place of absolute legal equality with the hitherto dominant classes," but the "equality in society, by legal compulsion, is neither to be attained nor desired." Alabama Republicans in 1874 in order to hold white votes denied in their platform any belief in mixed schools or any other mixed accommodations, asking only that "advantages shall be equal." They asserted that they wanted "no social equality enforced by law."[18]

One sign that the distinction between political and social equality was more than simply a way of denying blacks their rights is that blacks themselves made the distinction. In most of the consti-

17. J. G. deRoulhac Hamilton, *Reconstruction in North Carolina* (New York, 1914), p. 292; Adam Hedrick to Benjamin Hedrick, B. S. Hedrick Papers; Trelease, *White Terror*, p. xx.
18. David Gaffney Sansing, "The Role of the Scalawag in Mississippi Reconstruction," unpublished Ph.D. dissertation, University of Southern Mississippi, 1969, p. 71; Sarah Van Voorhis Woolfolk, "The Role of the Scalawag in Alabama Reconstruction," unpublished Ph.D. dissertation, Louisiana State University, 1965, p. 197.

tutional conventions, for example, the Negro delegates did not insist upon integration of the schools, and when the legal bans on intermarriage came up, Negroes were quick to say that they did not want miscegenation any more than whites. (What blacks uniformly objected to was punishment of blacks, but not whites, for crossing the color line.) As Francis L. Cardozo said in the South Carolina convention, "We have not said there shall be no separate schools. On the contrary, there may be separate schools, and I have no doubt there will be such in most districts." In fact, he thought Negroes would actually prefer separate schools, "particularly until some of the present prejudice against their race is removed." All that Negroes wanted was that where separate schools were prohibitively expensive, "those colored children who desire to go to white schools" should be allowed to.

Black spokesmen were well aware that white acceptance was still developing and ought not to be pushed too hard, too fast. "Some men with strong stomachs would call for their whiskey or brandy straight," one black Alabama Republican pointed out in 1874 in addressing his fellow Negroes; "others with weaker stomachs, require much water in it. So it is with the members of our party. Some of them can take Civil Rights unmixed already; others with weaker stomachs must take them in a diluted form for a while longer. We must wait until their stomachs grow stronger and must do nothing that will drive them off."[19]

Besides, as blacks well recognized, the first goal was the achievement of full civil and political equality. Hence when Joseph Rainey, a black congressman from South Carolina, spoke in behalf of the civil rights bill of 1874 he drew the same distinction that white Republicans in the South had drawn and for the same reason. "Now, gentlemen," he began, "let me say the negro is not asking social equality. We do not ask it of you, we do not ask . . . that the two races should intermarry one with the other. God knows we are perfectly content. I can say for myself that I am contented to be what I am so long as I have my rights. . . . Sir, we are not asking to be put on a footing of social equality. I prefer

19. Joel Williamson, *After Slavery: The Negro in South Carolina During Reconstruction, 1861–1877* (Chapel Hill, N.C., 1965), p. 220; Woolfolk, "Scalawag in Alabama," p. 198.

to choose my own associates. . . . We do not ask the passage of any law forcing us upon anybody who does not want to receive us. But we do want a law enacted that we may be recognized like other men in the country." He wanted, he said, to be able to stop, like other congressmen, at hotels and restaurants and be free from insult.[20]

Within the South the Scalawags demonstrated that they were prepared to support a number of Negro aspirations. All of the Southern states under Scalawag rule, for example, enacted Negro suffrage, which was required by the federal government, but they also provided for public support for Negro education, which was not required by the Reconstruction laws, and was generally resisted by Southern Conservatives. And when Conservatives, having been defeated in the attempt to require segregation in the schools, sought to prohibit mixed schools, as happened in North Carolina, the Radical whites in the constitutional convention refused to go along. The Radical whites, it is true, would not compel mixing of the races in the schools, but their refusal to prohibit it was deliberate. As W. W. Holden said later, "the delegates framed the constitution for the whole people of the state and for all time and did not wish to use the words white and black in it." The North Carolina convention, which was dominated by Scalawags, also refused to bar Negroes from office, though the Conservatives wanted to write such a prohibition into the Constitution.[21]

On the national level, Scalawags in Congress not only voted for the civil rights bill proposed by Radical Republican Charles Sumner of Massachusetts in 1874, but Charles Hays, a native Republican from Alabama, took the floor in the House of Representatives in support of the bill. After identifying himself as a former slaveholder, Hays said there was no threat to any white person in the bill. All that it would do was to give the Negro his legitimate rights. Even now in the South, he pointed out, you will

20. *Congressional Record*, 43rd Cong., 1st Sess., part 1, v. 2. Dec. 19, 1873, p. 344.

21. Remark of Holden reported by John A. Hedrick to Benjamin Hedrick, March 11, 1868, B. S. Hedrick Papers; Richard L. Hume, "The 'Black and Tan' Constitutional Conventions of 1867–1869 in Ten Former Confederate States: A Study of Their Membership," unpublished Ph.D. dissertation, University of Washington, 1969, pp. 495–96.

find in trains Southern white women "travelling and sitting side by side with colored women as nurses and servants. Is objection raised to this?" Hays asked. "Not at all. Does anyone feel debased by the negro there? Not at all. Why then should the case be changed when that negro buys a first-class ticket and travels alone?" (Hays probably knew that the answer to his question was that as subordinates the blacks could be accepted in any social situation; it was when they were accepted as civil equals that many Southern whites took offense. But here he was seeking to score a point against Southern whites who, under the circumstances, would find it embarrassing to admit the reason.) Besides, Hays went on, even if the Democrats are correct and the black is inferior to the white man, what harm will a civil rights act do to whites? It is often said further, he continued, that the antipathy between the races is so great in the South that such a bill would be dangerous. "I believe no such twaddle," Hays exclaimed. "Thousands of the most intelligent men of the South were born and raised upon the old plantations." They associated intimately and in every way with blacks. "Was there prejudice then? Was [the] cry against 'social equality' raised then? Never, sir; but now they are free and receiving the enlightenment of education for the first time and the fact is discovered that the negro, who molded our fortunes, built our railroads, erected our palatial mansions, and toiled for our bread, is a curse upon the face of the earth, and not entitled to the protection of society. Sir, for one, as a Southern man, I feel a debt of gratitude toward them."[22]

TO ACT FOR EQUALITY

Some Radical whites were prepared to act as well as speak in behalf of a policy of equality between blacks and whites. The most difficult test for white Republicans in the South came when whites who opposed Reconstruction organized themselves into paramilitary or terrorist organizations like the Knights of the White

22. Woolfolk, "Scalawag in Alabama," pp. 193–94; Sarah Van V. Woolfolk, "Five Men Called Scalawags," *Alabama Review*, XVII (1964), 53; *Congressional Record*, 43d Cong., 1st Sess., part 2, pp. 1096–97, Jan. 31, 1874.

Camellia, the Red Shirts, or the Ku Klux Klan. The object of such groups' activities was not only the blacks, but those whites who supported and worked with blacks. John C. Norris had been a Unionist in Georgia before the war; after the Surrender he joined the Republican party and was elected sheriff of Warren County in 1868. Even though members of the Klan ambushed him at one point, leaving him a cripple from his wounds, Norris refused to resign his office or stop making arrests of Klansmen who violated the rights of citizens. T. M. Shaffner, a Republican state senator in North Carolina and a native of the state, introduced a bill to suspend the writ of habeas corpus and to employ the state militia in suppressing the Klan in North Carolina. Because Shaffner's bill passed the legislature, the Klan marked him for death. The threats to his life became so unbearable that he left the state for Indiana.

The Klan was difficult for the Radical governments to suppress because its popularity among the masses of whites made it hard to obtain testimony against alleged Klansmen. And even when witnesses were available and willing, juries would not convict. As a result, Republican governments intent upon suppressing the insurgent violence proclaimed martial law under which juries were not needed. The warfare between the militia and the Klansmen that often ensued, however, could exact a high price. Radical Governor William Holden of North Carolina found this out when he sought to suppress the Klan with military force. The so-called Kirk-Holden war eventually suppressed the Klan in North Carolina, but it also was the occasion, if not the cause, for the impeachment and removal of Holden from office. William Brownlow, the Scalawag governor of Tennessee, also used military power to suppress the Klan. In 1869 he imposed martial law on nine counties and sent in the militia, most of which was recruited in east Tennessee. It was Brownlow's relentless pursuit of the masked night riders that caused the head of the Klan, General Nathan B. Forrest, in 1869 to call for the abandonment of masks—not the disbandment of the organization as is sometimes erroneously said.

Governor Powell Clayton of Arkansas, a carpetbagger, organized perhaps the most successful effort against the Klan. But before he managed to suppress the terrorist organization he had to turn to whites from the old Unionist areas of the state as well as to Negroes to obtain reliable militiamen. For a while, too, Clayton had difficulties obtaining guns for his troops, since the shipping firms, which were needed to bring in the guns, would not do so because they were sympathetic to the Klan. White and black troops fought together against the Klan, though usually in separate companies. At times, in short, Southern white men fought other Southern white men over the principle that black men were politically equal with white. And in Arkansas, Tennessee, and North Carolina the white friends of the black man's rights won—at least temporarily.[23]

The Klan was not particularly active in Texas, but lawlessness was endemic on the frontier. As a result, in 1870 the Scalawag governor, Edmund Davis, created a state police force to control the violence and lawlessness. The force was biracial, with about 60 percent white and 40 percent black. In the course of fourteen months, ending in September, 1871, the state police arrested almost 3,500 persons and jailed 638 persons for murder or attempted murder alone. It recovered about $200,000 in stolen property, too. During 1871 eight policemen were killed and four wounded in the line of duty. In the state archives today are hundreds of letters from citizens and groups, principally white, asking for help against secessionists, brigands, and terrorizers of blacks. The force, in short, was not simply a show.

The Conservative whites vigorously opposed the police force because it centralized power in the governor, but principally because it contained a large number of blacks with authority over whites, as the attacks on black policemen suggest. Davis used the police to protect the rights of blacks as well as those of whites. In two of the three times that he declared martial law, the murder of a black was the cause. Not surprisingly, one of the first things the Democratic legislature did when it came to power was to abolish the state police. One further sign that the hostility to the state police stemmed primarily from its biracial character is the case of Captain L. H. McNelly. As a state policeman McNelly was widely

23. Trelease, *White Terror,* pp. 161, 172, 196–97, 203, 226–27, 232–233.

condemned as inadequate, but later, when he joined the Texas
Rangers, an all-white outfit, he was recognized as a hero.[24]

A few white Southern Republicans completely accepted black
equality during the revolutionary days of Reconstruction. One
North Carolina Republican reported in 1867 that his sister was
then operating a free school for black children in conjunction with
a woman from New Jersey. Robert W. Flournoy of Pontotoc
County, and Joshua S. Morris of Claiborne and Warren counties,
in Mississippi gained notoriety because they not only worked
closely with blacks in the party but accepted them as equals.
Flournoy, for example, edited a newspaper entitled *Equal Rights*
at the same time that he was superintendent of schools in Pontotoc
County. "I have claimed the right for every colored man to send
his children to the same school as white persons do," he told a
congressional committee in 1870. Since black and white children
play together, he added, "I see no reason why it should poison
them to go to school together." James W. Hunnicutt of Virginia,
once a slaveholder, also became known as the public advocate of
the blacks and a personal practitioner of equality. Franklin J.
Moses, Jr., of South Carolina publicly and consistently supported
equality for blacks, whatever might be said against his corrupt rule
as governor of that state. Congressman Christopher C. Bowen of
the same state was said to receive blacks in his home. It is worth
noting that Flournoy, Hunnicutt, and Moses were all originally
from slaveholding families in South Carolina, at least two of which
were of high prominence. Their transformation into equalitarians
was therefore that more striking. John W. Stephens of North
Carolina was of a different origin; he was both poor and barely
literate. A wartime Unionist, he joined the Republican party after
the war and worked with blacks on the basis of equality from the
outset. His close association with Negroes aroused the hostility of
whites and particularly of the Klan. One night he was lured into an
empty room after a political meeting and killed.[25]

24. Ann Patton Baenzinger, "The Texas State Police During Reconstruction; a Re-examination," *Southwestern Historical Quarterly,* 72 (1969),
475–88; see also W. C. Nunn, *Texas Under the Carpetbaggers* (Austin,
1962), pp. 50–53, 58, 73–74, and ch. 3.
25. H. H. Buxton to Ralph Buxton, April 6, 1867, Ralph Potts Buxton
Papers; William C. Harris, "A Reconsideration of the Mississippi Scalawag,"

The number of white Radicals who went as far as Stephens or Flournoy or Moses in their acceptance of blacks were few, to be sure. But their existence suggests the breadth of the spectrum of adjustment white Southerners could make when the old molds were broken and a new fluidity and openness came into human relations in the South. In a sense the true measure of the change or the potentiality for further change lay not in such spectacular examples. It was to be found, rather, in the myriad of examples of whites and blacks carrying on the public business as they had never done before in the South and would not do again on such a scale for a hundred years. In the conventions and legislatures across the South black men talked, sometimes with sharp and embarrassing realism, and white men listened, perhaps answered, but continued to work with them. At the convention in Arkansas, for example, black men lectured former slaveholders on the fact that the existence of mulattoes in the society was the result of white, not black, sexuality. "The census of the United States shows that forty percent of us have crossed the line," one black delegate pointed out. "It is no fault of ours. No gentleman will lay it to our door. The intermixture has taken place illegitimately. Those gentlemen who so place themselves upon a pedestal of virtue, will not deny that this was wrong." The debate went on for several days, but without rancor or even personal attacks.[26] It was not without significance, too, that black men were now generally addressed as "Mister" in both the Republican press and the official records of the government. On a simple, but profoundly important level, these everyday events were also a measure of the way in which the Other South manifested itself during Reconstruction.

THE PRICE OF EQUALITY

White Republicans, of course, had to pay a price for their willingness to practice their new racial principles. Virtually every state

Journal of Mississippi History, XXXII (1970), 11; Sansing, "Scalawag in Mississippi," p. 72; Williamson, *After Slavery,* p. 294; Trelease, *White Terror,* pp. 212–13.

26. Paul C. Palmer, "Miscegenation as an Issue in the Arkansas Constitutional Convention of 1868," *Arkansas Historical Quarterly,* XXIV (1965), 105.

of the former Confederacy was convulsed at one time or another by groups of armed men who sought to punish or terrorize white men who were bold enough to side with blacks or to support Republican governments. There is no need to repeat the story of violence and terror here—it is fully told in Allen Trelease's recent *White Terror*. It is worth noting, however, that the acts of violence exerted a wide influence because of the permissive attitude taken by Conservative whites. When a Republican judge and a sheriff, for example, were murdered in Louisiana in 1868, a Democratic newspaper would not blame the murderers. Instead it suggested that the victims "have met the fate they deserved." It was too bad that people in the community were driven to such lengths to rid the community of "lawless tyrants and wrongdoers in their midst," the paper observed. "But who is to blame? Assuredly not we people of the South, who have suffered wrongs beyond endurance. Radicalism and negroism, which in the South are one and the same thing, are alone to blame," the paper explained.

The measures of the dangers and difficulties of being a Republican, like the measures of acceptance, are not to be found only in the spectacular acts of violence against persons, life, or property. The everyday discrimination, harassment, or hostility was hard enough to bear and could be devastating in itself. Whites who dared to vote Republican were ridiculed to their faces as "white niggers." George W. Ashburn of Columbia, Georgia, could not get a room in a hotel in his home town because he was friendly with his black constituents. It was the acceptance of blacks as political equals that fueled the deepest resentment among Conservatives. One old friend of W. C. Williams of Mississippi told Williams not to speak to him any more because "any white man who will go around with nigger clubs is too low to speak to a gentleman."[27] One Republican living in Mississippi wrote to Thomas Settle in 1872 that "even my own kinspeople have turned the cold shoulder to me because I hold office under a Republican administration." A Virginia Republican spoke for many others when he wrote in

27. Trelease, *White Terror*, p. xiv; Alexander, *Reconstruction in Tennessee*, p. 240; Nathans, *Losing the Peace*, p. 135; Trelease, *White Terror*, p. 76; Sansing, "Scalawag in Mississippi," pp. 48–49.

1868, "The Northern people have no idea of the animosity which exists against Union men in the South." Almost daily, he complained, Republicans are urged to leave the state. "I am a Virginian," he went on, "and I have no blood relations who are not Southern men and I assure you upon my honor there is a worse feeling in Virginia today than there was in March of 1861."

Given the threats, frauds, and violence visited upon white Republicans, it is understandable that many of them not only welcomed the Reconstruction Acts, but called also for federal legislation to protect the rights of whites and blacks at the ballot box. Indeed, knowing Republicans recognized from the beginning the need for federal protection. In July of 1867 one of the founders of the Republican party in North Carolina, Robert P. Dick, wrote from Greensboro that "there is a very bitter opposition to colored suffrage—and the political equality of the Negro. The Republicans here have to encounter the social prejudices of centuries," he warned. "And we must be kindly and generously sustained by our Northern friends or we will be overwhelmed." Four years later another North Carolinian declared to a Northern congressman, "A Union Man is Not Safe in these States. I think the Only Way that rebels can be Cut down in the South, is for Congress to take holt and See that the Law is prossecuted. . . . I can say to you with Safity that a Union man['s] Chance is Slender hear in North Carolina. All of the republicans look for Congress to aid them."

Given the inconveniences, not to say danger, of being a Republican, the assertion of one Mississippi Republican may well have been true: "a great many white men who would vote the republican ticket . . . never say anything about it publicly [and] are afraid of the odium, the denunciation, the persecution, the deprivation of patronage, and the loss of social position. . . ." And it was a fact that the lack of a secret ballot made men vulnerable to attack. Even someone as secure and prominent as Amos Akerman, the Attorney General of the United States, admitted in 1871 that the pressure was almost overpowering. He wondered if, in 1867, when he became a Republican, he "had foreseen the strength of the prejudice to be encountered, I should have had the courage to enter the field on the side which I believed both expedient and right. . . ."[28]

NATIVES VERSUS OUTSIDERS

The hostility of his neighbors may have been the principal burden a native white Republican had to bear in the South, but it was not the only one. A further consequence of the new openness of political and social life in the Reconstruction South was that many Northerners migrated to the region, seeking their fortunes and a new start in life. When they entered politics as Republicans these immigrants were quickly dubbed "carpetbaggers." Their presence among Southern Republicans also affected the future of the Scalawags.

In almost every state the conflict between the two groups of white Republicans was serious and divisive. In Alabama, for example, where the Unionists obtained access to offices after the defeat of the Confederates, the arrival of the Northerners seemed to threaten their recently acquired political power. Moreover, the Northerners encouraged the newly franchised blacks, upon whom they depended for votes. "What can a native Union man do, expect, or calculate on in the future?" David P. Lewis from northern Alabama asked irately of a fellow Scalawag in August, 1868. "The Carpetbaggers have already landed everything that is Republican in Hell. The possibility of building up a national party in Alabama in affiliation with the Republican Party, is utterly extinct," Lewis concluded rather prematurely. "The political offices, the University, Schools, all carpetbagged!" About the same time, the editor of a newspaper in the same part of the state was complaining that if "the present state of things goes on much longer,

28. J. F. Simmons to Thomas Settle, Nov. 21, 1872, Settle Papers; J. H. Clement to W. E. Chandler, Aug. 12, 1868, quoted in Leon Burr Richardson, *William E. Chandler, Republican* (New York, 1940), p. 114; R. P. Dick to T. D. Cox, July 6, 1867, in Padgett, ed., "Letters from North Carolina . . . to John Sherman," p. 374; A. E. Smith to B. F. Butler in Padgett, ed., "Letters from North Carolina to . . . Butler," p. 349; Sansing, "Scalawag in Mississippi," p. 44; Amos Akerman to James Jackson, Nov. 20, 1871, Amos T. Akerman Letterbooks. I am indebted for this reference to Elizabeth Studley Nathans of Duke University.

only a baker's dozen of us will be left up here, aside from the colored and the carpetbaggers." Actually, as Sarah Woolfolk has shown, the Scalawags dominated the state offices, including the highest in the state. What was really bothering native Republicans like Lewis was that they now had to share their newly gained power with outsiders and that these outsiders were often friends of the blacks in the party.[29]

Native white Republicans in North Carolina resented the intrusion of Northerners, too. One wrote in 1867 that he hoped congressional Reconstruction could be carried off without interference from the "secesh and adventurers. The permanent citizens of the State, those whose interests are here, ought to effect the work." By the end of Reconstruction, native leaders of the party were frank in their resentment over the offices held by Northerners in the state. "Not the least among our difficulties," wrote Daniel Russell to Thomas Settle in 1874, "is the fact that our Federal office Holders, composed almost entirely of the Carpet Bag class, are utterly inefficient, politically worthless and entirely selfish. Their devotion to the party consists in their love of the salaries and fees incident to the holding of Office. Take these away and they return North or to the enemy." Russell's indictment was no less severe than would be that of a Democrat. "Deserving men, good speakers and first rate politicians of our own people are thrust aside to keep these men in power," he complained.[30]

Because Tennessee had a Republican government even before the end of the war and without the necessity of congressional Reconstruction, the antagonism between Scalawag and carpetbagger came early. As one radical editor explained in February, 1868, to Thaddeus Stevens, "the loyalty of the northern born Tennessee radicals is not often questioned, but the native Tennesseans are jealous of such men aspiring to office and in many cases regard the northern Tennesseans as mere office hunting adventurers who come south with no intention of permanently residing here. That is why one section of the Radical party of Tennessee is often sneered at by the other as 'carpetbag fellows,' 'bummers,'

29. Woolfolk, "Scalawag in Alabama," pp. 93, 95, 62–63.
30. David Hogbin to Benjamin Hedrick, Sept. 20, 1867, B. S. Hedrick Papers; Daniel L. Russell to Thomas Settle, Sept. 16, 1874, Settle Papers.

and the like." The tenacity with which the Southern-born radicals clung to state office is measured by the assertion in a contemporary newspaper that only *one* of the general offices of the state was held by a nonnative, that all of the state's members of Congress were native, and that only ten of all the state legislators were Northern-born—and four of those were old residents of the state. Even on the local level, jobs were held principally by Southerners. Out of eighty-five county superintendents of education, sixty-three were Southern-born.

Although what has been said and quoted seems to suggest that at the heart of the contest between carpetbaggers and Scalawags was the search for jobs, that was more the result of the conflict than the cause. The real conflict came over the more sensitive issue of the Negro. The radical editor in Tennessee explained the antagonism to Thaddeus Stevens. "The radicals of northern birth having naturally more antislavery feeling and wishing to counter-balance the personal influence of those who are native Tennessee loyalists are more ready to sustain new rights or claim new privileges for the blacks than the other section of the radical party and as a result . . . have a larger share of the confidence of the colored population than others have. . . ."[31]

This different attitude toward blacks was also evident in the broader study of voting patterns that Richard Hume made of the ten state constitutional conventions. The 424 native whites in the conventions split 232 to 192 in favor of what Hume calls Radicalism, that is, the majority voted in favor of blacks and the disfranchisement of former Confederates. The 138 non-Southern whites who sat in the same conventions split 118 Radical and only 20 Conservative on the same issues. (Florida was the only state, Hume points out, in which the number of Conservatives among the carpetbaggers outnumbered the Radicals. In Florida, significantly enough, the antagonism between carpetbaggers and Scalawags was minimal during Reconstruction. The carpetbaggers in that state seemed to be more interested in economic development than in social change.) It is significant, too, that in no state did the number of Conservatives among black delegates even approach the number who were Radical.[32]

This difference in attitude toward blacks on the part of carpet-baggers and Scalawags cropped up again and again within the Republican organizations in the South. Daniel Goodloe, a good antislavery North Carolinian before the war, complained of it to his fellow antislavery North Carolinian, Benjamin Hedrick. The Northerners, Goodloe wrote in 1868, "evidently want to force social equality, as appears from the educational and other features [of the new state constitution], whatever they may publicly say to the contrary. John R. French [a carpetbagger] insists privately that there should *not* be separate schools for the white and colored children," Goodloe wrote. A native Texan Republican like Judge Charles Caldwell would not speak from the same platform with his fellow Republican George W. Smith. The reason was that Smith was a friend as well as a leader of blacks; yet Smith's personal life was exemplary, including the fact that he neither drank nor smoked. In the constitutional convention of Arkansas, John M. Bradley sought to have marriage between members of the two races prohibited in the constitution. On several other questions Bradley was undoubtedly a Radical; he had run as a Republican, he had voted for a carpetbagger as president of the convention, but on this issue he broke with his party. The carpetbaggers in the Texas convention, however, defended the right of black and white

32. Hume, " 'Black and Tan' Conventions," pp. 672–73, 682. Jack Benton Scroggs, "Carpetbagger Influence in the Political Reconstruction of the South Atlantic States, 1865–1876," unpublished Ph.D. dissertation, University of North Carolina, Chapel Hill, 1951, p. 325, writes: "Although political considerations contributed to carpetbagger concern with equal civil and political rights for Negroes, there remains little doubt that the Northerner was the chief sponsor of the Negro's cause during Reconstruction." Hume, " 'Black and Tan' Conventions," pp. 45–50, provides evidence for making the following revealing comparison. In the Alabama convention two votes were taken on opening public schools to blacks; the divisions were:

	First vote		*Second vote*	
	For	Against	For	Against
Southern whites:	20	20	14	18
Non-Southern whites:	24	0	23	1

Blacks voted unanimously "for" on both votes.

to marry. Once the convention was adjourned, Bradley supported other Republican policies.[33]

On clear-cut questions of racial equality the Negroes and carpetbaggers often came together on the same side, but at other times, the common Southern origins of blacks and native whites seem to have been controlling. When blacks in the South Carolina party demanded a share of the offices, for example, they tried to dislodge the carpetbaggers first. As one of the black leaders of the state, Beverly Nash, said in 1867, "We would rather have white people that have lived among us than strangers." And in the election of 1872 black voters preferred for governor the corrupt native Franklin J. Moses, Jr., to the scrupulously honest carpetbagger Reuben Tomlinson. (Moses's well-known egalitarian acceptance of blacks may well have played a role here, yet that same year the blacks of Charleston chose a native white over a carpetbagger for mayor.) In South Carolina, at least, as Joel Williamson has pointed out, the carpetbaggers were certainly the better educated of the two groups of white candidates, so that simple qualifications cannot explain the black preference for Scalawags. Rather, it seems to have been a case of Southerners of both colors standing together against the outsiders. When the crunch came with the violent overthrow of the carpetbag government in 1876 in South Carolina, a Negro leader told a Democratic Club that if the blacks could count on leaders like the Conservative patrician Wade Hampton to hold the whites to their promises of fairness to blacks, the Negroes would "grasp your hand and help you drive out the carpetbagger." Once again it is instructive to observe that the carpetbagger in question was Governor Daniel C. Chamberlain, a man of personal integrity and a genuine reform leader.[34]

The rivalry and often open conflict between carpetbagger and Scalawag during Radical Reconstruction reached significant proportions in some Southern states. The party organizations in Arkansas, Alabama, and Tennessee were deeply divided by the antagonism. The Unification movement in Louisiana, too, can be

33. R. D. Goodloe to Benjamin Hedrick, March 27, 1868, B. S. Hedrick Papers; Trelease, *White Terror*, p. 140; Palmer, "Miscegenation as an Issue," pp. 100–5.

34. Williamson, *After Slavery*, pp. 361, 409–10.

viewed as a conflict between natives and carpetbaggers, since the Republican government of the state was dominated by Northerners. And there, too, as in South Carolina, many Negroes sided with the natives, at least at the outset. The North Carolina party was always plagued by the division and particularly so in 1870, when a movement was begun among the natives to start a new Republican party with the carpetbaggers purged. Mississippi's Republican organization in the 1870's was also split by the antagonism, but there the Negroes supported the carpetbagger Adelbert Ames.

The rivalry played into the hands of the Democrats, of course. One Republican living in Alabama wrote in 1873, for example, that the bar of Mobile, which was dominated by Democrats, pressed carpetbaggers upon the federal administration as candidates for federal judicial appointments. "They do not want the Administration to appoint a native," the Republican wrote. "Their object is to make the Government as odious as possible to the people."[35]

The difficulties that Southern and Northern whites experienced in working together within the same party provide several insights into the South and Reconstruction. For one thing, they point up, once again, the differences between the South and the North and the persistence of these differences even during the fluid and open era of Reconstruction. Just as Southern antislavery men differed from Northern, so Southern Republicans seem to have differed from Northern, even when both operated within the social context of the South.

What those differences were precisely is not as easy to discern. But a clue is provided when it is recognized that the antagonism between Scalawag and carpetbagger was not automatic. Occasionally, outsiders could be accepted even by Conservative white Southerners in preference to Radical native whites. There were at least two such occasions of importance during Reconstruction. One was in 1869 in Mississippi when the Conservatives supported Louis Dent as a candidate for governor running against Southerner James L. Alcorn. Dent was a typical carpetbagger in every respect—except one. He had arrived in the state only after the war,

35. George M. Duskin to Thomas Settle, Nov. 23, 1873, Settle Papers.

he was a renter of land rather than an owner, and he was the brother-in-law of President Grant. The one characteristic of a carpetbagger that he lacked was that he did not take a stand in favor of Negro equality, which Alcorn did.

The second instance of a carpetbagger who was acceptable to Conservatives was Gilbert C. Walker, who ran successfully for governor of Virginia in 1869 under the auspices of the Conservatives. Walker, a lawyer from New York and Chicago, arrived in Virginia only in 1864, going into banking and manufacturing in Norfolk. He became a Republican only in 1868, having been a Douglas Democrat in 1860. Despite his "foreign" origins, Walker was intensely popular among Conservatives. While governor he was spoken of as the "noble Governor" by the Petersburg *Index* for being "the eagle by day, and the owl by night" in protecting the state against "birds of prey," that is, against carpetbaggers! After he completed his term as governor he was twice elected to Congress. As with Dent, it was clearly Walker's conservatism on the race issue and his desire to concentrate on the economic development of Virginia that removed the taint of carpetbagger from him. Otherwise he fitted well even the minor elements in the stereotype: he was a poor administrator, he was known to have a problem with liquor, and after Reconstruction he returned North![36]

A second insight that emerges from a recognition of the antagonism between Northern and Southern Republicans is a little clearer understanding of why a biracial political party did not flourish in the Reconstruction South. From the beginning of Reconstruction it was evident to realistic Southern Republicans that the party's future there depended upon the unity of its three principal groups. "We must keep together scalawags, carpetbaggers, and niggers," wrote a North Carolina Republican. "This is our safety—this is the hope of the South."[37] But making these three parts work together was difficult, not only because of ancient antagonisms between blacks and whites, but also because of almost equally ancient differences between Northerners and Southerners of the same race.

36. Garner, *Reconstruction in Mississippi*, p. 239; Maddex, *Virginia Conservatives*, pp. 74–75, 103.
37. Olsen, *Carpetbagger's Crusade*, p. 171.

In the end, the failure to unite the three elements doomed the Republicans to the status of a minority party in the upper South and to largely black members in the deep South. By 1876 the once bright hope of early Reconstruction, that out of the new order a powerful biracial political party would emerge, was gone. That year the white men of the South voted overwhelmingly Democratic.

The causes for the failure of the promise of Reconstruction do not really concern us here. It was never very likely that with luck or even with genius the Other South could have become the Majority South. Certainly the causes for failure are more complex than the split between whites within the Republican party. Any examination of the causes would have to include as well the violent and persistent hostility of the majority of white Southerners to the political equality of Negroes, of which the Klan's activities were the most visible measure. White Southerners also resented the interference of the alien North in their political and social life, of which the hostility toward carpetbaggers was but the tip of the iceberg. And finally, as the settlement of 1877 makes evident, the failure of the Republicans in the South is related to the North's failure of nerve and commitment. Northerners simply abandoned the protection of Negro political rights, which they had once insisted upon and which was the indispensable electoral foundation for a Southern biracial party.

The close of Reconstruction may have finished off the Republican dream of achieving majority status in the South, but the party was far from snuffed out. Not only did Negroes continue to vote, but thousands of white Southerners also voted and worked for Republican candidates and organizations. More important for the future was the additional fact that the social and economic sources of dissent and divergence within the South also remained. The powerful influence and authority of the federal government, it is true, was now removed. But the divisions within the region, as we have seen, stretched back long before the Fourteenth Amendment was even thought of. Out of those divisions would emerge new challenges to the traditional, Majority South. Let us turn now to those "Other Southerners," who in the years after Reconstruction spoke and acted on their own.

9

Southern Dissenters
on Their Own

The accession of Rutherford B. Hayes to the presidency as a result
of the so-called Compromise of 1877 has usually been interpreted
to mean that direct federal intervention in the political affairs of
the South was over. Actually that was true only of military intervention, for even after 1877 Northern Republicans continued
trying to win popular support for their party in the South. Moreover, the number of states in which military intervention was able
to take place had been declining for some time. By 1876, for
example, only three of the eleven former Confederate states were
still under Radical Republican rule and susceptible, therefore, to
military intervention. Indeed, ever since 1872, at least, it had been
clear that federal intervention would be sporadic rather than consistent. The split within the Northern Republicans, best illustrated
by the Liberal Republican movement in 1872, made evident that
the earlier Northern insistence upon a strong Republican party in
the South was weakening if it was not already dead. Northern
Republicans by the middle seventies had become quite cynical
about the "autumnal outbreaks" of violence, as President Grant
once referred to Southern elections. Many considered them as little
more than a means for perpetuating a few white Southern Republicans in public office rather than as a basis for a new party structure. Nevertheless, 1877 is as accurate a date as any for marking

the beginning of the period when Southern Republicans knew that they were on their own.

REPUBLICANS WITHOUT AN ARMY

What happened to the Republican organizations in the Southern states after 1877 usually varied according to the previous long-term history of each state party. For example, in North Carolina and Tennessee, where Unionists had been strong, and Scalawags numerous, the Republican party remained formidable, composed of large numbers of whites as well as blacks. In North Carolina, throughout the elections of the 1880's the Republicans regularly captured between 35 and 38 percent of the counties and fell behind the Democrats in the gubernatorial elections no more than 10 percentage points. One North Carolina Republican estimated in 1879 that the white Republicans in the state numbered 40,000, adding that among them were also some of the most prominent families in the state. As late as 1886 the Republicans elected fifty-seven members of the state legislature. Furthermore, Republicans remained sufficiently strong in that state to elect a governor in 1896.

Substantial numbers of white voters were also in the Tennessee Republican party. The white Republicans were concentrated in the eastern part of the state, where before the war the Whigs had clustered, and where during Reconstruction the Scalawags had been preponderant. Between 1870 and 1900 the Republican vote in Tennessee, of which fully half came from the eastern third of the state, ranged from 28 to 49 percent of the total. Under unusual circumstances the Republicans could even carry the state, as happened in 1880, when a four-way race permitted the Republican candidate to capture the governor's chair. That year, the Republicans won 41 percent of the vote. As one Tennessee Republican boasted, albeit a little inaccurately, in 1893, "We are the only state in the South with Republican Congressmen or with Districts that are reliable [*sic*] Republican and always elect Republican Representatives. . . ."[1]

1. Daniel J. Whitener, "The Republican Party and Public Education in North Carolina, 1867–1900," *North Carolina Historical Review*, XXXVII

In the deep South, however, the picture was quite different. There the rank and file of the party was overwhelmingly black, even though white men were usually the chief leaders. Furthermore, because a majority of the people in three of these states (South Carolina, Mississippi, and Louisiana) was black, the party was subjected there to both fraud and violence on an enormous scale in order to ensure that the white Democratic minority would control the government. Louisiana was a prime example of what this meant. In 30 of the 57 parishes in the state, for example, blacks outnumbered whites, but when the votes were counted many of these parishes went overwhelmingly Democratic. An extreme example of such fraud and violence occurred in Natchitoches Parish, where blacks outnumbered whites in the population by 3,000, but where in 1878 the Democratic vote was counted as 2,800 and the Republican as zero! In another black parish in which, again, not a single Republican vote was counted in 1878, more than fifty Negroes were killed and others driven from their homes during the campaign, according to a report by the local U.S. district attorney.[2]

In South Carolina the white Democrats not only drove out virtually all white men from the Republican party, but they also reduced the blacks who remained almost to political silence. In 1876, the year before Radical Reconstruction ended in the state, there were seventy-eight Republicans in the two houses of the legislature; two years later there were only eight. Between 1876 and 1896, when the Negroes were disfranchised in South Carolina, the Republican party in the state did not even bother to put up a candidate for governor. The dominance of the blacks in the party is shown, too, by the fact that between 1876 and 1895, all but two of the 32 Republicans who served in the legislature were black.

(1960), 391; interview with Stephen A. Douglas, Jr., in Washington *National Republican*, Oct. 27, 1879, clipping in Settle Papers, Folder 31; Verton M. Queener, "The East Tennessee Republican Party in State and Nation, 1870–1900," *Tennessee Historical Quarterly*, II (1943), 100; J. W. Baker to D. M. Key, Jan. 27, 1893, David McKendree Key Papers.

2. Otis Singletary, "The Election of 1878 in Louisiana," *Louisiana Historical Quarterly*, XL (1957), 46–47; Marguerite T. Leach, "The Aftermath of Reconstruction in Louisiana," *Louisiana Historical Quarterly*, XXXII (1949), 650–51, 659.

Thus when Negro disfranchisement was imposed in 1895 the Republican party virtually ceased to exist in South Carolina.

South Carolina's party, however, was not typical of the Republican organizations of the other states in the deep South. In all of them, to be sure, the vast majority of Republicans were black, but in most of them, unlike the situation in South Carolina, there were enough whites to make it worthwhile to try to attract more. The hope was that if more white voters could be won over, their very membership would counteract the charge that the Republicans were the party of the Negro. Black predominance was not a new problem, of course—it had already bedeviled the Republicans during Reconstruction—but with the return of the Democrats to power it was greatly intensified. By 1877 and after, the white Republicans had been cut down to the most loyal core.

Not the least of the white Republicans' problems in the deep South was that the Democrats did their best to see that the black label was firmly fixed on the Republicans. A white Mississippi Republican, for instance, complained in 1882 that national Democratic leaders in Mississippi "humbug the different administrations and keep up negro rule in the Republican party in order that fear of negro rule in the State may keep white men in the Democratic party. Between the upper millstone [of] Southern folly and the lower millstone of Southern crime we are ground to powder . . . ," he lamented. For the same reason, white Republicans in Mississippi opposed blacks' running for office because they believed few if any whites could be induced to vote for a black man. Always the important issue, contended Henry C. Niles, son of the Mississippi Unionist Jason Niles, was to attract whites to the Republicans. This was important not only in order to win elections, but to get the party out from under the charge of being black. Niles thought, too, that when Republican administrations appointed blacks to federal offices in the states it was undoubtedly "pleasing to the Negro," yet at the same time "it cuts off all hope for recruiting our ranks from the whites."[3] The party, in short,

3. James Welch Patton, "The Republican Party in South Carolina," in Fletcher Melvin Green, ed., *Essays in Southern History* (Chapel Hill, N.C., 1949), pp. 93–94; Willie D. Halsell, ed., "Republican Factionalism in Mississippi, 1882–1884," *Journal of Southern History*, VII (1941), 93–94, 89–90; see also Willie D. Halsell, "Democratic Dissensions in Mississippi, 1878–1882," *Journal of Mississippi History*, II (1940), 123–35.

was truly caught between the millstones: the desire to gain white support and the need to retain black interest and support.

The same point was made by a Louisiana Republican in advising Henry C. Warmoth, the former carpetbag governor of the state, who in 1889 was readying himself to run for governor again. Warmoth was advised to keep the well-known Republican faces in the state in the background of his campaign and to permit only new adherents—presumably whites—to speak in behalf of Republicans. Otherwise, the writer predicted, "the announcement will be made from hundreds of foul mouths that an attempt is made to rally the negroes as a unit against the whites." And if that is done, "in an instance, every timid, courageless *white man* falls back into the ranks of his old political associates, and the contest goes on, in the name of democracy vs. negroes."[4]

In other states of the deep South, like Georgia, Texas, and Alabama, where the blacks were not a majority of the potential voters, the problem of winning white support was no less acute. Often, as in Georgia where General James Longstreet was a chief of the party, relations between the former Scalawags and the blacks were not cordial. (Virtually all of the Republican parties in the Southern states were led by old Scalawags. The principal exceptions were Texas and Louisiana.) Georgia Republicans had never had a strong white base to begin with, but Longstreet, despite his national prestige, was not able to improve the situation. Moreover, as a man who had never been fully reconciled to black political equality, he did not enjoy the full support of black Republicans. In 1884 he went so far as to flirt with the idea of forming separate Republican organizations for blacks and whites. This was too blatant an insult to be acceptable to black Republicans and was soon dropped. Yet the idea of abandoning the Negroes was always attractive to certain white Republicans in the South. The Alabama Republican party, which was so weak after 1876 that for almost ten years it did not even run a candidate for governor, in 1889 tried Longstreet's tactic, but with no more success. The Louisiana Republicans made a brief effort in the same direction in the early nineties but again without gaining any whites.

Texas Republicans were unusual in not manifesting this effort to

4. E. North Cullum to Henry Warmoth, Aug. 20, 1889, Henry Clay Warmoth Papers.

escape the black label. The principal reason was that the party there, after 1883, was headed by a Negro, Norris Wright Cuney, one of the South's major political leaders. Like most Republican organizations in the Southern states immediately after Reconstruction, the Texas party had been led by a Scalawag, Edmund J. Davis, the Reconstruction governor. When Davis died in 1883, he was succeeded by Cuney. Cuney remained the Republican boss until 1896. As late as 1894, the Texas Republicans ran a black for governor; he received 55,000 votes.[5]

Naturally any effort to exclude blacks from the Republican party in the South was doomed as long as the Negro was protected in his right to vote; few Negroes, after all, could be induced to vote regularly Democratic. Yet as long as the Republican party was overwhelmingly black, few whites could be won to its banner in the deep South and not even very many in the upper South. From a party standpoint, of course, these two facts made it difficult if not impossible to look forward to Republican victories in the South. And without victories there would soon be no party.

The only hope lay in an issue or issues that transcended the traditional appeal to racial solidarity. Then the division of parties by race might be overcome. Such issues entered Southern politics twice in the quarter-century between the end of Reconstruction and 1900. One time was in the nineties with Populists, and the other was in the eighties with the Virginia Readjusters. Neither of these groups was Republican, though as we shall see, both were to have important connections with Republicans. Populism convulsed the lower as well as the upper South. The Readjuster movement occurred in only one state of the upper South. Yet as a dissenting movement it was significant enough to have repercussions across the region. The Readjusters swept into power in Virginia in the election of 1879 as a challenge not only to the reigning Democratic party but to the idea of a white party. For the Readjusters

5. Olive Hall Shadgett, *The Republican Party in Georgia: From Reconstruction Through 1900* (Athens, Ga., 1964), p. 87 and passim; Paul Casdorph, *A History of the Republican Party in Texas, 1865–1965* (Austin, 1965), p. 46; Robert Miller Saunders, "The Ideology of Southern Populists, 1892–1895," unpublished Ph.D. dissertation, University of Virginia, 1967, p. 114n.; William Warren Rogers, *The One-Gallused Rebellion: Agrarianism in Alabama, 1865–1869* (Baton Rouge, 1970), pp. 48–55.

were the most successful political coalition of whites and blacks organized in the South between Reconstruction and the 1960's.

THE RISE OF THE READJUSTERS

It was no accident that the most successful biracial political movement should arise in post-Reconstruction Virginia. That state had never really been ruled by a Radical regime at all, having moved from military Reconstruction in 1867–68 directly to Conservative or Democratic rule. As a result, unlike white Southerners in other reconstructed states, Virginians had few of the real or imagined memories of Radical oppression or so-called Negro domination. It is true that Virginia, like all other Southern states, had had to accept Negro suffrage, but that innovation in Virginia was never the threat to white political control that it was in the states of the deep South. In Virginia blacks made up only about two-fifths of the population, while in five of the states of the deep South they were either a majority or very close to it. In short, Democrats might warn about Negro domination, as they frequently did, but in Virginia the danger lacked the final, clinching argument from numbers that it possessed in the states of the deep South.

Virginia also differed from most other former Confederate states in the rigid conservatism of its ruling Democratic party. The most obvious manifestation of that rigidity was Virginia's stand on the question of the state debt. After the Civil War most Southern states recognized that the debts which had been contracted before the war and during Reconstruction could not or ought not, for a variety of reasons, to be met in full. Many Southerners thought that the Reconstruction debts, for example, had not been incurred for good or valid purposes. Many more thought that the financial difficulties of the Southern states, because of the devastation and dislocation of the war and emancipation, precluded paying the debts in full. This doubt was reinforced when the depression of 1873 hit. As a result, most of the Southern states, when white Conservative governments came to power after Radical Reconstruction, worked out arrangements for reducing or, in some cases, repudiating their debts.

The Conservatives of Virginia, burdened with an exaggerated sense of state honor, refused to make such a practical compromise. To them a debt was sacred, to be honored in full, even if, as they quite readily admitted, other needs of the state, like the construction of roads or the maintenance of the public schools, had to be slighted or even abandoned. One Conservative, for example, said in 1878 that he would rather see a bonfire made of every school in the state than to see the bill to reduce the debt pass the legislature. The Conservative governor was not quite as extreme, but he clearly preferred the repayment of the debt in full over support for education. "Our fathers did not need free schools to make them what they were," Governor Frederick Holliday told the legislature in his message vetoing the debt adjustment bill. "Free schools are not a necessity. The world, for hundreds of years, grew in wealth, culture, and refinement, without them. They are a luxury, adding, when skillfully conducted . . . to the beauty and power of the state, but to be paid for, like any other luxury, by the people who wish their benefits."[6] It was not for nothing that the Conservative Democrats were called Bourbons, after the royal house of France, which, at its restoration, was said to have learned nothing and forgotten nothing.

It was this intransigence, this refusal to acknowledge the claims of today against those of yesterday, that was the soil out of which the Readjusters sprang. For it was Holliday's veto of the debt adjustment bill in 1878 that moved a large number of Democrats out of their traditional party to form a political coalition dedicated to passing a bill to readjust the debt, as partial repudiation was euphemistically called. Hence the name Readjusters.

"THE NOBLEST LITTLE ROMAN OF THEM ALL"

General conditions, however, do not completely account for the Readjuster movement. They leave out of the accounting the movement's remarkable leader, William Mahone.

6. On Southern state debts in general see B. U. Ratchford, *American State Debts* (Durham, N.C., 1941); Allen W. Moger, *Virginia Bourbonism to Byrd, 1870–1925* (Charlottesville, 1968), pp. 34–35; Raymond H. Pulley, *Old Virginia Restored: An Interpretation of the Progressive Impulse, 1870–1930* (Charlottesville, 1968), p. 35.

Who was this man whom Richard Wise, the son of Henry A. Wise, the old antebellum governor of the state, described as "the noblest Roman of them all"?[7] On the surface Mahone was not the kind of man one would pick out to lead the rebellion against the Virginia oligarchy. A graduate of Virginia Military Institute, a slaveholder, an ardent secessionist before the war and a Confederate general during the war, Mahone was a thorough as well as a native Virginian. In 1864, moreover, he became a minor hero of the war with his successful leadership in the Battle of the Crater outside Petersburg. For that exploit he was promoted to major general on the battlefield by Robert E. Lee himself. Later it would be said that Lee's estimation of Mahone was so high that Lee had designated him to command the Army of Northern Virginia should he himself be killed. Mahone's friends also liked to recall that at Appomattox Mahone's division stacked more guns and reported more men fit for duty than any other division in the Army of Northern Virginia. Short of his life, Mahone had given everything to the Lost Cause. Moreover, during Reconstruction he supported the Conservative Democrats, not the newly formed Republicans. About him, in short, there was nothing of the Scalawag, and his Virginia birth precluded his being a carpetbagger.

Yet if some of the facts of Mahone's life seemed to fit him for membership in the Virginia establishment, other aspects promised a quite different role. In appearance alone Mahone was far from the stereotype of the Virginia gentleman. A writer in the Washington *Post* in 1881 described him as "a very small, thin man, weighing ninety-two pounds. His attenuated frame, about which . . . a suit of plain black broadcloth clothes hung in folds and wrinkles, is surmounted by a head of good proportions. Long iron-grey hair, brushed down over the forehead, almost conceals the upper part of the face. A pair of sparkling blue eyes shine from beneath projecting eyebrows. A finely cut aquiline nose is the most prominent feature of the face, as the mouth and chin are hidden from view by a long, iron-grey moustache and beard which extends far down upon his vest." Mahone had more the build of a wiry

7. Richard A. Wise to John Wise, Nov. 7, 1879, in William Mahone Papers.

gnome than that of a conventional leader of Virginians. As his thin form suggests, Mahone during all of his adult life suffered from dyspepsia. Even during the war he had kept a cow and hens with him to provide the special food his delicate stomach demanded. The thinness of his body was almost legendary. When his wife was informed during the war that he had been wounded in battle, though assured it was only a flesh wound, she cried, "Flesh wound? It can't be a flesh wound; the General hasn't any flesh!"[8]

Although born in agricultural Virginia in 1826, Mahone came from neither the yeoman nor the planter class. His father was a merchant and tavern owner; only occasionally did he dabble in real estate or farming. Mahone grew up close to the site of Nat Turner's rebellion, and his father, curiously enough, in the light of Billy's later leadership of blacks, had played an important role in suppressing it. In later years the Bourbons would say in derision that Mahone was a poor white—a description that infuriated him only partly because it was not true. Yet his family was not wealthy, either, for Billy was able to attend V.M.I. only because he received a state scholarship.

Much more important than his family background in accounting for the little general's later rebellion against the Bourbons is his almost obsessive interest in railroad construction. The interest began early, with his employment as civil engineer for the Orange and Alexandria Railroad in 1849, soon after his graduation from V.M.I. When Virginia seceded in 1861, Mahone was only thirty-five years of age, but by then he was already launched upon a successful career as a railroader, having been chief engineer of one road at twenty-four and president of another at thirty-three.

Upon the defeat of the Confederacy, Mahone returned immediately to railroading. In a remarkably short time he established himself as the leading railroad entrepreneur in the state. By 1867 he was president of three railroads in southern Virginia and was working to consolidate them into a single line to be called, grandly enough, the Atlantic, Mississippi and Ohio Railroad. At that time

8. Richmond *Whig,* March 15, 1881, clipping in Scrapbook XIX, William Mahone Papers; Nelson Morehouse Blake, *William Mahone of Virginia, Soldier and Political Insurgent* (Richmond, 1935), p. 45. I have relied on Blake's thorough biography for the facts of Mahone's life.

a friend commented that Mahone then controlled more miles of
track than any other railroad man in America, including Commo-
dore Cornelius Vanderbilt, of the New York Central. Despite his
undeniable drive to consolidate lines, Mahone was more than
simply an organizer of railroads; he was equally involved in their
operation and construction, as his training as an engineer would
lead one to expect. One of his delights, for example, was to ride
over the tracks of his lines on a handcar, inspecting the roadbed.
While he was president of the Atlantic, Mississippi and Ohio he
made several trips in that way over the full length of the road.

It was Mahone's interest in railroads in particular and Virginia's
economic development in general that brought him into politics.
He soon found that without political support many of his efforts of
an economic or business nature would not receive the necessary
backing. Only through an act of the legislature, for example, was
he able to consolidate his railroads into the Atlantic, Mississippi
and Ohio. He also had a longtime interest in bringing immigrants
to Virginia to hasten its industrial development. In 1868, for
example, he participated in a convention called to promote direct
trade with Europe. That same year he was also president of a
society to encourage immigration into Virginia and North Carolina. In 1879 he put himself on record as favoring a state immigration agent to stimulate immigration. Not surprisingly, he also
supported the protective tariff as a means of protecting wages of
labor and the iron industry, which he hoped to develop in Virginia.
In 1884–86 he corresponded with James M. Swank, the secretary
of the American Iron and Steel Association and a prime lobbyist
for a protective tariff. Swank supplied Mahone with funds and
literature in the campaigns of the 1880's. Mahone, in turn, publicly supported the protective tariff.[9]

As his activities in behalf of economic development show,
Mahone was no traditionalist, no Southern Shintoist wedded to the
mindless worship of an agricultural past. When the Bourbons

9. For evidence of Mahone's interest in the tariff see his letter to William
Burwell, Jan. 16, 1884, in Letterbooks, and the letters of James M. Swank
to Mahone, Oct. 20, 1884; Oct. 20, Nov. 10, 1886, in William Mahone
Papers.

equated the payment of the state debt with morality Mahone dismissed the point with the remark: "This twaddle about the honor of the state is sheer nonsense." In sum, despite his complete support of the Confederacy, Mahone was a new man, one of those innovators who wanted to move the South into a new and more progressive channel now that the war was over and lost. "I have thought it wise to live for the future," he wrote in 1882 to a fellow Confederate, "and not the dead past . . . while cherishing honorable memory of its glories. I have thought that we should look to the future for life, power and prosperity—practical policies and not to theories. . . ."[10] He was a proponent of a new South in the best sense of that phrase. Mahone's interest in Virginia's economic development provided the thrust and the justification for the dissenting political organization he helped to create and successfully led.

The Bourbons, too, advocated economic development. Indeed, their principal justification for their position on the debt, when they were not talking about the state's honor, was that developmental capital would not come to Virginia if the public debt were not paid to the last dollar and on time. "To repudiate is to stain her [Virginia's] honor, to shut out immigration and capital which would otherwise come here," said a Conservative governor, "and to inflict upon the state damages and losses many times greater . . . than the thirty millions of debt." William E. Lamb, the mayor of Norfolk, made the same point. "Let the shadow of repudiation rest upon our state and who would trust us?" he asked. "Our own capitalists would send their surplus means abroad, and all hope of foreign aid would be a delusion and a snare." Unlike the Readjusters, however, the Bourbons evidenced more concern about the foreign or Northern bondholders than about the actual and present circumstances of the people of Virginia. Development for the Bourbons became an end in itself instead of being a means for improving the lot of the average Virginian. As one Readjuster wrote, "Honor won't buy a breakfast."[11]

10. Pulley, *Old Virginia Restored*, pp. 38–39; William Mahone to Thomas T. Munford, July 22, 1882, Munford-Ellis Papers.
11. Jack Maddex, Jr., *The Virginia Conservatives, 1867–1879: A Study in Reconstruction Politics* (Chapel Hill, N.C., 1970), pp. 259–60.

THE READJUSTERS

Although popular dissatisfaction with the complacency of the Bourbon Democrats had been growing for some time, even the onset of the depression of 1873 did not set off a revolt. As late as 1877, Mahone himself, when passed over for the Conservative nomination for governor, still willingly supported Frederick Holliday as the least objectionable of the Bourbon candidates. In office, however, as his comment on the public schools being a "luxury" revealed, Holliday showed himself to be as insensitive to the needs of ordinary Virginians as his predecessors.

In February, 1879, soon after Holliday's veto of the debt reduction bill, the new party organized itself. A convention of self-proclaimed "Readjusters" met in Richmond to draw up a platform and nominate candidates for the legislature in the election that fall. The program was to enact a measure that would provide for the scaling down of the debt; the candidates were to stand on that principle.

The call to the Convention was issued "without distinction of color." Most of the two hundred delegates were white, but some Negroes were present, too. William T. Jefferson, one of the black delegates, not only expressed strong anti-debt sentiments but committed himself to political cooperation between black and white as well. "As to the debt," he told the assembled delegates and speaking for his fellow blacks, "we don't want to pay a cent of it. We think we paid our share of it, if it ever was justly chargeable upon us, by long years of servitude. And, then, as Virginia has been reconstructed in her territory [by which he meant the creation of West Virginia during the war] and in her government, we think that the debt should be reconstructed too. (Applause.)" Then he moved to the question of relations between the races. "We are humble citizens—the humblest in the Commonwealth—and we treat white people invariably with a great deal more courtesy than we receive, because we are anxious not to offend you, and to win your good will. We are for peace, and we accept the overture made to us as heartily as it is tendered, for we feel that your interests and our interests are identical. (Applause.)"

The Readjusters were not unmindful of the seriousness of the decision to call a convention without regard to color. As one white delegate said, "the Readjusters had been sneered at for seeking the aid of the colored citizens. He desired nothing better than to add all the colored voters to the ranks of those who were fighting the battles of popular rights and interests. If the colored people are for re-adjustment, they have as much right in the Convention as anybody," he proclaimed to applause. People in Richmond had told him that "we should not waste education on the 'd——d niggers,' " he said. Yet, he went on, "let the colored people stand fast by the Re-Adjusters and the Re-Adjusters will see to it that education shall be provided for the children of all colors." Other whites spoke along the same lines.[12]

The Readjusters' decision to include blacks in their movement sprang, of course, not so much from a newly awakened sense of justice toward the former slaves as from the recognition that if the ruling Bourbons were to be defeated, black votes would have to be won over. As William Jefferson pointed out, blacks and the mass of whites certainly had a common cause, given the character of Bourbon rule. For even as Jefferson spoke, the state was on the verge of bankruptcy after years of economic stagnation under the financial policies of the Bourbons. By the end of 1878 scores of schools were closing or already closed, white as well as black, because the Bourbons had been using the school funds to meet the payments on the debt. Although the state constitution and an act of the legislature prohibited the diversion of educational funds, the Bourbon state auditor was doing just that. In February, 1879, the school fund was already over a million dollars in arrears. Perhaps as many as half of the school population—some one hundred thousand pupils—were shut out of school. Even the Bourbons' own superintendent of public instruction denounced the policy, which was depriving children of education and the state of trained citizens. Mahone's commitment to public education for both races was already on public record. "You rightly conjecture that I am the friend of the public school system of Virginia," he wrote in a public letter in June, 1877, "and my matured conviction is that it

12. *Report* of Convention of Readjusters in Scrapbook IX, William Mahone Papers.

should be effectually nurtured." Furthermore, he wrote, "the best interests of the State demand that the large class of persons recently admitted to the privilege of citizenship [Negroes] should receive careful and ample instruction."[13] An expanded public education system for both races was an integral part of Mahone's vision for the reinvigoration of Virginia's economy.

The general's contribution to the Readjuster cause went beyond statements. His energy and remarkable organizing ability were major contributions. His voluminous correspondence, now preserved at the Duke University Library, is a monument to his industry and meticulous attention to the details of political organization. It was not unusual for him to write fifty to seventy letters a day, in his own hand, day after day during the weeks of a campaign, a copy of each one being kept. All of the letters were indexed in a letterbook. Furthermore, each piece of incoming correspondence was annotated as to its author, place of origin, and a brief statement of contents. This information was then transferred to a large journal, presumably for ready reference. It seems that even the humblest person received a personally written answer from Mahone, though the incoming mail was enormous in quantity. Undoubtedly this almost compulsive dedication to detail was one source of Mahone's reputation as a political boss or tyrant. There was little that happened in the party about which he did not know or instruct. Some of his incoming correspondence, for example, makes evident that his agents were rarely free to arrive at important decisions without consulting him.

Thanks to Mahone's organizational ability, and the many devoted party workers in the field, both black and white, the Readjusters won an overwhelming victory in the contest for the legislature in the fall of 1879. The blacks in the tidewater region—most of whom were Republicans—and the whites in the western part of the state—most of whom were Democrats—deserted their regular parties to vote for the Readjuster candidates. Both the house of delegates and the senate went Readjuster. Mahone's organization won fifty-six seats out of a hundred in the lower

13. Maddex, *Virginia Conservatives,* p. 264; Ratchford, *State Debts,* p. 204; Moger, *Virginia,* p. 36; Pulley, *Old Virginia Restored,* p. 33; Moger, *Virginia,* p. 29; Blake, *William Mahone,* p. 149.

house and twenty-four out of forty in the upper. Eleven blacks were elected to the former and two to the latter. Mahone himself was then selected by the new legislature to serve as United States senator from Virginia.

The victory of 1879 was exceeded two years later when the Readjusters captured once again the two houses of the legislature and then topped that with the election of the governor as well. That same year, 1881, the legislature filled the second United States Senate seat with the western leader of the Readjusters— Mahone was from the eastern part of the state—Harrison H. Riddleberger. Finally, to bring the Readjusters' triumph to a new climax, in 1882 the new party won six of Virginia's ten seats in the U.S. House of Representatives. Thus in the course of three years the Readjusters had captured the legislature twice, the governorship, the two U.S. Senate seats, and a majority of the state's delegation to Congress. It was the most extensive rebuff to Democratic rule in a Southern state since Reconstruction. In fact, it has not yet been equaled in any Southern state.

A POPULAR UPRISING

The Readjuster campaign was truly a grass-roots movement. Few of its leaders, except for Mahone and a handful of Republicans and Democrats, were well known in politics. In private the Conservatives viewed the movement as dangerously class-conscious. One Conservative, for example, wrote to Governor Kemper that Mahone was seeking "to unite with the negro and ignorant white men to control the state." The well-known educator Jabez L. M. Curry frankly explained the Readjuster strength as the result of "ambition for place, communism, ignorance, and a little honest delusion." After campaigning himself in 1879, he concluded that Denis Kearney, the incendiary workingmen's advocate in California, "would have been applauded by some in every audience I spoke to."

The Readjusters, in turn, proudly proclaimed their interest in the poor man, white or black. One of the party's addresses to the Republicans asserted "that the Readjuster party has done more in one brief year of power towards liberalizing public sentiment, abolishing caste legislation, restoring the poor man his rights . . . than the Republican party has been able to do in all the years of its existence in the South." Undoubtedly, too, many poor whites and blacks voted for Readjusters to express their hostility toward the establishment in both parties. Certainly the Readjusters' whole approach to politics was innovatively popular. Mahone astonished traditional politicians by sending speakers and workers into the remote corners of the state, bringing to the polls men who had not voted for years or perhaps never. The popular politics practiced by the Readjusters was reflected in the turnouts on election day. In 1879 the total vote in the state was merely 143,000, but by 1881 it was up to 213,000, and in 1883 it stood at 276,000. The effect of Mahone's methods was also evident in a comment by a party worker who wrote the chief in 1884 that "the day has been when I was the only white man who voted our ticket at Whitehall—now at this precinct & Blackwell's we have 157 white voters. I am sure the democratic party will never change any of these men and am equally as confident that they cannot break our colored ranks."[14]

The dividing line between Funders or regular Democrats and Readjusters was sharp, socially as well as politically. The bankers and large businessmen were clearly Funders—with the exception, of course, of the leading railroad man in the state, Mahone himself. Generally, city dwellers, businessmen, planters, and white men living in the black counties were Funders. The Readjusters were generally poor farm people, fairly prosperous yeoman farmers in the Shenandoah Valley, "hillbillies" in the southwestern part of the state, together with a large number of Negroes and a few poor whites in the eastern plantation counties. John S. Wise, a son of the antebellum governor Henry A. Wise, and a Readjuster, put the division differently, but no less revealingly. He said, with only a little exaggeration, that the old Whig areas went Bourbon while the old Democratic areas of the state were Readjusters. The scores of letters Mahone received from semiliterate whites and blacks further attest to the extent to which the Readjusters reached Virginian voters who had been excluded from or ignored in politics

14. Pulley, *Old Virginia Restored*, p. 36; Maddex, *Virginia Conservatives*, p. 274; flyer in Scrapbook XXXII, William Mahone Papers; W. B. Bailey to William Mahone, Nov. 24, 1884, William Mahone Papers.

before. Not even Populism penetrated as deeply into the lowest levels of the political structure as the Readjuster movement.

The success of the Readjusters was in large part dependent upon the willingness of many blacks to respond positively to the movement, despite the early efforts of Republicans to hold the blacks to their traditional allegiance. It did not take long, however, for the Republican leadership to recognize the real threat the Readjusters posed to the Democrats. Moreover, in some counties the Readjusters deliberately supported Republican candidates to demonstrate their willingness to cooperate with anti-Bourbons. In turn, the black Republicans voted heavily in 1879 and after for Readjusters. As a result, a victory like that in 1881 could be celebrated with the cry: "INTOLERANCE, BIGOTRY, AND HATRED BURIED FOREVER. THE COLORED VOTE COULD NOT BE BOUGHT!" Even before that outburst, a Boston newspaper observed that Mahone's victories had shown that "the enfranchisement of the colored man had at last been made real in one of the lately rebellious states."[15]

Something of the commitment of the Readjusters to Negro participation in politics comes through in a letter written to Mahone from a supporter in Norfolk in 1880, just a year after the first Readjuster victory. The writer, C. Billups, expressed his support for Mahone's policy of moving in a new direction, but was cautious about going too far. He had no doubt, however, about our "obligation to execute faithfully the laws of our land respecting all classes of our people." Not only was there an obligation to do so, he said, but "wise policy calls for such a course of action. This is now so manifest that an open plea for its practice is no longer misconstrued to the injury of any." But a decision to go beyond that "must first be calmly canvassed among the leading *white people* of our state and *this calm* and dispassionate consideration must *for a time,* have a somewhat private and quiet growth." The writer's implied priority of first consideration to whites was not accidental. "I say 'white people,'" he explained, "not that I wish to ignore the negro or forget that he is an element in the body politic, but I named the *white because* no party can permanently

15. Flyer, Scrapbook XXIX, William Mahone Papers; Boston *Traveller,* March 15, 1881, quoted in Richmond *Whig,* March 22, 1881, clipping in Scrapbook XIX, William Mahone Papers.

succeed without a preponderance of that influence." Moreover, he continued, "the best interest of the white people of our state is what we desire. . . . We want them to so understand it and work with us." Although this placed the emphasis upon whites, Billups made clear that "success for the white man requires no injustice to the Negro. On the contrary we cannot do justice to ourselves if we are unjust to him. . . . He was faithful in a moment of trial, his labor we can make valuable to us and we can well afford to deal justly and even liberally by him."[16] These were fully radical sentiments in the South of the late nineteenth century.

THE READJUSTER ACHIEVEMENT

The identity of interest between ordinary white and black Virginians, on which the Readjuster movement and successes rested, would be put to a crucial test in 1883. Before then, however, the Readjusters were prepared to act on that identity of interest. Once in power, the Readjusters indeed tried to "deal justly and even liberally" with blacks as well as whites.

First they carried out their promises as Readjusters. They scaled down the debt as they said they would, yet in such a responsible manner that even the Conservatives in later years did not seek to reverse the decision. In order to increase the revenues for expanding the social services so shamefully neglected by the Bourbons, the Readjusters raised assessments and taxes on corporations. Between 1880 and 1881, for example, the assessments on railroads and canals jumped 150 percent to compensate for the years of undervaluation by the Bourbon government. At the same time, the Readjusters brought some tax relief to the farmers by cutting the general property tax rate by 20 percent.

The increase in revenues gained from higher assessments and taxes on business was first of all applied to the improvement and expansion of the schools for both races. (The Readjusters never advocated or practiced racial integration of the schools.) Between 1879, the last year of Bourbon rule, and 1880 the number of

16. C. Billups to William Mahone, Nov. 22, 1880, William Mahone Papers.

schools in Virginia almost doubled, while the number of children attending school more than doubled. The increase in the number of Negro children in school from 36,000 to 69,000 was not quite up to that for children in general, but it was sufficient to show that the Readjusters were taking seriously their promises to blacks. The number of black schools increased from 675 to 1,256. The final report of the Readjuster superintendent of public instruction in 1886 further attested to the commitment of the Readjusters to education for blacks. After noting that Negro education in Virginia was by then only fifteen years old, the superintendent pronounced the Negroes' progress "wonderful—deserving of the highest praise —and shows conclusively that they have the capacity to acquire an education, and that all they need is fair school facilities to enable them soon to remove the burden of their illiteracy from the body politics."[17] Mahone himself was publicly committed to Negro education, as his support of the Blair education bill in the Senate showed. The Blair bill, which was a national political issue of the 1880's, would have used federal funds to support education. Since the federal funds were to be apportioned on the basis of illiteracy, the South would have received the greater portion of the money. A stated intention behind the bill was to assist in the schooling of the former slaves, who were recognized as a responsibility of the nation and not of the South alone.

The Readjusters supported higher education for blacks in Virginia, too. When a black member of the legislature in 1882 presented a petition from 150 Negro citizens asking for a Normal and Collegiate Institute, the legislature, which was dominated by white Readjusters, appropriated $100,000 for the purpose. That marked the founding of what today is Virginia State University at Petersburg, the first state-supported black college in Virginia. In 1885, John Mercer Langston, the nationally known black orator and educator, was invited by the Readjuster administration to head the new Negro institution. Langston had been a supporter of the Readjusters, having campaigned for them in Virginia in 1881 and 1882. When the Conservatives returned to power in Virginia they fired Langston from his office.

17. [Virginia] Superintendent of Public Instruction, 15th *Annual Report* (1886), p. 93, in Scrapbook XXXV, William Mahone Papers.

Important as educational opportunity was for Virginia's Negroes, the Readjusters' attention to blacks went beyond that. A new lunatic asylum for Negroes was built (along with one for whites) so that scores of mentally ill persons could be released from the common jails. The Readjusters also abolished the poll tax, which had been used by the Bourbons to disfranchise thousands of poor blacks—and whites. The punishment of crimes by whipping was also ended by the Readjusters. The Bourbons had introduced whipping as a means of both disciplining and disfranchising blacks. The suffrage was denied to anyone convicted of a crime that was punishable by whipping. The Readjusters also opened to blacks dozens of jobs in government that had heretofore been denied them. Blacks now served as clerks and other minor functionaries in government as well as guards at the state penitentiary and as policemen in the towns. Blacks also sat on juries and school boards for the first time.

When to these reforms are added minor ones like the outlawing of dueling and the improved mechanics' lien law, the reforming character of the Readjuster regime is evident. That character is also seen in the renovations made in the University of Virginia, which was not only an all-white, upper-class institution, but a hotbed of Conservative sentiment among both faculty and students. The newly appointed Readjuster Board of Visitors measurably improved the finances of Mr. Jefferson's university, leaving it in 1886 with a surplus of $13,000. Even so, the efficient board was still able to carry out extensive repairs and refurbishings long left unattended to by the preceding tight-fisted Bourbon regime. According to the student newspaper even the food improved under Readjuster governance! The Board of Visitors also modernized the curriculum and sought ways to widen the opportunities for poor students to enter the university. Despite the initial difference in political views, the new board, faculty, and students soon got along very well. As a result the foundations for a modern graduate school were laid then.

A recent historian of the Readjuster board's activities sums up both the educational and the general outlook of the Readjuster movement. The Board of Visitors, writes James T. Moore, "brought a new spirit of innovation and efficiency to the campus.

In a broader sense, moreover, the Readjusters' actions at the school displayed in microcosm their entire state policy. They did not attempt revolutionary or destructive changes in either the state government or the University; they sought, instead, to modernize both, to make them more responsive to the changing needs of the state."[18]

WIDENING RIPPLES

Even before the extent or nature of the Readjuster reforms was known, the spectacular electoral victories had captured the attention of the South and the country. As the leader of the movement, Mahone was catapulted into a new role as "the hope of the South." Whites as well as blacks suddenly envisioned new opportunities for their backward region in the midst of an expanding national economy. Perhaps, after all, it was possible to break the color line in politics and to shake off outdated and useless economic attitudes and practices that kept Southern society sluggish and its people poor. The novelty of the Readjuster victories was not lost on knowing observers. "The significance of the victory in Va.," wrote Andrew J. Kellar privately, "is that it was won under Southern leadership and so clearly cut is the work that Republican leaders cannot claim it as a party triumph. . . ." What particularly pleased Kellar was that Mahone and the Readjusters had been able to keep "aloof from the caucuses of the old war parties. . . ." Kellar was a Tennessee Unionist who, after the war, had played a central role in bringing about the Compromise of 1877, which had brought Rutherford B. Hayes to the White House. For years, Kellar had been seeking a Southern leader who could link dissenting and forward-looking Democrats in the South with moderate Republicans in the North. Obviously, in Mahone, Kellar thought he had found the man he was looking for.

J. Willis Menard, a prominent black editor from Florida, for his part, recognized the potentialities the Readjusters offered Southern Negroes. "Mahoneism," Menard wrote, is "the acceptable middle ground between impracticable Radicalism and intolerant Bour-

18. James T. Moore, "The University and the Readjusters," *Virginia Magazine of History and Biography,* 78 (1970), 101.

bonism, on which any patriot willing to sacrifice small personal prejudices and resentments for the peace and prosperity of his Country or Section, can honestly and honorably stand. . . ." Menard was here alluding to the Readjusters' partial repudiation of the state debt, an act that did not sit well with the financially traditional Northern Republicans. "The materials, forces and agencies for a political 'tidal wave' at the South are ripe and ready . . . ," Menard exuberantly, if prematurely, prophesied; "let those become united and utilized, and made to develop a thousand Mahones!"[19]

Less prominent Southerners, too, showered Mahone with congratulations and thereby revealed how many dissenting Southerners there were—waiting for a leader. "The lesson taught by this brilliant victory will extend itself to the entire South," wrote a Kentuckian, "and as Kentucky Republicans who have long looked forward to the time when there would be a 'breaking up' of the 'Solid South,' we extend our thanks. . . ." From Mobile, Alabama, an "old Confederate soldier" rejoiced at the Readjuster victories. "It is to such gallant and fearless leaders as yourself that the Southern States must in the future look for a better condition of things. . . . We regret there is not a *Mahone* in every Southern state." In Nashville, Tennessee, the Readjuster victory in 1881 was called "the Waterloo of Bourbonism," while in Wilmington, North Carolina, a newspaper oblivious to the Nashville metaphor labeled Mahone "the Napoleon of the South's Grand Vindication." A Louisianan, speaking in Washington, D.C., called the victory of 1881 "the precursor of a break up in the Solid South," saying it "proclaims the political emancipation of the Southern people." Lincoln freed the slaves, the speaker went on, but he had not freed the whites from the tyranny of the Southern oligarchy. "Mahone has appeared to finish the work of Abraham Lincoln," he concluded. A Radical Republican editor in 1882 in North Carolina emphasized the Readjuster acceptance of blacks. In Virginia under the Readjusters, wrote the Wilmington *Post,* "the colored man was

19. A. J. Kellar to E. J. Harris, Nov. 12, 1881, with E. J. Harris to W. Mahone, Nov. 15, 1881, in William Mahone Papers; letter from J. Willis Menard, April 20, 1881, to *National Republican,* in Scrapbook XVIII, William Mahone Papers.

treated. . . . as a human being, he was recognized as a factor in the body politic, was put in office according to his ability, and made to feel that he was part and portion of the Commonwealth."[20]

Outside the South, the Readjusters' successes were appraised only slightly less extravagantly. "The Republicans in other Southern states should follow the example of their brethren in Virginia," advised the Warren, Ohio, *Tribune* in February, 1881, "and unite with liberal Democrats under competent leadership. . . . Every state needs a Mahone." About the same time a New Jersey Republican wrote Mahone that "this victory is not only for Virginia, but for the whole South—or I might say for the whole country; . . . it means a government *'of the People—for the People—and by the People.'*" George B. Cowland, an Indiana politician who knew the South well, wrote a friend in 1880 that "the South has only produced one *statesman* since the war, and that the new Senator from Virginia, General Mahone. He seems to have grasped the great fact that the South, with her great natural wealth, can be and ought to be made rich, as powerful, and as prosperous as the most favored part of the country. . . ." He then proceeded to make a rationale for Mahone's politics that echoed Mahone's own. "He has laid the basis for a future fair ballot and honest count in Virginia, upon which foundation all else can be built up, but without which no structure better than a shanty can ever be raised." A New York City Republican paper summed up the achievement of Mahone and the Readjusters while measuring the surprise of that achievement. "He has done what appeared to be impossible in this generation," contended *Truth* in September, 1880. "He has made one strong and harmonious political party of native Southern Democrats, negroes and Republicans."[21]

Mahone's success in 1879 and after produced more tangible

20. Sam F. Spencer and W. Nick Vaughn to William Mahone, Nov. 12, 1881; Henry C. Thooner to Mahone, Nov. 11, 1881; W. R. Hamby to Mahone, Nov. 12, 1881, William Mahone Papers; Wilmington *Post,* Nov. 13, 1881; R. Hutcheson, *Lesson of the Virginia Election* (n.d., n.p., but of speech given on Nov. 28, 1881), copy in pamphlet box of William Mahone Papers; Wilmington *Post,* Aug. 6, 1882.

21. Warren *Tribune,* Feb. 7, 1882, Scrapbook XXVIII; James Thornton to William Mahone, 11th month 18, 1881, William Mahone Papers; Blake, *William Mahone,* p. 204; New York *Truth,* Sept. 17, 1880, in Scrapbook XIII, William Mahone Papers.

consequences, too. He personally came forcefully to the attention of Northern Republicans and the nation as a whole when he took his seat in the United States Senate in March, 1881. By casting his vote in the evenly divided Senate with the Republicans, he permitted the South's traditional political enemy to organize the Senate. The excoriation of Mahone for his apostasy by Southern Democrats was almost unending as well as vicious both on the floor of the Senate and in newspapers throughout the South. But as a result, and no doubt as he intended, Mahone received from the grateful Republicans the chairmanship of the Committee on Agriculture, which was of intense interest to him, and membership on three other Senate committees. Some Readjusters also received lucrative federal jobs in Washington. In 1880 and early 1881 Mahone worked behind the scenes to extract promises of support in Virginia from James Garfield, the newly elected Republican President. Garfield was fearful of what he considered the Readjusters' repudiationist tendencies, but he also recognized that Mahone and his Readjusters offered a better chance of defeating the Bourbons decisively than the regular Republicans. Ever since the end of Reconstruction the Republicans had wrestled with the question of how to build a party that could win in the South—and they would be wrestling with the issue until the end of the century. Considerations of that kind undoubtedly played a large role in Mahone's receiving a share of the federal patronage in Virginia—an aid that was quite welcome in view of his extensive and growing state organization. As Garfield wrote in his diary in April, 1881, "I shall do enough for Mahone to help him against the Bourbons but not to abandon our organization."[22]

Throughout the South the practical significance of the Readjusters' victories was to spark similar movements in a number of states. Many Democrats in the Southern states had their own internal reasons for being dissatisfied with Bourbon rule, just as the Democrats in Virginia who became Readjusters had the debt and the schools. But Mahone's example was a catalyst even if it was not always a first cause of the various Independent candidates and movements that flared up in Mississippi, Georgia, North

22. Vincent P. De Santis, "President Garfield and the Solid South," *North Carolina Historical Review,* XXXVI (1959), 461.

Carolina, and Texas between 1880 and 1884. In some states the Independent movements antedated the Readjusters, it is true. This was particularly so where the Greenbackers were active in 1877 and 1878, as in Texas. On the whole, however, the Readjuster victory was a turning point for dissident Democrats throughout the South. In Mississippi, for example, men spoke of James R. Chalmers, because of his break with the Democrats in 1882, as "the Mahone of Mississippi." Chalmers had been a Confederate general and Democrat, but that year he was elected to Congress as an Independent. Unlike Mahone, however, Chalmers had no local issue of overriding importance to unite Republicans, Greenbackers, and Democrats, though he did receive financial and patronage support from an eagerly optimistic Republican administration in Washington. Moreover, Chalmers was no obvious friend of black men and the regular black Republicans in the state neither trusted him nor supported him.

An Independent movement developed in Georgia, too, where James Longstreet, the Republican leader, sought to make political connections between the new dissidents and the Republicans soon after Mahone's success in 1881. The leaders of the Georgia Independents were Dr. William H. Felton and his wife, Rebecca, both of whom had long been critical of the Georgia Democracy. Mild reformers themselves, the Feltons were energized by the victory of the Readjusters in Virginia. Both Feltons were active in opposing the convict lease system and in support of cheap money. In 1882 they sought, unsuccessfully, as it turned out, to divide the Democrats by running Alexander Stephens, the former vice-president of the Confederacy, as the Independent candidate for governor. Although in the 1890's Rebecca Felton would emerge as a defender of lynching of Negroes, in the early 1880's she and her husband bravely talked of not fearing the Negro's political power. In 1882, for example, she denounced the Democrats for their "crusade against the colored race," and predicted "evil results" would flow from it. At the very least, she argued in emulation of Mahone, the state's industrial progress would suffer. As with Independent movements in other states, the Georgia Independents indirectly supported Negro participation in politics by calling for a free ballot and a fair count. Although the Feltons were still active

290 THE OTHER SOUTH

in Georgia politics in the 1890's, they were not at first friendly to
the Populists. Nevertheless, as a perennial dissenter, William
Felton did finally run for Congress as a Populist, but he was
beaten. Not surprisingly, the Feltons were admirers of Thomas
Watson, the great Georgia Populist, if only because they, like
Watson, were opponents of banks and hard money.[23]

The Independent movement in North Carolina emerged first in
1881–82, calling itself the "liberal" party. It began as an antipro-
hibition movement, but soon moved on to opposing monopolies
and favoring the Blair bill in support of federal aid to education.
As a dissident Democratic movement, seeking enough new votes to
defeat the traditional party, the new party called for equal political
rights for all men, regardless of race. Like other independent
movements in the South, the "liberals" of North Carolina received
support from both national and local Republicans, but the dissident organization did not survive beyond 1884.

There were also Independent candidates and groups in Alabama, Texas, South Carolina, and Florida in the early 1880's.
William M. Lowe of Alabama ran as a Greenbacker for Congress
in 1878 and was elected; he repeated his victory in 1880, receiving
support from Republicans. In 1882 the Greenback-Independent
candidate for governor in Alabama received more than 46,000
votes, almost all of them in the northern old Unionist and Republican part of the state. That same year an old Greenbacker in Texas,
Wash Jones, also ran for governor, receiving more than 100,000
votes out of 250,000 cast. Jones, like Mahone, thought the South

---

23. The standard and an exemplary work on this period is C. Vann
Woodward, *The Origins of the New South, 1877–1913* (Baton Rouge, 1951),
on which I have relied often, even though Woodward underplays the importance of Mahone. For a recent and sensitive analysis of the Bourbon
mind see Paul Gaston's *The New South Creed* (New York, 1970). I have
also used for the Independents Willie D. Halsell, "James D. Chalmers and
'Mahoneism' in Mississippi," *Journal of Southern History*, X (1944), 48–49,
52–53, 56–58; Judson Clements Ward, Jr., "Georgia Under the Bourbon
Democrats, 1872–1890," unpublished Ph.D. dissertation, University of North
Carolina, Chapel Hill, 1947, p. 122; Shadgett, *Republican Party in Georgia*,
pp. 70–74, 147; Rebecca Felton, *My Memoirs of Georgia Politics* (Atlanta,
1911), pp. 380–81; John E. Talmadge, "The Death Blow to Independentism
in Georgia," *Georgia Historical Quarterly*, XXXIX (1955), 37–47;
Josephine Bone Floyd, "Rebecca Latimer Felton, Political Independent,"
Georgia Historical Quarterly, XXX (1946), 14–34.

should emulate the North in its economic development. Hence he stood for encouragement to immigration and investment as well as free schools, free ballot boxes, free speech, and enforcement of federal laws in the South. None of the Independents, however, even approached the success of the Readjusters.

Mahone's successes gave hope not only to dissident Southerners but to national Republicans as well. Garfield may have had some doubts, as we have seen, about supporting Mahone over the regular Republican organization in Virginia. But Garfield's successor in the White House in 1881, Chester A. Arthur, had none. Arthur's outlook was reinforced by his Secretary of the Navy, William E. Chandler, who had long been concerned about the fate of blacks in the South as well as about the diminishing prospects of his and their party in the South. With Chandler's encouragement, Arthur threw his considerable patronage and prestige behind Mahone in Virginia and behind Independents throughout the South in the elections of 1882. That year Arthur turned over to Mahone alone 200 offices in the Treasury Department, 1,700 in the Post Office, 70 in the federal courts, and an unspecified number at the Norfolk navy yard.

Most national Republican leaders supported Arthur and Chandler in their abandonment of the regular Republican organizations in the South, but not all. James G. Blaine, for example, who was still worried about repudiation, did not. Perhaps the Republicans most reluctant to follow Arthur's new policy were the black leaders in the South, for they were the ones who were being abandoned. The well-known Northern black editor T. Thomas Fortune was especially outspoken in opposing Arthur's policy. Yet even the blacks came around when the example of the Readjusters was examined. In 1883, for example, Fortune himself, once so opposed to any abandonment of Republican organizations, wrote that the Readjuster victories in Virginia had "revolutionized the state so that it is no longer a heaven for whites and hell for blacks."[24] The year 1882 turned out to be, however, the high point not only of the Independent movement throughout the South, but of the Readjusters as well.

24. Stanley P. Hirshson, *Farewell to the Bloody Shirt: Northern Republicans and the Southern Negro, 1877–93* (Bloomington, Ind., 1962), pp. 116, 118.

THE BOURBON COUNTERATTACK

No Independent movement was as successful as the Readjusters. Only in Virginia did the Independents do as much as win the state government; the most that the Independents in other states accomplished was to elect an occasional congressman or a few members of the legislature. But if the Readjusters were the most successful they were also the most vulnerable. No other anti-Bourbon movement had gone as far as the Readjusters in appealing to and winning the Negro vote. That very success was the Readjusters' principal weakness. Political cooperation between the races in the South, as the Scalawags had found out, exposed its white practitioners to charges of endangering white supremacy. The Bourbons of Virginia had not been slow to take advantage of the weapon of race. "Rally to your own color and colors . . . ," urged a Democratic flyer during the campaign of 1880. "Remember the strength and color of your foes. . . . Men of Virginia! White Men of Virginia!! Remember the fight in your State will settle the political question of either white or colored supremacy. Which shall it be?" Even during the highly successful campaign of 1881, one of Mahone's political workers reported that race was the principal Bourbon argument in his district. "It was the nigger—represented in every phase of social equality that could be imagined to drive off the whites—their [Bourbons'] only hope—but thank God and yourself we have won the day. . . ."[25]

During the campaign in the fall of 1883 the Bourbons made a concerted effort to drive the wedge of race between black and white Readjusters. Whether all the elements in the effort were planned or were only the result of skillful exploitation of chance events is not clear. Yet it is significant that in 1883, for the first time since the Readjusters came into being, the Conservatives agreed with them on the question of the debt. For in that year the Conservatives promised that if they were returned to power they would not repeal the Riddleberger act, which had scaled down the debt. In effect, then, in appealing to race the Bourbons were saying

25. Flyer, Scrapbook XIII, William Mahone Papers; John E. Bradford to William Mahone, Nov. 23, 1881, William Mahone Papers.

that the only issue that divided the two parties now was the question of the Negroes in politics. For if the debt issue, which had brought the Readjusters into existence, was no longer a bone of contention with the Democrats, then the presence of black men in the Readjuster party was the principal difference between Readjusters and Democrats. Furthermore, as we shall see, the exquisite timing of the appeal to race suggests that something more was involved than the simple exploitation by the Bourbons of a chance opportunity. In short, it is not unlikely that the opportunity was created rather than merely seized.

The first part of the appeal to whites on grounds of color was certainly planned. A Bourbon flyer entitled "Mahone's Game" asserted, for example, that Mahone intended to have a civil rights act passed in Virginia because the U.S. Supreme Court had recently declared the federal Civil Rights Act unconstitutional. "Every white man who votes for Mahone and his gang," the circular read, "goes for making the negro his equal socially, and gives Mahone a legislature to carry out the African plan." That plan, apparently, proposed to do "what Congress cannot do and what the Constitution of the United States does not allow. . . . A Mahone legislature will turn you and your wives and children over to mixed schools, mixed marriages and miscegenation."[26]

Another circular, headed by the title "Coalition Rule in Danville," hit the same target, only harder. Danville was a small town at the western edge of southside Virginia, where blacks were in the majority. The circular purported to be signed by white merchants, mechanics, and manufacturers of the city, who were complaining about the circumstances under which they had to live when Negroes were a political majority. It was asserted, for example, that Negroes held a majority of the seats on the city council, and that four of the city's nine policemen were black. (These apparently, were the first black policemen in the city's history.) Furthermore, the circular contended, twenty out of the twenty-four stalls in the town market were held by blacks, a situation that was said to be driving North Carolina tobacco farmers from the Danville market. It alleged, moreover, that blacks paid almost no taxes yet received

26. Flyer, Scrapbook XXXI, William Mahone Papers.

substantial amounts of public funds for their schools and dominated the town judiciary and police force.

Finally, the circular came to the sensitive question of racial etiquette, emphasizing Negro insolence toward whites. *"Negro women* have been known to *force ladies* from the pavement," the circular reported, "and remind them that they will 'learn to step aside the next time.' *In several instances white children* have been struck by grown negroes. . . . It is a very common practice for the negroes who are employed about our houses to allude to white ladies and gentlemen as *men* and *women,* and to negroes as *ladies* and *gentlemen.* This is a practice almost without exception with the negro women. They do it to irritate and throw contempt upon the white race." Nor could an improvement in the future be expected, the circular implied. The blacks intended to incorporate a Negro settlement within the town limits and thereby obtain sufficient votes to overwhelm the whites. The scheme would thus make it *"impossible for any white man to hold office in the town. We know this is their plan."*

The circular closed with a plea for racial solidarity: "Now fellow-citizens of the Valley and Southwest, we cry out to you in our affliction to deliver us from this awful state *of humiliation and wretchedness.* . . . Help us, fellow citizens, by voting for the Conservative-Democratic candidate for the Legislature, for *unless they are elected we are doomed."* As a friend and lieutenant of Mahone's reported, the Bourbons were making an unprecedented effort. Many were speaking every night, he noted, and "Nigger, nigger, nigger, with the Danville Circular as the only theme."[27]

The actual situation in Danville was quite different from the circular's description. Blacks sat on the city council, it is true, but they held four, not seven seats; furthermore, the blacks had voted with the whites to elect a white chairman. The chairman was stigmatized by the Conservatives as a carpetbagger, but he had actually lived in Virginia for eighteen years. Moreover, only two of the policemen were black, and the city controlled only twelve of the twenty-nine market stalls, the preponderance of them being owned by white men who freely rented them to whites and blacks. Fur-

27. "Danville Circular," Scrapbook XXXI; C. A. Heermans to William Mahone, Nov. 3, 1883, William Mahone Papers.

thermore, the tobacco business of Danville had actually risen under Readjuster government. The true measure of the so-called black domination of Danville was that twenty-three of the city officials were Democrats, fourteen Readjusters, and two independents. Thirty-nine were white and only eight were black, though Negroes constituted a majority of the city's population.

Before the facts could catch up with the circular, however, a new event provided a powerful clincher for the Bourbon appeal to racial allegiance. It is this close timing that lends credence to the Readjuster assertions of a deliberate Bourbon plan. On November 3, just three days before the election, violence between unarmed blacks and armed whites broke out in Danville. A later report by local Democrats blamed Negro insolence and provocation in the face of white forbearance. The results of the violence, however, seem to bear out the Readjusters' assertion that the source of the riot was white aggression against blacks. Even the Democrats' report counted seven blacks wounded, four of them mortally, as against only two whites injured. Other reports listed six blacks killed and ten wounded. The Readjuster governor sent troops to maintain order, but as one Readjuster wrote Mahone, they fraternized with the whites rather than apprehending those who had shot down the Negroes.[28]

The outbreak in Danville was immediately capitalized upon by the Bourbons. Two days later one of Mahone's workers telegraphed that his part of the state was "being flooded by Circulars," the content of which is "an inflammatory misrepresentation of the row in Danville; . . . the object is to . . . draw the color line." Another, in the far southwestern part of the state, reported that the circulars were printed "by the tens of thousands" and the Bourbons ran "their printing press here all day last sunday and by nightfall had at least a dozen horsemen started to every neighborhood in this and Craig counties." By Monday night the people

28. Discussion of the Danville riot is based on the variety of materials in the Mahone Scrapbooks, including clippings from Richmond *Whig*, Nov. 30, 1883; *Daily Register* (Danville?), undated, statements of witnesses and reports; Charles E. Wynes, *Race Relations in Virginia, 1870–1902* (Charlottesville, 1961), pp. 129–33; D. H. Pannill to William Mahone, Nov. 10, 1883, William Mahone Papers tells of behavior of militia at Danville.

were "worked up to the belief that the whole state was to be overridden by the negroes if the Readjuster party was successful." Even some stalwart Readjusters he knew "turned a deaf ear to all persuasion and would hear nothing, fully bent on voting the only ticket they believed would save the state from Negro domination." From Pearisburg, in the mountains, came the familiar report of a massive change in opinion as a result of the circular, which told "of the 'insurrection' at Danville." The report gave the Bourbons "a lever by which they forced the color line into the contest with powerful effect, at a time that was too late for us to authoritatively deny, or in any way explain it."[29]

And the Bourbon tactic did work. One of Mahone's workers reported that those precincts in his district which received news of the riot were lost to the Readjusters, while those that did not see the circular stood firm. A Readjuster from the mountain town of Covington wrote that "the 'Nigger' cry was kept up so incessantly and howled so fiercely that many of our people became really frightened, & some men here who have been true Republicans since the war voted against us." The reports to Mahone, in themselves, coming as they did from ordinary Virginians, made evident that not all white Virginians feared black voters or could be stampeded by a Danville riot. One Readjuster from a western county wrote that there was much bribery and "bulldozing," but that "the negroes voted Solid with us but the poor white men was [sic] afraid to vote their sentiments and to day they are afraid to put their name [sic] to a certificate" of fraud. "The cold [colored] people stood like a wall but the white Readjusters could not stand the storm," he recalled. From the southside came a familiar litany: "the canvass was not upon legitimate legislative questions, either of the past or the future, but the principal argument of the funders was mixed schools, mixed marriages, mixed society, and a war of races. They knew that they were infamous lyes when they were circulating their reports and papers." Even where the count "was as usual a fair and honest one," a Mahone supporter wrote

29. Telegram from Miner F. Chamberlain to William Mahone, Nov. 5, 1883; W. O. Wesson to Mahone, Nov. 9, 1883; James B. Peck to Mahone, Nov. 22, 1883, William Mahone Papers.

from the southside, the effect of the riot was sharply felt. "The great falling off in our vote was attributable . . . to the raising of the false issue of negro vs. white man," he told Mahone; "our candidate being a colored man and theirs a white man gave enough plausibility to the issue to cause hundreds of white men who had heretofore voted with us—to change about and join the Bourbons."[30]

The suspicion that the Danville riot was deliberately provoked by the Bourbons was often voiced. "Had they not have gotten up that riot in Danville we would have carried this county," wrote one lieutenant in the west. Instead, he continued, "the white leaders of our party got scared at the Danvill [*sic*] riot. . . ." Mahone heard enough of such claims that he wrote soon after the election, "I hear that the Danville Massacre was discussed . . . before it came to pass. Is this true—if so furnish me the facts—sustained by affidavits."[31]

Many of the reports to Mahone dwelt on the often brutal method used against the Negroes. In the process, these ordinary white Virginians revealed their own sympathy for and appreciation of blacks as political associates. "I know of a number of Negroes that will loose [*sic*] their homes on account of their polatics," wrote one worker from the southside. "The Funders in a number of places rode around the day before the Election and told the Negroes if they went to the Election they would be shot." He went on to estimate that "at least 160 negro votes" were lost by fraud, another 60 because the Negroes were bribed not to vote. The Bourbons, he insisted, stole still other votes by liberally dispensing whiskey and leading drunken Negroes to the polls "like Sheep to the Slaughter; the trouble with us [is that] we have no one to prosecute the offenders. Our courts, attorney and judge are both

30. Anonymous sheets of paper in Scrapbooks, Mahone Papers, containing reports on reaction to Danville riot. S. M. Dickey reported, p. 87, that where the circular went, there the Readjusters lost; A. A. McDonald to William Mahone, Nov. 10, 1883; J. G. Saunders to William Mahone, Nov. 20, 1883; James D. Clay to Mahone, Nov. 19, 1883; Robert T. Thorpe to Mahone, Nov. 17, 1883, William Mahone Papers.

31. Steward M. Lewis to William Mahone, Nov. 8, 1883; William Mahone to H. Southworth, Nov. 17, 1883, Letterbooks, William Mahone Papers.

against us." Another reported that in his district, too, there was much attempted bribery, but "all honor is due to our colored voters only one in 224 was lost to us. This was largely due to the labors of two or three colored workers to whom I wish particularly to call your attention as they have worked without any reward." Mahone himself was intensely angered by the Bourbon methods. He explained the defeat as resulting from the "diabolical methods and murders of the Bourbons. . . . These and the incendiary Danville address re-inforced by the murders perpetrated there on unoffending, unarmed fleeing colored people—and the fiendish use made of these, that stampeded the white people—" and gave the Bourbons victory.[32]

Robert W. Hughes, an old friend of Mahone from railroading days and a Republican from the days of Reconstruction, told Mahone that half of the 30,000 votes the Readjusters lost were taken away "by cajolery and threats of proscription. Say what you will," Hughes went on, "a large class of Readjusters voted in a manner both treacherous and cowardly towards their party." The other half of the lost 30,000 votes Hughes attributed to the defection of the "poor whites" who could not or would not pay their poll tax in the past, but who in this election, "when hissed on to a war upon the negro, voted 'to put the nigger down.' . . ." (Thanks to the Readjusters, of course, there no longer was a poll tax.) Unlike Mahone, Hughes did not think the blacks were intimidated. Indeed, he, like other observers of the election, was impressed by the behavior of the blacks. "Almost throughout the state, they voted fully the usual strength and with a quiet and manly courage and unanimity that I cannot but admire. Efforts were indeed made to intimidate them, but they were in the main unsuccessful," he concluded.[33] Hughes's evaluation was probably the correct one; it was the white Readjusters who had caved in— under the pressure of the appeal to race.

The election of 1883 was close in votes—the Bourbon majority was only 18,000 out of 267,000 votes cast—but nearly two-thirds

32. James D. Clay to William Mahone, Nov. 19, 1883; T. B. Parham, Nov. 9, 1883, to William Mahone; William Mahone to W. P. Dryden, Nov. 11, 1883, Letterbooks, William Mahone Papers.
33. Robert W. Hughes to William Mahone, Nov. 25, 1883, William Mahone Papers.

of the seats in the two houses of the legislature went to the Funders. The Readjuster era in government had come to an end.

Undoubtedly fraud and intimidation were a part of the explanation for the Bourbon victory, as Mahone and his lieutenants maintained. Yet those electoral crimes were not new in 1883, especially in the post-Reconstruction South, and the Bourbons certainly had no monopoly on their commission, either. At least two things were new, however. One was the Danville riot, and the other was the Bourbons' acceptance that year of the Readjusters' position on the debt. Thus in the campaign of 1883, unlike the previous ones, the Bourbons abandoned the one issue that had brought Negroes and whites, Democrats and Republicans, together in the Readjuster party while, at the same time, the Bourbons forcefully pressed home, with the Danville Circular and riot, the one issue that was capable of dividing a coalition that had now lost its original principal cement. From that Bourbon strategy issued the victory of 1883.

No one was more aware of the fraudulent character of the Bourbon appeals to white supremacy than the blacks themselves. "After thinking over our defeated," wrote one half-illiterate black supporter to Mahone, "I thought I would write to think how we was defeated by the Democrat party saying that Colored people want to uprise against the white people." It was the patent absurdity of the charge that most irritated him. "We did not think of it when from 1861 to 1865 and I don't see why they should think of it now when there are three whites to one Colored in Virginia. We was a great protection for their family during the War. We gave them bread when they were hungry and gave water when they were thirsty and we would hudalley [hide away?] their family from the federal troops when they would come through. They themselves would be afraid to stay and protect then would be laying in the mountains among the rock and bushes, dogging [dodging] and hiding from the federal troops, we yet were braver soldiers than they yet. . . . They know very well we did not want mixed marriadges or mixed school. We know it was not healthy for old Virginia, that was the only way they could carry the election in Virginia and they would go around and asked the low classes of people: war are you going to put your wife & children in the hand

of the Negro. . . . Gen we will stand by you thought thik and
thin and hope you wie by us."[34]

AN INESCAPABLE CHOICE

The defeat of 1883 confronted Mahone and the Readjusters
with a fundamental and, as events turned out, far-reaching decision. The delicate but heretofore successful coalition had been
disrupted along its weakest fault line, that of race. From the
beginning, of course, it had been recognized that the Bourbons
would draw the color line. As one Mahone supporter wrote after the
defeat of 1883, "No party can ever succeed in Virginia that
accepts issue on the color line. Why, I can scarcely tell, but a
Virginian sovereign is more afraid of a negro voter than the devil
is of holy water." Nevertheless, without the black vote, the victory
over the Bourbons could not have been accomplished in the past
and could not be expected in the future. The blacks, on the other
hand, could not be counted on to vote with Democrats for long;
they had a strong historical allegiance to the Republican party.
Furthermore, over the long run national support would be forth-
coming for a reform party in Virginia, or anywhere in the South
for that matter, only from a Republican administration in Washington. Certainly no national Democratic administration would
support an anti-Bourbon party composed of whites and blacks in a
Southern state. Ideologically, too, the Republicans seemed more
congenial. As one Southern Republican wrote in 1881, "the Republican party is the friend and patron of free schools, while the
Democracy has been their inveterate enemy. The Republican party
advocates internal improvements . . . and by appropriations
have lavished millions upon millions in developing the North,
while the South has always opposed. . . ." If Mahone wants to
help Virginia's economy, the writer concluded, "could he do otherwise than ally himself with the appropriation, in opposition to the
sentimental party?"[35]

34. M. Spurlock to William Mahone, Nov. 27, 1883, William Mahone
Papers.
35. C. A. Heermans to William Mahone, Nov. 9, 1883; letter signed
"Republican" to Nashville, Tennessee, *Banner,* Nov. 22, 1881, clipping in
Scrapbook XXVIII, William Mahone Papers.

As a result of the defeat of 1883, however, Mahone received advice on both sides of the question of whether he should take his Readjusters into the Republican party. W. C. Elam, the editor of Mahone's Richmond *Whig*, was sure that no good would result from a move into the Republican party. For if such a move were made, "a large proportion of the white conservative strength we have left" would be driven away. All that the Republicans would bring would be more blacks, when what the party needed was white men. Those Negroes who refuse to stand back ought "to be sent to the Bourbons. We can well afford to swap negroes for white men," he concluded. (Interestingly enough, Elam immediately qualified that harsh judgment by assuring Mahone that the party "will be still for the equal rights and interests of white & colored citizens." The political subordination of blacks, in short, would be only a tactic to achieve the larger end.)

Richard A. Wise, one of Mahone's closest friends and a son of the antebellum governor, took the opposite view. He suggested that the party "call a convention at once and declare ourselves National Republicans. . . . This is the game, and the only one by which we can in the future hope to control the negro vote. The tariff question will aid us then and the Republican party will aid us."

On balance it did seem clear that if Mahone wished to reform Virginia's economy and politics, he had little choice except to affiliate with the Republican party. In a way, he had anticipated his dilemma even before the election of 1883. The previous summer he had written to James Longstreet that if the Readjusters lost in the fall it might well "be the end of hope and effort all over the South for the formation of a party in favor of the Union and . . . the education of the children and the honest and cheerful recognition of the civil and political rights of all citizens."[36]

Not surprisingly, therefore, in April, 1884, in time for the Republican National Convention of that year, Mahone's Readjusters met in convention in Richmond and proclaimed themselves Republicans. But Mahone's hope that his decision would bring to his forces increased and continuing support from a national Re-

36. W. C. Elam to William Mahone, Nov. 18, 1883; Richard A. Wise to William Mahone, Nov. 9, 1883, William Mahone Papers.

publican administration was doomed to disappointment. That year
Grover Cleveland became the first Democratic President elected
since 1856.

The meaning of the setback was reflected in a remark that
Mahone himself had made even before the election. "Democratic
success in the Presidency," he wrote in December, 1883, "would
be fatal to us in Virginia." And two years later, after local defeats
in 1884 and 1885, he was sure of it. "Our hope for any remedy
must be in the return of the Republican party to power in Washington, full and complete in 1888. Then it will be possible to lift
the heavy hand of bourbonism here by a federal election law that
will at least free the ballot and secure honest returns in all Federal
elections."[37] In short, in 1884 just at the time Mahone was
embarking upon his daring experiment in affiliation with the
Republican party, he lost whatever possibility of support and
federal protection a Republican administration could provide.

The defeat of the Republicans nationally in 1884 also shook the
commitment of some of Mahone's white followers in Virginia,
many if not most of whom had been lifelong Democrats. It was
one thing to be a Readjuster, that is, a dissident Democrat, temporarily out of the harness, but it was quite a different thing to be a
Republican. Soon after election day in 1884, a Readjuster from
the western and white part of the state wrote Mahone, suggesting
that perhaps it was time for the little general to abandon the
Republican affiliation and return to the Democratic party. "You
were mistaken," he wrote, to think that the Republicans were going
to control indefinitely the federal government, and "you took upon
yourself the odium and suffered the abuse and vituperation of a
majority of the white people of the state," believing that such was
the best way "to break up the solid South and destroy Bourbonism
in our own state." But obviously, the correspondent continued,
that approach was not working. "You had the courage" to leave
the Bourbons; "now you can, with no more courage, return to do
the same thing." The return of Mahone to the Democratic party,
he predicted, "would scare the Bourbons to death." Besides, he

37. William Mahone to James Longstreet, July 7, 1883; William Mahone
to T. T. Fauntleroy, Nov. 6, 1885, Letterbooks, William Mahone Papers.

added, a return to the Democrats would ensure Mahone's reelection to the United States Senate.

In a full and candid statement of his own emancipation from the past and from blind allegiance to region, Mahone turned down the suggestion. First of all, he wrote, he had never had much interest in political office for himself. Reelection to the Senate, therefore, was not a decisive issue. It was the future of Virginia that concerned him. "Upon the abolition of slavery," the former Confederate general declared, the interest of Virginia was transformed "and became common with that of the Republican states of the Union. . . ." The growth and power of the state was now "dependent upon the economic policies of the Republican party." It had been his hope that by uniting with the dominant party in the North, "a flood of settlers and capital" would come to Virginia, thereby advancing "the wealth of her people and the power of the commonwealth." This hope, it is true, he went on, was being frustrated by Bourbon victories, but it still did not seem to him to be in the interest of Virginia for him and his followers to rejoin the Democrats.

His reasons were not entirely economic or developmental. Evidently Mahone had a belief in the national destiny and principles that kept him a Republican. He could not believe that the North would acquiesce in the illegalities characteristic of Southern elections. Even if principle did not preclude it, he said, practical politics did. "It is out of reason to suppose that the union people of the North and West will submit to subordination to the South, by such methods as gives to that section the controll [sic] of the government." All one needed to understand that fact was to put oneself in the position of a Northerner. Furthermore, he said, it simply cannot be in Virginia's interest "to stand in with a sectional party or sectional government," which is what the Democrats were. To join the Democrats "will take the country back to the policies and sentiments and predjudices [sic] which brought on the war of secession and surely Virginia wants no more [of] such a period and consequence." The crux of the matter, he argued, was that the Bourbons found it "impossible . . . to realize that there was an Appomattox and to appreciate the generosity and forbearance of the successful section in the contest concluded there."[38] Mahone, in short, was like those Scalawags for whom the war had marked a turning point in the history of the South and in their own outlook on the future. The trouble was that Mahone was wrong about what the nation or the Republican party would do about electoral illegalities or violence. Neither the nation nor the party was prepared to protect black and white in the free exercise of the suffrage. The former Confederate general was more of a nationalist and believer in Republican principles than the national party itself.

As long as Mahone lived—he died in 1895—he never changed his mind about the need to stay with the Republicans and the Negroes. To the end of his life he continued to work for a Republican victory in Virginia, or, when the occasion arose, as we shall see, a Populist victory. For his first objective always was to defeat the Bourbons. He was never again able to achieve the kind of victory won by the Readjusters, but even as a Republican Mahone's leadership was impressive. In 1886, for example, Republicans captured seven of the ten congressional seats in Virginia. And in the presidential canvass of 1888, Mahone brought Virginia within 1,500 votes of victory, even though the state's electoral machinery was in the hands of the Democrats. That year the national Republicans had emphasized the tariff as an issue that they hoped would be able to transcend the divisions over race in the South. The Republicans did not come as close to victory in other Southern states as in Virginia, but there were some surprisingly close contests. In North Carolina, for example, the Republicans came within 13,000 votes of victory, out of a total of 285,000; in Tennessee the Democratic margin of victory was only 20,000 out of 304,000. In the upper South, at least, the Republicans were by no means dead.

As a Republican, just as when he was a Readjuster, Mahone was the boss of the party; nothing happened in the Republican party of Virginia without his knowledge or approval. Many of his old Readjuster friends and lieutenants deserted him, as the old victories receded into the past. Sometimes they abandoned him out

38. Floyd B. Hurt to William Mahone, Nov. 20, 1884; William Mahone to Floyd B. Hurt, Dec. 8, 1884, Letterbooks, William Mahone Papers.

of ideological or political disagreement, but not infrequently simply out of distaste for his dictatorial ways. He could not have been an easy man to get along with, for he was too dedicated and driven himself to be ingratiating or overly generous with others, especially when they disagreed with him. Yet it seems likely that the frustrations, defeats, and calumny he endured, which were monumental, go far to account for his dictatorial ways. He was determined that he would win by will, if nothing else.

In 1889 Mahone himself ran for governor. By then whatever personal ambition for office he may have had—and it was never strong—was spent. Yet he threw himself into the campaign with vigor. He campaigned in behalf of a protective tariff on the ground that it would aid the development of Virginia's industries and protect the wages of its industrial workers. The Virginia Knights of Labor newspaper supported Mahone on the grounds that he would bring prosperity and development to Virginia. But others saw in his campaign the old question of the Negro. Educator Jabez L. M. Curry wrote his son that the election would "decide whether Mahone & negroes are to dominate. . . ." And Mahone did appeal to blacks as well as whites. In the western white counties, despite their demonstrated susceptibility to appeals to white supremacy, he deliberately raised the issue of "black domination." "This pretended concern for the safety of our civilization," which the Bourbons profess, he told an audience in Abingdon, "is merely to mislead and turn away the more thoughtless and gullible of our population from the exercise of their political rights in the direction of their own convictions and interest. It is employed as a mere scarecrow to excite prejudice and fear, in the hope of diverting the white working man from casting his ballot for the candidate he honestly prefers." In twenty-two legislative districts where blacks are a majority, he pointed out, seven were represented by white Democrats, ten by white Republicans, and five by colored Republicans. "Whence, then," he wanted to know, "comes the menace to our civilization by the presence of the colored man, to whose care and keeping the lives of our wives and children were largely and safely entrusted during the sectional war?"[39]

39. Jabez L. M. Curry to Manly Curry, Oct. 31, 1889, Jabez Lamar Monroe Curry Papers; *Vital Virginia Issues* (n.d., n.p.), Abingdon speech, Sept. 23, 1889.

J. L. M. Curry wrote his son on the eve of the election that he
wished "every black person could be colonized in Africa. There is
no peace nor safety for us, nor prosperity, while they remain as co-
citizens." Mahone's position was quite different. "The colored man
is here to stay," he told his audience at Abingdon. "He is an
essential factor in and to our labor system. His place cannot be
supplied." Rather than being an obstacle to prosperity, as Curry
contended, the Negro "is in great measure the life-giving power to
all our industrial pursuits," Mahone asserted. Five years before, in
a speech in the Senate, Mahone had referred to blacks as essential
to Virginia's "fields of industry as the machinery of New England
is to her factories." And simply because the Negro's labor was so
important, Mahone believed it followed that "the more we enlarge
his capabilities and stimulate his efforts the greater will be his
contributions." On this principle rested Mahone's interest in and
concern for Negro education. Moreover, the place that Mahone
envisioned for the Negro in the "New Virginia" was more than
that of simply a field hand or agricultural worker. "We want here
no condition of serfdom," he told his predominantly white audience in Abingdon in 1889, "if we would advance our civilization
and promote the peace, happiness and prosperity of all." Blacks,
in short, would be included in all phases of his New Virginia.[40]

Mahone's phrase about serfdom comes close to a "private
maxim" of George W. Cable, probably the most outspokenly
liberal white Southerner on the question of Negro rights of his day.
"There is no room in America for a peasantry," wrote Cable in
regard to blacks. Cable's defense of Negro rights was sufficiently
strong and liberal that he felt compelled in 1885 to leave the South
permanently to live in the North. His views on the Negro caused
Southerners for years to abuse and harass him as a traitor to his
race and region. Yet it is instructive in seeking to understand in
context the ideas of Mahone and the Readjusters to recognize that
even the racial ideas of Cable fell short of an unequivocally
modern conception of equality between blacks and whites. Early in

40. J. L. M. Curry to Manly Curry, Oct. 31, 1889, Jabez Lamar Monroe
Curry Papers; *Vital Virginia Issues;* James Hugo Johnston, "The Participation of Negroes in the Government of Virginia from 1877–1888," *Journal
of Negro History,* XIV (1929), 267.

his career as a writer Cable had frankly admitted: "Yes, the black race is inferior to the white." But, he insisted, the proper response to that fact was "magnanimity, not scorn." By 1888 he had advanced considerably beyond that position, but his view was still somewhat ambiguous. "For all that is known the black is 'an inferior race,' " he wrote in his essay "The Negro Question," "though how, or how permanently inferior, remains unproved." What bothers blacks, however, he emphasized, is that they are not judged on their "person, dress, behavior, character, or aspirations." They are judged as if "the African tincture, much or little, were itself stupidity, squalor, and vice."[41]

THE LITTLE GENERAL AND BLACKS

Mahone's personal attitude toward Negroes was never as advanced as Cable's, but it was not simple either. Certainly it moved beyond merely recognizing the presence of blacks in society or of seeking to capitalize on their votes or exploit their labor. Long before he had become a political leader in need of black votes, Mahone had condemned President Hayes's Southern policy, which intentionally by-passed black Republicans while seeking to forge an alliance between Southern white Conservatives and Northern Republicans. What was significant about Mahone's condemnation was that one of his reasons was the harm inflicted on Negroes by Hayes's approach. The policy's "misconception of the interests and destiny if not of the rights of the colored people are [sic] fanatical," he wrote.[42] It is not without significance, too, that in his private correspondence he never denigrated Negroes or used the word "nigger," though several of his correspondents did. He was careful, also, to address even a poorly educated Negro as "Dear Sir."

41. Lucy Leffingwell Cable Bikle, *George W. Cable: His Life and Letters* (New York, 1967; orig. pub. 1928), p. 156; George W. Cable, *The Negro Question*, ed. by Arlin Turner (Garden City, N.Y., 1958), pp. 29, 126.
42. William Mahone to James G. Halladay, March 29, 1877, Letterbooks, William Mahone Papers. See Wynes, *Race Relations in Virginia*, for the general pattern of Negro-white relations in Virginia, including under the Readjusters.

Mahone's attitude toward blacks was often sentimental, at other times patronizing. The sentimentality appears again and again in his private letters and seems to stem from his conviction that Negroes had been especially—almost inconceivably—loyal during the war, particularly in a war that was fought to keep them in slavery. After the defeat of 1883, for example, he wrote to the Republican Attorney General Benjamin Brewster that "the time must come, or our civilization fails, when men will cease to condemn the work of the creator by refusing to crusade against the weak and lowley [sic] because his skin is black. Of all men the Southern brave man should cheerfully exercise a tender care for the colored people." At another time his concern for the contradiction between the treatment accorded blacks and their wartime loyalty was made even more explicit. "To me as a Virginian, a former slave-owner, and an ex-Confederate, the saddest feature of this reign of terror is the sufferings [sic] it has inflicted upon the negroes here," he wrote in 1883. "This unfortunate people have had a fate as black as their skins." Brought to this country against their wills and then enslaved, and "now, when they act on their rights voluntarily accorded to them, they are shot down like dogs for party purposes by the beneficiaries of their toil for centuries."

Although Mahone had been a slaveholder, he was convinced, he wrote one correspondent in 1883, that "it was the blight of human slavery that beat" the Confederacy. "The hand of God all mighty was against [us] for the sin of Slavery." A similar retribution, he was sure, awaited those in his own time who "oppress the lowly, the weak of his creation. These unfortunate people defended our homes during the war, they fed our armies, our wives, daughters . . . while we were fighting to keep them in bondage. God forbid that I shall ever allow myself to be drawn into an act of unkindness toward them," he vowed.[43]

Sentimental as Mahone's views may seem to us today, they were echoed by other Southern white friends of the Negro. Atticus

43. William Mahone to Benjamin Brewster, Nov. 11, 1883, Letterbooks, William Mahone Papers; Letter of William Mahone, Nov. 14, 1883, in Wilmington, North Carolina, *Post*, Nov. 23, 1884; William Mahone to A. H. Wood, Nov. 17, 1883, Letterbooks, William Mahone Papers.

Haygood, the Methodist bishop of Georgia, one of the South's most eloquent and consistent defenders of black aspirations, expressed such views in his book *Our Brother in Black* (1881). He developed the point at some length in a speech at Chautauqua, New York, in August, 1883. "The Negro's conduct during the war makes one of the most wonderful chapters in the world's history," he said. But he did not see this as simply a sign of benevolent white treatment, as many whites were prone to do. The Negro knew quite well what the war was about, Haygood emphasized; moreover, he had been "praying for freedom for generations." Furthermore, he had been encouraged to violence "that would have made the stories of Hayti and San Domingo tame. . . ." Yet the blacks did not rise; they grew the crops that fed the armies and they protected the families of the absent soldiers. "Why was this so?" Haygood asked. "Some will say it was the natural submissiveness of Negroes, but that did not stop San Domingo and Hayti . . . ," he correctly pointed out. The answer that Haygood gave may also have been Mahone's: "the great majority of the slaves did truly love the white people. . . ."[44]

Nor did Mahone conceal his paternalism toward blacks. The Negro's labor was so important to Virginia, he once told a Boston audience in a public letter, that the Readjusters hoped "to make the colored man feel his identification with us, and to stimulate in him the feeling of contentment by wise and generous care and consideration that there may be prevented the calamity to the South of a heavy emigration of the colored people."[45] No wonder Negrophobic conservative Democrats like J. L. M. Curry thought the general a menace to Virginia!

If, despite his sentimentality and patronizing of blacks, Mahone had a better appreciation of blacks than many of his white Southern contemporaries, he was still a white Southerner himself and a practical politician. He was well aware that most white Virginians were less liberal on the subject of Negro rights than he was. Moreover, he recognized that this limitation was particularly evident

44. Atticus Haygood, *Pleas for Progress* (Nashville, 1889), p. 27.
45. Richmond *Whig*, Feb. 11, 1882, clipping in Scrapbook XXVIII, William Mahone Papers.

among poorer whites. "The lack of opportunity and knowledge on the part of the white laboring people of the South," he wrote privately in 1886, "are [*sic*] the seat of the predjudice [*sic*] of that class . . . against the colored race. . . ." Nevertheless, he thought that it was to the interest of workingmen to have "the labor of the colored race" raised to "a higher plane." Meanwhile, however, he cautioned, it was necessary not to arouse the prejudices of the whites. "Our colored people must now realize," he wrote after the defeat of 1883, "that to preserve their liberties they must let us lead—they must not over burthen us. Predjudices are still to be consulted. Time will subdue them—but we must be wise not to fight them—even with reason—nothing vs [against] them avails." Five years later, acting on his own advice, he resolutely refused to support the campaign for Congress of the well-known Negro educator and Republican John Mercer Langston.

The candidacy of Langston, to be sure, was of complicated origin and character. It derived from several factors: from Langston's own ambition now that the Bourbons had removed him from his post at the Negro College at Petersburg; from the desire of some black Republicans in Virginia for recognition in office, and from the general hostility within the Republican party of Virginia toward Mahone's iron rule. Langston lost in the balloting, but he was seated by the House of Representatives because of election frauds. Mahone, however, protested Langston's seating. "Our growth to the extent of full seventy thousand whites, drawn from the Democratic ranks," he boasted in 1890 in explanation of his opposition, "has been acquired by refusing to put colored candidates up for places that excite lingering prejudices and the foolish fear of negro supremacy." He asserted that Langston's candidacy in 1888 had been the cause for scaring off sufficient white votes to lose the state to the Democrats.[46] There is no sure way of knowing whether that was in fact the explanation for the near-miss in 1888, but Mahone obviously saw the Langston candidacy as confirmation of his view of the dangers inherent in moving too rapidly against the force of racial prejudice. It is worth noting, too, that

46. William Mahone to James M. Swank, Oct., 1886; William Mahone to John Booker, Nov. 17, 1883; William Mahone to John Sherman, March 28, 1890, Letterbooks, William Mahone Papers.

some Negro leaders, among whom was included Frederick Douglass, concurred in Mahone's opposition to Langston's candidacy.

As Mahone's open opposition to Langston's candidacy made evident, the little general never denied his paternalistic approach toward blacks in politics. When he was asked by a newspaper man in 1889 about a rumor that the newly elected President, Benjamin Harrison, would appoint a Negro to his cabinet, Mahone snapped that there was no possibility "whatever. The time has not come for that." He did not think that a Negro should run against a white man for Congress, either, having in mind, no doubt, Langston's attempt. "The colored man is entitled to all the rights that properly belong to him," he said, "but his place is not at the extreme front yet." Rather, he suggested that Negroes concern themselves with "industrial and educational" enterprises. And though Mahone was careful to make clear that the Negro must not seek places in society for which he was not presently fitted, he insisted that the Negro "must be educated, and he must assist in educating himself by appreciating and availing himself of the advantages that are afforded him by public or private agencies."[47] Mahone, in short, did not align himself with those increasingly vocal Southern whites of the time who were opposing education for Negroes—those men who said that to educate a Negro was to spoil a good fieldhand.

Like other Southern white friends of black aspirations, Mahone moved beyond mere self-interest in thinking about the future of black people in the South. He felt that the white South owed a debt to Negroes—a debt that could be repaid only with kindness, generosity, and recognition of the political and civil rights of blacks. He saw blacks not only as human beings but as human beings who had suffered from having worked and lived in a white South. His views were paternalistic and admittedly limited regarding equality between the races. He neither preached nor practiced equality of rights. Yet it also seems certain that if Mahone's views had prevailed, limited as they were, the future of black people in the South would have been considerably brighter than it turned out to be during the years of lynching, disfranchisement, and legal segregation that followed.

47. New York *World*, Jan. 18, 1889, clipping in Scrapbook XXXIX, William Mahone Papers.

THE LESSONS OF THE READJUSTERS

There were undoubtedly other white Virginians who felt as Mahone did, especially after the experience of working with Negroes in the Readjuster Crusade. Certainly it comes through in the many letters from Mahone's supporters, some of which have already been quoted. It was also evident in the defense of the blacks of Danville, which a Readjuster newspaper made soon after the riot in 1883. The *Valley Virginian* was a white county paper in the western part of the state, but it appreciated, nonetheless, the responsibility shown by the blacks in politics. The paper asked its readers whether any town or city in Virginia in which the whites constituted a majority could "have exercised one-tenth of the moderation on the race question that the negroes of Danville have displayed." Then it went on to become specific, asking whether a white majority would have taken merely a fraction of the seats on the city council as the blacks did in Danville where they constituted a majority of the citizens. Nor is it sufficient, the paper continued, to plead the prejudice of the whites as extenuation. Put the blame where it belongs, the paper urged. "Ignorance is the soil where passion and prejudice attain their rankest growth. . . . Ignorance breeds excess. Intelligence fosters moderation."[48]

Mahone and his Readjusters and Republicans were not modern integrationists. Yet in at least one Southern state they succeeded in bringing whites and blacks together into the same party, and they mounted a powerful challenge to the reigning Democrats. As Orra Langhorne, a Virginia Republican and dissenter in her own right, wrote in 1888 for the Boston *Times,* "the whole country" owes Mahone a debt. He did more than break the Bourbon hegemony, she declared. The fact that "the negroes of Virginia can vote today, and that our public schools . . . are in active operation and bringing countless blessings to Virginia, is due to the energetic, though somewhat arbitrary methods of Mahone." She went on to predict that in time it would be recognized "that General Mahone has come nearer to statesmanship in this generation than any of

48. *Valley Virginian* (Staunton), Nov. 15, 1883, Scrapbook XXXI, William Mahone Papers.

the public men who have striven for leadership in these troubled times." Orra Langhorne came from an old Virginia family—of Unionist and antislavery background, it is worth noting. For years she wrote for the *Southern Workman,* a publication of Hampton Institute, where her concern for blacks was frankly expressed, as it was in the article she wrote for the Boston *Times.*[49]

Langhorne was not the only Virginia liberal of the 1880's to be stimulated by the Readjuster effort in behalf of blacks. Another was Lewis Harvie Blair, a Richmond merchant of aristocratic family. In 1889 Blair published *The Prosperity of the South Dependent upon the Elevation of the Negro,* in which he argued forcefully for full civil and political rights for blacks if Virginia were to advance its economy. In the course of his book he pointed to the period of the Readjuster government to show that the Commonwealth under "so-called Negro rule" not only survived, but "in the opinion of many, was much benefitted."

With the exception of the two essays by George W. Cable on the Negro—"The Freedman's Case in Equity" (1885) and "The Negro Question" (1889)—Blair's book is the boldest and most penetrating argument against the subordination of the Negro written by a white person living in the South before 1900. Like Cable before him, Blair forthrightly advocated mixed schools. Equally significant was the fact that one of the arguments he advanced against segregated schools was that they harmed black children because they perpetuated a sense of caste. Blair, in short, was not simply concerned with the effects upon whites. He well recognized that mixed schools were dreaded by most whites, but he was confident that the dread would prove as "chimerical" as the dread that had once accompanied Negro emancipation or voting, but which was subsequently "dissipated by experience." It was also significant that Blair thought that mixed schools would improve the quality of intellectual activity among Southern whites. He apparently believed that one reason Southerners had shown "little intellectual development, apart from law and politics, is that the

49. Undated clipping, but identified on back as Boston *Times,* Aug. 1, 1886, Scrapbook XXXVIII, William Mahone Papers. For more writings by this Virginian dissenter of the Age of Mahone see the valuable collection of her writings: Orra Langhorne, *Southern Sketches from Virginia, 1881–1901,* ed. by Charles E. Wynes (Charlottesville, 1964).

whites have been possessed of the idea that the height of superiority is a white skin, and that they have been content with that kind
of eminence. Mixed schools, will, in time," he predicted, "emancipate us from this fallacy. . . ."

Blair's book was hardly noticed when published and quickly fell
into an abyss of obscurity. Yet Blair was a part of that Other
South of which the Readjusters were a prime example. (Later, in
the early twentieth century, Blair repudiated all that he had so
incisively argued in his book, a victim, it can be surmised, of the
increasing pressure of racism after 1900.) [50]

Although Mahone and the Republicans never won the state
again after the defeat of the Readjusters in 1883, those earlier
victories and Mahone's uninterrupted dedication to the Republican
cause and the cause of the Negro in Virginia stood as a constant
threat to the Democracy. It is not surprising, therefore, that
Mahone and his Readjusters were viciously attacked then and
later. In private, a Virginian wrote to his sister in 1882 that he
could not believe that Mahone would dare show his face at the
Memorial Day services that would take place the next day.
"Mahone would be a welcome figure probably in some Federal
Cemetery . . . but I fancy that the brave Union men who honour
their dead, would spurn him from their midst as an informer & a
renegade. . . . Mahone's deceit, treachery, & amazing effrontery
are so palpable as to recoil from his support some of his hitherto
staunchest partisans," he went on. "I am told the creature is afraid
to show himself to his own people, & well he may be." One of
Mahone's friends wrote him in 1883, "you are hated with a venom
and hatred not known or comprehended by fair-minded men."
Many years later one of Mahone's conservative opponents confessed: "Possibly I am not doing Mahone justice in this sketch of
him, because I hated him and he is the only man I ever hated."
And the Chicago *Inter Ocean* observed in 1885, after noting
Mahone's achievements, that "no public man was ever more

50. Lewis H. Blair, *A Southern Prophecy: The Prosperity of the South
Dependent upon the Elevation of the Negro* (Boston, 1964), pp. 99, 148–49.
For background on Blair see the introduction to the new edition of his book
by C. Vann Woodward, and Charles E. Wynes, "Lewis Harvie Blair, Virginia
Reformer: The Uplift of the Negro and Southern Prosperity," in C. E.
Wynes, ed., *The Negro in the South Since 1865* (New York, 1968).

cordially hated or bitterly maligned . . ." than Mahone. The reason for that hatred, the paper went on, was "because he recognized the negro's right to the ballot and stood heroically and aggressively for it." More recently, Allen Moger, a Virginia historian of his state, has recalled that in the early years of the twentieth century, when he "was growing up in eastern Virginia few people remembered Mahone and the Readjusters. Those who did spoke of him with horror. He had prostituted the Negro vote. He had threatened Virginia with Negro-Republican rule. . . . The worst charge that could be brought against an opposition candidate," Moger writes, "was that he had been associated in any way with Mahone and the Readjusters."[51]

For those Southerners of the late nineteenth century who were interested in breaking the stranglehold of the Democrats, the lessons to be drawn from the Readjusters would seem to have been at least two. The first was the need for an issue of such widespread importance that it could unite blacks and whites, Democrats and Republicans. In Virginia, the question of the debt with its implication for public education had provided that issue for the Readjusters. The second lesson, as the failure of other independent movements in the South revealed, was the need for a dynamic and dedicated leader. Only a Mahone, it would seem, could have taken the Readjusters into the Republican party as he did and still mount a campaign that almost carried the state for the Republicans in 1888. There was to be no comparable leader in any Southern state for the remainder of the century. But there was to be an issue of even greater transcendence than the public debt or the schools. It was the great agricultural depression of the 1890's. It would affect the whole South, not a state here and there. This was the issue that produced the Populist upheaval at the end of the century—itself the last great example of the Other South for another half-century.

51. George M. Wallace to Charlotte Tapscott, May 23, 1882, John Clopton Papers; F. U. Northup to William Mahone, Nov. 16, 1883, William Mahone Papers; Blake, *William Mahone,* p. 171n.; Chicago *Inter Ocean,* Nov. 12, 1885, clipping in Scrapbook XXXV, William Mahone Papers; Moger, *Virginia,* p. 69.

10

The Last Great Dissent

The decade of the 1890's was one of upheaval, North and South, in cities and countryside, among industrial workers and dirt farmers. For that reason, if for no other, it is easy to lump Southern Populists with Northern and to consider both as farmers in common revolt against growing dominance by industry. Historians, like many of the participants at the time, have been prone to do just that. To do so, however, is to lose sight of the special character of the Southern Populists, who were more like Scalawags and Mahone's Readjusters than they were like rebellious farmers in Kansas or South Dakota.

A RENEWED RECONSTRUCTION

During the Populist revolt in the South, men were forcefully reminded of earlier conflicts, before and during the War, and especially during Reconstruction, when class and racial antagonisms threatened the social order. One Alabama Democratic paper, for example, asserted that the Populists were to be found "in the mountain coves, where ignorance and superstition, suspicion and envy reigned, where deserters and mossbacks flourished during the war, where moonshiners and feudists stalked at large." A Southern Populist told a Northerner in 1896 that to be a member of the People's party in the South "may cost me my life. I can return home only at that risk. The feeling of the Democracy against us is one of murderous hate," he contended. "I have been shot at many times. Grand juries will not indict our assailants. Courts will give us no protection." And murders were as common as they had been during the last days of Reconstruction. During the campaign of 1892 in Georgia it was said that fifteen men had been killed for their politics. The killings in Mississippi in 1894 reminded men of the desperate days of 1875, when Radical rule was violently overthrown. All over the South in the 1890's the Democrats appealed to race in opposing the Populist party because the new party threatened the one-party system that had been forged during Reconstruction. "The man blessed with a white cuticle," said one Virginia Democrat in 1892, "is false if he does not in this emergency cooperate with the Democratic party. As my father used to say, 'deserters since the war are worse than deserters during the war!' Let them feel the weight of Democratic condemnation," he urged.[1]

Years later, in 1910, Tom Watson, the best-known Southern Populist, emphasized the special problems confronted by Southern, as contrasted with Western, Populists. He compared his electoral difficulties with those of Nebraskan William Jennings Bryan. "Consider the advantage of position Bryan had over me," Watson wrote. "His field of work was the plastic, restless, and growing West; mine was the hide-bound, rock-ribbed Bourbon South. Besides Bryan had *no everlasting and overshadowing Negro Question to hamper and handicap* his progress: I HAD." A Georgia Democrat also remarked in later years that the illegalities and violent measures taken to defeat the Populists were as justified as those that had been employed to end Reconstruction. "We had to do it," he contended. "Those d—— Populists would have ruined the coun-

1. Joseph H. Taylor, "Populism and Disfranchisement in Alabama," *Journal of Negro History*, XXXIV (1949), 418; Theodore Saloutos, *Farmer Movements in the South, 1865–1933* (Berkeley and Los Angeles, 1960), p. 146; C. Vann Woodward, *Tom Watson, Agrarian Rebel* (New York, 1938), p. 237; Albert D. Kirwan, *Revolt of the Rednecks: Mississippi Politics, 1876–1925* (Lexington, Ky., 1951), p. 96; William DuBose Sheldon, *Populism in the Old Dominion: Virginia Farm Politics, 1885–1900* (Princeton, 1935), pp. 87–88.

try!"[2] In the minds of traditional Southerners, that is loyal Democrats, the Populists were as bad as Scalawags or Readjusters: traitors to the party of Jefferson, to the South, and to the white race.

CONSERVATIVE ROOTS

If Populists ultimately came to be dissenters in a class with Republicans and Readjusters, they certainly did not start that way.[3] Prior to becoming Populists the great majority of them seem to have been much like the average Southerner. All the well-known leaders of the Southern Populists, for example, had been Democrats: Marion Butler of North Carolina, Tom Watson of Georgia, Thomas Nugent of Texas, John Tetts of Louisiana, and Reuben Kolb of Alabama. The only Populist leader of significance who had been a Republican was John B. Rayner of Texas. But he was a Negro and would hardly have been a Democrat before he became a Populist. Benjamin F. Brian, the president of the Louisiana Populist Convention of 1891, had been an Independent in 1880–84, but the residents of Winn Parish, where Brian lived, were scarcely typical Populists, as we shall have occasion to notice later. Joseph C. Manning, the outspoken and radical Alabama Populist, claimed that becoming a Populist "was just in me; I was

2. Woodward, *Tom Watson*, p. 220; Alex Mathews Arnett, *The Populist Movement in Georgia* (New York, 1922), p. 184.
3. Populists themselves, even in retrospect, did not always recognize the similarity between Scalawags and themselves. Witness, for example, the remarks of a radical Populist writing in 1924: "When the carpet-baggers invaded the South, the vicious and evil-disposed among them started a propaganda of social equality among the Negroes and the disreputable scalawags in poisoning the Negroes against the whites. The Negro was slow to accept the theory of social equality. Respect for the white man was a part of his nature. He had never known freedom, and respect for the superior race that had held him in slavery was a part of his being. The Negro's respect for the superior race and his reverence for the white women of the South held him in check and it was not until he was brought face to face with the vices and corrupt practices of the disreputable politicians who coddled him that the Negro lost respect for the white man." William Henry Skaggs, *The Southern Oligarchy* (New York, 1924), pp. 320–21.

never a Bourbon Democrat."[4] Yet it is not clear what he had been if not a Democrat. His father and brothers were lifelong Democrats, and there is no evidence he had been a Republican. The traditional political origins of most Populist leaders were stressed also by the historian of Virginia Populism. He observed that if a Populist leader had been politically active during the Readjuster period he was likely to have been a Conservative, not a follower of Mahone.

The Populists themselves often emphasized their Democratic and conservative origins. "The People's Party is composed of the most conservative elements of the old parties," wrote the North Carolina leader Marion Butler in 1894. "It is composed of men who want the present wrongs righted by due process of legislation and execution of law. The old party machines are to-day playing the part of anarchists by refusing to observe and execute laws, and playing the part of traitors and tyrannists by passing laws in the interest of the few against the interest of the many."[5] One scholar has found that the Populists in the Texas legislature during the 1890's averaged five years older than the Democrats. And this difference was not simply because of the advanced age of a few. Fourteen of the Democratic legislators were younger than thirty, while out of forty-four Populist legislators, only one was less than thirty.

TO BECOME A POPULIST

Why did men become Populists, especially when to break with the dominant Democratic party was fraught with real danger to the man who was so bold? The obvious and traditional answer, of course, is that they were farmers who found the depression of the late 1880's and early 1890's intolerable. And it is true that almost all the Populist leaders came out of farm organizations like the

4. Jerrell H. Schafner and William W. Rogers, "Joseph C. Manning: Militant Agrarian, Enduring Populist," *Alabama Historical Quarterly*, XXIX (1967), 8.

5. H. Larry Ingle, "A Southern Democrat at Large: William Hodge Kitchin and the Populist Party," *North Carolina Historical Review*, XLV (1968), 179.

Farmers' Alliance or The Wheel. When the unhappy farmers saw that their economic problems were not being solved or alleviated by private organizations, and that the possible solutions required governmental intervention or support, they turned increasingly to politics. Then, when it became evident that the traditional political instrument of Southern farmers, the Democratic party, was not sufficiently sympathetic, many looked to another means for influencing government, that is, to a third party. In the South, only fifteen years after Reconstruction, it was not easy to make a break to a third party. One Alabamian who had been a Democrat for forty years said that in deserting his party for the Populists he had "never performed a more painful duty." A Virginian who became a Populist recalled that "it is like cutting off the right hand or putting out the right eye."[6] In those days, after all, to be a white Southerner was to be a Democrat, and vice versa.

Farm unrest and dissatisfaction with the economic status quo were deep and widespread in the South of the 1890's, but it is a measure of the loyalty to the Democratic party that in some states the People's party never did become popular. Usually this was because the Democratic party responded positively to the farmers' needs. Or, put more precisely, the farmers' needs were found to be less weighty when measured against the dangers of splitting the white vote. South Carolina, for example, never had a Populist party of significance, though it did have a farmers' movement. Its political manifestation, however, was the Democratic party under the leadership of "Pitchfork Ben" Tillman. Florida, Arkansas, and Tennessee did not have important Populist organizations, either. But in Texas, North Carolina, Georgia, Louisiana, and Alabama the agrarian revolt was no less than a political and social earthquake, and in Virginia and Mississippi it was at least a major tremor.

One way of getting at why Southerners became Populists is to look at the reasons offered by those who did join the party. Some of the leaders, of whom William H. Kitchin of North Carolina was an example, joined the Populists because they were simply fed up with Grover Cleveland, the conservative Democrat in the White

6. C. Vann Woodward, *The Origins of the New South* (Baton Rouge, 1951), p. 244.

House. As one Virginia farmer said in 1892, Cleveland's nomination "snapped the last cord which binds free men to the Democratic party." Actually it took Kitchin until 1894 before his hostility to Cleveland moved him to the Populist party. Since the roots of his shift were conservative, he sought to prevent the party from standing for anything more radical than free silver and the repudiation of Grover Cleveland. Not too surprisingly, therefore, in 1896 he went back to the Democratic party.

More characteristic of the motives behind the Populism of the leaders was that expressed by Thomas Lewis Nugent, the Populist candidate for governor of Texas in 1892 and 1894. Nugent said that he left the Democratic party to become a Populist because his old party had forsaken its principle of "Equal rights to all, special privileges to none." His conversion to Populism was derived from his sympathy with the farmers' cause, and, unlike Kitchin, he remained a Populist until his death.[7] Frank Burkitt, the leader of Mississippi Populists, was a leader in the Farmers' Alliance and a delegate to the constitutional convention of 1890. Nugent left the Democratic party in 1889, but Burkitt was still trying to support the farmers' cause within the Democratic party as late as 1891. That year he was so outraged by the Democrats' counting out of the farmers' candidate that he joined the Populists. Marion Butler of North Carolina, like so many of the Populist leaders, came out of the Farmers' Alliance, too. Butler was distinguished among the Populists by his youth. Nugent was in his sixties when he became a Populist, but Butler was only thirty-three years old when he headed the state Populist party, the national organization of the Southern Alliance, and was a senator from North Carolina.

The conclusions drawn from these examples of the background of Populist leaders are borne out by what systematic studies exist on the background of the Populist elite. An analysis of 126 Populist leaders in Texas, for instance, reveals that about half of the group were farmers and only one-quarter lawyers. On the other hand, about half of the Democratic leaders were lawyers. An analysis of Texas legislators reveals even more dramatically the

7. *Ibid.*, p. 179; Ingle, "Southern Democrat," pp. 179–82; Wayne Alvord, "T. L. Nugent, Texas Populist," *Southwestern Historical Quarterly,* LVII (1953), 65–81.

difference between the backgrounds of the leaders in the two parties. In 1894, about 73 percent of the 22 Populist legislators were farmers, while fewer than 22 percent of the Democrats were farmers. In three legislatures in Texas during the 1890's, 48 percent of the Democrats were lawyers while there was not one among the Populists. As these figures suggest, Populist votes in Texas were concentrated in the poor farming areas rather than in agricultural sections in general.

When Populists entered the Virginia legislature in 1891, one historian of the state has written, that body contained more farmers and fewer lawyers "than any in Virginia for twenty-five years." One-half of the Populists elected to the Louisiana legislature in 1896 were listed as planters or farmers. And in Louisiana, as in Texas, Populism was strongest in those parts of the state where the small farmers were located, that is, in the northwestern, western, and southwestern parts of the state. "Populism never gained much of a foothold in the cotton parishes of the delta, or in the sugar parishes," one of its leaders later remarked. The recent historian of Populism in Alabama finds a similar pattern. The character of Alabama Populism is complex, Sheldon Hackney warns, "but the single most powerful predictor of Populism in a county was the rate at which farm tenancy increased in the county during the decade of the 1890's."[8]

The other side of the coin of the farmer basis of Populism was the lack of support given Populist candidates in the cities of the South. This was certainly true in Virginia and Louisiana. Populism was never strong in New Orleans, for example. In fact in 1892 the Populist candidate for governor received 71 votes out of 40,000 cast in that city. Roscoe Martin, the historian of Populism in Texas, demonstrated that there was a high correlation between Populist strength and the absence of towns in a county. In east Texas, for example, three counties had high Populist percentages, but counties on either side of them showed low Populist support;

8. Alwyn Barr, *Reconstruction to Reform: Texas Politics, 1876–1906* (Austin, 1971), pp. 149–50; Allen W. Moger, *Virginia: Bourbonism to Byrd* (Charlottesville, 1968), p. 102; Melvin Johnson White, "Populism in Louisiana During the Nineties," *Mississippi Valley Historical Review*, V (1918), 14–15; Sheldon Hackney, *Populism to Progressivism in Alabama* (Princeton, 1969), p. 25.

these latter counties had sizable towns. The same pattern was discernible in Georgia, where the counties with substantial towns consistently returned a Populist vote of less than 45 percent while neighboring counties without cities went heavily for Populism.

Given the farmer background of so many Populist leaders and voters it is not surprising that Populists displayed a characteristic that was also noticeable among Scalawags. Many of the Populist leaders were political nobodies before they ran for office. None of the eight legislators elected on the Populist slate in 1892 in Texas, for example, had served in the legislature before; in 1894 only two out of the twenty-two elected that year had previously been a legislator. By contrast, 30 percent of the Democratic legislators were repeaters. In fact, so fresh were the Populist officials in Texas that Roscoe Martin concludes that it may account for their higher rate of corruption! They were simply more naïve and more politically inexperienced than the Democrats. When Hackney tried to identify the origins of the Alabama Populist legislators in 1894 he could do so for only nine of the thirty-five. Yet he uncovered the origins of thirty-six of the sixty-five Democrats. Not one of the Populist legislators was either a lawyer or a college graduate, while fourteen of the Democrats had graduated from college and half of them were lawyers or judges. Twenty-eight of the Democrats in the Alabama legislature—out of sixty-four—had been officers in the Civil War, but only nine of the thirty-three Populists had been officers, although almost all of them were Confederate veterans.

Given the newness of the Populists to politics, it is not surprising that some of their heads of state tickets were virtual unknowns. Robert Tannehill, the Populist candidate for governor in Louisiana in 1892, was a fairly prosperous sawmill and cotton gin owner, but he was almost a stranger outside of Winn Parish; the only office he had held before was that of sheriff. That same year the Populist candidate for governor in Arkansas was J. P. Carnahan, a schoolteacher who had almost no experience in politics.

Although many Populists were political unknowns and many Populist voters were marginal farmers, the Populist leadership, like the Republican leadership during Reconstruction, was not confined to the lowest levels of Southern society. Many of the leaders may have been farmers, but they were, nevertheless, often quite well-to-do. Tom Watson, the Georgia leader, for example, was one of the largest landowners in Georgia; he was said to have had more tenants on his land than his grandfather had slaves. Reuben Kolb of Alabama was not only commissioner of agriculture, but a successful seed-house owner as well. Marion Butler may have been born on a farm, but he was also a graduate of the University of North Carolina. The Populist candidate for governor in Virginia in 1893, Edmund Randolph Cocke, was reputed to be the wealthiest farmer in southside Virginia. Moreover, as his name suggests, Cocke, like several other Virginia Populists, derived from one of the first families of the state.

A PARTY OF NATIVE PROTESTANTS

Since the South as a whole was overwhelmingly Protestant and native born, it is to be expected that the Populists were almost entirely Protestant. But it was an active Protestantism. The earnestness of Populists, wrote a Texas newspaper in 1892, "bordering on religious fanaticism, has a touch of the kind of metal that made Cromwell's round heads so terrible a force in the revolution that ended with bringing the head of Charles I to the block." The party convention of Texas opened with a prayer in which it was declared that "God is with the Populists in their efforts to regain their liberty and escape from the bondage in which they had been placed." And when James Field, the national Populist candidate for Vice-President, was campaigning in his native Virginia in 1892, he not only exhorted his listeners to recognize the connection between the Populist principles and those of 1776, but he commanded them to "read your Bible every Sunday and the Omaha Platform every day in the week." Cyclone Davis of Texas went further when he insisted that "the Bible is our model." Populist meetings seemed to observers often like religious revivals, so intimately did politics and religion come together.[9]

9. Roscoe C. Martin, *The People's Party of Texas: A Study in Third Party Politics* (Austin, 1933), p. 85; Sheldon, *Populism in the Old Dominion,* p. 76; Charles A. Cannon, "The Ideology of Texas Populism, 1886–1894," unpublished M.A. essay, Rice University, 1968, pp. 79–80, 28.

Ministers were also conspicuous in the movement. In North Carolina, for example, the Reverend P. L. Groome aroused the animus of the Democratic party because he used the *North Carolina Christian Advocate,* which he edited, to push Populist principles. He not only advocated an inflated currency as a "vital interest of humanity," with which many Democrats could agree, but he also expressed doubts about erecting new factories when they employed people at low wages and for long hours. His theme, he acknowledged, was "applied Christianity," which meant "that the warfare against evil should be initiated by the Church and the religious press" and carried on until the state acts. Another North Carolina minister, Cyrus Thompson, became secretary of the state's Populist party. His public attacks on the failure of the church to confront social problems as a Christian duty struck a responsive chord in some Populists. "You are the first man in all my knowledge," wrote one, "that has yet arraigned the pulpit for its inactivity and silence on the side of the reform of the day." Populist leaders in the state publicly and privately supported Thompson when he came under attack from conventional clergymen.

The use of what amounted to social gospel arguments from Populists was most evident in the speeches of the Texas leader Thomas L. Nugent. Nugent was not a conventional Protestant, since he was a Swedenborgian. Moreover, he saw Christ as more than simply the Redeemer. "The Christ of history is not an ecclesiastic, nor a politician, nor a cultural theorist," he said in one speech. "He was a 'man of the people.' " To Nugent, Christ was not a creator of a new orthodoxy or system, but an opponent of dogmas. "I am not a theologian, nor even a member of any church," Nugent pointed out, "yet in this wonderful man and his work I see the ideal reform . . . giving his life to the work of arresting the evil tendencies inherent in the world's social and political institutions." Nugent's social gospel approach to religion was the result of his own thinking, since he apparently did not read

---

Michael Paul Rogin, *The Intellectuals and McCarthy: The Radical Specter* (Cambridge, Mass., 1967), pp. 179–80, also emphasizes the revivalist and "grass roots" aspects of Populism.

or even know about the great social gospel writers who were then transforming Protestantism, especially in the North.[10]

Wherever and whenever Populists espoused a social gospel approach it came under attack. Religiously based criticisms of social conditions helped to undermine the status quo in the minds of conservatives, just as attacks on the Democratic party or doubts about the validity of white supremacy struck at the supports of the Bourbon South. During his campaigns for governor, Nugent was attacked for his religious unorthodoxy, and in North Carolina the Reverend Groome and others like him found themselves under attack from fellow clergymen as well as from the leaders of the Democratic party. Orthodox church leaders asserted that "sound money" (gold) and "sound morals" went hand in hand. One clergyman even contended that the church ought to "align itself with the powers that be," for that would prevent social disorder.[11]

Because Populists were overwhelmingly Protestants, their popular appeal was restricted. There were only a few areas of the South where Catholics were strong—in southern Texas and coastal Louisiana—but where the census showed many Catholic churches, there the party was correspondingly weak. For example, in eleven Texas counties, in which 82 percent of the church members were Catholic, the Populists harvested few votes. In 1894 the Democratic candidate for governor received from these counties six times the number of votes that were given to his Populist opponent. In that same year, in Louisiana, the French Catholic parishes of Lafayette and St. Martin cast not a single Populist ballot. The Catholics well knew that most of the Populist leaders were Baptists. As a consequence, in Louisiana and Texas, the Populists often felt called upon to deny that they were anti-Catholic. (Unfortunately, not all Southern Populists were prepared to make that denial. In Georgia, for example, the party came out in favor of separation of church and state, which in the political context

10. Frederick A. Bode, "Religion and Class Hegemony: A Populist Critique in North Carolina," *Journal of Southern History*, XXXVII (1971), 417–38; Nugent's speech is in Norman Pollack, ed., *The Populist Mind* (Indianapolis, 1967), p. 303; Alvord, "T. L. Nugent," pp. 72–73.
11. Bode, "Religion and Class Hegemony," pp. 424–25.

was a friendly signal to the American-Protective Association, a violently anti-Catholic organization.)[12] Even in Texas the Populist interest in Catholic voters was not high. One Texas leader asserted in 1896 that there existed a large territory south of the Nueces River, which embraced eight counties, into which no Populist speaker or organization had gone except at Corpus Christi and Laredo.

It was not only Catholic Mexican-Americans that Populists failed to enlist in the cause. To the Swedes and the Czechs in Texas the Populists paid scant more attention in their organizing drives than to the Mexican-Americans. Populists did try to recruit the Germans, but with no more success. Only one county of the five that contained 50 percent or more Germans went Populist in the 1890's, and that was in 1896 when the Populists endorsed the Republican presidential candidate. (Most Texas Germans were Republicans.)

One reason for the failure to win support among Texas Germans was that Populists were so Southern that they could not always keep their unfamiliarity with ethnic voters out of their speeches. Thus a leader could blithely refer to Germans as the "base element in our country." Or a voter could write to a Populist newspaper asserting that "the worst and most dangerous part of the population of the United States are foreigners . . . we want neither Bohemians nor Chinamen." Another reason was that Germans were wary of Populist intentions. The large number of Protestant preachers in the party and the presence of a former leader of the Prohibition movement in the party's state councils made the Germans fear for their beer halls. The German language press ridiculed the Populists as backwoodsmen or laughable rustics.[13] An exception to this general failure with ethnic voters was the strong support that the Populists received from foreign-born miners in northern Alabama in 1892 and 1894.

12. Robert Saunders, "The Transformation of Tom Watson, 1894–1895," *Georgia Historical Quarterly,* LIV (1970), 343.

13. William Ivy Hair, *Bourbonism and Agrarian Protest: Louisiana Politics, 1877–1900* (Baton Rouge, 1969), p. 244; Barr, *Reconstruction to Reform,* pp. 152–53; Martin, *People's Party in Texas,* p. 107; Cannon, "Ideology of Texas Populism," p. 93.

FRIENDS OF ALL WORKERS

An explanation for the exception in Alabama seems to lie with the diligent efforts the Populists made to enlist the support of organized labor. Although there were not many unions in Texas, the leaders of the few labor groups that existed in the state were strongly represented among Populist speakers. For their part, the Populist party in Texas advocated an eight-hour day for public employees, improvements in the mechanics' lien law, and removal of convict labor from competition with free labor. And Populist legislators did introduce bills in behalf of industrial labor, though they were invariably voted down. In Tennessee, too, the Populist platform opposed the convict lease system because of its competition with free labor, and advocated the prohibition of child labor in factories.

Alabama Populists also pushed labor legislation like removal of convict labor from the coal mines and the prohibition of children under thirteen years of age from working in the mines. The party condemned the Democratic governor's use of state troops against miners and railroad workers during the strikes of 1894. Populists in the Alabama legislature were not always consistent in supporting labor bills, but they were about as consistent in this regard as they were on other reform legislation in which they had a more direct interest.

At bottom, of course, the Populists were a farmers' party, not a labor party. The support they gave to industrial labor derived from their self-conception as the advocates of all workingmen, urban as well as rural. As a result they often spoke and wrote as if they were an arm of the proletarian revolution. And some historians have been taken in by their rhetoric. The fact was that the Populists were reformers rather than revolutionaries. Despite their undeniably radical rhetoric, their principal concern was to help the farmer get better prices for his crops and to reduce the costs of the things he had to buy. Indeed, their best-known, though not most important, plank—free silver—was just that. By inflating the currency, free silver was intended to reverse the downward movement of farm prices and thereby increase the farmer's income. A more important proposal, particularly to Southern Populists, who devised it, was the so-called subtreasury plan. It provided that the government would set up warehouses in every county, to which farmers could bring their wheat, cotton, or other crops for storage. On the basis of that collateral, farmers were to be lent money by the federal government at a very low rate of interest. Since most farmers usually borrowed money to tide them over until harvest time, the subtreasury plan would reduce interest charges, which were a major cost in farm operation.

The subtreasury plan was widely recognized as the most radical proposal of the Populists. Generally, Southern farmers were more interested in the subtreasury plan than Northern farmers. The Virginia farmers pronounced it more important than free silver, for example. Many Southern Democrats who were sympathetic to the farmers' plight could and did support free silver, especially as 1896 approached, but few Southern Democrats supported the subtreasury. Zebulon Vance, an important Democratic senator from North Carolina, for example, in 1892 introduced a bill to enact the subtreasury plan, but he admitted that he could not vote for it. Even some Populist groups found the subtreasury too radical. The state Populist convention of Georgia under the leadership of Tom Watson in 1895 dropped the subtreasury plan from its platform. So did the state party in Tennessee in 1892.[14]

Populists also came out for control and sometimes ownership of railroads and other corporations. In practice, however, they were much less radical than some of their rhetoric made them seem. In Alabama, for example, the Populist legislators divided eleven to eight to stop the establishment of a regulatory commission for railroads, a position that was favored by the railroads and a division that was about the same as that among the Democratic legislators. Reuben Kolb, the farmers' candidate for governor in 1892, and later a Populist, did not agree with those who said he was for the people and against corporations. "I am friendly to corporations, and I am also friendly to the best interest of the men whom

14. Saloutos, *Farmer Movements in the South,* p. 120; Saunders, "Transformation of . . . Watson," p. 343; Daniel Merrett Robison, *Bob Taylor and the Agrarian Revolt in Tennessee* (Chapel Hill, N.C., 1935), pp. 170–71.

the corporations employ," he said. "Individuals cannot develop our mineral resources, cannot easily build furnaces and factories. Corporations are, therefore, necessary to the working men and to the general well being of the community. I am not fighting corporations," he emphasized. "I am trying to be just to all. My election will work no harm to organized capital." Thomas L. Nugent, the Populist candidate for governor in Texas, was more outspoken than Kolb against monopolies. Yet Nugent saw large enterprises as no more than excesses of capitalism, not integral evils that called into question the whole system. Even big corporations, he said, were acceptable if they were moderate in their behavior and were not unfair to competitors.[15]

The Populists did not object to the system; they merely wanted a fair chance to prosper under it. They had been led to believe— for they were fervent followers of Jefferson and other early patriots —that America was the home of opportunity. A chance to realize that promise was what they felt was being denied them and which could be theirs if the principles of Populism were put into practice. They were not revolutionaries; they were just people who asked that the rules of the system be obeyed. And if the rules were honored, the Populists believed, all would be well. In fact, it was the Populists' belief in the validity of the rules that made them so prone to see conspiracies and cabals around them. It was those people who did not play by the rules that caused the trouble for those who did. It was not the fault of the system, but of those who did not live up to it. Since, in the mind of the Populists, the rules of the social and economic game were fundamentally sound, it followed that the failure of the farmers and other workers to make a decent living was because certain Americans or foreigners conspired to prevent the system from working as it was intended.

To conclude that Populists in the South, like Populists elsewhere in the nation, were reformers, not revolutionaries, is not enough. True as that conclusion may be in regard to Populists as a whole, it leaves us without an adequate understanding of the Populists as Southern dissenters. Perhaps the most important fact about South-

15. James F. Doster, "Were Populists Against Railroad Corporations? The Case of Alabama," *Journal of Southern History,* XX (1954), 397; Alvord, "T. L. Nugent," p. 80.

ern Populism, as we have seen already, is the intense hostility and fear that it aroused. Older men were transported back to Reconstruction by the violence and conflicts of the Populist era, and even men who were too young to have lived through the earlier days could not help but recognize the dangers. "More or less . . . the man who broke with his old party and joined our ranks has been under a ban," remarked Marion Butler in 1896. "He has been subjected to every sort of persecution, petty and great, that it was in the province of his neighbors to bestow. In the South it was social ostracism. . . ."[16] It could also be injury or death. What was it, then, about Populism that aroused such hostility?

THE POPULIST THREAT

The explanation for this hostility and fear cannot be found in any particular plank of the Populist platform. Many Democrats often supported one or more Populist ideas. Free silver, for example, which was a prominent Populist proposal, was eventually taken up by the Democratic party itself, while on the other hand, as we have seen, not all Southern Populists accepted the radical subtreasury plan. The real threat of Populism lay in the fact that the new party cut like a knife into the going politicosocial order of the South. By contesting with the dominant Democratic party, the Populists made possible for the first time since Reconstruction a functioning two-party system. (Mahone had done that in one state, but Populism promised to do it in the whole South.) The Populists first of all threatened the dominance of the Democrats, which was sufficient in itself to arouse the Democratic machines throughout the region. Behind that threat, however, lay much more than a danger to bureaucrats' or politicians' jobs and offices, however important that may have been to some Democrats. Behind it lay the rejuvenation of the Republican party—the party that had brought on Reconstruction.

Historians of Populism have not been able to ignore the connection between Populists and Republicans, of course. But they have generally minimized the significance of the connection, seeing it as

16. Carl Snyder, "Marion Butler," *Review of Reviews* (Oct., 1896), p. 432.

little more than a matter of political expediency. When C. Vann Woodward, for example, discussed the efforts at fusion or cooperation between the two parties, he described "the binding force [as] . . . plainly expediency, and the only principle Republicans and Populists proclaimed in common was the demand for 'a free ballot and an honest election.' "[17] Yet it is worth emphasizing that it was just this common demand for free and honest elections that threatened the Democrats and the Bourbon South. More important still, historians have too often forgotten that without Republicans the Populists would have been much less successful. One can go even further: it was the example as well as the presence of the Republicans that served as a stimulus to the Populist effort to challenge the Democratic dominance of Southern politics. Ultimately, as we shall see, the Populists were forced to become, as Southern white Republicans were already, true dissenters from the Southern tradition, rather than merely reformers within the standard political order.

In some states Republican support for farmer groups began before the nineties. In Arkansas in 1888, for example, the farmer-dominated Union Labor party candidate for governor was supported by the Republicans. As a result, and despite much fraud, he came within 15,000 votes of the Democratic winner. Two years later the vote for the Union Labor party was just as big. From 1890 on, the Democrats raised the race issue in Arkansas to protect their one-party domination of politics. Therefore, when the Republicans in 1892 refused to join with the newly formed Populists, the Populist candidate for governor came in behind the Republican in the election. At that juncture the Democratic state government moved to disfranchise blacks, the mainstay of the Republican party. Thereafter, the Populist party made no headway in Arkansas.

In Texas, too, the fortunes of Populism were tied closely to the Republicans. In 1894, for example, Jerome Kearby, a Populist candidate for Congress in eastern Texas, carried Dallas, city and county, and almost the whole congressional district with the help of Republican votes. Yet Thomas Nugent, who was running at the same time for governor as the Populist candidate but without

17. Woodward, *Origins of the New South*, p. 276.

Republican support, lost the city of Dallas by 1,400 votes and the county by 2,300. When the Republicans did *not* nominate rival candidates in these counties in 1896–98, the Populists picked up new votes. But once the Republicans entered candidates in those counties the Populist vote fell sharply. When the Republicans put a full ticket into the state competition in 1900, Populism died in Texas.

During the early years of Populism in Virginia, Mahone was still the leader of the Republicans. (He died in 1895.) The one congressional candidate that the Populists probably elected in 1892, though he was actually counted out by the Democratic machine, was the man whom Mahone supported and against whom a Republican candidate did not run. In the election of 1893 for governor, Mahone did not put a Republican candidate into the field on the ground that the election of a Populist "means fair voting in Virginia." As a result, the Populist candidate's vote jumped by 70,000 votes from the election a year before. Significantly, the Populist strength in Virginia was in the southside and in the southwestern counties, where Republican votes had long been concentrated. The ten Populists who were elected to the state legislature were from these areas; they had had no Republican opponents in their campaigns. The significant contribution of the Republicans to Populist success in Virginia was demonstrated in the congressional elections of 1894. No fusion between Populists and Republicans was worked out that year; as a result, the total Populist vote was only 10,000, even though several of the candidates were the leading farm spokesmen of the state.[18]

The closest the Populists came to success in Louisiana was in the governor's race in April, 1896, when Populists joined with Republicans. The fusion candidate was John N. Pharr, a white Republican sugar planter of considerable wealth. Pharr is an authentic Other Southerner aside from his willingness to associate with Populists. In the course of a long political life he had been a Whig, a Democrat, a Prohibitionist, and, finally, a Republican. Although sixty-seven years of age in 1896, and worth at least three-

18. Robert Saunders, "Southern Populists and the Negro, 1893–1895," *Journal of Negro History,* LIV (1969), 257; Sheldon, *Populism in the Old Dominion,* pp. 101–3, 108–10.

quarters of a million dollars, he advocated a number of Populist planks, including free silver. To some Republicans he was more of a Populist than a Republican. The Democrats hated him for being willing to run with the support of blacks, who, it was never forgotten in Louisiana Democratic circles, constituted a majority of the population. Pharr defended his position before whites. "I was reared with the Negro and worked side by side with him for twenty odd years," he said once. "I may say for all my life I never have found him other than a good laborer and as honest as most other men. If he has cut a bad figure in politics, we are to blame for it." Old-line Democrats were horrified at the mixing of the races in the campaign. "At the Pharr meeting yesterday," wrote conservative William Porcher Miles, "Henry McCall conducted his wife on his arm through the seething mass of black bucks . . . redolent with the genuine African odor (the day being warm) and seated her with the handful of 'ladies' present. Ye Gods! He must be crazy. . . ."

Vilifications of Pharr and other Fusion candidates that year were common. Fusion meetings were broken up by stink bombs and shootings. A Populist print shop in one town was burned, and in another the Board of Health harassed Fusionist candidates by putting them in jail for violation of obscure health ordinances. In that year alone there were twenty-one lynchings in the state, one-fifth of all the lynchings in the whole United States.

Pharr was defeated by 26,000 votes out of 206,000 cast. That his defeat was the result of fraud seems obvious from the fact that the Democratic candidate's largest majorities came from those parishes where Negro registration was heaviest and despite the fact that Pharr was a well-known Republican. Pharr carried twenty-five of the thirty-two predominantly white parishes in the state and four of the black ones.

Fraud had been so patent in the election that the months between the election and the meeting of the legislature, when the illegalities could be protested, were filled with the danger of civil war. Armed whites and blacks threatened to assault the parish courthouses to obtain the ballot boxes. When a group of black Fusionists seized a ballot box in one parish, the militia was called out. In another parish, the killing of two white men also brought out the militia. One rumor said that nine thousand angry white Populists from the hill country were preparing to march on the state capital. In the end, however, as had occurred in Alabama in 1894 when similar frauds had been perpetrated by Democrats against Populists, the Louisiana Fusionists decided not to resort to armed rebellion. Instead they relied on the fairness of the legislature, even though it would be dominated by Democrats. The legislature, however, refused to investigate the returns. With that decision the Populist movement collapsed in Louisiana.[19]

Undoubtedly the most successful electoral effort by Southern Populists took place in North Carolina. Again, however, that success was dependent upon Republicans, those creations of Reconstruction, those whites who had long cooperated with black Southerners. Early in the 1890's the Populists in North Carolina worked out a fusion arrangement with the Republicans. As a result, the two parties won both houses of the legislature in 1894 as well as the supreme court and state treasurer offices. (In 1892 when there was no fusion, the Populists captured only 18 percent of the vote, while the Republicans won 35 percent.)

FUSION IN NORTH CAROLINA

The greatest triumph over the Democrats came in 1896. The Populists, it is true, nominated their own candidate for governor instead of endorsing the Republican nominee, Daniel L. Russell. But below the level of governor, the two parties informally worked out a fusion or joint ticket, which carried the state. Populists and Republicans overwhelmed both houses of the legislature, and Russell outran his Democratic opponent by more than 8,000 votes, even though the Populist gubernatorial candidate had drawn away 31,000 votes. If not many white Populists voted for Russell, even fewer blacks voted for Guthrie, the Populist, for just before the election he had counseled the party to fuse with the Democrats, rather than with the Republicans! On the other hand, it was

19. The quotation from Pharr is in Perry H. Howard, *Political Tendencies in Louisiana* (rev. and expanded ed., Baton Rouge, 1971), p. 183; the quotation from Miles is in James Amedee Gaudet Papers, William P. Miles to Henry Eustis, April 20, 1896; see also Hair, *Bourbonism and Agrarian Protest*, pp. 252, 260–68.

the Republican "angel," millionaire Benjamin N. Duke of the Tobacco Trust, who kept the Populist state organ of Marion Butler solvent. During 1896 Duke secretly contributed $1,000 to the *Caucasian,* which was apparently unable to survive without this support.[20]

The victory of fusion and Russell in North Carolina was the second example since Reconstruction of a successful political alternative to the Democratic party. In North Carolina, in the 1890's, as in Mahone's Virginia in the 1880's, the trick depended upon a coalition between white Democratic dissidents and black and white Republicans. For in both instances the Republicans had brought more to the fusion than black votes, important as they were. Since blacks did not constitute a majority in either state, a victory over the Democrats required substantial defections among the whites. In Virginia the controversy over the debt had supplied the issue that could do it; in North Carolina the concern over the plight of the farmer was the needed push. But in both instances, the prior existence of a black-and-white Republican party was the foundation. As recently as 1888 the Republican vote in North Carolina had reached 134,000, which was 25,000 beyond the number of black males over twenty-one according to the census of 1890. In short, even if one made the unrealistic assumption that every black entitled to vote cast a ballot in 1888, the white Republicans would number 25,000. Actually, estimates of the number of white Republicans ranged from 60,000 to 92,000. The figure of 75,000 was not an excessively high estimate of the number of white North Carolinians who could be counted on to oppose the Democrats, even without the issue of farm reform to energize them.

But if the Republicans were essential to the Populists for such a victory, to discerning and alarmed Democrats it was equally evident that without Populist support the Republican success in

20. On the election of 1896 in North Carolina see Helen G. Edmonds, *The Negro and Fusion Politics in North Carolina, 1894–1901* (Chapel Hill, N.C., 1951), pp. 26, 37, 53–56; Duke's support of the *Caucasian* can be followed in the Benjamin Duke Papers, particularly W. F. Stroud to Benjamin Duke, April 2, 1896, Thomas Settle to Benjamin Duke, April 18, 1896, W. H. Worth to Benjamin Duke, April 18, 26, 1896, and in Duke Letterbooks: Benjamin Duke to W. H. Worth, April 20, August 5, 1896.

capturing the governorship for the first time since Reconstruction would have been impossible. It was this role of putting into power the hated Republicans and humiliating or endangering the Democratic organization that caused so many white Southerners to view the Populists with hostility. It was the willingness to risk bringing Republicans back into power that reminded good Democrats so forcefully of Reconstruction and moved them to take up again the violent reprisals that had been so successful in that earlier crisis. Supporting Republicans or helping them to achieve office by splitting the white vote, as in North Carolina, was certainly a sin in the eyes of Democrats. But the cardinal sin of Populism was that it brought blacks to power.

IN SUPPORT OF NEGRO SUFFRAGE

Behind the fear and hatred of the Republican party was the fact that the party depended upon and supported Negro suffrage and officeholding. Not only had the Republicans introduced the idea of political equality for blacks, they had become in the deep South a largely black party. And in South Carolina, Louisiana, and Mississippi, where blacks constituted a majority of the population, political equality meant a black electoral majority. It was largely because of this fear that there were virtually no Populists in South Carolina at all and that in Mississippi the Populists were always weak.

White Populists were all too well aware of the damage association with blacks might do to their cause. Yet, as they surveyed a political scene in which the Democrats were unwilling to adopt a legislative program helpful to the farmer, they saw no alternative. A similar conclusion had been reached by the Readjusters a decade earlier in regard to another economic issue. The Populists, in short, were no more ideologically committed to equality for blacks—even political equality—than most other Southern white men. Moreover, unlike the Scalawags, the Populists had no political experience with, or commitment to, Negroes. The white Republicans of the South not only had a historical and ideological obligation to blacks, they also had a dependence upon black votes for election. Most Populists, on the other hand, were former

Democrats. In time they might have reached the same conclusion that the Republicans and many Readjusters did after they had worked with blacks. They might have come to recognize that the South's best future lay in political cooperation between black and white rather than suppression of one by the other. But at the opening of the nineties, as Populists looked to Republicans and blacks for support and votes, they still had not reached that point. They simply were willing to ignore some old prejudices in exchange for a chance to defeat the Bourbons.

Once it is recognized that Populists began with little or no ideological commitment to black political equality, then the lengthy debate among historians as to the degree of sincerity of Populist appeals to blacks can be put into a realistic and historical context. The historians' debate has been able to last so long because the evidence has been so ambiguous and even contradictory. Populists supported and denied blacks at the same time. We shall look at some of this evidence a little later in this chapter. But here it is simply worth noting that such conflicting statements and behavior are to be expected when a deeply accepted social ideology like white supremacy is being undermined, but not being confronted directly by a clearly articulated counter ideology. The Populists were not philosophical egalitarians; they were simply Southern farmers who wanted to defeat the Bourbons, and they needed black votes to do it. And as we shall see, too, when the Populists sought to develop an ideological conception of race relations by drawing a distinction between political and social equality, their practical approach to the question of the Negro resulted only in confusion and inadequacy.

The significance of the Populist movement in the South, however, lay not in the consistency of its behavior, the clarity of its ideology, or the purity of its motives, but in the fact of its challenge to the existing racial-political order from whatever motive. In the 1890's, for the third time since Appomattox, white Southerners out of the necessities of their history and society challenged the political rigidities of the one-party system, which white supremacy had demanded and constructed. The challenge was admittedly not intended to change race relations, but by its very nature it could not fail to do so. For if the new party was to succeed, blacks would have to be induced to vote Populist, and to do that they would have to be worked with, appealed to, and recognized. In the context of the late nineteenth-century South that fact alone was a threat to the racial status quo. And if that racial order were disrupted, even a little, who could say what more far-reaching changes might follow?

WANTED: BLACK POPULISTS

The novelty of the Populist appeal for Negro votes is reflected in the fact that the farmer organizations from which the Populists derived had shown little or no interest in Negroes. There was a Colored Farmers' Union in the South, to be sure, but it had no formal organizational connection with the white farmers' groups. Furthermore, in Louisiana in 1890, most of the legislators who had been elected by the Farmers' Union voted without complaint for a bill making segregation compulsory on trains in the state. Similarly, the Alliancemen who sat in the Georgia legislature in 1891 voted for Jim Crow legislation and primary election restrictions against blacks. In both Louisiana and North Carolina, it is worth noting, too, the official newspapers of the farmers' organizations were entitled *The Caucasian!*

Once the farmers moved into politics, however, their interest in Negroes noticeably quickened. The most obvious form this new interest took was to assert the black man's right to vote his political conscience. For some Populists that was a major concession in itself. William H. Kitchin, for example, had been a Negrophobic Democrat before he became a Populist in 1894. He had often spoken publicly against black civil and suffrage rights. Yet as a Populist he said, "We must lay prejudice aside and come together, regardless of party or color, and make one common fight for our common interest."[21]

Other Populist leaders made deliberate appeals or promises to blacks, particularly in regard to schooling. Frank Burkitt, the Populist candidate for governor in Mississippi in 1895, pledged his party to provide free public schools for a term of four months each

21. Ingle, "Southern Democrat," p. 189.

year "for equal benefit of all the children of the state without regard to race, color or condition in life, and if the present law, honestly enforced, does not meet this, then such changes will be made as may be necessary to give every child in the state equal opportunities to attain a common school education." The platform of the Texas Populists in 1894 similarly favored "an effective system of public free school for six months of the year for all children. . . ."[22] It specified that each race would have its own trustees and control its own schools, for no Populist, like no white Republican, favored integrated education. The North Carolina Populists also promised four months of free public schooling for both races.

The commonest kind of Populist appeal to blacks was to assert that only through the Populists would Negroes receive their due as poor people. "You colored men," read the state platform of the Louisiana Populists in 1891, "you must now realize that there is no hope of any further material benefit to you in the Republican party, and that if you remain in it you will continue to be hewers of wood and drawers of water in the future as you have been in the past." A year later the party strengthened its class appeal to blacks. "We declare emphatically that the interests of the white and colored races of the South are identical. . . . Equal justice and fairness must be accorded to each."[23]

No Populist became better known for his appeal to blacks than Thomas Watson of Georgia. Elected to Congress in 1890 as a farmers' candidate, Watson went on to become one of the leaders of the People's party in the South and in the nation. In 1896 he was the national party's candidate for the vice-presidency. Because he is so well known, he has been subjected to much analysis by historians, particularly since 1938, when C. Vann Woodward published a biography of him in which he emphasized the strong class appeals made by Watson and the Populists in general. As one examines Watson's words and record it is evident that he was hardly a friend of what today is called integration, but it is also clear that he was quite willing to encourage Negro political equality in an effort to defeat the Democrats.

22. Pollock, ed., *Populist Mind,* pp. 396–97.
23. Hair, *Bourbonism and Agrarian Protest,* pp. 218–22.

Watson could be quite paternalistic in making his appeals to blacks. In 1892, for example, he detailed to a black audience his help to blacks in the past. Then he went on: "I pledge you my word and honor, as a man and as a representative, that if you stand up for your rights and for your manhood, if you stand shoulder to shoulder with us in this fight, you shall have fair play and fair treatment as men and as citizens, irrespective of your color." In modern terms, of course, this was an outrageous statement, for why should blacks have to stick their necks out—which is what Watson meant by standing up for their manhood—in order to be treated fairly? On the face of it, blacks ought to have been treated as citizens regardless of what their behavior was. But in the context of the South of the 1890's Watson's promise was a small revolution. It was in recognition of that political fact that his statement was greeted by the blacks with "Great Cheering," as the reporter phrased it. Besides, in another part of the same speech Watson put the issue more directly and less patronizingly: "My friends, this campaign will decide many things, and one of the things it will decide is whether or not your people and ours can daily meet in harmony, and work for law, and order, and morality, and wipe out the color line, and put every man on his citizenship, irrespective of color."[24]

Perhaps the best-known example of Watson's appeal to class as a counter to race appears in his article published in 1892 in the national magazine *Arena*. Watson advanced the same argument in the South, but his *Arena* article brought to national attention the Populist effort to win blacks and whites on grounds of a common class interest. "Now the People's Party says to these two men [black and white], 'You are kept apart that you may be separately fleeced of your earnings. You are made to hate each other because upon that hatred is rested the keystone of the arch of financial despotism which enslaves you both. You are deceived and blinded that you may not see how this race antagonism perpetuates a monetary system which beggars both.'"[25] This is the closest, incidentally, that Watson or any other Populist came to saying that

24. Pollock, ed., *Populist Mind,* pp. 378–79, 379–80.
25. C. Vann Woodward, "Tom Watson and the Negro," *Journal of Southern History,* IV (1938), 17–18.

racial prejudice and hostility were deliberately created to gain advantage for the dominant economic interests.

BEYOND RHETORIC

Words, one might say, are cheap. And that has often been the response of some skeptical historians to Populist statements in behalf of Negro rights. There are two responses that need to be made to that skepticism. One is that even to make the remarks in the context of the late nineteenth-century South is at once an act of audacity and a shift in ideology that ought not to be ignored. Words, as well as deeds, may change men's minds and even their behavior. The second point is that the words were not alone. Populists did act to put them into practice. One such act was an incident connected with Watson himself in 1892. H. S. Doyle, a black preacher who had been speaking in behalf of the Populists, came to Watson pursued by angry white Democrats. Watson offered Doyle a place to stay and sent word into the countryside that he needed armed support. Ultimately two thousand white men came to Watson's plantation, prepared to defend a black man's right to speak against other white men. As C. Vann Woodward wrote in describing the incident, "the spectacle of white farmers riding all night to save a Negro from lynchers was rather rare in Georgia." At the conclusion of the incident Watson said, "We are determined in this free country that the humblest white or black man that wants to talk our doctrine shall do it, and the man doesn't live who shall touch a hair of his head, without fighting every man in the People's Party."[26]

Not all of the behavior in support of black rights was as dramatic as the Doyle incident, to be sure. Sometimes it was nothing more than accepting blacks as political associates, as when the Arkansas Populist Convention met in 1892 with eleven of the 170 delegates being Negroes. Eighty-two of the white delegates, it is worth noting, too, were Confederate veterans. In the Georgia state convention of 1894 there were twenty-four black delegates and one was on the executive committee.

26. C. Vann Woodward, *Tom Watson, Agrarian Rebel* (New York, 1938), p. 240; Woodward, "Tom Watson and the Negro," pp. 22–23.

As during the Reconstruction, the rise of a rival party to the Democrats produced a new intimacy and mingling among the races at barbecues, picnics, suppers, and speakings. When the national Populist candidate for President, James B. Weaver, came to Raleigh, North Carolina, in 1892, he was escorted to the park in which he was to speak by 300 white men and 50 black men mounted on horseback. Reuben Kolb, the Populist candidate for governor of Alabama, spoke in Opelika in 1892 to a crowd of eight thousand, of whom a quarter were blacks.

One immediate consequence of the mingling with and the speaking to blacks in public was that all white men, Democrats as well as Populists, at least up to a point, had to moderate the expression of their hostility toward blacks. As occurred during Reconstruction, Democrats made appeals to blacks, too, inviting them to barbecues and picnics and making them promises. Occasionally the Democrats showed more interest in black voters than the Populists did, a development that was one of those unintended, but potentially significant, consequences that sometimes follows a break in an established racial-political order. Carried on long enough, it even might have worked a permanent change in outlook and social behavior. Whites might have begun to become familiar with and therefore accepting of black participation in politics.

A more concrete measure of the impact of Populist appeals to Negroes was the violent reaction from Democrats. When the Populists in Arkansas, for example, condemned lynching of blacks, the party came in for sustained and severe attacks from the Democratic newspapers. One of them made quite clear that it took seriously the Populist appeals to blacks. In fact the paper contended that it was their very concern for blacks that would ensure their defeat. "This is a white man's country, and white men are going to rule it," asserted the *Arkadelphia Siftings* in 1892, "and when the third party opened its arms to the Negro at its State Convention, it invited its certain death at the polls next fall." Democrats in Alabama took equally seriously the 1892 platform of the Populists (then still calling themselves Jeffersonian Democrats), which demanded the protection of the political and legal rights of Negroes. The Democrats denounced the Jeffersonian Democrats as traitors. In Louisiana the Democrats ridiculed the

Populists for having picnics with blacks, and particularly for sitting down to eat with them. "We can no longer depend upon the solidarity of the white race," complained the *Tensas Gazette* in 1896.[27]

The new willingness of some white Southerners to work with blacks in the political arena under the aegis of Populism was evident too in gestures that were often cautious and even timid, but which seemed to be leading to a new biracial cooperation. One example was the nomination and election of a Negro delegate from Virginia as assistant secretary at the St. Louis convention of the Populist party. Two hundred white Southerners voted for the black, while a single Alabamian voted no. Another instance occurred at the Arkansas state convention of the party, when a resolution denouncing lynching and arguing that criminals must be punished only in the courts was passed unanimously. The resolution had been introduced by a black delegate. The Populists in the Alabama legislature were quite willing to vote against bills to punish tenants for breaking their work contracts even though they knew that the tenants in question would be blacks. The Fusionist lower house in North Carolina (Republicans and Populists) responded generously to the request of a black member that the house pass a resolution of respect for Frederick Douglass, the Negro leader, who had just died. Innocuous as this incident may seem, it was used as the basis for a major attack upon Populists. The Democratic critics erroneously asserted that no notice had been taken of Robert E. Lee's birthday. (In actual fact, a black member had proposed adjournment in honor of Lee.) For years thereafter the Douglass resolution was brought up in North Carolina and other Southern states as an example of what political cooperation between whites and blacks entailed.

The Fusionist regime in North Carolina provided a number of examples of black-white cooperation. The fact that two blacks sat in the Fusionist legislature and a black was assistant doorkeeper was not lost upon white Democrats. Under their regime no blacks at all had been in North Carolina's legislative halls. It is true that North Carolina Populists did not issue any statement in support of

27. Groves, "Negro Disfranchisement in Arkansas," p. 205; Shafner, "Joseph C. Manning," p. 13; Hair, *Bourbonism and Agrarian Protest,* p. 238.

black officeholding, but it is also a fact that more blacks ran for and held office during the Fusion years, 1894–98, than ever before. The number of blacks who held office is not known, but at the time it was said that as many as one thousand Negroes held office in the state, and no one denied it. Undoubtedly the great majority of the offices were minor, like justice of the peace. For even after 1896, when a Republican occupied the governor's chair in Raleigh, he appointed, by his own count, no more than eight blacks to state offices. Yet even that cautious approach, as we shall see a little later, aroused enormous hostility from Democrats.

A revealing vignette of the way in which whites and blacks responded to the novel and fluid political relationship occurred at the Texas Populist Convention of 1891. A white man tried to deny blacks representation on party committees, even though Negroes were members of the convention. At that point a black delegate rose. "The negro vote will be the balancing vote in Texas," he pointed out. "If you are going to win, you will have to take the negro with you. . . . You must appoint us by convention and make us feel that we are men." The white president of the convention expressed his agreement by saying, "I am in favor of giving the colored man full representation. He is a citizen just as much as we are, and the party that acts on that fact will gain the colored vote of the South." The convention then elected two blacks to the state executive committee of the party.[28] Negroes remained on the committee until 1900. The Texas party was distinguished also by having a former slave as one of its principal organizers and orators. John B. Rayner, born a slave in North Carolina, came to Texas in 1881 as a Republican. In the 1890's he was one of the most effective Populist workers, addressing not only black meetings but white audiences as well. The historian of the Texas party cites him as one of the six most prominent Populist leaders.[29]

When it is recalled that Southern Populists were largely small farmers, usually from the more remote and unsophisticated areas

28. Woodward, *Origins of the New South*, p. 256.
29. For further information on Rayner see Jack Abramowitz, "John B. Rayner—A Grass-Roots Leader," *Journal of Negro History* (1951), 160–93, and Martin, *People's Party in Texas*, p. 126. It is fascinating to speculate that Rayner, who came from North Carolina, was related to the North Carolinian Whig-Unionist Kenneth Rayner, perhaps even his natural son.

of the South, the mixing between black and white at these political
gatherings is even more remarkable. Ordinarily it was the small
farmer, the man without much education, but with many problems,
who least understood or felt a connection with blacks. Often these
small farmers were not even familiar with blacks in their everyday
lives, since most of them did not live among Negroes as the whites
of the Black Belt did. Thus when the Populist convention of
Louisiana met in 1892 with 24 of the 127 delegates being black, it
was a new sight and experience for many of the white Populists
from the hill country, where almost no blacks lived. At that convention two blacks were placed in nomination for the state ticket,
but then some more cautious black delegates questioned whether
such a ticket might not be too stiff a dose of biracial politics for
white Louisianans to take. They asked that the black nominees
withdraw. The whites said nothing, leaving the delicate matter to
the blacks to decide. Both blacks withdrew. Both of them, however, were then made members of the state executive committee of
the party.

Consistently throughout its history the Louisiana Populist party
stood firm against efforts to disfranchise Negroes through constitutional amendments. Virtually all of the Populist leaders defended
the right of Negroes to vote as long as their ballots could be freely
given and honestly counted. One Louisiana Populist leader told
another Southern Populist that in his state free elections were more
important than free silver. Even after the defeat of April, 1896,
the Populists did not abandon the defense of black suffrage. Part
of this persistence, of course, stemmed from the clear recognition
that only with Negro votes could the reigning Democratic party be
overthrown. But some of it must also have stemmed from a sentiment expressed by one Populist: "We are in favor of fighting
wrong to the bitter end." Not much can be concluded from a single
example, it is true, but it is worth noting that in the Louisiana
Constitutional Convention that disfranchised Negroes in 1898,
there was a single Populist delegate. He refused to sign the completed constitution.[30]

An even more dramatic example of the persistence of white
Populist support for black suffrage occurred in Grimes County,

30. Hair, *Bourbonism and Agrarian Protest,* p. 274.

Texas. All through the 1890's black and white Populists in this east Texas county worked together politically, including the election of a Populist white sheriff, who appointed black deputies. The unity of black and white lasted until white Democratic terrorists killed one black leader and seriously wounded and drove out the white sheriff, Garrett Scott, and his family. As late as 1970 a descendant of Scott's defended that cooperation between blacks and whites. "They said that Uncle Garrett was a nigger-lover," his niece remembered. "He wasn't a nigger-lover, or a white-lover, he just believed in being fair to all, in justice."[31]

THE DANGERS OF POLITICAL EQUALITY

To concentrate on examples of Populists' defenses of black participation is to present a distorted and therefore misleading picture of what was going on in the South of the 1890's. The evolution of a working relationship between blacks and whites in the same political organization was much more uneven and fluid than a catalog of such examples suggests. Individuals as well as groups of Populists shifted on the question during the decade. Indeed, it is this shifting on the race question that has allowed historians to maintain contrary positions on Populists' attitudes and behavior toward blacks. The fact is that, for reasons already suggested, Populists were ambiguous on the subject, often inconsistent, and sometimes hypocritical.

Certainly Populists expressed their belief in Negro subordination in politics. As one Virginia Populist wrote to a party paper in 1894, "This is a white man's country and will always be controlled by whites." Only in Virginia did the Populists make an effort to include Negroes in their state organizational clubs. Yet in less than a year they, too, shifted to separate clubs for whites and blacks, as was the practice in all the other state Populist organizations in the South. Not surprisingly, there was not a single Negro delegate present at the Virginia Populist Convention of 1893.[32] Before the

31. Lawrence C. Goodwyn, "Populist Dreams and Negro Rights: East Texas as a Case Study," *American Historical Review,* 76 (1971), 1442–47.
32. Woodward, *Origins of the New South;* Saunders, "Southern Populists and the Negro," pp. 240–41.

Alabama Populists sought out the Negro vote they tried to interest the Democrats in the idea of a white primary, thus eliminating the need for Negro votes. But the Democrats twice rejected the overtures because they wanted to use the Negro voters in the Black Belt counties to outweigh their Populist opponents in the northern, white counties of the state. And when the Populists and Jeffersonian Democrats of Alabama met in joint convention in 1894, they literally expelled a Negro Republican leader who sought to address them in behalf of a possible fusion ticket. Yet at other times, the Alabama Populists went out of their way to seek Negro votes and support. The Populists of Mississippi, too, assumed a liberal attitude on Negro rights in their platform of 1895, but that same platform was silent on the subject of support for Negro suffrage, and the ticket that year did not include a single Negro candidate.

The range of attitudes that the Populists could assume on the question of the Negro is neatly shown by the Alabama farmer party. When the Alabama House of Representatives passed a bill for separate but equal facilities on trains, the bill went through without dissent, though a number of Populists sat in the House. Indeed, there was almost no discussion on the measure. Nor was the issue of segregation simply a settled one at that time, for the Negro press protested strongly against the pending legislation. Populists simply did not think the issue concerned them. Yet in 1894 the Jeffersonian Democratic–Populist fusion party took a strong stand in its platform against any restrictions on the voting rights of blacks and in support of special protections for blacks. It announced that "we are in favor . . . of having the general government set apart sufficient territory to constitute a State, given exclusively to the colored race, to which they may voluntarily go, and in which they alone shall be entitled to suffrage and citizenship."[33] Although one might suspect that a desire to separate whites and blacks lay behind such a plank, it is worth noting that the separation was to be voluntary, a distinction that makes it closer to a modern black nationalist position than to one of simple segregation.

33. Pollock, ed., *Populist Mind,* pp. 391–92.

Another indication of Populist uncertainty or even desperation on the question of Negro suffrage and officeholding was the backhanded way Populists defended themselves against Democratic charges of favoring blacks. The gambit usually took the form of accusing the Democrats of being more friendly to blacks than the Populists. A favorite ploy was to refer to the fact that Frederick Douglass, the black leader, and his white wife had once been invited to the White House by Democratic President Grover Cleveland. Marion Butler, the North Carolina Populist leader, expatiated upon this fact for pages in an article entitled "Committed to Miscegenation." Cleveland also came under attack for having given jobs to blacks. "No Negro was ever promised any political position by Populists," asserted a Populist newspaper in Birmingham, Alabama, in 1896. "Mr. Cleveland gave the best paying office in the United States, except his own, to a negro, besides others of high honor." At another time, the same paper denied the charges of social equality levied against Populists by writing that "we are farther from advocating or practising social equality than any ballot box stuffer alive. Our objection does not relax at the going down of the sun. We have got no children at the Tuskegee normal school or kindred there."[34]

Probably the most common form that the ambivalence of white Populists assumed toward black suffrage was to deny that there was any danger of Negro domination. Tom Watson spelled out the groundlessness of the fears in such a way that his own sense of white superiority was obvious. " 'Dominate' what? 'Dominate' how? 'Dominate' who?" he asked. "It takes Intellect to dominate: haven't we got it? It takes Majorities to dominate: haven't we got them? It takes Wealth to dominate: haven't we got it?" As Watson made clear, there could be no doubt that, given their advantages, the whites would always rule in the South. Trying to shame those who uttered the cry of Negro domination, he fell back upon an appeal to white supremacy: "What words can paint the cowardice of the Anglo-Saxon who would deny 'equal and exact justice' to the ignorant, helpless, poverty-cursed Negro in whose ears the clank of chains have scarcely ceased to sound." Then came the

34. Saunders, "Southern Populists and the Negro," p. 250; Pollock, ed., *Populist Mind*, pp. 392–93, 388.

near-racist clincher: "No power on this earth will ever reverse the decree of God."

That Watson's appeal was at least paternalistic and perhaps tinged with racism was clear from the remarks he once directed to a predominantly black audience. You ought to be ashamed to allow white men to buy your vote, he told his listeners. "You are doing nobly in the way of educating your children; your daughters are *beginning* to dress nicely and behave themselves decently, and be respected, and now will you throw all this away in a campaign that your false leaders have been bribed to delude you?"[35]

When Watson addressed a national audience he emphasized, just as Mahone had done ten years before, the economic and social importance of blacks in the South. "They are a part of our system and they are here to stay," Watson wrote in *Arena* magazine in 1892. To believe, as some white Southerners do, that blacks are a dying race is false, he asserted. Nor were mulattoes increasing in number. "Miscegenation is further off (Thank God) than ever. Neither the blacks nor the whites have any relish for it," he assured his Northern readers, who believed the same thing. Once again he denied any danger of "Negro supremacy." As things now stand in "this country there is no earthly chance for Negro domination unless we are ready to admit that the colored man is our superior in will power, courage, and intellect."[36] Obviously, Watson, for one, was not ready to admit it.

Other Populists were equally willing to deny any danger from black domination. At the farmers' convention at Cincinnati in 1891, which supported the formation of a third party, there was a delegation from Winn Parish in upstate Louisiana. The chief of the delegation, Hardy Brian, presented a monster petition, signed by 1,200 voters of Winn Parish, in support of a third party. The number was especially striking since it was only 131 shy of the total number of males eligible to vote in the parish. When Brian was asked whether he feared black domination from a third party in Louisiana, he boldly answered, "The race cry doesn't scare

35. *Ibid.*, pp. 398–99, 379; emphasis added.
36. Thomas E. Watson, "The Negro Question in the South," *Arena*, VI (1892), 543, 550.

us."[37] It is true that there were few blacks in Winn Parish, yet for Southern whites like Brian and Watson to deny the danger of black domination was courageous and hopeful even if the denial originated in a sense of white superiority.

Sometimes the appeal for black support took the form of recognizing that blacks must, in the nature of things, benefit from the Populist cause and therefore ought to support it. "Whatever victories we may win, whatever we may accomplish for the benefit of agriculture or productive industry," observed the Birmingham *People's Weekly Tribune* in 1896, "the colored man will have an equal share with us in those benefits. We cannot prevent it if we would. Likewise, if we are defeated, the colored man will have an equal share with us in the woes of that defeat. No matter with which party he votes he cannot prevent that. . . ."[38] Undoubtedly, it was the recognition that black farmers were indeed in the same economic boat as white farmers, regardless of the sincerity of Populist interest in Negroes, that moved many blacks to support Populist candidates.

The heart of the Populist argument in behalf of political participation by blacks was that it would not threaten white supremacy. It was, said one Alabama Populist, simply "making a practical application" of Booker T. Washington's famous metaphor of the fingers of the hand, which Washington had set forth in his Atlanta Exposition speech in 1895. Washington's views, the Populist noted, had received high praise from traditional white Southerners for being practical and helpful to both races. In cooperating with the Republicans "for the purpose of restoring the purity of the ballot, of having once more honest elections and majority rule," the Populists said that they were doing no more than following Washington's advice. One North Carolina Populist made clear in a private letter to Marion Butler in 1900 that support for Negro rights did not go beyond the suffrage. "I am not in favor of the Negro," the writer began, "but I do believe in giving the pore negro his dues. I live in Dunn, N.C. where they say you [Butler] wold never be aloud to speak in no more. And this negro I want to

37. Hair, *Bourbonism and Agrarian Protest,* p. 212.
38. Pollock, ed., *Populist Mind,* p. 389.

tel you [about] went to register and [they] wold not let him and
he came to me and told me about it."[39]

For some sophisticated Populists the justification for black
suffrage derived from what George Frederickson has called roman-
tic racialism—that is, the idea that in some ways Negroes were
superior to whites, though those ways were not necessarily ones
the white man would want to emulate. Usually they consisted of
"soft" or "feminine" traits like faithfulness, or patience. Joseph
Manning, a radical Populist from Alabama, justified Negro
suffrage on these grounds in a speech in 1903. During the Civil
War, Manning said, the Negro was not and "he is not now, and
had never been, turbulent or anarchistic as a race. No people on
earth would have deported themselves during the Civil War as did
the Negro, and no other race would have" remained faithful to a
society "then ruled by a passionate belief, sustained by an unyielding prejudice, that the Negro should never himself either be a free
man or the owner of a free man's home." Later, another Alabama
Populist, William Skaggs, defended blacks in the same terms.
"Never has there been a race whose leaders, almost without exception, have struggled with more patience and forbearance, or more
heroically than the leaders of the Negroes in America, not only for
the uplift of their own race but also for the maintenance of peace
between two races," he wrote in his book *The Southern Oligarchy*.[40]

No one, however, put more forcefully or clearly the assumption
that underlay the relationship between blacks and whites in the
Populist party than Tom Watson. At his best, Watson was without
sentiment or illusion. (By 1895, however, his best was behind him,
for after that year he was having increasing doubts about working
with blacks.) He did not expect to convert whites to appreciation
of or even sympathy with blacks, nor did he expect blacks to
support Populists out of gratitude. After all, he pointed out, "gratitude may fail, so may sympathy and friendship and generosity and

39. *Ibid.*, p. 388; Robert F. Durden, *Climax of Populism: The Election
of 1896* (Lexington, Ky., 1965), p. 167.
40. Joseph C. Manning, "Letting the South Alone: Class Government
that Defrauds Whites and Blacks," speech before Middlesex Club, Boston,
Grant Night, April 27, 1963 (n.d. n.p.), pp. 4–5; Skaggs, *Southern Oligarchy*, p. 421.

patriotism; but in the long run, self-interest *always* controls. Let it once appear plain that it is in the interest of a colored man to vote with the white man, and he will do it. Let it plainly appear that it is to the interest of the white man that the vote of the Negro supplement his own, and the question of having that ballot freely cast and fairly counted, becomes vital to the *white man*. He will see that it is done." On this ground Watson confidently predicted that "the People's Party will settle the race question."[41]

Watson was right when he said self-interest would be controlling. What he forgot, however, is that not all interests are equally powerful. When he talked of self-interest he meant concrete economic concerns, that is, class interests that white and black farmers had in common. But there was another interest that white men had, and it was even stronger than class. Watson and the Populists knew that, too, and they feared its power. As a result they sought to erect additional defenses against it.

THE FEAR OF SOCIAL EQUALITY

That powerful interest was the belief in the superiority of the white race. Like the Scalawags and Readjusters before them, the Populists sought to allay white fears of compromising that belief by drawing a line between political equality, which they defended, and social equality, which they scoffed at as not worth discussing, much less fearing. "The man who alludes to Social Equality" when talking about Negro suffrage "insults the intelligence of those to whom he talks," declared the *People's Party Paper* in 1892. "Social equality is a question which every citizen settles for himself. The law never did, and never can, interfere with it." ("Social equality does not exist now among the whites," Republican Thomas Settle had asserted in 1867, "and no law has ever attempted to regulate that matter. . . . Every man chooses his own company. The virtuous form one association and the vicious

41. Watson, "The Negro Question," pp. 546–47. Robert Miller Saunders, "The Ideology of Southern Populists, 1892–1895," unpublished Ph.D. dissertation, University of Virginia, 1967, p. 175, shows Watson's increasing conservatism by 1895.

another. This matter regulates itself, law cannot do it.") Tom
Watson himself phrased the argument this way: "No statute ever
yet drew the latch of the humblest home—or ever will. Each
citizen regulates his own visiting list—and always will."[42]

During the Populist years, again as during Reconstruction,
Negroes also developed a case that would support the distinctions
that their white allies were drawing. And again the aim was to
allay the fears of the majority of whites that white superiority was
being threatened. "Now, let me tell you, Mr. Editor," wrote a
black Georgian to a Populist newspaper in 1892, "we don't want
to rule the government; we don't want to come into your family;
we don't want to enter your schoolhouses or your churches. But I
tell you what we do want: We want equal rights at the ballot-box
and equal justice before the law" and a better economic situation.
Some Negroes went further in supporting the distinction between
political and social equality. "The Negro does not seek among
other races what he does not have in his own," wrote J. C. Price,
president of Livingstone College in North Carolina, in 1891.
"There is no social equality among Negroes, notwithstanding the
disposition of some whites to put all Negroes in one class. Culture,
moral refinement, and material possessions make a difference
among colored people as they do among whites," he emphasized.
Grant the Negro his civil and political rights, he went on, and the
Negro will be quite content to remain with his own people. "When
a train stops for refreshments, and the Negro enters a dining
room," Price observed, "he does not go there because he is seeking
social contact with whites, but because he is hungry." The question
of social equality, he concluded, "will take care of itself in the
future as it has in the past."

Price was undoubtedly sincere and honest when he asserted that
"the Negro has no idea that in demanding his political and civil
rights he is seeking an arbitrary social equality with any other
race." Southern whites may say he is, Price went on, but as a
Negro himself he thought that "ninety-nine hundredths of the
Negroes of this country" agreed with him. "Social equality is in the

42. Pollock, ed., *Populist Mind*, p. 375; Watson, "The Negro Question,"
p. 550.

brain of the alarmist rather than in the mind of the Negro," he concluded.[43]

Despite Price's assertion, the line that Populists and Scalawags tried to draw between political and social equality was inadequate on two counts. The barrier that the Populists and Price sought to erect, as the quotations make clear, was essentially a class barrier. But class barriers can operate only when there are class differences. Price inadvertently pointed up the issue even as he was attempting to show that blacks did not seek social equality. Before the Civil War, Price declared, "a poor white man was as much a social pariah as a free colored man. The aristocracy took no notice of him as a social equal." Since the war, that barrier between classes of whites has remained, Price continued. "This class of white men have all their civil and political rights, but no one asserts that they are trying to force themselves into social equality with the dominant classes of the South." If poor white men cannot force themselves upon the upper class, he concluded, then surely the Negroes, who were of a lower social class, could not either.

Price's argument was also the basic premise on which George Washington Cable, the Southern novelist and racial liberal, rested his argument in behalf of Negro rights. Southern critics of his devastating essay "The Freedman's Case in Equity," published in 1885, charged him with advocating "social equality." Nothing, he retorted in a subsequent essay, "The Silent South" (1888), could be more wrong. "Social Equality," he asserted flatly, "is a fool's dream." He wanted no more of it than did "the most fervent traditional of the most fervent South. . . . Social equality can never exist where a community, numerous enough to assert itself, is actuated, as every civilized community is, by an intellectual and moral ambition." Cable, like Price and Watson, declared that "no form of laws, no definition of rights . . . can bring it about. The fear that this or that change will produce it ought never to be any but a fool's fear."[44]

It is tempting to argue that this appeal to class may have been

---

43. Pollock, ed., *Populist Mind*, p. 395; J. C. Price, "Does the Negro Seek Social Equality?" *Forum*, X (1891), 562–63, 558–59.

44. *Ibid.*, p. 562; George W. Cable, *The Negro Question*, ed. by Arlin Turner (Garden City, N.Y., 1958), pp. 53–54.

peculiarly Southern. After all, the South's social structure has always been more defined and rigid than the North's. If class barriers could be substituted for race consciousness, the South's society was undoubtedly the best prospect. But for the majority of white Southerners class barriers could not do the job they wanted done. For what Price and Cable and the Populists overlooked was that poor whites did not have a class position from which to repel Negroes. The mass of whites, like the mass of Negroes, were in the same class. They possessed no class differences with which to construct a barrier. The protection or security that poor whites would have against competition from, or association with, blacks was solely through an appeal to color or race.

But this was not the principal weakness of the appeal to class barriers. More significant was the fact that the distinction between social and political equality was artificial. For when the concept of "social equality" is scrutinized, it turns out to be no more than the right to choose one's own friends. When Price, restating Cable's point, said "that no legislation in either church or state can give [the Negro] arbitrary admission into the best society, white or colored, and that no congressional enactments can regulate the affections,"[45] he and Cable, and the Populists, who said the same thing, may have been stating a truism, but they were certainly not speaking to the issue. No poor white farmer in the South thought for a minute that any law could compel him to have friends or intimates he did not like. But he did think that if blacks were accepted as equal in everything except as intimates, there were, then, no distinctions between the races.

Yet to the poor white farmer racial distinctions were vital. In the mobile, open society of the nineteenth century each man had to prove himself, to establish his own place in the social order. Who you were, where you stood, and where you were going were not inherited or ascribed by custom; they were the result of one's own efforts. At the same time, the society placed much value on upward movement, competition, and achievement. In such a fluid society it was imperative to seek distinctions wherever they could be found. The most obvious and the easiest to assert was color. A white man could look to his skin and ancestry to provide at least

45. Price, "Does the Negro Seek Social Equality?" p. 564.

some standing in the mobile and competitive social order of the nineteenth century.

Middle- and upper-class Southerners, the poor white man knew, could rely upon their class differences to provide status and to keep blacks at a distance. The whites of the upper classes may not have believed any more strongly in black equality than the lower class, but they did not have as urgent an interest in arguments of racial difference or inferiority. As Price pointed out, they relied, instead, upon their class positions. Lacking such advantages of class, the poor white farmers had no way of keeping blacks at a disadvantage except by appeals to racial differences. This was what racial consciousness accomplished for them. What they feared, in short, was not that a civil rights law would compel them to associate with blacks, but that the removal of a sense of racial difference would leave them without standing in a society in which standing was important. Moreover, a long history of seeing blacks as slaves and inferiors was not easy to forget or ignore. They had been brought up to see blacks as inferior. Perhaps, therefore, it is not so surprising after all that, in the end, and despite the Populist counter effort, most Southern whites fell back upon their traditional belief in the superiority of white skin and ancestry.

And when we understand why most white Southerners found it difficult to abandon their ideas of racial superiority we also understand why the Scalawags, Readjusters, and Populists did not advance more sophisticated—or modern—arguments against racism. For they were a part of the same world. What is more remarkable is that those white Southern dissenters were able to go as far as they did in the direction of acceptance of Negroes. It is not given for many men and women to transcend their history; most are lucky if they can make even a few changes in their vast and varied inheritance from the past. The Populists and Republicans of the South were among those exceptions.

These three unsuccessful efforts by white Southerners to counter race allegiance by class appeals should remind us of another fact. Class and race are certainly among the elemental allegiances, but in the American South of the nineteenth century, class appeals when placed in opposition to race allegiance have been like a summer breeze against a juggernaut.

THE BLACK RESPONSE

Given the ambiguity of many Populists toward Negroes, it is to be expected that some blacks in the South would not find the Populist appeals persuasive. There is some evidence, for example, that blacks supported the Democratic candidate for governor in Georgia in 1896 because he had taken a strong stand against lynching while the Georgia Populists had done little for blacks, despite the support Negroes had given them in 1892 and 1894. Texas blacks, too, were not friendly to Populists, if only because their leader, Norris Wright Cuney, the head of the state Republican party, did not approve of Populist principles. Republicans in Texas gave the Negroes more recognition than the Populists were prepared to give them. In 1894, for example, the Republican candidate for governor was a Negro, and he received 55,000 votes. These were votes, of course, that the Populist candidate Thomas Nugent was thereby denied. Many Negroes, too, must have felt in 1896 that free silver and the money question in general were not of immediate interest to them. As the black poet Paul Laurence Dunbar put the matter:

> An hit ain't do so't o' money dat is pesterin' my min'
> But de question I want answehed's how to get at any kin'.[46]

Yet, a number of Southern Negroes did see in the Populist effort to work with Republicans an overall gain. And the reason they would is not hard to discover. Given the situation in which the black Southerner found himself, any support from white Populists for the cause of a free ballot and an honest count was worth sustaining. Some black men said just that, publicly. "The one and only advantageous political course of the Negro, under present existing affairs," wrote a black Texan in 1892, "is to support the people's party. . . . The people's party is not heard to say that 'this is a white man's government' but this is a people's government."

46. Durden, *Climax of Populism*, p. 106; Jack Abramowitz, "The Negro in the Populist Movement," *Journal of Negro History*, XXXVIII (1953), 269, 287.

And there were other signs that many Negroes voted Populist. At the 1892 Populist convention in Texas a former slave stood up to observe "that the Negro holds the balance of power, and the democrat and republicans are trying to hold him down. You should remember that these parties intend to keep the Negro out of this reform movement if they can. . . ." Democratic newspapers, in turn, sometimes publicly worried about the successes of the Populists in appealing to blacks. The Atlanta *Constitution* in 1894 concluded that in Pike County, Georgia, 60 percent of the Populist vote was from Negroes. "For some reason not known," the paper commented, "the Populists have been able to do much better with negroes than was counted on." It was also striking that in Macon County, Alabama, where Tuskegee Institute was located, 63 percent of the vote went to Reuben Kolb, the farmers' candidate for governor in 1892. H. S. Doyle, the black preacher who came to Tom Watson for protection from Democratic lynchers, later commented on the impact that the incident had on black Georgians. "After that Mr. Watson was held almost as a savior by the negroes," Doyle told a Congressional committee. "The poor ignorant men and women who had so long been oppressed, were anxious even to touch Mr. Watson's hand, and were often a source of inconvenience to him in their anxiety."[47] In the Marion Butler Papers are hundreds of letters from blacks in which they tell of the harassment visited upon Negroes after 1896. They wrote to Butler, as the head of the Populist party in the state, because they knew Populists were fighting against the disfranchisement of blacks. To these Negroes the Populists were valued supporters even if they were self-interested.

The importance of the relationship between blacks and Populists, or between Republicans and Populists, was nowhere more evident than in Butler's state of North Carolina. There cooperation between blacks and whites, between Republicans and Populists, achieved a degree of success duplicated nowhere else in the South. As we have seen, the coalition of the two parties captured both houses of the legislature in 1894 and again in 1896. In addition, in 1896 the Republican candidate for governor, Daniel L. Russell,

47. *Ibid.*, pp. 267–69, 275–76; Woodward, "Tom Watson and the Negro," p. 23.

defeated the Democratic candidate for the first time since Reconstruction. These victories in North Carolina were the closest that a black-white political coalition came to equaling the Readjuster victories in Virginia in 1879 and 1881. Nor does the similarity between the two coalitions end there. The overthrow of the North Carolina Fusionists, like that of the Readjusters in Virginia, was carried out through fervent appeals to white solidarity. The city of Wilmington in North Carolina played a role in that overthrow that was curiously similar to that of Danville, Virginia, in 1883 in the defeat of the Readjusters.

THE WILMINGTON RIOT

The story of the race riot that broke out on November 10, 1898, in the port city of Wilmington, located at the mouth of the Cape Fear River, has yet to be fully told. Its general purpose and results, however, are clear. In fact, it was considerably more than a "riot." Its organizer and leader, Alfred M. Waddell, referred to it as a "revolution." And in a literal sense it was precisely that. The origins of the riot were embedded in the victories of the Populist-Republican fusion tickets in 1894 and 1896. That triumph had brought important changes to Wilmington. In 1897, for example, the legislature altered the government of the city from an elected city council to one in which half of the ten members were elected and half appointed by the governor. As a result, in 1898 the city council consisted of four blacks and six whites. The irony of this change, which white Democrats opposed unsuccessfully in the courts, was that the legislature's power to control city and county government had been written into the state constitution after Reconstruction as a way of ensuring white control of the black counties in the state. Little had the Democrats, who drew up that constitution, foreseen that in the future a Republican governor might use that same power to support a black-white coalition in a predominantly black city like Wilmington. As early as 1897 plans were laid by white Democrats to overthrow the new city government.

An event in the summer of 1898 provided an occasion for whipping up white sentiment against the black majority. During the 1890's Wilmington had a black middle class of substance, consisting of a number of lawyers, educators, craftsmen, public officials, and even two black newspapers. In 1898 the one of those two newspapers still being published was Alex Manly's *Daily Record*. On August 18, 1898, the *Record* published Manly's answer to a vicious defense of lynching of blacks that the Georgia Independent Rebecca Felton had made. Felton said, "if it needs lynching to protect woman's dearest possession from the raving human beasts—then I say lynch; a thousand times a week if necessary." In his public reply, Manly pointed out that blacks were not the only rapists. But what most aroused the Democratic whites was Manly's frank discussion of Southern interracial sex. It was not always clear, Manly observed, that poor white women "are any more particular in the matter of clandestine meetings with colored men, than are the white men with colored women. Meetings of this kind go on for some time until the woman's infatuation of the man's boldness bring attention to them, and the man is lynched for rape." In the eyes of Southern whites this kind of remark from a black was bad enough, but when Manly went on to suggest that lower-class white women were not the only ones attracted to black men, he was indeed raising the "unmentionable." "Every negro lynched is called 'a big, burly, black brute,'" Manly declared, "when in fact many of those who have been thus dealt with had white men for their fathers, and not only were not 'black' and 'burly' but were sufficiently attractive for white girls of culture and refinement to fall in love with them as is well known to all."[48]

The article in the *Record* did not attract immediate attention, but as the elections approached in the fall, it was widely publicized and denounced throughout the state. It would provide the focal point for the "riot" in November.

All through the fall, the Fusion government in North Carolina was an object of attention in the South and the nation. On October 6 and 7, for example, the Atlanta *Constitution* published two long articles on the threat to white supremacy posed by the government

48. Josephine Bone Floyd, "Rebecca Latimer Felton, Champion of Women's Rights," *Georgia Historical Quarterly*, XXX (1946), 83–84; *Wilmington Daily Record*, Aug. 18, 1898, copy in Daniel L. Russell Papers, Folder 19.

in North Carolina. "The white race and the black race in North Carolina are engaged today in a momentous struggle for supremacy," one of the articles contended. The Negroes were depicted as united and aggressive, hoping "to repeal the laws against intermarriage between the races and mixed schools and all other laws which, in any manner, shape or form, provide for separate accommodations for whites and blacks." These intentions, the article continued, may be denied publicly, but there could be no doubt of their truth. "This is the solution to the race question which the negroes are attempting for themselves," the article concluded. Contrary to the article, the Fusionists did not even run candidates in the local city or county elections in a futile, if commendable effort to allay the racial fears of the whites. Such caution on the part of the Fusionists and blacks, however, did not prevent the largest newspaper in the state, the Raleigh *News and Observer,* from printing, almost daily, exaggerated or fabricated stories of mistreatment of whites by Negro policemen in Wilmington or of alleged insolence to whites in other North Carolina cities that also had black majorities. Not surprisingly, the Richmond, Virginia, *Dispatch* drew a historical analogy. "The contest in North Carolina reminds us very much of the mighty effort the Democrats of Virginia made in 1883 to throw off the yoke of Mahone. . . . The North Carolinians are engaged in another such struggle."[49]

Shortly before the election, Alfred M. Waddell, a fervently anti-Negro Democrat of Wilmington, denounced the Fusionist regime in violently racist terms. His speech was printed in full in the *News and Observer.* Waddell's subject was the insolence and misrule of blacks. The only solution to the problem, he contended, "is to make it impossible for a negro ever to hold office in this State. They, and they alone," he declared, "have made the issue" by voting their color. The whites, on the other hand, have been paying all the taxes for the social services of the community while blacks dominated the government. This forbearance and generosity on

49. Olive Hall Shadgett, *The Republican Party in Georgia: From Reconstruction through 1900* (Athens, Ga., 1964), p. 120; Edmonds, *The Negro and Fusion Politics,* pp. 160–63; Raleigh *News and Observer,* Oct. 5, Nov. 6, 7, 8, 1898. Richmond *Dispatch* quoted in Raleigh *News and Observer,* Oct. 7, 1898.

the part of the whites, he said, "is without a parallel in human history," but it must have its limits. Waddell and his followers resolved to establish those limits, "if we have to choke the current of the Cape Fear [River] with carcasses. . . . The time for smooth words has gone by, the extremest limit of forbearance has been reached." From now on, Waddell concluded, Negro domination will be only "a shameful memory."

Waddell was more than a speaker in the cause. Behind the scenes for some days the "Secret Nine," a committee of whites, had been meeting to draw up a "Declaration of White Independence." The Declaration called for the closing of the *Daily Record* and for Manly's permanent banishment from the city. Waddell was made the head of a Committee of Twenty-five who were to carry out the Declaration. Election Day was selected as the occasion.[50]

The appeal to white solidarity worked as effectively in Wilmington and North Carolina as it had in Danville and Virginia fifteen years before. The victory was so overwhelming that one prominent Democratic politician, Charles B. Aycock, wrote privately, "It is a glorious victory that we have won, and the extent of it frightens me."[51] And it ought to have frightened him, but for a different reason than he had in mind.

The same day that Aycock wrote—November 10—Alfred Waddell began his "revolution" in Wilmington. That morning at 8:30 a group of four hundred armed whites with Waddell at their head appeared before the offices of the *Daily Record*. Their intention was to destroy the presses and the offices. On election evening, two days before, Waddell's Committee of Twenty-five had summoned before them thirty-two of the leading Negroes of the city. Waddell then read the declaration to them and demanded that by 7:30 A.M. on the tenth Manly be gone from the city and his paper closed. When no agreement was received from the Negroes, the whites moved against the newspaper office, one hour after the deadline had passed.

50. Raleigh *News and Observer,* Nov. 6, 1898, p. 10, carried Waddell's speech; Edmonds, *Negro and Fusion Politics,* pp. 166–67.

51. Joseph Flake Steelman, "The Progressive Era in North Carolina, 1884–1917," unpublished Ph.D. dissertation, University of North Carolina, Chapel Hill, 1955, p. 187.

In the course of demolition the building was set afire. The outbreak of fire convinced the Negroes that their homes would be burned as well. Panic swept the Negro community, and scores of blacks fled the city. Even John C. Dancey, the U.S. Collector of Customs and a longtime resident of the city, fled with his family to Salisbury. Armed whites now roamed the streets, seeking out obstreperous blacks and insisting upon complete control of the city. A group of blacks who refused to disperse was fired upon; three were killed. A Negro who was said to have shot at and wounded a white man was hounded down to his home and his body riddled with bullets after he allegedly confessed to the shooting. Since the Negroes, like the whites, had been arming themselves before the election, widespread bloodshed was a real possibility. Militia companies were rushed into the city as well as a unit of U.S. naval reserves to establish order. When quiet was restored that evening, between eleven and thirty Negroes were dead; Waddell's own estimate was the higher figure. No whites were killed, and only three were wounded, two of them not seriously. No whites were arrested.

On the following day the soldiers still patrolled the streets, though few people ventured out of their houses. Six Negro leaders of the town were placed on a northbound train and told not to return. Many other blacks of repute and accomplishment left voluntarily out of fear or despair. Several whites who had been associated with the Fusionist government were also ordered to leave. Strangely enough, the governor of the state, Daniel L. Russell, a Republican, took no action to interfere with the vigilantes. He did not even declare martial law. One newspaper reported that at the height of the riot Russell had agreed to influence the Fusionist mayor and city council to resign if that would restore peace.

It is not certain whether Russell made the offer, but no such intervention on his part was necessary. The insurgents carried through their revolution within legal forms. Each alderman was ordered to resign by the "revolutionists"; as each did so, the remainder of the city council chose a successor from a list of names provided by the vigilantes until the entire membership was "changed legally," as the friendly *News and Observer* phrased it.

"They resigned in response to public sentiment. The new board is composed of conservative Democratic citizens. The Mayor and Chief of Police then resigned and the new board elected their successor, according to law."[52]

The leader of the coup—and now the mayor—Alfred Waddell, was pleased with his handiwork. "I certainly shall not answer the newspaper lies about our revolution," he wrote one correspondent. The northern newspapers widely condemned the Wilmington affair, but in the South it was more often seen as a necessary, if harsh, method for removing Negroes from office. "I verily believe our action here has gone very far towards settling the 'race problem,' " Waddell wrote another correspondent. "Election frauds which we in this honest old State have never resorted to, are fraught with evil and demoralization and I have always despised them. The good old Anglo Saxon way of patiently awaiting until government becomes intolerable, and then openly and manfully overthrowing it is the best."[53]

Other local observers were not so sure. Professor of history John Spencer Bassett, then teaching at Trinity College in Durham, North Carolina, seemed almost to be answering Waddell's remark. "We are crowing down here like children because we have settled the Negro question," he wrote to a fellow professor. "We don't see that we have not settled it by half. At best we have only postponed it." He warned his friend against believing too much about "Negro rule in N.C. When this campaign started, I had heard nothing of the evils of Negro rule. I took pains to ask about from many sources. I learned that in some of the Negro counties there were magistrates, a few county commissioners, and some school committees. In no case did I hear that they were disposed to abuse the privilege." The riot in Wilmington he described as "justifiable at no point, a riot directly due to the 'white man's' campaign." Bassett went on to say that it was, furthermore, totally unnecessary, since within two months the new Democratic legislature

52. Raleigh *News and Observer*, Nov. 11, 12, 1898; Edmonds, *Negro and Fusion Politics*, p. 89.
53. A. M. Waddell to E. A. Oldham, Nov. 29, 1898, Edward A. Oldham Manuscripts; Alfred M. Waddell to Thomas Nelson Page, Dec. 1, 1898, Thomas Nelson Page Papers.

could have been counted on to change the situation in Wilmington. Waddell's revolution was apparently an effort to retaliate with violence against blacks, Populists, and Republicans. Bassett also did not think that "many white people who understand things in the State believe the charge" that the blacks began the shooting. Years later, Josephus Daniel, whose newspaper, the *News and Observer*, had helped to whip up the winds of racial animosity, admitted that the Negroes certainly "did not fire until four hundred armed white men led by Colonel Waddell marched to the *Record* office to destroy it."[54]

Two months after the riot in Wilmington, the Republican-Populist fusion government in North Carolina came to an end. It was the last as well as the most successful of the Populist efforts in the South. What is the meaning of that burst of biracial politics called Populism in the history of the South?

FROM POPULISTS TO REPUBLICANS

In the United States as a whole Populism may have been an uprising of farmers against an increasingly industrial America, but in the South it was that and more. For, like other manifestations of Southern dissent, Populism in the South differed from the national form. For one thing, Southern Populists, as Tom Watson pointed out, had to confront the race question, which no Northern Populists had to do. For another, the Populist movement in the South was a part of a long tradition of dissent from oligarchic rule that was absent from Northern Populism. Many of the antislavery leaders like Cassius Clay and Hinton Helper had been a part of that dissent before the war, as had many of the Unionists before and during the war. Certainly the underlying pulse of the Reconstruction and Readjuster periods had been the drive to bring forward new men and new outlooks to the South. Southern Populism, in short, was a culmination of several earlier efforts to transform the South from within. And like almost all of them—the notable exception was that of the Unionists—it, too, got entangled in the question of the Negro's place in Southern society. No

54. Edmonds, *Negro and Fusion Politics*, pp. 150–51, 172–73.

Populist took what today would be spoken of as a liberal position on the Negro, but then few antislavery Southerners had either. For again, the dissent of the South turns out to be like the South as a whole—more conservative and cautious than the rest of the nation.

There is another measure of continuity between Populists and previous dissenters. What happened to Populists after the crusade was over bears a similarity to the behavior of some white Southerners during Reconstruction. Probably most of those who voted Populist during the 1890's went back to the Democratic party whence they had come. Certainly among the leaders there was a movement back to the Democrats. That was true, for example, of Reuben Kolb of Alabama and Tom Watson of Georgia. In the case of Watson his abandonment of Populism was almost total. He not only became a leader of the Democratic party, but he also became known nationally for his violent hatred of Negroes, Jews, and Catholics. Only in his eccentric defense of the Bolshevik Revolution in Russia immediately after the First World War was there a residual glimmer of his dissenting Populist principles. Melford W. Howard, who had also been conspicuous in the 1890's as a radical Populist congressman and propagandist for the movement, followed Watson's model. In the 1920's Howard became an admirer and defender of Mussolini's Italy.

That the Populists should move back to the Democrats is not really surprising, of course; most of them had begun as Democrats. What does seem significant is the number of Populists who went on to become Republicans. Marion Butler of North Carolina, for example, became a Republican in 1904, when it was finally clear that Populism had no future. It made sense, of course, to make that move in North Carolina, where the largest contingent of white Republicans in the South was located. But even in Alabama, where white Republicans were considerably less numerous, there was a significant movement of leaders into the Republican party after 1896. Sheldon Hackney, the most recent historian of Populism in that state, says that becoming a Republican was the second most popular choice of a political future for Alabama Populists. (The first was withdrawal from politics.) Prominent among the several

Populist leaders in Alabama who became Republicans was Joseph C. Manning, one of the founders of the party in that state and an early Populist and radical. Manning's activities after 1896 stand in contrast to Watson's course. Manning never abandoned his Populist belief in cooperation between black and white. In 1903 he praised those "true and brave men in the mountains and valleys of the South [who] had no fear of Negro domination then and . . . have no fear of Negro domination now. The white man with the black heart is more hurtful to the cause of good government and is more to be feared than the humble man of the black skin," he declared. He continued to speak out against Negro disfranchisement, as did another former Alabama Populist, William Skaggs. In the twentieth century Manning was singled out by a Northern Negro newspaper for his consistent support of black voting rights in the South. He did not leave the South until 1914 and always considered blacks and whites equally oppressed by the ruling Bourbons of the region—even when they called themselves "Progressives."[55]

The fate of Populists in Alabama has significance beyond Manning. As Sheldon Hackney has pointed out, few Alabama Populists became Progressives in the twentieth century, though there was a significant progressive movement in Alabama as in the rest of the South. That fact further helps to delineate the nature of the Populists as a part of the Other South. Progressives were not dissenters in the same sense that Republicans or Scalawags or Populists were. The Progressive movement in the South stood for change, to be sure, but change within the framework of the established society. It did not contemplate disturbing the relationships between the races. The Populists, like the Scalawags, were revolting against a political social oligarchy, a part of whose base of power was the suppression of the Negro. The Progressives did not disturb that power base even though they were interested in reforms. Their reforms were of a kind that could be initiated without altering the traditional political patterns. Indeed, the Progressives in some Southern states were often responsible for dis-

55. Manning, "Letting the South Alone," p. 15; Shafner, "Joseph C. Manning," pp. 31–32.

franchising the Negro, if only because in that way they could get on with the economic reforms in which they were principally interested.

Another reason for seeing a continuity between Populism and Republicanism among the voters is again provided by Hackney's study of Alabama. He finds no statistical correlation between the Populist vote in the 1890's and the Republican vote in 1888. That is, Republicans were not a prime source of Populists. But there is a significant correlation between Populist votes in the 1890's and the vote for Republicans in 1902, suggesting that many former Populists by 1902 were voting Republican. By that date, recently enacted disfranchisement legislation had removed most Negroes from elections so that the correlation principally involved whites. The pattern was especially dramatic in seven counties. All of the seven counted fewer than 10 percent of their votes for Republicans in 1888. All but one of these counties went 50 percent or more for the Populists in 1896; the single exception voted 45 percent Populist. In the election of 1902 these seven counties voted on the average of 23.4 percent Republican as against an average of 2.4 percent in 1888.

There are no equivalent studies of what happened to Populists in other Southern states. There are scraps of evidence, however, to suggest that hard-core Populists were sufficiently deviant from the Southern tradition that they did not simply fall back into the Democratic party, even though the vast majority of Populists had once been Democrats. In Texas, for example, many Populists joined the Socialist party in 1900 and after. In 1912, Socialists in Texas won 25 percent of the Democratic vote in fifteen counties of the state. Four of these were western counties with a very small vote. But of the remaining eleven, all had been strongly Populist in the 1890's. Four of them had been among the strongest Populist counties in Texas.

Louisiana, too, showed a continuity of sorts between Populism and twentieth-century radicalism. As Grady McWhiney has shown, one out of every fourteen Louisianans (5,249) in 1912 voted for Eugene V. Debs, the Socialist candidate, or about 1,500 more than voted for William Howard Taft. Seventy percent of that Socialist vote came from the hill counties where Populism had been centered. Winn Parish, where Huey Long was born and raised, was strong for Populism in the 1890's and for Socialism in 1912.[56]

Finally, there is another continuity that links Populism with earlier Southern history. In Alabama, Mississippi, Louisiana, Texas, and Georgia, the old conflicts between white counties and black counties clearly persisted. In state after state the Democratic machines of the black counties used Negro suffrage to overwhelm by fraud the Populist challenge from the white counties. Indeed, it was this historic conflict within many Southern states—a conflict that began in the antebellum years—that made the Populists, like the Scalawags before them, so interested in appealing to blacks and in protecting them in their right to vote and to have a fair count. Thus in Alabama the forty-five white counties of the north voted down the constitution of 1901, which disfranchised Negroes. Through fraud and manipulation of the black vote, the black counties pushed the constitution through. Always the dissident whites recognized that if they could enlist the blacks in their cause the historic domination of the black counties might be broken. But, historic as the conflict may have been throughout the nineteenth century, victory consistently went to the traditional South. The subordination of black people was always more important in the politics and society of the South than the divergent interests of white men. That was the ultimate continuity in the history of the South. It is the central theme of which U. B. Phillips wrote almost fifty years ago, the insistence that the South "shall be and remain a white man's country."

After the great upheaval of the 1890's the majority of Southern white men resolved that such a threat to white supremacy must not recur. By almost common consent, the Southern states disfranchised the Negroes, though in such a way that thousands of poor white men lost the vote, too. For the poll tax, literacy test, and "understanding" clause screened out some whites along with many blacks. The argument was made that with Negroes no longer voting, white men would now be able to divide in politics as they

56. Grady McWhiney, "Louisiana Socialists in the Early Twentieth Century: A Study of Rustic Radicalism," *Journal of Southern History,* XX (1954), 315–36.

did in interest. But that did not happen. Instead of cleansing and invigorating politics in the South, black disfranchisement riveted the one-party system even more firmly upon the region. The end of Populism brought not a new life to the politics of the South but apathy.

With the opening of the new century, in short, the great period of Southern dissent on a widespread and organized basis came to an end. It was not that there were no more dissenters from the Majority South, for, of course, there were. Courageous individuals like John Spencer Bassett, Andrew Sledd, and William E. Dodd continued to speak out for a different South in the years before the First World War,[57] just as Lillian Smith, James McBride Dabbs, and Ralph McGill would in the 1930's and 1940's. But for the first fifty years of this century, there was no large-scale dissent in the South comparable to the great popular movements of the nineteenth. The second half of the twentieth century, however, presents a different story. That story began in 1954 and it is a continuing one today, but its telling deserves another book and another author, for the story of the Other South has no end so long as there is a South—and that, too, promises to endure for a long time.

57. For a recent study of some of the dissenters of the early twentieth century see Bruce Clayton, *The Savage Ideal: Intolerance and Intellectual Leadership in the South, 1890–1914* (Baltimore, 1972).

Location of
Manuscript Collections Cited

Amos Tappen Akerman Letters. Alderman Library, University of Virginia, Charlottesville, Va.

James Lusk Alcorn Papers. Southern Historical Collection, Chapel Hill, N.C.

Edward Porter Alexander Papers. Southern Historical Collection, Chapel Hill, N.C.

C. W. Broadfoot Papers. Southern Historical Collection, Chapel Hill, N.C.

Ralph Potts Buxton Papers. Southern Historical Collection, Chapel Hill, N.C.

Eli Washington Caruthers Papers. Manuscripts Room, Duke University Library, Durham, N.C.

Washington Sanford Chaffin Journal. Manuscripts Room, Duke University Library, Durham, N.C.

Charles Lyon Chandler Papers. Southern Historical Collection, Chapel Hill, N.C.

J. F. H. Claiborne Papers. Southern Historical Collection, Chapel Hill, N.C.

W. J. Clarke Papers. Southern Historical Collection, Chapel Hill, N.C.

Thomas W. Clawson Papers. Manuscripts Room, Duke University Library, Durham, N.C.

John Clopton Papers. Manuscripts Room, Duke University Library, Durham, N.C.

Jabez Lamar Monroe Curry Papers. Manuscripts Room, Duke University Library, Durham, N.C.

Benjamin N. Duke Papers. Manuscripts Room, Duke University Library, Durham, N.C.

William Gaston Papers. Southern Historical Collection, Chapel Hill, N.C.

James Amedeé Gaudet Papers. Southern Historical Collection, Chapel Hill, N.C.

Daniel Reaves Goodloe Papers. Southern Historical Collection, Chapel Hill, N.C.

Benjamin S. Hedrick Papers. Manuscripts Room, Duke University Library, Durham, N.C.

William Woods Holden Papers. Manuscripts Room, Duke University Library, Durham, N.C.

David McKendree Key Papers. On microfilm at Southern Historical Collection, Chapel Hill, N.C.

James Longstreet Papers. Manuscripts Room, Duke University Library, Durham, N.C.

William Mahone Papers. Manuscripts Room, Duke University, Durham, N.C.

Munford-Ellis Papers (Thomas T. Munford Division). Manuscripts Room, Duke University Library, Durham, N.C.

Jason Niles Diaries and Journals. Southern Historical Collection, Chapel Hill, N.C.

Edward A. Oldham Manuscripts. Manuscripts Room, Duke University Library, Durham, N.C.

Thomas Nelson Page Papers. Manuscripts Room, Duke University, Durham, N.C.

Richmond M. Pearson Papers. Southern Historical Collection, Chapel Hill, N.C.

James Graham Ramsay Papers. Southern Historical Collection, Chapel Hill, N.C.

Daniel L. Russell Papers. Southern Historical Collection, Chapel Hill, N.C.

Thomas Settle Papers. Southern Historical Collection, Chapel Hill, N.C.

William D. Valentine Diaries. Southern Historical Collection, Chapel Hill, N.C.

Henry Clay Warmoth Papers. Southern Historical Collection, Chapel Hill, N.C.

Acknowledgments

The systematic work on this book began in 1964, but it has been interrupted by other tasks from time to time. In the course of those ten years I have incurred a number of intellectual and other debts to persons and institutions. It is my pleasure now to at least acknowledge the generous and indispensable help I received even if I cannot fully discharge my obligations.

Undoubtedly basic to the whole endeavor was the financial support I received during the academic year 1964–65 through Fellowships from the American Council of Learned Societies and Vassar College, which enabled me to spend a year in the South. Virtually all of that time I worked in the Southern Historical Collection at Chapel Hill, North Carolina, and in the Manuscripts Room at Duke University. My tasks there were lightened by the cordial welcome and knowing assistance of Dr. Carolyn Wallace and Professor James Patton at the Southern Historical Collection and of Dr. Mattie Russell and Mrs. Virginia Gray at the Manuscripts Room at Duke. I am also indebted to Joel Williamson, Professor of History at Chapel Hill, for his friendship, interest in, and conversation about The Other South, of which he himself is a part. My thanks go also to Cass Canfield, Jr., of Harper and Row, who has been patiently waiting many years for this manuscript without ever losing his interest in its subject and who has served as my friendly editor on this book. I want to thank Mildred Owen for her excellent copyediting, which often went far beyond the call of ordinary duty, much to my benefit. Catherine Grady Degler took time to read portions of the manuscript so that its prose is clearer and sharper than it would otherwise have been. As always, the reader will be as grateful for that assistance as I am. Helpful, too, were Charles Cannon and John Dibbern of Stanford University and Professor John Mering of the University of Arizona, who read particular chapters and gave me the benefit of their expert knowledge. Gloria Guth provided help in surveying the periodical literature when I needed that help badly; I thank her for her careful assistance.

I am especially grateful to Mr. H. P. McGill of Petersburg, Virginia, for granting me permission to use the papers of General William Mahone. Without those papers this book would lack a central episode in the history of The Other South.

Vicki Cooper has more than earned my thanks for her expeditious typing of the manuscript and her interest in the South today along with The Other South. I want also to express my appreciation to The Institute of American History at Stanford University for helping to defray the cost of preparing the manuscript for publication.

For the errors that undoubtedly remain, despite this array of help, I am solely responsible.

May 1973

CARL N. DEGLER

Index

Populist party (*Cont'd*)
  free silver issue, 321, 328, 331,
    358
  and labor, 327–31 *passim*
  Protestants, appeal to, 324–27
  and Republican party, 269, 304,
    331–38 *passim*, 344, 351, 358–
    67 *passim*, 369
  subtreasury plan, 329, 331
  see also individual states
Potter, David, 2, 117, 118, 163, 164
Preston, William, 37
Price, J. C., 354–55, 356, 357
prisons, 219
  convicts as labor, 289, 328
Progressive party, 368–69

Quakers (in the South); antislavery,
    27, 28–29, 90; *see also* Janney,
    Samuel McPherson

Rainey, Joseph, 247–48
Raleigh *News and Observer*, 362,
    364–65, 366
Raleigh *Register*, 21
Raleigh *Standard*, 144, 173, 201,
    242
Randolph, John, 101
Randolph, Thomas Jefferson, 31–32,
    65–66, 79, 92, 93
Rayner, John B., 318, 345
Rayner, Kenneth, 89, 115
Reade, Edwin G., 212
Readjuster movement (Va.), 269–73
    passim, 275–304 *passim*, 306,
    309, 312–16 *passim*, 318, 331,
    337, 338, 353, 357, 360, 362,
    366
  Danville circular and riot, 293–
    99 *passim*, 312, 360, 363
  and Republican party (nation-
    wide), 269, 288, 291, 301–02
  see also Mahone, William
Reconstruction, 5, 53, 65, 168, 191–
    263, 270, 366, 367
  carpetbaggers, 194, 198, 199, 229,
    256–63
  constitutional conventions, 195–
    98, 203–04, 206, 207, 208, 209,
    211, 216, 218, 219, 220, 222,

226, 227–28, 230, 232, 235, 238,
    246–47, 248, 253, 258–59, 259–
    60
  disfranchisement of whites, 193,
    196, 198, 204–08 *passim*, 258
  Southern Claims Commission,
    178–83 *passim*
  terrorism and terrorist organiza-
    tions, 212, 249–51, 253–56, 263
  see also Republican party (in
    the South)—Scalawags and
    Reconstruction
Reconstruction Acts, 204, 222, 232,
    234, 255
Red Shirts, 250
Reid, Robert, 18–19
Reid, Whitelaw, 230
Republican party (in the North and
    nationwide), 52–53, 70–71, 114,
    209, 261–62, 264
  and blacks, 27, 52–53, 84, 217,
    237, 244–45
  Civil Rights bill (1874), 248
  election (1856), 71, 89
  election (1860), 51, 70, 89, 125,
    136, 158, 159, 160, 163
  election (1864), as Union party,
    149
  election (1868), 208, 223–24, 232,
    233
  and Independent movements, 290,
    291, 300
  and Readjuster movement, 269,
    288, 291, 301–02
Republican party (in the South)—
    before Civil War, 53, 156, 168
Republican party (in the South)—
    Scalawags and Reconstruction,
    1, 4, 5, 53, 168, 173, 187, 191–
    263, 292, 316, 323
  and blacks, 7, 53, 192–93, 195,
    198, 199, 205, 207–20 *passim*,
    224–63 *passim*, 304, 334, 336,
    337, 338, 353, 355, 357, 368,
    370
  and carpetbaggers, 194, 198, 199,
    229, 256–63
  constitutional conventions, 195–
    98, 203–04, 206, 207, 208, 209,
    211, 216, 218, 219, 220, 222,

Republican party (*Cont'd*)
226, 227–28, 230, 232, 235,
238, 246–47, 248, 253, 258–59,
259–60
and education, 65, 218, 219, 226,
243, 246, 248, 249, 252, 259
election (1872), 195, 216
former Democrats, 216–17
former Whigs, 192, 212–16
terrorism and terrorist organizations, 212, 249–51, 253–56, 263
and Unionists, 203–07, 209, 212,
217, 231–32, 256, 265
see also individual states
Republican party (in the South)—
after Reconstruction), 7, 8,
263–69, 300–05 *passim*, 312,
314, 315, 332, 333
and blacks, 265–69 *passim*, 300,
340
election (1888), 304
election (1920), 7
election (1972), 7
and Independent movements, 289,
290
and Populist party, 269, 304, 331–
38 *passim*, 344, 351, 358–67
passim, 369
see also individual states
Rhett, Robert, 112, 114, 125, 126
Rice, David, 18
Rice, Samuel, 209, 217, 224
Richmond *Dispatch,* 362
Richmond *Enquirer,* 86
Richmond *Whig,* 86, 95, 239, 301
Riddleberger, Harrison H., 279
Ritchie, Thomas, 86
Roane, William H., 25–26
Robinson, John, 231
Ruffner, Henry, 50, 93
*Address to the People of West
Virginia,* 50, 54–55, 62–63, 64,
78, 86–87, 95
Russell, Daniel L., 229, 244, 245,
257, 335, 336, 359–60, 364

Scalawags *see* Republican party (in
the South)—Scalawags and
Reconstruction
Schurz, Carl, 70

Scott, Anne, 76
Scott, Garrett, 347
Scott, Gen. Winfield, 114, 175
secession, 2, 159–60, 163–67
Alabama, 130, 131, 164, 170
Arkansas, 134, 165, 167, 171
Constitutional Union party, 159,
160, 161
cooperationists, 112, 125, 133,
164, 170, 177, 178
Democratic party, 110, 114–15,
158, 159, 160, 161
Florida, 164
Georgia, 128, 164, 170
Louisiana, 164, 178, 182, 230
Mississippi, 177
North Carolina, 134, 139–40, 143,
144, 165, 167, 172
South Carolina, 103, 125, 127,
129, 138, 144, 147, 150, 163
Tennessee, 134, 136, 148, 150,
164–65, 167, 172, 173
Texas, 132, 163
Virginia, 120, 134, 165–66, 166–
67, 182, 183–84
Whig party, 96, 111
see also Confederacy; Unionists
Semmes, Raphael, 235
Settle, Thomas, 173, 201, 204, 208,
216, 218, 226, 227, 229, 237,
242–43, 254, 257, 353–54
Seward, William A., 27, 113, 120–
21, 153, 156, 211
Shackleford, C. C., 199
Shaffner, T. M., 250
Sharkey, William L., 177, 214–15,
217
Sherman, John, 70, 72
Sherman, Gen. William T., 170
Skaggs, William, 368
The Southern Oligarchy, 352
slavery: American party and lack
of stand, 115, 116
compensated emancipation, 52–
53, 61, 84, 183
Constitutional Union party and
lack of stand, 158–59
John Brown's raid, 87, 88, 89
Nat Turner rebellion, 13–14, 15,
16, 26, 34, 35, 273

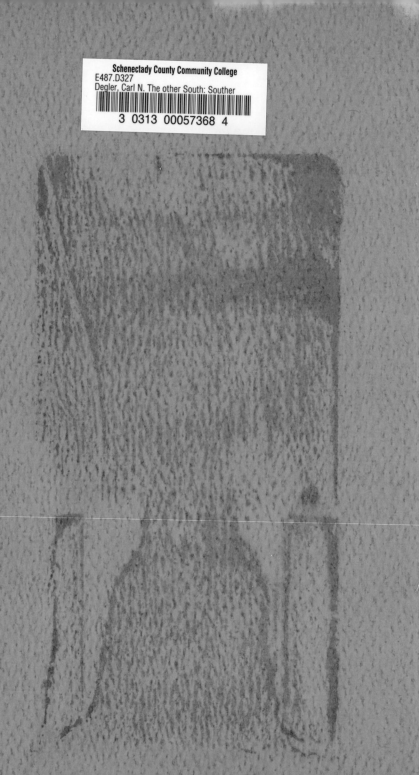